RADICAL FORMALISMS

Also available from Bloomsbury

ARISTOPHANIC HUMOUR
edited by Peter Swallow and Edith Hall

PINDAR AND THE SUBLIME: GREEK MYTH, RECEPTION,
AND LYRIC EXPERIENCE
by Robert L. Fowler

THE POLITICS OF FORM IN GREEK LITERATURE
edited by Phiroze Vasunia

RADICAL FORMALISMS

READING, THEORY, AND THE BOUNDARIES OF THE CLASSICAL

Edited by
Sarah Nooter and Mario Telò

BLOOMSBURY ACADEMIC
LONDON • NEW YORK • OXFORD • NEW DELHI • SYDNEY

BLOOMSBURY ACADEMIC
Bloomsbury Publishing Plc, 50 Bedford Square, London, WC1B 3DP, UK
Bloomsbury Publishing Inc, 1385 Broadway, New York, NY 10018, USA
Bloomsbury Publishing Ireland, 29 Earlsfort Terrace, Dublin 2, D02 AY28, Ireland

BLOOMSBURY, BLOOMSBURY ACADEMIC and the Diana logo
are trademarks of Bloomsbury Publishing Plc

First published in Great Britain 2024
This paperback edition published 2025

Cover image: *Winged*, 1999, by Michael Richards (1963–2001).
Bonded bronze and metal. Reproduced courtesy of the Michael Richards Estate.
Photograph by Oriol Tarridas

A catalogue record for this book is available from the British Library.

Library of Congress Cataloging-in-Publication Data
Names: Nooter, Sarah, editor. | Telò, Mario, editor.
Title: Radical formalisms : reading, theory and the boundaries of the classical /
edited by Sarah Nooter and Mario Telò.
Description: New York : Bloomsbury Publishing Plc, 2024. |
Includes bibliographical references and index.
Identifiers: LCCN 2023028743 (print) | LCCN 2023028744 (ebook) |
ISBN 9781350377431 (hardback) | ISBN 9781350377479 (paperback) |
ISBN 9781350377448 (pdf) | ISBN 9781350377455 (ebook)
Subjects: LCSH: Comparative literature—Classical and modern. |
Classical literature—History and criticism. | Classical literature—Influence.
Classification: LCC PN883 .R33 2024 (print) | LCC PN883 (ebook) |
DDC 880.9—dc23/eng/20230830
LC record available at https://lccn.loc.gov/2023028743
LC ebook record available at https://lccn.loc.gov/2023028744

ISBN: HB: 978-1-3503-7743-1
PB: 978-1-3503-7747-9
ePDF: 978-1-3503-7744-8
eBook: 978-1-3503-7745-5

Typeset by RefineCatch Limited, Bungay, Suffolk

For product safety related questions contact productsafety@bloomsbury.com

To find out more about our authors and books visit www.bloomsbury.com
and sign up for our newsletters.

CONTENTS

Contents

FIGURES

FOREWORD: A WORD BESIDE

Sarah Nooter

Adrienne Rich's 2007 poem "Tonight No Poetry Will Serve"[1] offers a searing indictment of US policy in the Middle East, ending here with the brutal choking of "noun":

> verb force-feeds noun
> submerges the subject
> noun is choking
> verb   disgraced   goes on doing
>
> now diagram the sentence

How do we do what Rich commands us to? How do we diagram the sentence of our lives in systems, political and otherwise, that we did not choose but nonetheless live in and through? How do we find resistance to the forms that contain us, the grammar of our language, the limits of our thoughts? Have we not always, in fact, depended on poetry and other arts to offer this resistance? Have we not always formulated it not only through clear and manifest content, through its phonic materiality, but also through the gut-punch of a sometimes very slight break in form?[2] For *form* is many things, but one is the expectation of a pattern. It is the forming of a letter-shape into a "type" in printing that allowed each letter to be seen and heard consistently again and again and again. Form offers the actuality and illusion of predictability, concord, sameness, conformity.

The final words of Rich's poem display the torture that we came to know the US government was perpetrating. It was known primarily through the shorthand phrase "waterboarding"—a term for the use of water to suffocate, to simulate and threaten death by drowning. Read about the choking Ovid threatens in the suffocating lines described by Tom Geue in his chapter, and then imagine an arm of the world's most powerful superpower holding down your head in a breathless space. Rich's poem shows not just the act of torture, but the facelessness of the systems—the legal system, the linguistic system—that allowed and authorized this torture, turning names, agency, responsibility, guilt into "verb" and "noun" and "subject." And look, too, at the extra spacing around the word "disgraced." Here we pause—we must pause—and think about the world within and surrounding the word "disgraced," think about how the time has warped. When we pause, do we breathe? Is there space for breath? "Noun" cannot breathe; can we? Can we break away?[3] Can we make this stop by the disapprobation of disgrace? No, for the verb "goes on doing." Yet the brief space for pause, breath, respite resists—if subtly—the power of the systems that are maintained through oppression.

This is the radical work of form. Radical formalism is its recognition.

*   *   *

On September 17, 2022, over dinner, one of the radical formalists, if I may call the diners that, politely accused certain others of a lack of restraint, a tendency in their research to veer off, self-indulgently, into the strange. More precisely, perhaps: that the idea of simply opening up further possibilities in the text, not nailing down one interpretation, was not a responsible path through the work—the work meaning both the work that one was reading and the work of classics. Moreover, discussions the day before had revealed divisions in thinking on a variety of interpretive, political, and aesthetic issues, including on how we viewed our engagement with "classics," on what "form" might actually mean, let alone "formalism," what the word "radical" implied, and on the different theorists we were reading. It would be safe to say—maybe it is the only safe thing to say—that "radical formalism" is not one approach but several, or rather one that splinters outward from an initial set of readings, considerations, and a certain framework that we first constructed together. Hence our "formalism" became plural: *formalisms*. Ours is not the last word, and was not meant to be, but is rather an invitation or incitement to go deeper into the archive and arch further back into examining our own practices of reading: what forms do we construct and maintain? What structures do we expose and which ones do we break down? Can we make manifest the questions, roots, histories, and presences in which we dwell by inscribing the impossible within the possible, even at the risk of summoning the strange?

The strange might also be found in simply the range and (dis)order with which we present our findings. As Mario Telò explains in the Introduction, we have made "a collective effort to rethink formalistic approaches to Greek and Roman literatures through the experimentalism of close, keen, earnest encounters with critical theory and, in particular, with Black poetry and art." But we also have tried to be upfront about the impressionistic angling of our endeavors. We have chosen to eschew the normative mode of starting with, and thus privileging, the oldest text under discussion and moving forward to the outer reaches of the field from there. The chapters of this volume start, rather, with Patrice Rankine's transhistorical tracing of the Icarus myth in the work of Black artists and writers, as well as that of Homer, Apollodorus, Euripides, Vergil, and Ovid. Our other earliest chapters take an equally long and wide view of "classics" and, moreover, make material forms central to their questions of positionality. Thereafter, a reader finds collocations of readings in Greek poetry and philosophy, an Antiguan-American novel, Romantic verse, Black American poetry and music, ancient Greek theater, Latin odes, satire, and elegy, and epic both Roman and Hellenistic. These are fifteen individual takes on a theme, results of the provocations to push against the resistant and unsettling aspects of form that we have felt push at us, the places of nearly excessive pressure on language, on the materiality of sound, on pauses and breaks. One can imagine many more responses in this vein, and we hope to see these take shape.

*   *   *

The volume is divided into four sections, whose headings revolve around the term "form": *Shaping Forms, Proximate Forms, Forms (Un)becoming,* and *Forms Unfurling.*

Shaping Forms evokes both the originary act of encounter with the "classical" and the work we do in shaping what we find there. Moreover, form in this sense is a matter of material, a thing with contours. If Shane Butler takes us to the question of how we meet, absorb, and hear our texts and histories, Patrice Rankine and Allannah Karas invite us inside the creative, Oedipal act: what bodies inform the formation of new embodiments? Where Rankine shows that Michael Richards tended to use the imprint of his own body to serve the contours and mythologies he was shaping, Karas exhibits the work of blending and distinguishing embodiments to re-inscribe the marginalized into our canons: formative reformations indeed.

The second section of our book, *Proximate Forms*, looks at forms as they sit side by side with one another, as they touch and, in touching, change. Their proximity is process, it is chemical, reactive; the reader's eye or ear triangulates. If all encounters are dynamic, then no conclusion is conclusive, no form is set, no radical is so rooted it cannot be deracinated. So Alex Purves shows us how the fissures in the sense of just one word that splits on the juncture of awake/asleep have a centrifugal force, spinning from a small formation of verses out into infinities of experience and interpretation. My chapter likewise focuses on just one sound-object in Aristophanes' *Birds* as it becomes distended and extended by the language and song that surrounds it. Tom Phillips and Ren Ellis Neyra demonstrate how past works arc over present encounters, whether illuminating or shadowing through aspects as small as the turns of words, and as great as the clash of historical constraint.

The study of form reveals both the movements of formation and deformation, as the section called *Forms (Un)becoming* explores: one form comes into being as another comes unstrung. Victoria Wohl shows how Heraclitus' lines resist pure flow, even as an interrupted river, revealing both a lack of full formation and the subtle hint of its fruition, framing this tension as a formative philosophical position. Efrossini Spentzou displays the world of Statius' epic as one where only gaps of meaning can give rise to radical formation and formulation. Sarah Olsen's Electra, like Lucy Alford's Gwendolyn Brooks, erects the construction that she simultaneously exhibits as unsettled and precarious: the invocation of an event, a set of rhythms, a building that will fall, lives that will not be protected, shelters that will not be shored up. The text maintains them in their evanescence, creating a negative imprint of a missing form.

And what if form mumbles, murmurs, moans? What if we admit imprecision, improvisation? What if our forms lose their contours? Won't things slip through, slip out? Perhaps yes. In *Forms Unfurling*, we look to the opening of forms that results from their recognition. Victoria Rimell's incisive meditation on/at the threshold of both poetry and our engagement as classicists takes us to the proems of Horace and to the radical alterity exposed in initial encounters. Tom Geue brings us into the tightly wound elegiac formations of Ovid's *Ibis* so as to push his readers to resist the fixing, or affixation, of formal constraint. Sean Gurd shows Mackey playing with the tendency of form to melt toward conformity, and challenges us instead to transform and deform, as we come to the edge of what we hear and formulate as system, objectivity, syntax. In the final chapter of the volume, Mario Telò displays the fantastical unfurling of affordances in language when it is loosed from rigid expectations, the (dis)abled body escaping its boundaries through a gorgeous indulgence of excesses that break the skein of formal patterns.

*   *   *

Eve Kosofsky Sedgwick, and then again Stephen Best, suggest a manner of reading that eschews the "dualistic thinking" of traditional critique, which seeks to get "[b]ehind, beneath, beyond" the work in question, turning that work into an "effect," an "object" whose depths we must plumb to extract the truth. The term "beside" instead suggests an "open-sourced program" that deals in the "additive and accretive," with a push or a bow toward "plenitude."[4] Accordingly, this volume invites readers to encounter the forms of texts, songs, poems, objects of art, histories and archives, with an eye toward the formations, transformations, reformations, deformations, and all those other form-[ ]s, that initiate the life, the life-i-ness or aliveness, of the classical in its ancient and contemporary instances, its arcane and everyday instantiations. Here, in these meetings, we have privileged the affect of subjectivity, subjunctivity, positionality; exposed debatable and dubious positions; we have confused at times and at times affronted. Our hope has been to expose, in the words of Kevin Quashie, "an astonishing intimacy."[5] Such an intimacy is vulnerable to the problematic politics of being, to accusations ranging from radicality to banality, to interruptions and disruptions, into the sentences under which we live, and which we are compelled to diagram.

*   *   *

At the start of this brief statement, I offered the ending of "Tonight No Poetry Will Serve." But if you have read this far, you deserve the start of the poem too:

Saw you walking barefoot
taking a long look
at the new moon's eyelid

later spread
sleep-fallen, naked in your dark hair
asleep but not oblivious
of the unslept unsleeping
elsewhere

As we saw at the start of this preface, the poem ends with an indictment, the expression of searing disappointment with an appalling government and a world that sanctions such cruelty. But it is important too to see how it is framed from a place of deep, quiet intimacy, from the crux of asleep and awake (as per Purves in this volume), "asleep but not oblivious," from the tender openness of "walking barefoot" and "naked in your dark hair," from the living look at the "new moon's eyelid."

When I think of such intimacy, and such resistance through form, my mind goes to one of antiquity's most lauded works, namely Sophocles' *Oedipus Tyrannus*. In one of the more breathtaking moments of the play, the chorus express their grief over the loss of their leader. The final stanza (antistrophe β) of this stasimon goes like this (1213–21):

ἐφηῦρέ σ’ ἄκονθ’ ὁ πάνθ’ ὁρῶν χρόνος,
δικάζει τὸν ἄγαμον γάμον πάλαι
τεκνοῦντα καὶ τεκνούμενον.
ἰὼ Λάϊειον <ὤ> τέκνον,
εἴθε σ’ εἴθε σε
μήποτ’ εἰδόμαν·
ὡς ὀδύρομαι
περίαλλ’ ἰὰν χέων
ἐκ στομάτων. τὸ δ’ ὀρθὸν εἰ-
πεῖν, ἀνέπνευσά τ’ ἐκ σέθεν
καὶ κατεκοίμησα τοὐμὸν ὄμμα.

It found you out against your will, seeing all: time.
It judges marriage not
a marriage in which begetter was begot.
Oh child of Laius,
o that, o that
I had never seen you.
For I mourn
pouring out an exceeding cry
from my mouth. Truth be
told, it was from you that I drew breath
and closed my eye in sleep.

Here is a song of love, which closes as the "eye" closes to go to sleep—a remembered sleep of peace? Or the sleep of pain, loss, death into which the chorus now symbolically enter? Note, as per Wohl's Heraclitus, how the song stutters (*agamon gamon . . . / eithe s'eithe se*) in an inarticulate gasp of pain. Note too that the chorus' "exceeding cry" (like Brooks's "exceeding sun"?)[6] is said to "pour" out of its systemized limits, break its boundaries. In the end, though, the song comes down to breath—for it was "from you that I drew breath" (*anapneusa*). In Homeric literature, this word means *respite*: breathing room, a pause, a break. In Pindar, the breath is understood to come from the source and start of life (*Nemean* 7.5). And here, in Sophocles, bodies merge, the song pulls back, and life is allowed in a brief, precarious suspension, a fleeting prefiguration of Nathanial Mackey's "radical pneumaticism."[7] It is just one moment before the gaze of time arrives, full of decimating judgment, replicated but not replaced by the chorus's singular, lone I/eye. There is just this breath, this break.

Notes

1. Rich 2012, 25. Used by permission of W. W. Norton & Company, Inc.

2. See, for one, Moten (2003, 1) on the resistance offered by Blackness as "an ongoing irruption that anarranges every line— ... a strain that pressures the assumption of the equivalence of personhood and subjectivity." When, in Rich's poem, the "noun is choking," the field of battle, the matter of value, is the potential for this "object" (in Moten's terms, or "commodity" in Moten on Marx) to get a breath and *speak*: "we can think how the commodity who speaks, in speaking, in the sound—the inspirited materiality—of that speech, constitutes a kind of temporal warp that disrupts and augments not only Marx but the mode of subjectivity that the ultimate object of his critique, capital, both allows and disallows ... for if the commodity could speak it would have an intrinsic value, it would be infused with a certain spirit, a certain value given not from the outside" (11, 13).

3. See Mackey 2021a, 22: "That none of us is guaranteed our next breath is a truth that has to sit alongside another, equally obvious, which is that precarity has been and continues to be unequally distributed, some groups serving, for others, as a sacrifice to it or a shield against it." See Gurd on Mackey in this volume.

4. Best 2018, 62.

5. Quashie 2021, 77.

6. See p. 191 in Alford in this volume. These lines in Sophocles are highly contested; the version printed here is the emendation of Burges, as found in Lloyd-Jones and Wilson 1990, ad loc. Translations are my own.

7. "A poetics of breath is all the more palpably evident in black music, particularly the music of wind instruments, a radical pneumaticism in which the involuntary is rendered deliberate, labored, in which breath is belabored, made strange. Breath becomes tactical, tactile, textile, even textual, a haptic recension whose jagged disbursements augur duress ... Granted solidity, audiotactility, does breath become less airy and thus less fleeting, less ephemeral? Is radical pneumaticism as much a holding action as an elegiac lament?" (Mackey 2021a, 9–10, 13).

INTRODUCTION
RADICAL FORMALISM: A QUASI-MANIFESTO

Mario Telò

A left and right arm, cast from bronze, join to form a disembodied unity, complete with hands in repose, not surrender, or in determined action. Five items, similar in form, hang from the figure, but they do not quite dangle. Upon close examination, these feathers have pierced the would-be flesh all the way through, so that their sharp, arrow-like tips protrude, extending inches above the floating sculpture, their edges rubbing up against skin, animal detritus becoming one physical form with the human (disem)body . . . As in most of Richards's work at the time of his death on 9/11/2001 in the Twin Towers, the metaphor, or form, in question is not only sculpture, but also the myth of Icarus, ideally suited for the artist's interest in "the simultaneous possibilities of uplift and downfall," in this case, "in the context of the historical and ongoing oppression of black people."[1] . . .

As Richards described his sculptural process, "in attempting to make [the] pain and alienation [of Blackness] concrete, I use my body, the primary locus of experience, as die from which to make casts. These function as surrogates, and as entry into the work." . . . Racial inequity, the oppression of Black people, and the pain and alienation of the experiences of Blackness are narrative points of entry into artistic expression.

With these words, Patrice Rankine, one of the contributors of this book, captures the harrowing formal intensity of the artistic experimentalism of Michael Rolando Richards, who died while working in his studio on the ninety-second floor of the World Trade Center's North Tower. *Winged* (1999) is an uncanny prefiguration of Richards's own passing at the hands of flying anti-heroes, re-enactors of Icarus' self-annihilation. The enfoldment of hanging arms punctured by winged arms (feathers? arrows?)—potential instruments of liberation—expresses, in its lack of closure, a line of flight bound up with proliferating wounds and angular constriction. As Rankine puts it, Richards's sculpture takes the form of "an impasse or permanent stalemate between Western civilizing narratives and Black[ened] being, or . . . an appeal to another way of knowing beyond European epistemology." Richards's *Winged* is emblematic of the agenda of this book, a collective effort to rethink formalistic approaches to Greek and Roman literatures through the experimentalism of close, keen, earnest encounters with critical theory and, in particular, with Black poetry and art.

In modeling a reconceptualization of the literary in classical antiquity in light of what we call "radical formalism," we aim to present untrodden interpretive avenues that problematize current approaches to the phenomena of poetic expression usually referred to as "form."[2] We are indebted to the work of Victoria Wohl, Simon Goldhill, Phiroze Vasunia, and others, who have brought the "politics of form" to the center of scholarly discourse in classics. However, ours is not an intervention in the politics of form in Greek and Roman literature, in the entanglements of form and politics within the specific cultural or generic contours of two delimited textual archives.[3] Rather, it is an attempt to rethink formalism as a mode of reading[4] these archives at this precise moment—one in which an overdetermined sense of a global crisis has coincided with a no-longer postponable disciplinary reckoning for classics and the humanities as a whole with methodological logics (positivism, empiricism, historicism) that perpetuate, or fail to challenge, normative politics, with the attendant -isms and -phobias.[5] The innovative force of reception studies that do not shy away from critical-theoretical engagement can beneficially inflect established modalities of reading the "originals," which still largely operate with implicit or explicit, weak or strong reconstructive aspirations, with programmatic or unstated re-inscriptions of intentionalism, with axiologies of plausibility that curtail the interpretive and affective possibilities afforded by the untimeliness of the ancient.[6] Our goal is, in other terms, to locate underexplored (or disavowed) theoretical complexities in formalistic approaches to Greek and Latin texts, suggesting ways in which such complexities can be made integral to the practices of reading. Radically reading for form implies dramatizing, in the thick of analysis, the interpreter's usually suppressed sensations of disorientation and dispossession, which arise in the effort to translate an encounter with formal effects and impressions into an interpretive structure. Aestheticized internalizations of the dis- or re-assembling in formalistic reading yield disorientation and dispossession, the quintessential feelings of radical politics in *the undercommons*.[7]

The term "radical" as we see it captures the possibility of "uprooting" current views of classical poetic form. We envision sustained methodological projections (not mere excursions or detours) outside the field of mainstream classics, beyond the temporal bounds of antiquity, beyond the safety of historicist limits, beyond empiricism's illusion of immediacy, even beyond the dichotomy of "paranoid" and "reparative" reading.[8] What the book aspires to accomplish is in line with the aesthetic programmatics that, in her contribution, Lucy Alford finds in Gwendolyn Brooks's *In the Mecca*, a poem collection that "builds housing insecurity into its very form, while also leveraging that very formal precarity toward a new poetics that combines elegiac witness and social reflection with formal demolition." Form is radical insofar as it realizes itself in its own unforming, its undoing—within a word, within a line, within a poetic whole. It engenders mutually dispossessive encounters between an interpreted object and an ostensible interpreting subject, giving an apparent structure to the breaking of verbal structures in the process of reading. "In its break with received forms such as sonnet, ballad, and rhymed quatrains," Alford writes, *In the Mecca* "also formally manifests the poet's own intentional break with or demolition of the house of the poem—breaking down the very forms that had housed her language and thinking up to that point." The primary position that, among these encounters, we reserve for Black classicisms and Black theory is programmatic of the radical politics underlying this project—politics conceived as the art of the impossible, a continuous inscription of the impossible within the possible (as in the interplay, generated by poetic form, between the verbal given on the page and imaginative infinity). In what follows I will place some of the case studies analyzed in the individual chapters against the backdrop of recent theoretical interventions in theater and film, as well as in literary studies.

For film theorist Eugenie Brinkema, "radical formalism" designates a hermeneutic practice that "involves … reading the form of the films, light, montage etc., but also thinking about … abstract forms such as toroid, list, design, diagram or grid as a kind of thinking as well."[9] Identifying affect with pure form—instead of seeing it as a somatic force, the material basis (or pretext) for subsuming interpretation into what she would regard as a kind of embodied contextualism or corporeal presentism[10]—is, in her view, an opportunity to "retur[n] to the *roots* of formalist analysis, and exten[d] their reach."[11] The radicality of this apparently non-radical regression—which is captured by her programmatic titular statement, "We Never Took Deconstruction Seriously Enough"— results in the cultivation of an unapologetically, drastically anti-representational formalism, one, in her words, "utterly indifferent to context, allegory, all provocations of putting … representational depths … to work."[12] While we endorse neither Brinkema's anti-somatism nor her anti-political posture—which is, inevitably, political—we are sympathetic with her anti-representational orientation, which is not incompatible with close reading, but pushes us to distance ourselves from its canonical configurations, to reconsider its practices, to reject the reassuring temptation of pure descriptivism, and to commit to making form "surprising and speculative."[13] The emphasis on the "speculative" is especially important at a moment when, in classics, references to the post-critique and the "new sincerity" seem to have legitimized empiricism and descriptivism—neither critical nor post-critical, but often acritical.[14] According to Marjorie Perloff, "To be a poet … is to draw on the verbal pool we all share but to choose one's words and phrases with an eye to unexpected relationships—verbal, visual, sonic—that create a new construct and context—relationships that create infrathin possibilities."[15] It is in the opening of these possibilities, which I would characterize as "minor" or "minoritarian," that the speculative quality of poetic form resides, together with its power to disorient, unsettle, to upset the relational apparatus of ordinary perception.

In her chapter, Victoria Rimell offers an illuminating example of how to deterritorialize established interpretive models through the speculative force of form, dramatizing the possibilities offered by form as an "unfinished formalization/Gestalt," as an opening of radical, unpredictable relationalities within the text and between text and reader. She finds such an opening in the programmatics of Horatian beginnings, disrupting the anti-speculative mood enforced by conventional readings of such programmatics, their preemption of an affective experience of formal disorientation. As she puts it, "[t]he Latinist works to convert the act-event of inauguration, with its fresh, relational formalizations, into static topics, patterns, and declarations of authorial-generic identity that are only dynamic insofar as they are seen to activate paths within a plottable complex of tradition." In this way, "the 'programmatic' curtails astonishment by harnessing a predictable future and projecting that closure onto the work's opening, so that meaning is not per-formed as (im)possibility but pre-formed as disciplinarily codified knowledge." This use of programmatics for reinforcing familiar epistemic modes, for reducing the practice of reading to the discovery of the codified and known, and for disavowing the effect of unconditional disorientation, of interpretive dispossession, exemplifies what form is for classical philology—as Rimell says, "a static functional device, an innovation dissected from affective vitality and from the overt movements of the proem's becoming, as we enter into it." Starting from the consideration that "it is hard to fit either/or into the format of traditional literary criticism ... because writing takes its thread from the medium of a single, looping line," Alex Purves splits the space of interpretation into two simultaneous and autonomous paths, visualizing the disavowed inevitability of reading sideways or dually—"across the page if with a facing page translation, or across the desk or screen to a lexicon or a commentary." The outcome of her re-engagement with Sappho's most famous nocturnal scene is a conceptualization of reading as an in-between state, a kind of *sleepwaking*, the precarious vigilance of eyes always at risk of losing sight in the middle, "through the incoherence of a world seen in double."

Similarly, in his analysis of Pindar, Tom Phillips pushes against the "tendency to conceive poetic form as resultative, as the outcome of prior intentions or structures which are regarded, in different ways and in differing degrees, as determining form's ontic character." For Phillips, Pindaric form can be conceptualized as a complex of "tentative apprehensions" that challenge pretenses to "epistemic mastery" and turn reading into a kind of formal thinking. Notwithstanding certain simplistic views of "surface reading," reading for form is always, to an extent, an exercise in overanalysis or in "too-close-reading."[16] Speaking of the film image, D. A. Miller conceptualizes "too-close-reading" as the practice of "observing ... some striking *failure of transparency*," "a marked resistance to the immediacy of our knowing what to see."[17] This "failure of transparency" shakes the image; it opens "fracture points in the image's presumed obviousness." The "speculation" in speculative formalism—which is the reading of "radical formalism" that we have privileged so far—is, despite its catoptric resonances, a rejection of pure reflection, or what Fred Moten calls the "refusal" characteristic of "re-reading," which he identifies with "the degenerative decomposition of readerly anticipation" and with "the *speculative*, disruptive irruption of what is, as 'is' is anoriginally displaced by 'as.'"[18] To embrace the speculative, as Brinkema's, Perloff's, and Moten's versions of radical formalism suggest, means to strive toward a failure of transparency by lingering on minimal, seemingly idle phenomena, which, if heeded, if turned into objects of hyper-attention, can allow us to make the very stubbornness of form interpretively relevant.[19] This stubbornness can proliferate but also preempt relationality, as illustrated by Ren Ellis Neyra in their reading of Jamaica Kincaid's engagement with the Ovidian and Romantic background of daffodils, a flower whose colonial legacy disturbs the imagined paradigm of relation, and forestalls subjective recovery after the scene of disturbance.

Differently from Brinkema, Craig Dworkin connects "radical formalism" with a version of radical politics, adapting the concept from the "radical praxis" of Bruce

Andrews, a representative of the L-A-N-G-U-A-G-E poets.[20] Radical praxis, in Andrews's view, "involves the rigors of formal celebration, a playful infidelity, a certain illegibility within the legible: an infinitizing, a wide-open ex-uberance, a perpetual motion machine." There is something politically radical in the very idea of illegibility, of disruption of the legible in the practice of writing and reading poetry. This illegibility conforms to a notion of anti-functionalism, which we find for example in Alan Ruiz's Adornian theorization. For Ruiz, "radical formalism" is to be located in objects' ability to withstand their designated function, in their radical reluctance to do what they apparently are for. Andrews's illegibility and Ruiz's anti-functionalism point to the radicality, the illegibility of the useless.[21] Stefka Mihaylova has applied the phrase "radical formalism" to the theater of Suzan-Lori Parks and Sarah Kane.[22] As she observes, "Proposing that formalism may illuminate a radical theatrical approach to race is, of course, counterintuitive." Yet "the history of formalism … contains important insights about the limits of historicist approaches in rethinking art and identity in socially efficacious ways."[23] Mihaylova connects the artistic experiments of Parks and Kane with the intellectual and political experiences of the Russian formalists:

> the theory of estrangement, which saw every person as a potential artist, at least theoretically pitted individual agency against the "compulsory mimesis" of socialist realism. In other words, the regime's response to formalism transformed it into a situated and embodied practice of antitotalitarian resistance. This is the kind of formalism that I see Parks and Kane practicing in their playwriting, and it is motivated by factors similar to those that radicalized Russian formalism: the limits of materalist contextualization for critically staging race and a reaction against the "compulsory mimesis" of established ways of staging the racially marked body.[24]

One can make the argument that, while, in his own writing, Marx modeled forms of radical formalism, infusing stretches of his prose with anti-representational intensities, with expressive approximations of the revolution,[25] socialist realism rigidified the irreverence and unruliness of formalistic speculation into "compulsory mimesis," a counterpart, in its constraining force, of historicist contextualism.

Joseph North sees the still-dominant historicist/contextualist paradigm as informed by a neoliberal wish to collapse the humanities into the social sciences, as well as by a normative fantasy of establishing a safe barrier between "then" and "now." For North, anti-contextualism encompasses the radicality of aesthetic immersion, valorizing an impressionism rejected or disavowed by historicist hermeneutics, that is, an attentiveness to the idiosyncratic effects or the particular, unruly pressures exercised by an art object on our perceptive apparatus in the moment.[26] The social-scientific politics of the "useful" can and should be countered by a full, fearless re-evaluation of what North calls "the affective intimacy of the critic's own subjective inwardness with the text"[27]—a strategy for dwelling on effects of readings whose formal disruption, beyond conventional notions of the useful, is precisely the metapolitical message. In this frame of mind, the ostensible objectivity of historicist hermeneutics, the effort to separate the ancient "original" from later accretions and thereby preserve its integrity, is replaced by an embrace of anachronism, which cannot be separated from interpretation as such.[28] As Sasha-Mae Eccleston and Dan-el Padilla Peralta observe, the traditionally philological idea of a textual analysis "disembedded from the world around it, untainted by contemporary feelings, biases, and agendas" reinscribes well-established practices of race-based disciplinary exclusion in classical studies.[29]

The positivistic notion of responsibility toward antiquity—based on the dream of unmediated access, of excluding subjectivity and temporal situatedness from the interpretive act, of separating reception from what is construed as unbiased scholarship—can be replaced here by a novel, negative sense of responsibility.[30] If we conceptualize ancient culture, or a Greek or Roman artifact, textual or otherwise, in Levinasian terms as the face of the Other, the locus of the ethical encounter, we can regard historicist contextualism as the transformation of the face into a name, the reduction of "the idea of infinity," which is the face, but also, in a sense, form's infinitude, to a finite, limited representation.[31] The face, Emmanuel Levinas says, "cannot become a content, which your thought would embrace," because, as he adds, "the relation to the Infinite is not a knowledge, but a Desire."[32] This "desire" is the feeling that allows the "interpersonal relation" to safeguard ethical infinity or incomprehensibility, the dynamic irresolution of the inbetweenness expressed by *inter-* and illustrated in many of the chapters. Using the phrase "resistant form," Jacques Rancière emphasizes, instead of relationality and inbetweenness, "a force of disindividualization."[33] In the word "disindividualization," the "dis-"—the impetus of rupture as such, the negative force of the "illegible," of making no sense[34]—has an agency and importance in itself, autonomous from the "new forms of individuation" or "new worlds of possible sense making" that it may give rise to.[35] As a hermeneutic judgment, "uselessness"—intrinsic to the rhetoric of the useful—establishes hierarchies of what counts and what does not for the interpretive exercise, but it may conversely be reclaimed as the resistance of form, a locus of radical anti-normativity.

In our emphasis on de-formation, speculation, and radicality, our approach expands and differs from Caroline Levine's *Form: Whole, Rhythm, Hierarchy, Network* (2015), an important book that has had a strong influence in classics (and is discussed by a few contributors here). Levine takes an approach that she characterizes as more New Critical than deconstructionist, though not necessarily anti-deconstructionist. In her first chapter, she favors formal wholes and totalities as politically progressive shapes, playing up "their power to hold things together," their dynamic ability to "brin[g] together conflicting elements."[36] Reacting against the conventional association of formalism and anti-politics while making a case for form as a channel of emancipatory politics, Levine points out that "wholeness" and "unity" are valued not only in the aesthetic-political imaginary of liberal democracies but also, for example, in the Marxist theorizations of Georg Lukács. What seems problematic in this assumption is the equation of form with unity or wholeness, which she posits by taking Cleanth Brooks's *The Well Wrought Urn* as a privileged figuration of New Critical hermeneutics.[37] But what if we consider form as a liminal space between construction and destruction, doing and undoing, or as the ongoing process of de-formation occurring in this space?[38] As Paul Saint-Amour puts it in a review of Levine's book, "Forms only participate in socially transformative work through their evasion," that is through texts' evasion of the very forms they inhabit (genre, meter, etc.) and, I would add, through form's evasion, its flight from the agencies (text, "author," context) that deploy it.[39] Levine's assimilation of form to a "bounded enclosure" seems to reinscribe notions of authorial control and intentionality, without considering the radical autonomy of form, its nomadism.

The book's impact may be due to its main limitation, that is, "liberal-ecumenical vision of formal complexity," in Tom Eyers's phrase.[40] Although in her discussion of rhythm, Levine adds elements of dynamism and mutability to her political aesthetics, the plural(istic) rhythms that she speaks of as "jumbled and constantly altered, each, thanks to the others, incapable of imposing its own dominant order,"[41] still operate within a system, a unity. We might say, however, that rhythm, with its etymological liquidity (from the verb *rheô* "flow"), entails an anti-systemic, anarchical notion of dissolution, an intrinsic threat to the regular, structured cadence crafted by the patterns and repetitions. Even repetition itself, with its death-driven orientation, brings a chaotic impulse into rhythm, de-forming form,[42] as we see, for example, in Tom Geue's analysis of the torturously claustrophobic, constricted metrical atmosphere of Ovid's *Ibis*, and in Sarah Olsen's consideration of the aesthetic forces of "disintegration and proliferation," "expansion and accumulation" in Sophocles' *Electra*. Levine's approach may generate or legitimize, unintentionally, an assimilation of form to conformism, the danger that Sean Gurd discusses in his reassessment of Greek poetic and performative genres in light of Nathaniel Mackey's theoretical interventions and his poetic output. As Gurd observes, for Mackey, "the alternative to 'conformist form' is a music that emphasizes the 'notional' rather than the 'notational,'" that is, an "open form"—"improvised, intonationally free, noisy and uncomposed." Mackey's form "not only allows for forms to occur within the realm of reference, but it also implies that reference may itself be mostly or entirely formal."

In this collection's theorizations of radical formalisms, we are particularly influenced by Fred Moten's notion of "the black radical tradition" as "a sociopoetic activity," that is, as an "improvisational, anarchically principled (dis)organization," materialized in poetry and music (especially jazz), or "a poetics of recombination marked precisely by an ongoing anarchic seizure, excess and intensification."[43] Moten's notion of Blackness as "the extended movement of a specific upheaval, an ongoing irruption that anarranges every line,"[44] evokes conceptual fields and critical-theoretical imaginaries that can foster a radical reconceptualization of ancient poetic phenomenologies. Sound, a topic that traverses many of the chapters of the book, can be construed, à la Moten, as "the transference of a radically exterior aurality that disrupts and resists certain formations of identity and interpretation by challenging the reducibility of phonic matter to verbal meaning or conventional musical form."[45] Emblematized by the figure of the "shriek," which Moten labels as a "(phono-photo-porno-)graphic disruption,"[46] sound—"a venerable phonic propulsion, the ontological and historical priority of resistance to power and objection to subjection"—enables form's de-forming agency.[47] In my own chapter, a re-examination of the Talos episode in Apollonius' *Argonautica*, I resort to

Moten's idea of "socio-poetic insurgency," an "improvisational … principle of (dis) organization," to theorize a glitchy, metallic formalism, which I connect with the ethics and aesthetics of disability. In his exploration of John Addington Symonds's Victorian classicisms, Shane Butler lingers on Tennyson's "Break, Break, Break," an echo of "the repetitive, percussive force of the [Homeric] sea against the shore," wondering "Was a distinctively Black sound already at work … in the sonic imaginary, phonographic *avant la lettre*, of Britain's poet laureate?" Butler advocates for a practice of "postcritical hylomorphism," which includes "the liberation of form itself from even the most seemingly natural of formalisms." Moten's view of sounds as "anarchic seizure" is also relevant to Victoria Wohl's reading of the irruptive force of the stutter in Heraclitus' fragments. Wohl borrows from Gilles Deleuze the idea of the stutter's deterritorializing pressure, its opening of language to the nonsensical threat of a foreign idiom—like the "unruly idiom" that, in her Deleuzian reading of the Hypsipyle episode in Statius' *Thebaid*, Efrossini Spentzou sees emerging in the collapse of the epic code, in the proliferation of moments of "becoming–woman."

In her retheorization of poetic onomatopoeia through her own affective and interpretive engagement with an Aristophanic avian voice, Sarah Nooter tracks the flying, nomadic persistence of an aural phenomenon, which she suggestively reads alongside one of Tracie Morris's sound poems: "Though the sound is itself the same each time, its meaning—the meaning that envelops it—is constantly moving: it is first an onomatopoeic interjection, then an iconic illustration, then seemingly both at once but within a more distanced fictional frame, until finally it is transformed into a transformative, theriomorphosizing, divine exclamation." Seen from a radically formalistic perspective, this iconic, hypermimetic onomatopoeia might be likened to the "cry of verse" that, at the beginning of *Poetics of Relation*, Édouard Glissant connects with the sound of the marine abyss in the Middle Passage.[48] Heeding the ways that form makes and unmakes itself, realizes itself in and as de-formation, means being attentive to an overdetermined "cry"—something calling for a hermeneutic apprehension that wanders, encompassing but going beyond figures of nonsensical or mimetic sound. A practice of "critical-sensual, visceral-formalist reading"[49] can connect us with intimations of metapolitics by enabling an imaginative encounter with the radicality of the impossible.

Radical Formalism is also the title of a recent poetry collection of Richard Kostelanetz, the author of a "novella" entitled *In the Beginning*, which presents itself as an alternative alphabet, consisting of a list of letters and non-sensical combinations.[50] Here "radical formalism" recalls the experimentalism of the Hellenistic and late-antique *carmina figurata*—poems becoming drawings, versifications suggesting the contours of pictorial or quasi-diagrammatic structures—which modern criticism dismissively judged as emblematic of Alexandrian (or generically "late") *art pour l'art*, "empty" formalism.[51] The time might have come to revisit this critical position and to contemplate reading for the metapolitical implications of these fanciful, "decadent" experiments. Some of them are in line with the procedures of exuberant collage, jarring juxtaposition, quirky and queer overlaying, ironical accumulation that Allannah Karas analyzes in the engagements of Emma Amos and Robert (Bob) Louis Thompson with signature works of Greco-Roman sculpture and painting, engagements that, as she puts it, "model … creative forms of resistance."

In his book *Poetic Aliveness, or a Poetics of Being*, Kevin Quashie theorizes Blackness as subjunctivity, which he defines as "the doubt and vitality of leaning into one's relationality, the animating of being through the expressiveness of might-be"; "an expression of desired or conditional action" that can "create or manifest a scene for happening"; and "a capacity of wandering and wondering."[52] For us, practicing radical formalism means locating (un)productive zones of subjunctivity; it means turning reading into a deterritorialized space or a space for intense aesthetico-political deterritorialization, for affirmative processes of de-formation, for *poiêtic* (that is, world-making), or *poethic* dismantling.[53] It means performing the minor or minoritarian gesture of proceeding "without guarantee,"[54] unconditionally, sensitively or over-sensitively welcoming the imaginative potentialities of the literary and, especially in the case of antiquity, pursuing the (post-)critical opportunities of achronies and out-of-joint synchronies, while emancipating ourselves from fantasies of return, restoration, reconstruction.

Notes

1. See Nonnenberg 2019.

2. Some of the points made in this Introduction are derived from the Introduction of Telò 2023b.

3. See Wohl 2015, Goldhill 2020, and Vasunia 2022a and b.

4. As Brinkema observes, form is, inevitably, "the root of all reading." See Olsen's chapter.

5. See, esp. Rankine 2019, Eccleston and Padilla Peralta 2022, and Umachandran 2022. See also below.

6. As Gunderson (2021, 200) observes, in classics "readings that suspend the role of the author are branded with various excommunicatory marks: errant, stupid, faithless, anachronistic … [S]uch labels serve as angry rhetorical gestures that summarily dismiss interpretive avenues." On the untimeliness of the ancient, see esp. Porter 2000, 2005, and The Postclassicisms Collective 2019.

7. Moten and Harney 2013.

8. The distinction goes back to Sedgwick 2003; but, on the trouble of identifying Sedgwick's legacy solely with the reparative, see Berlant and Edelman 2019. On the debate see, with different orientations, Love 2010, Kurnick 2018, Edelman 2022, and Mueller, forthcoming; on the relation between the reparative and reconstruction, see Nooter 2022. There is a danger that, in classics, certain versions of reparative reading may turn into the reinscription of empiricism: see Telò 2025.

9. Brinkema 2019, 73.

10. Brinkema 2014.

11. Brinkema 2014, 37.

12. Brinkema 2016, 94.

13. Brinkema 2019, 69. According to Brinkema (2022, 178), "the text … is a model of the absolute

necessity of a radical formalism. In its staging of forms interpreting and engaging with other forms to generate unforeseen possibilities, it gives rise to a nonanthropomorphic, antihumanist model in which forms and structures speculatively grapple with other logics." Porter's anti-Platonic, anti-humanistic paradigm of materialistic formalism is, in a sense, a kind of radical formalism in its own right (2010). Speaking of Kant, De Man (1996, 128) notes that "the radical formalism that animates aesthetic judgment in the dynamics of the sublime is what is called materialism."

14. On the entanglement of the "new sincerity" with neoliberal ideology, see Lambert 2020.

15. Perloff 2021, 6.

16. On the much-influential concept of "surface reading," see Best and Marcus 2009, and the important intervention of Purves (2016). On overanalysis, see McEleney 2021.

17. Miller 2021, 15.

18. Moten 2017, 266 (my emphasis).

19. Eyers (2017) offers important discussions of "word" and "world" that have inspired my notion of the stubbornness of form.

20. Dworkin 2003 ("Radical Formalism" is the title of Dworkin's introduction); see Andrews 1996, 51.

21. See Ruiz 2016, 237. For a critique of the utilitarian rhetoric of the "useful" and a re-evaluation of the "useless," see Ahmed 2019; for Ahmed, "to queer use can be to linger on the material qualities of that which you are supposed to pass over." See also Moten and Harney 2021 for a critique of what they call "the usufruct of man."

22. Mihaylova 2015, 213–31.

23. Mihaylova 2015, 214.

24. Mihaylova 2015, 221.

25. See Comay 2021 and Telò 2023b (Introduction).

26. On anti-contextualism and archaic Greek lyric, see Budelmann and Phillips 2018.

27. North 2017, 167.

28. See Bassi and Euben 2010, ix: "Determined by disciplinary regimes . . . the notion of an original source . . . becomes the basis on which ends or outcomes are predicted," but "the power dynamic inherent in this predictability, expressed in the naturalized notion that a culture's origins are predictive of its final or present form, requires rethinking." As they put it, "'The Greeks' do not exist outside of or prior to [scholarly] practice; in this sense they are always emerging" (x). See also the Postclassicisms Collective 2020, chs. 1.4 and 2.7.

29. Eccleston and Padilla Peralta 2022.

30. See Bassi and Euben 2010, xiv: "We cannot erase the traditions that mediate our understanding of a text . . . But this is neither a failure nor a pathology. It merely urges us to make every condition of our reading the subject of conscious reflection while recognizing that we cannot bypass what the text has become or where we are located sociologically and historically as readers of it." As the scholars of the Postclassicism Collective put it, "Thinking we have reached out to the Other, we in fact enclose ourselves in a narcissistic fantasy of self-reference" (2020, 38). Putting the matter in somewhat different terms, I would point to the aspiration to assimilate the Other into our own cognitive apparatus when we aspire to comprehend it. Comprehending, that is, capturing, containing, is an assimilationist operation.

31. See Levinas 1969, 198: "The face speaks to me and thereby invites me to a relation incommensurate with a power exercised, be it enjoyment or knowledge."

32. Levinas 1985, 92.

33. Rancière 2011, 117.

34. Comparing Rancière's notion of "resistant form" to the formalism of the L-A-N-G-U-A-G-E poets, Fisher (2013, 166) observes that "Language Poetry does not depend upon opening up new possibilities for life, but rather in holding the rupture itself by way of sustained presentations of the unrepresentable, the 'impossible' and the 'illegible.'"

35. Fisher 2013, 168.

36. Levine 2015, 26–31.

37. C. Brooks 1947. My impression is that some versions of New Criticism, in a proto-structuralist and even proto-poststructuralist fashion, see form as a privileged site not just of tensions but of intrinsically broken wholes: see, among others, Barzilai and Bloomfield 1986 and Berman 1988.

38. As A. Benjamin puts it, "A politics of form is always a politics of forming" (2022, 106), where, in my view, the gerund *forming* is poised between formation and de-formation.

39. Saint-Amour 2020.

40. Eyers 2018; Serpell (2017, 1236) speaks of the book's "latent conservatism," its lack of interest in what Serpell calls "weird" forms, and in the way in which "time—as it stutters, swerves, slips, steeps—reforms and deforms form, occasionally moving us toward radical political ends." See also Lesjak 2019 on Levine's optimism. While MacPherson (2017, 1218) takes issue with Levine's concern with form's power to "impose a powerfully homogenizing, unifying order on the social" (2015, 80), I, like others, am more concerned with Levine's excessive attachment to "wholes": see also Olsen's and Rimell's chapters. Brinkema (2022, 259) sees "radical formalism" as the domain of *disaffordances* insofar as it "open[s] up a thinking of nonunderstanding, finitude, limit, passage, the not-something, arrival at the nothing, abeyance, inaudibility."

41. Levine 2015, 81.

42. See Telò 2020b, 17–18, 269–70.

43. Moten 2018, 17, 36, and 51.

44. Moten 2003, 1.

45. Moten 2003, 6. Foundational contributions to sound studies in classics are: S. Butler 2015 and 2018; Gurd 2016, 2018a and b; and Nooter 2012, 2017, 2018, 2019a and b, 2020.

46. Moten 2003, 14.

47. Moten 2003, 12.

48. Glissant 1997, 9: "We know ourselves as part and as crowd, in an unknown that does not terrify. We cry our cry of poetry. Our boats are open, and we sail them for everyone." See also the "cry of art," which figures broken glass, in Gwendolyn Brooks's poem "Boy Breaking Glass" as discussed by Best (2018, 55–62): on this poem, see Alford's chapter.

49. Neyra 2020, 34.

50. Kostelanetz 2018.

51. The most important representative of this Hellenistic "extreme" experimentalism is Simias of Rodi: see esp. Gurd 2022. There is a tendency to consider Simias' compositions as "marginal" or "anti-canonical" or "minor": see the title "Marginal Aberrations?" of the relevant section in the state-of-the-art treatment of Fantuzzi and Hunter (2004). From a Deleuzian-Guattarian viewpoint, this "minoritarian" character makes this formalistic experiments acts of resistance: in spite of its denigratory connotations, "ab-erration" expresses a nomadic motion. Similarly

to Simias' *technopaignia*, the *morphogrammata* of the fourth-century CE Latin author Optatianus Porphyrius have been relegated to the margins until recently: see, esp., Levitan 1985, Lobato 2017, Squire 2017, and Goldhill 2020, passim. Recent re-evaluations of these works have compared their experimentalism to the artistic avant-garde of the twentieth century.

52. Quashie 2021, 59, 82.

53. I owe the term "poethic" to Ferreira Da Silva (2014, 91), who theorizes a "Black Feminist Poethics" imagining an "existence toward the beyond of Space-time, where The Thing resists dissolving any attempt to reduce what exists—anyone and everything—to the register of the object, the other, and the commodity."

54. See Brinkema 2022, 21: "Reading without guarantee always risks defaulting on the contracts that purport to stabilize and restrain signification."

PART I
SHAPING FORMS

CHAPTER 1
MYTH, FORMALISM, AND BLACK EXPRESSION: THE CASE OF ICARUS

Patrice Rankine

Myth is a form separable from but related to poetry, drama, literature (e.g., the novel and then types of novels, the short story), or art (sculpture, painting, etc.). The formal study of myth—what Claude Lévi-Strauss called a "symbolic form"—is not in itself a new observation.[1] Tracible to the Cambridge ritualists and the advent of modern anthropology, the usefulness of myth as symbolic form appealed to such Black writers and artists in North America as Edmonia Lewis and Ralph Ellison.[2] The relationship of a particular myth, the story of Icarus, to Black aesthetic experience and expression is a proposition I advance and for which I give a few concrete examples: the work of Michael Richards, and Helen Oyeyemi's *The Icarus Girl*. Icarus as a Black expressive trope is not fixed, any more than was Icarus as a counterpart to Athena and her city in the classical period. It is precisely myth's impermanence, its malleability to time, place, function, and meaning, that makes it an appealing means of individual expression and group cohesion, affording it a psychological, political, and radical function.[3]

I return to myth as a kind of formalism throughout this chapter, but the proposition that Icarus becomes a radical formation for certain African American writers and artists—signifying, among many other things, an impasse or permanent stalemate between Western civilizing narratives and Black[ened] being, or even as an appeal to another way of knowing beyond European epistemology—requires some definitions and parameters. I use the terms "Black" and "African American" somewhat interchangeably to refer to a configuration of a people, marked and recognizable by an historical and shared experience of enslavement, abjection, and the resulting struggle for personal and collective freedom and nobility. Paul Gilroy's naming of the cultural production of this people "the Black Atlantic" has served an important critical function, notwithstanding recent critiques of Gilroy's heteronormative examples.[4] The Black Atlantic makes visible the roots and routes from which meaning has been made and foregrounds home and diaspora as central tropes.[5] From Phillis Wheatley's eighteenth-century poetry in the British colonies of North America to those of Mutabaruka in Jamaica, Steve McQueen's *Small Axe* film anthology chronicling experiences of migration to England, or Manuel Zapata Olivella's Columbian novels, Black existential expression is transatlantic though not monolithic—so that "America(n)" refers to the entire New World. Early twenty-first-century critique has arrived at the idea of the "Black[ened]" being,[6] denoting, among other phenomena, the conditional and processual nature of racial construction, namely that a Black person is first made by others, as not-human (e.g., Thomas Jefferson's "black" and "slave"), abject, and then reclaimed in the dignity of such expressions as "Black is beautiful." It is worth considering Stephen Best's observations that such reclamation is an affective choice. A beautiful conflagration, or disintegration, is a contravening wish, which David Walker's prayer (that there be "none like us" ever again in the history of humankind) conveys. As Best sees, both the suffering and sublimity of Black[ened] being is singular, as much death and destruction as beauty and meaning. As Best puts it, "there is and can be no 'we' in or following from such a time and place . . . . what 'we' share is the open secret of 'our' impossibility."[7]

As it pertains to the particular encounter of Black writers and artists with Icarus, there are several examples, including Richmond "Barthé's" 1945 figurine of Icarus as the Tuskegee Airmen, who fought for the United States in the Second World War only to return home to segregation and second-class citizenship, a topic to which Richards returns;[8] Malcolm X's reference to himself as Icarus in his autobiography, a story he likely learned in his earlier years while in prison, another shared experience of the Black Atlantic;[9] Toni Morrison's trope of flight in *Song of Solomon,* which draws from African American folklore but is heavily invested in the classical trope;[10] Ralph Ellison's *Invisible Man* and, from what we can tell, the novel he had been writing for some decades when he died in 1994, extended passages of which have been collected in *Three Days Before the Shooting.*[11]

The story of Icarus functions on the same register or frequency as the processes that define a person or group as Black. These narratives are myths, narratives that bring grounding, cohesion, and significance, not fixed for one time but mutable, given to conventional or radical formations.[12] Michael Richards's sculptures and Oyeyemi's novel are two examples of the convergence of these myths, i.e., Black[ened] being and Icarus: one instance from the end of the twentieth century, the other the beginning of the twenty-first, the former from the United States of America, the latter from England, one a visual form, the other narrative. In each case, the myth of Icarus brings about radical formations through the estrangement that unexpected juxtapositions can cause, as was the case in antiquity, i.e., through the queerness that Eve Sedgwick expresses in the idea of the "beside."[13]

Winged

A left and right arm, cast from bronze, join to form a disembodied unity, complete with hands in repose, not surrender, or in determined action (Figure 1). Five items, similar in form, hang from the figure, but they do not quite dangle. Upon close examination, these feathers have pierced the would-be flesh all the way through, so that their sharp, arrow-like tips protrude, extending inches above the floating sculpture, their edges rubbing up against skin, animal detritus becoming one physical form with the human (disem)body (Figure 2). Being bronze, these cybernetic, inoperable wings on lifeless arms evoke the poetry of Bob Marley, "Misty Morning:" "The power of philosophy floats through my head: light as a feather, heavy as lead."[14] The sculpture is surprisingly small, slight even at 38" wide, the two arms extend from the center of my chest to the tip of my middle finger (and I am 5'11). Juxtaposed to the light, almost dainty artwork, "heavy as lead" is paradoxical, a state that the material conveys, bronze being a weighty metal.

Regarding the heaviness of the subject of *Winged,* as the curators of his work, Alex Fialho and Melissa Levin, convey, "materially and conceptually, Richards used the language

Figure 1 Michael Rolando Richards, *Winged* (1999). Bonded bronze and metal, 20 x 38 x 4 inches. Courtesy of Pérez Art Museum, Miami.

of metaphor in his art to investigate racial inequity and the tension between assimilation and exclusion."[15] As in most of Richards's work at the time of his death on 9/11/2001 in the Twin Towers, the metaphor, or form, in question is not only sculpture, but also the myth of Icarus, ideally suited for the artist's interest in "the simultaneous possibilities of uplift and downfall," in this case, "in the context of the historical and ongoing oppression of black people."[16] Eerily haunting is that with *Winged*, we are in a way experiencing Richards's own flesh—haunting especially given the likely disintegration of that flesh in the cinders of the World Trade Center heat after the incineration of two airplanes melted the metal structure of the buildings, which toppled as if in a planned demolition. As Richards described of his sculptural process, "in attempting to make [the] pain and alienation of [Blackness] concrete, I use my body, the primary locus of experience, as die from which to make casts. These function as surrogates, and as entry into the work."[17] Racial inequity, the oppression of Black people, and the pain and alienation of the experiences of Blackness are narrative points of entry into artistic expression.

As an aesthetic form, sculpture follows Derek Attridge's analysis of poetry, in *The Singularity of Literature* (2004), as essentially a practice of estrangement, one for which formalism is a vehicle, as he demonstrates through a reading of the political and ethical meaning that South African writer Mongane Wally Serote performs in "The Actual

Figure 2 Detail of Michael Rolando Richards, *Winged* (1999). Bonded bronze and metal, 20 x 38 x 4 inches. Courtesy of Pérez Art Museum, Miami.

Dialogue." As he writes of literature, "otherness and singularity arise from the encounter with the words themselves, their sequence, their suggestiveness, their patterning, their interrelations, their sound and rhythms" (107). As it pertains to form, "there is no moment, not even a theoretical one, at which it is possible to isolate a purely formal property" (199). So, too, Richards's *Winged* depends, for its political and ethical meaning, on juxtaposition, or the besideness of Sedgwick that Best believes aligns Blackness and the queer, an "otherness," or estrangement, which is a formal quality of the sculptural art.[18] The disembodied limbs of *Winged* are as much a rupture from perceived normalcy as the glossy, ghostly white finish over the five busts of *A Loss of Faith Brings Vertigo*, Richards's 1994 installation (Figure 3). New images superimposed onto busts again invoke the pain and alienation of Black being in the United States. The words on four pedestals read, "When I was young I wanted to be a policeman," recalling the childhood game of "cops and robbers."

Along with images of protest and state-sanctioned violence covering these faces, indeed Richards's own Black face, given what we know of his method, the words on the centerpiece pedestal give voice to alienation: "A loss of faith brings vertigo" (Figure 4). The bust resting on this pedestal bears the image of Rodney King, brutally beaten in 1991 at the hands of a Los Angeles police officer, "like a target," as one reviewer puts it.[19] The formal attributes of the installation correspond with its content: the estrangement in

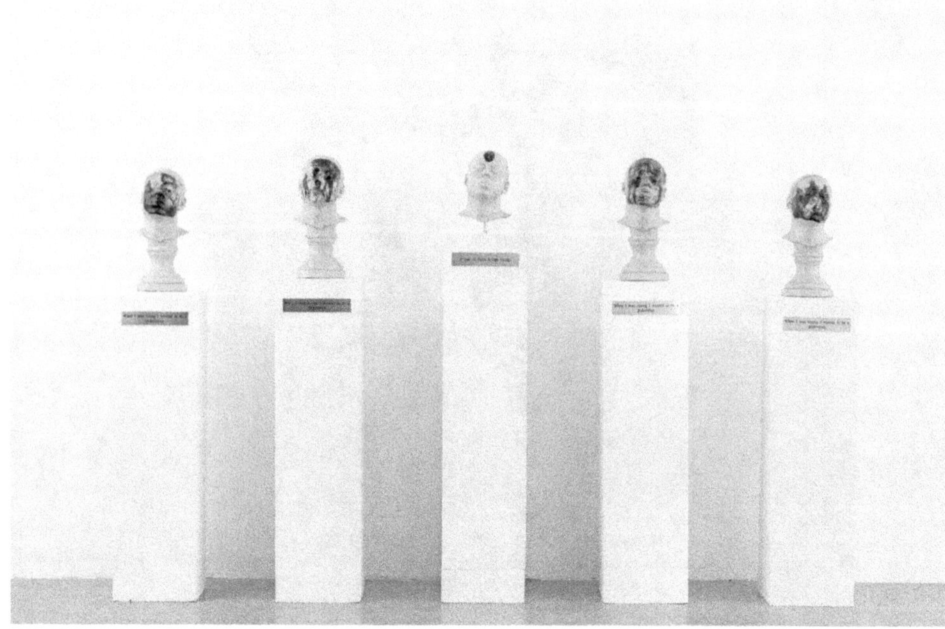

Figure 3 Michael Rolando Richards, *A Loss of Faith Brings Vertigo* (1994). Photograph by Oriol Tarridas. Photograph courtesy of the Museum of Contemporary Art, North Miami and The Michael Richards Estate.

repetition, the faciality, the expectation of sameness that differences in position, angle, and visual overlay disrupt.[20] These busts recall the copper Obalufon masks from fourteenth-century Ife, which Suzanne Blier describes in terms of fluidity, where "the very qualities of representation and differentiation enhance aspects of the real and imaginary in ways that prolong visual interest in these objects and enrich our experience of them."[21] As with Obalufon, so with *A Loss of Faith*: material, representation, repetition, and perspective are some of the formal features that result in its captivating estrangement.

Vertigo whirls the viewer back around to the stabilizing, or orienting, narrative dimension of the visual medium, the myth of Icarus that across Richards's pieces represents the purported "uplift and downfall" of Black life. Rather than turn to an indiscreet idea of "classical mythology" as the source of Richards's inspiration, it is worth amplifying the idea of myth as symbolic form, inhabited and revived with each distinct iteration. Myth is a sign system that "does not exist,"[22] independent of its social and ethical content. Building on Ferdinand de Saussure's structural work on language, Lévi-Strauss designated "mythemes" as parallel to phonemes in language. One interpreter of Lévi-Strauss describes the process as follows: "Since signs, and mythemes, are arbitrary, they have no meaning in and of themselves but only in relation to other elements in the system, in Saussure's view through their difference from other signs with which they are in systematic relation."[23] Further, the symbolic form known as myth is simply a "repertory of

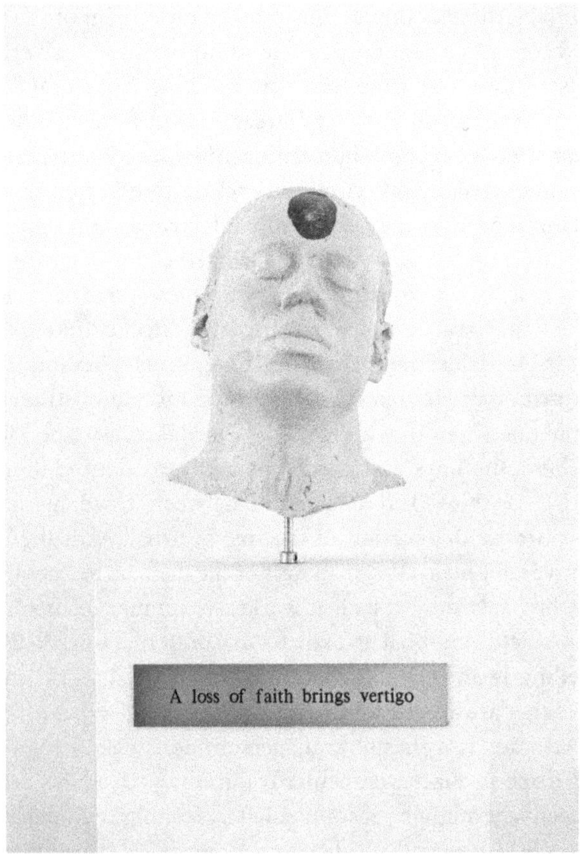

Figure 4 Detail of Michael Rolando Richards, *A Loss of Faith Brings Vertigo* (1994). Photograph by Oriol Tarridas. Photograph courtesy of the Museum of Contemporary Art, North Miami and The Michael Richards Estate.

ideas," or a set of patterns, wherein "things really deep down and really far away become one another. Everything has an opposite, and many things become their opposites."[24] Things "deep down" surfacing anew, or that which is "far away" being brought up close denote the Derridean play on difference/*différance*. In the symbolic form of myth, any meaning upon which a narrative might seem to arrive is deferred, as new arrangements arise. Hans Blumenberg (1988) referred to this process as the "work on myth" to denote its ongoing, incomplete, fluid reality, its vertiginous aliveness.

Icarus

It is worth pointing to a few instances of Icarus as mytheme in what has come to be understood as its classical context, prior to Richards's deployment. Rather than serving as an account of Richards's reception of the idea of Icarus, which he could have taken from any number of sources, these examples illustrate the movement of the symbolic form, its adaptability to new contexts, and some possible affinities with Black vernacular traditions. The Icarus story is a subset of narratives having to do with the crafted work, already in antiquity. That is, stories of Icarus always already point to an almost posthuman and metapoetic self-consciousness about human ingenuity. The commentary on craft, like a midrash, accompanies, secondly, reflections on enclosure and expansiveness, colonization and enslavement, but the tropes are also, thirdly, affective or nostalgic: the pubescent joy and effervescence of a first dance of youth or spring, the glee of gazing on a gilded work, the heated jealousy of artistic or romantic rivalry, or the anguish of the loss of a loved one.

Icarus is not the first character in the narrative that we encounter in ancient literature and art. Rather, it is Daedalus, the craftsman likened to Hephaestus, the demiurge who fashions Achilles' armor in Homer, *Iliad* 18: "On it the famous paraplegic designed a dance floor like the one when in wide Knossos Daedalus fashioned for Ariadne of the beautiful locks. There, the boys and much-courted girls danced, holding each other's hands by the wrist" (590–4). The association between Daedalus and Hephaestus is noteworthy, an ecphrastic duplication of the role of artist. As if the mimesis were not enough, the narrative later likens the quickness of the dancers to a ceramicist who "sitting at the wheel spun by his hands," tests if it works. As spinner of the narratives that take shape on Achilles' shield, the poet is akin to the potter, a worker like Hephaestus or Daedalus. Storytelling is an indelible feature of the crafted work, and Achilles' shield contains narratives that are also in some relationship to its formal function.[25]

As much as Daedalus is a master craftsperson, he is also a fugitive, and fugitivity becomes a useful trope in Black vernacular traditions.[26] Daedalus is a landless exile, a condition that, affectively, might be accompanied by feelings of hopelessness and despair, or at least melancholy. A descendant of the royal house of Athens through Erechtheus, Daedalus arrives at Crete as a runaway, having slain his nephew, alternately named Talos, Calos (in Pausanias), or Perdix (Sophocles' *Camicans* and Ovid's *Metamorphoses*). Apollodorus tells the story as follows:

> When the corpse was discovered, he was tried in the Areopagus. After being condemned, he fled to Minos. There he helped Pasiphae, who had been smitten with the bull of Poseidon, by building a wooden cow, and he constructed the labyrinth, where every year the Athenians sent seven boys, and as many girls, as food for the Minotaur (3.15.8).

It is difficult to separate Daedalus' work as craftsperson from his status as fugitive to Crete. He is on the run, moreover, because of jealousy, as Apollodorus tells it, his fear that his nephew, through his *euphuia*, his "skill," will supersede his status as student (*mathêtên onta*). Fugitivity, enslavement, and sacrificial victimhood enclose Daedalus. The annual sacrifice of fourteen young people to the Minotaur and associated stories, such as that of Theseus slaying the beast, speak to some historical relationship between the two cities.[27] In its mythic form, the practice begins with the murder of Minos' son, Androgeus, in Athens, after his victory in the Panathenaic Games.

Into this fraught world of his father enters Icarus. As part of a cycle of violence (or pattern of behavior), Icarus' demise was a foregone conclusion. Imagine Icarus on the therapist's couch: a murderous, fugitive father, who in aiding Pasiphae is betraying his host, her husband, Minos; a patron/craftsperson/father given to jealousy, who inappropriately and unnecessarily perceives a rivalry with a young person he should have nurtured, as student and kin; and all of this before Daedalus' evident problem of Promethean, human craft challenging the laws of nature. There are narrative gaps in the story, such as the reason for Daedalus' sudden flight from Crete, but Minos' displeasure at the architect's assistance of Pasiphae would be enough of an explanation.[28] In the fragment from Euripides' *Cretans*, Pasiphae defends her love for the bull with whom she conceives the Minotaur and, in contrast to her, Minos' adamant nature is confirmed in Plato and Plutarch. Whatever the case, Daedalus must hasten from Crete, and he plots with his son Icarus alongside.

The earliest representations of Icarus' flight and fall are on a black-figured vase (likely a hydría) from the sixth century BCE.

Figure 5 Terracotta lekythos (oil flask), attributed to the Icarus Painter (second quarter of the fifth century BCE). Metropolitan Museum of Art, New York, Fletcher Fund, 1924.

The shard, from the Acropolis, Athens, shows two winged feet as if running, with the name "Ikaros" inscribed. The fragment is from a vase depicting the birth of Athena from Zeus' head, another demiurgic innovation, which Hephaestus aids.[29] The pot reactivates the Homeric kinship between Hephaestus and Daedalus, and here too the artistic form and its narrative content are inextricably bound. Daedalus is to Hephaestus as Hephaestus is to Athena. As such, Icarus' connection to Athens is also evident in the "imaginal" associations chosen.[30] Whereas his father is akin to a god, Icarus is likely always already a representation of limits. On a terracotta lêkythos from the end of the fifth century BCE (Figure 5), a bird devolves downward toward a crouched man, his wings in inverse or chiasmal relationship to the bird with which he is associated. Icarus' demise, which is part of a broader network of narratives linking Athens and Crete, is by classical times a repeated trope.

Exile, fugitivity, and ingenuity are thematic for the father; an added feature in Vergil is the grief of a father at the loss of his son. In the *Aeneid*, Aeneas arrives at the cave of the Sibyl, at Euboean Cumae, where he sees a shrine that Daedalus has dedicated to Apollo, a thanksgiving offering for his safe passage from Crete. The poet juxtaposes the father's success to grief for his son, a relationship that in this context recalls that between Aeneas and Anchises, whom the son carries on his shoulders from a burning Troy:

> Daedalus, the story goes, having fled the kingdom of Minos, fettered with wings dared to entrust himself to the sky. He floated along an unusual path to cold Northern climes, and at last he stood lightly above the Chalcidian summit. To you, Phoebus, once restored to land here he consecrated his oar of wings and established a huge temple: on the doors the death of Androgeus; then the children of Cecrops, a pity, ordered to pay as yearly tribute the bodies of seven sons. The urn for drawing lots was there. On the other side the land of Crete faces the elevated sea, where there is the excruciating lust related to the bull. Pasiphae is falsely hidden, and the mixed breed, double-natured offspring, the Minotaur, is present, a testament to unnatural passion. Here that labyrinth that causes disorienting vertigo, the architect's work. For now Daedalus himself, pitying the great passion of the queen, solved the tricky pathways of the building by guiding one's blind steps with thread. Icarus, you also were to have a great part in the affair, were the pain to have allowed it. Twice Daedalus tried to fashion your misfortune in gold, and twice your father's hands faltered (6.14–33).

There are several noteworthy aspects to Vergil's comprehensive narrative that carry over to the myth's later reception. Daedalus has, after all, consecrated a shrine, the *immania templa* (19), to Apollo, a monument that serves as if a compendium of the Cretan narratives. The shrine is one of the architect's several successes, which include the wings themselves, by which he can fly (*ausus se credere caelo* 15); the wooden cow, the *furtum* (24), in which Pasiphae hides to consort with the bull; and the labyrinth (27), a puzzle for which Daedalus also provides the solution (*dolos resolvit* 29). What he cannot accomplish, however, is a rendering of Icarus, and his repeated failure (twice, *bis*, 32, 33) conveys a trauma, the father's inability to come to terms with the loss. Given the failure to represent, the story of Icarus is here told through apophasis or praeteritio, a presence through absence. Daedalus, who fled Athens for the murder of his nephew, is remorseful about this death of the second youth, his son, now that he has completed a second journey. Androgeus, Minos' son, is here a third loss of a son. Despite Daedalus' failure to represent his own grief, as demiurge he is otherwise distinguished, a maker to be counted among the gods: just as the Minotaur is a testament to Venus' power (*Veneris monumenta nefandae* 26), Daedalus too has left monuments—this one to Apollo, the labyrinth, and also the gift of flight, notwithstanding the necessary losses that come with such experimentation.[31]

All these excerpts are examples of the relationship between form and content. Ecphrasis is a consistent mode of storytelling across the instances cited, but in each context the mythemes serve functions specific to its teller. Whereas in the *Iliad*, Daedalus' craft was a testimony to handiwork of the god Hephaestus, and in the Athenian pottery the presence of the eponymous goddess, also a craftsperson, was central; these deities are absent from Vergil's telling of the story. The association of craft and divinity remains palpable in the *Aeneid*, but here Apollo and Venus are more appropriate associations for Daedalus. These are Roman visitations of the divine, the former the god of the military triumph of Octavian at Actium, the latter his immortal ancestor, as he is her son Aeneas' descendant, as Augustus. Mythemes are not only in the characters of Daedalus, Apollo, etc., but they are also present in the imagery, as will become clearer in how Oyeyemi deploys imaginal connections to gold in *Icarus Girl*.

As it pertains to the narrative's affective pull, the mistake (or liability) that comes to be associated with Icarus is still absent from Vergil's narrative; guilt rests on the father in the *Aeneid*. The loss of a son would be gruesome. Daedalus' successful flight to Cumae attests to the power of his craft, or at least to fate (again, *ausus se credere caelo* 15), but there is always an underside to triumph. Emotion tied to Daedalus corresponds with that for Aeneas, which aligns Vergil's Icarus with Androgeus, Dido, and others lost in the founding of Rome. Figured as personal loss in the *Aeneid*, there is in Ovid's telling in *Metamorphoses* a new emphasis on the potential harm that technical innovation can bring, along with marvel at the very processes of production.[32] Rather than the trauma of the father over the loss of his son, Ovid now focuses on Icarus' behavior, even if the authorial voice does not fully commit to any judgment of the son's inattention to this father's instruction.

Like the exiled poet himself, Daedalus "hating his long exile and moved by a yearning for his native land, was closed in by the sea" (182–5). In his desire to escape from Crete, Daedalus, a *homo faber*, surveys his options, focusing on natural, elemental components consistent with the Epicurean understanding in Lucretius.[33] He chooses the vast sky: "'Let him block the land and sea. The sky is absolutely open. That's the way we will go. Minos owns everything, but he does not own the skies'" (185–7). Plato had already given us Minos the tyrant, and Ovid makes good use of that mytheme, paralleling the literary trope of his—the poet's and his character's—exile at the hands of an absolute despot. The sympathy for Daedalus continues, as he renders clear instructions to Icarus, who "stands nearby and, unaware (*ignarus*) that he is handling threats to his life, now smiling ear-to-ear, took the plumes, which moved about with the breeze. Now he was softening the bright wax with his thumb, and then impeding the marvelous work of his father with his playfulness" (195–200). Daedalus warns Icarus of the middle course between the heat of the sun above and the sea below (*"medio" que "ut limite curras, / Icare," ait "moneo"* 203–4). Icarus' fall is a result of youthful indiscretion: "When the boy began to delight in his bold flight, he deserted his leader. He was led away by desire for higher heights and took that path" (224–5). Seeking to reach the sky or the stars might be "programmatic for the *hybris* theme,"[34] and the error is consistent with Greek hamartia, if hybris translates harshly. Hoefmans puts it poignantly: "Being a parent makes one vulnerable through his/ her children. Daedalus, composed as he may be as the self-contained artisan, cannot avoid the test and the failure of his values when he exposes his son to an endeavour he himself is up to, but apparently not this too young child."[35]

Before returning to the potential of Black receptions that Richards's *Winged* signals, it is worth considering Pieter Bruegel's 1560 painting (Figure 6), for its resonances with Ovid as well as its departures from the epic narrative. Like Roman wall paintings of the first century CE, which tend to depict "Icarus in the act of falling or both the falling and the dead Icarus,"[36] Bruegel demonstrates a fascination with Ovid's manneristic attention to surrounding details. Bruegel can depict curious departures visually in ways that Ovid cannot, even in a detailed narrative. At first glance, the viewer of the painting might seem optically to enter Ovid's text: "Someone while casting the knotted net for fish, a shepherd leaning on his staff, or a farmer on his plough, each one sees these men [Icarus and his father] and marvels. Each onlooker believed he beheld gods, since none could touch the sky" (217–20). In keeping with artistic form, Bruegel paints a landscape in which sky, land, and sea somewhat supersede the human presence, along with inventions that might seem to parallel concepts of innovation: Dutch sailing vessels, a ploughshare, and buildings in the distance. The painting toys with perspective and depth of field to convey different points of emphasis from those of Ovid. Although Bruegel depicts the fisherman, farmer, and shepherd, unlike in the epic narrative, none of these people seems particularly rapt at Daedalus' feat or Icarus' plunge into the sea. Only the shepherd stops his activity to look toward the sky, and from the vantage point of the painting's viewer, this figure is looking off to the left, in the opposite direction, his back turned as Icarus' feet appear at bottom right register. We might believe Bruegel has seen the Icarus hydria, were it not for the pot's late twentieth century reemergence, or the lack of wings on Icarus' feet. The painting is almost melodramatic, affective or melancholic neither from the perspective of those within the landscape, who seem to miss Icarus' fall, nor that of the painting's viewer, who struggles to find Icarus, almost as if in a game of his insignificance. As much as Bruegel might be drawing from Ovid, Lyckle de Vries argues that Bruegel's painting is as resonant with his Roman antecedents as with the fourteenth-century *Ovide moralisé* and sixteenth-century emblem books of Gilles Corrozet and Johannes Sambucus, the former of which "advises the reader not to stray from the golden mean," the latter also depicting "among other figures, a falling Icarus."[37] Whereas before the rise of Christianity a winged man might be associated with Pegasus, Hermes or Athena Nike, by the sixteenth-century Lucifer, the fallen angel, is as much in play. According to one

Figure 6 Pieter I Bruegel, *Fall of Icarus*. Royal Museums of Fine Arts of Belgium, Brussels, inv. 4030. Photo: J. Geleyns.

overambitious reading (which de Vries recounts), "the floundering figure in the water is supposed to be a fallen devil with wings and claws."[38] There is no reason to push this interpretation because Christian themes are already no doubt present. The ploughman's focus suggests the virtue of labor, as he reaps, as it were, "by the sweat of [his] brow" (Genesis 3:19).

The Icarus Girl

To return to Black Atlantic receptions, I end with Helen Oyeyemi's *The Icarus Girl*, which again demonstrates, first, estrangement, otherness, difference/*différance* that results from being placed beside; and, secondly, that this juxtaposition can itself be radical. Estrangement, new associations, is itself a means of change, or a rerooting. *The Icarus Girl* was the debut novel of Nigerian-born writer Helen Oyeyemi, whose family moved to London when she was four. Nineteen when she wrote the book, Oyeyemi channels the angst of identity formation, as a process never fully complete even in adulthood.[39] Like the eight-year-old protagonist of her novel, Jessamy Harrison, called Jess, Oyeyemi was a voracious reader, awkward around others, and struggled with being between two cultures. As Oyeyemi puts it, "I was a real mess at school. I got a bit of a reputation for being the weird girl, the girl who'd go silent randomly and just kind of write down replies to people's questions in a book."[40] The affective experience of alienation belies the celebration of hybridity that often accompanies an accomplishment like *The Icarus Girl*, which was widely celebrated and nominated for awards. Oyeyemi describes herself being deeply depressed as a child and overdosing at 15, owing at least in part to the isolation of not finding others with whom she could relate, whether in life or in books, "especially in the classics," as she characterizes it. Although with *The Icarus Girl* Oyeyemi "wasn't really aware that I was writing a first novel," the narrative becomes a site for the formal mediation of her experiences. As Jordan Stouck puts the case, "the novel form invokes expectations, even if these are not always fulfilled, of exposition, climax and denouement so that in using this form, Oyeyemi places her character on a trajectory of change and process."[41] The Icaran fall, however, is a narrative resolution that some critics have found unsatisfactory, variously describing it as predictable, hasty, or implausibly constructed.[42]

Oyeyemi's Yoruba setting surfaces throughout the novel. Jess has a ghostly female double, Titiola, whom she names TillyTilly for fear of mispronouncing the Nigerian name.[43] TillyTilly haunts the boys' quarters of the ancient compound belonging to Jess' Nigerian grandfather. Freedom, flight, and escape are repeated, Daedalian themes, and the novel also evokes enclosure and confinement. The title provides the primary means of structuring *The Icarus Girl* as allusive to ancient narratives, and a plethora of other fragmented images scatter across the book. Flight, for example, is figured from the novel's first pages, when Jessamy, the daughter of Sarah Harrison, a woman of Yoruba ancestry, and her white, English husband, Daniel, travel from England to Nigeria. Other motifs proliferate early on, from an allusion to Jess as Dorothy from *The Wizard of Oz*—"she tried not to think about clicking her heels together, then watched her feet to see if the heels clicked independently"—to an embroidered, dreamlike pattern on a stranger's *iro ati buba*, a traditional women's garment: "Yellow snakes, coiled up like golden orange peel, sprang from the beaks of the vivid red birds with outstretched wings which soared across the royal blue background of the woman's clothing."[44] In a riff that intertwines myths not elsewhere associated, the woman is as much Yoruba embodiment as evocative of Medusa: "Jess kept her eyes fixed on the woman, caught by her gaze, gradually growing frightened, as if somehow she could not look away or let this woman out of her sight. Would that be dangerous, to *not* look while being looked at?"[45]

The Icarus theme itself flickers like light in the novel, now taking form, now scattered and barely visible, e.g., the gold that figures both in ancient narratives and Oyeyemi's. Recall that in Vergil, Daedalus draws his story in gold, although the representation of Icarus eludes him. Similarly, Ovid's narrative announces the blazing fire of the sun, which melts the waxen wings when Icarus flies too close, against his father's instructions. Gold, as precious metal and as rays of the sun, could be part of any story or landscape, but in *The Icarus Girl* its infrathin connection ties the Greek and Roman tropes to West African antiquities,[46] evoking the majesty of a region from which gold and other materials were extracted, until the Black[ened] bodies of human beings became the commodity of international, capitalistic, transatlantic trade. Jess' Yoruba name is Wuraola, which means gold. Her grandfather's compound, which "had been this way since the 1870s," is labyrinthine, Minoan, such that the "houses stopped light from reaching the centre, forcing it to push through at angles and in chinks, which was why the inside of her grandfather's house was often so dim and in shadow, except for the top floor and the balcony roof, which during the day were bathed constantly in waterfalls of gold."[47]

Beyond a case study in classical reception, the novel reveals myth to be a ubiquitous, melded form. While the title *The Icarus Girl* would suggest Greek or Roman sources, the narrative moves alongside the Romantics, Samuel Taylor Coleridge's "Kubla Khan" (1797, 1816) the first explicit reference to the breadth and depth of Oyeyemi's associations, from which she allows the precocious and well-read Jess to draw, her mother a professor of literature. The title of Coleridge's poem suggests eastern, Mongolian sources, but its "woman wailing for her demon-lover" is just as evocative of Pasiphae and the Minotaur. "Kubla Khan" makes Jess "think of . . . you know, when something's so different and weird that when it touches other people it makes them different and weird too."[48] This is to be beside. Such is the otherness, or the estrangement, that art, literature, and myth can effect. Jess names the phenomenon "holy dread," which approximates something akin to what the narrator of the *Aeneid* describes Daedalus as experiencing (and how Aeneas views the monument), a depth of emotion that interrupts activity. Put otherwise, holy dread is sublimity, reaching outside of reality's vertiginous pull to take wings and fly, or as Richards suggests in an unpublished installation, it is to achieve "escape velocity" (from the title of an unpublished work). Flight has this implication for human beings, given the potential gravity of our winglessness. In *The Icarus Girl*, the individual identity of an eight-year-old requires flight to reconnect her to part of her familial, ancestral ties. In England, she is incomplete, so given to quietude and her books that she is awkward in school and visits a therapist. But neither is she complete in Nigeria. Stouck describes this being in between as "abject hybridity," denoting the impossibility of laying oneself beside another when the self is never a fully formed phenomenon. Stouck reminds us that "we need to read in-depth for the losses embedded in hybrid experience."[49]

Oyeyemi figures these losses, the "lived experiences of humiliation and self-loathing" that can be located "within Julia Kristeva's narrative of abjection,"[50] in hybrid terms, through the trope of Icarus' fall now set beside a Yoruba one. As the story progresses, Icarus' fall figures this abjection. In the novel, Jess discovers that she had a twin that was lost at birth, named Fern. In keeping with a Yoruba practice that the family had abandoned, they carve an Ibeji doll, "as a substitute for the deceased twin."[51] The Ibeji protects the living against untimely intrusions from the dead, or the third-space of the bush, where spirits live. The Ibeji can also be a protector of leaders, which puts Jess at the center of the heroic narrative. Within this cosmology, TillyTilly is not simply an imaginary friend. Rather, she is the ghostly spirit that roams until Jess can master this outside force. She does so in part not through any intellectual understanding or physical touching, a laying beside or a moment of infrathin contact. Rather, TillyTilly inhabits Jess, and Jess eventually consumes TillyTilly. This consumption, a beautiful death of self not unlike David Walker's "none like us," is vertigo—the fall of Icarus now figured in terms of the impossibility of resolution in the wake of abject hybridity.

Flying Home

I have foregrounded myth as a formal consideration, and by way of some concluding thoughts, it is worth opening the conversation beyond the authors and artists in this chapter. *Flying Home*, for example, is the title of collected short stories of Ralph Ellison written between 1937 and 1954, featuring the story from which the series takes its title. In these stories as well, Icaran flight is a central mytheme. I return to Ellison, even as I included *Invisible Man* and *Three Days Before the Shooting...* in the opening survey of Black authors and artists interested in the Icarus myth, as a way of reiterating the recurrence of tropes of flight and homeward journeys. In these stories, as in the art and literature that I have discussed throughout the chapter, I would draw attention to three considerations for further work on Icarus and other mythemes in Black art and literature.

First, attention to form is important. Richards and Oyeyemi convey a sense of the mytheme in the hands of a sculptor and a novelist. Throughout the chapter, Icarus and his paternal forerunner, Daedalus, have recurred in ancient epics, including Homer, Vergil, and Ovid. Bruegel offers a view of the two-dimensional, visual form, different from but in some ways related to sculpture. If we take formalism seriously, then considering how they occasion different aspects of the mythemes—different perspectives and meaning—is paramount. In this chapter, I have approached myth as an epiphenomenon that allows entry into and regress from other forms, even noting similarities among the forms—e.g., sculpture and literature both bring estrangement through laying unlikely phenomenon beside one another.

If attention to form is the first concluding observation, the note on periodization is also of importance. Richmond "Barthé's" 1945 figurine of the Tuskegee Airmen as Icarus might seem to land upon similar symbols, and yet they function differently, even as expressions of a particular experience of Black people. Briefly, the fragmentation of the body in Richards's study of Icarus seems visually to contradict the upright posture of the "Barthé's" figure. There are several possible reasons for this difference, but the early twenty-first century framework of Afropessimism, not entirely available to Barthé, provides some language for grappling with Richards's new existential reality. To period (or time) we might add space, as in some ways Richards and Oyeyemi might be considered of the same period and yet from different geographical locations. I have used the Black Atlantic framework to travel this distance, and yet there is some friction in this. The Black Atlantic blurs distinctions between colonial experiences; a Yoruba descendent living in England is not the same as a Jamaican immigrant living in Queens, New York, although these experiences might be said, through the Black Atlantic, to share some attributes. A deeper study of the Icarus trope across these authors and artists would attend to the moves between place and time, and even secular and sacred, as modernity sheds mythic language accompanying these figures in ancient times, e.g., "priest," "sacrifice," "sacred," etc.

A final consideration for broader study is the issue of affect. The effervescent joy of the young dancers on Achilles' shield in Homer's *Iliad*, which Hephaestus crafts and that alludes to Daedalus, clashes against the ineffable grief of Daedalus the father in Vergil's *Aeneid*, who cannot bring himself to recreate the loss of his son Icarus—so real is representation, so affective (and effective) the reproduction. Other emotions include the childlike impatience of Ovid's Icarus. Are these emotions the same as those Richards evokes in his work, or the various feelings that Oyeyemi surveys in her novel, from Jess' impatience to her fierceness? Does Icarus' Ovidian responsibility speak directly to Black agency and self-determinacy, as Malcolm X indicates in his autobiographical association with Icarus? Or, as Daniel M. Gross argues in *The Secret History of Emotion* (2006), are we speaking about different phenomena once we cross the divide of time? I present these and other questions for future study.

Notes

1. For an overview, see Doniger 2010.

2. A body of scholarship concerned with Black engagement with the classics, from literature to theatrical performance, has proliferated over the past two decades, including Rankine 2006, Walters 2007, Goff and Simpson 2008, Greenwood 2010, Cook and Tatum 2012, Roynon 2013, Rankine 2013, Hairston 2016, Malamud 2019, and Barnard 2021. Some of these works have a tangential interest in myth, but none takes on the form directly per se.

3. Bottici's arguments in 2007 and elsewhere are too complex to expound upon here, but she develops a political theory of myth as bringing groups or collectives "grounding" and "significance." Since "there is not a single 'self' that can tell the whole story" (241), the group is reliant on others to complete—to future—the narrative, and this is the "danger" to which plurality points (242). She challenges the scientific basis of political philosophy as a discipline, arguing that "a purely rational model of society risks being a model for a world that does not exist" (2007, 1).

4. Gilroy 1993. For critiques, see, for example, Tinsley 2008.

5. See Hall 2021.

6. See Z. Jackson 2020 and Wilderson III 2020.

7. Best 2018, 22.

8. See Smalls 2018 for a nuanced treatment that takes into account classicism and gender. At the conference where this paper was initially presented, the session facilitator Kenneth Warren raised an important question about periodization as it pertains to these works. It is worth noting how different Barthé's 1945 work is from Richards's at the turn of the century. The reasons why are beyond the scope of this paper, but I hope to take these topics up in my extended work on Icarus in Black aesthetic traditions.

9. See Alexander 2020.

10. See Rankine 2006 and Roynon 2013.

11. See Roynon 2021.

12. See Bottici 2007. Frazer Tessema also deserves credit for an unpublished undergraduate essay on the Icarus theme in *Invisible Man*.

13. See Best 2018, 62. On "flight" as a figuration of radical formalism, see also Phillips's and Nooter's chapters.

14. The song is from the 1978 album *Kaya*, Bob Marley and the Wailers.

15. See Nonnenberg 2019.

16. Nonnenberg 2019.

17. Edalatpour 2019.

18. See Best 2018, 62.

19. Barone 2016.

20. To borrow from Marjorie Perloff's analysis of literature, these differences can sometimes be infrathin (2021). On Deleuze and Guattari's notion of faciality in art, see Blier 2017.

21. Blier 2017, 251.

22. Edmunds 1990, 1. Edmunds's volume includes several important contributors, among which Claude Calame's essay on the birth of Cyrene is notable: "Since Calame holds that there is no such thing as 'Greek mythology,' that 'myths' are available only as particular texts in particular genres, he shifts the focus from the utterance [énoncé], which would be the myth as found, say, in a handbook of mythology, to the enunciation [énonciation], which is, for the purposes of his essay, three odes of Pindar, *Pythians* 4, 5, and 9" (1990, 275–6). Calame establishes the notion of canonic schema, e.g., the relationship between distant authors like Pindar and Apollodorus in their mythmaking, which, as Edmunds argues, establishes a kind of énoncé, the "mythology" writ large that Calame asserts does not exist.

23. Philen 2005, 223. Philen goes on to say that "the workings and meaning of myth operate analogously to the way meaning is produced in linguistic signs: through relationality and difference" (225).

24. The citations are from Doniger 2010, 197, 199.

25. Homeric and archaic narratives move toward casting the worker or craftsperson as noble, notwithstanding the demiurge's fortune with beggars, wanderers, and the enslaved. Hephaestus' disability status, tied to his identity as a craftsperson, might bring a certain singularity and awe, but it is also the source of humor and scorn (*Iliad* 1); on form and disability, see Telò's chapter. In contrast, Odysseus' unwillingness to work with his hands separates him from Eumaeus, notwithstanding the latter's role in disrupting perceptions of nobility and status in the second half of Homer's *Odyssey*. In keeping with these narratives, Daedalus is not enslaved, but his presence in Crete is more curious than we might initially suspect.

26. See, for example, see Moten and Harney 2004.

27. This is not a topic that seems to have interested classical scholars recently, but for longer-standing work see Mylonas 1940. Although historical specificity is lacking, from the perspective of the original rupture to which these stories might point, they serve a similar function to the artwork of Obalufon, as Blier describes it: "If art in ancient life is shaped, as I argue, in large measure by difficulties incurred in a devastating early civil war that pitted families and neighborhoods against one another, these artworks also served in the aftermath of these events as visual loci to help repair the fractured center. These objects, in short, not only helped to heal this center, but also were a means to recall and commemorate the critical roles played by leading figures on both sides of the contestation and its resolution" (2017, 17).

28. See Gantz 1993 for an overview of sources, which include many not listed here, such as Plutarch.

29. As Beasley wrote, "without the inscription one would have guessed Hermes, or rather Perseus" (1927, 225). Beasley affirmed that "the Birth of Athena is a subject which, like the Birth of Erichthonios, and the Maker of Pandora, unites Athena and Hephaestus. There was space for another subject: he [the artist] chose the story of Daedalus—the great craftsman, pattern of all those who make daedal things—and his intrepid son Icarus" (227).

30. Along with Bottici (2014), I use "imaginal" here to convey the real-world images and associations that mythemes invoke, independent of their truth-claims. As Bottici puts it, "in

contrast to imagination and imaginary, the concept of the imaginal emphasizes the centrality of images, rather than the faculty or the context that produces them; therefore, it does not make any assumptions about the individual or social character of such faculty" (5).

31. The *remigium alarum* in line 19 is worth pausing on, the paradoxical phrase being like the ship's oar that Odysseus founded on the remotest land as a witness, perhaps a *monumentum*, to Poseidon. This founding symbol comes into play in the Calame article on Cyrene, cited above, in Edmunds 1990.

32. The following passage from *Metamorphoses* echoes aspects of the attention to craft already noted from Homer: "He put the feathers in order beginning from the smallest, with the short ones following the long, so that you would think they had grown on an incline. Just as the old Pan pipes rise little by little with their uneven reeds. In this way he fastened them in the middle with twine and at the bottom with wax, and he bent them in the middle on a curve with care, so that they really looked like wings" (189–95).

33. See Hoefmans 1994, especially 149–56.

34. Hoefmans 1994, 146.

35. Hoefmans 1994, 158.

36. Blanckenhagen 1957, 82.

37. de Vries 2003, 7.

38. de Vries 2003, 8.

39. I am thinking here of the work of Appiah, especially but not exclusively 2018.

40. Sethi 2005.

41. Stouck 2011, 93–4.

42. Stouck 2011, 106.

43. See Stouck 2011 on naming and the loss of identity that accompanies hybridity.

44. Oyeyemi 2005, 8–9.

45. Oyeyemi 2005, 9.

46. On the infrathin, see Perloff 2021.

47. Oyeyemi 2005, 33.

48. Oyeyemi 2005, 57.

49. Stouck 2011, 90.

50. Stouck 2011, 89.

51. Stouck 2011, 89.

CHAPTER 2
FUGITIVE COLOR: FROM TROY TO THE BLACK ATLANTIC[1]

Shane Butler

A Hero Screams

A plaque on the façade of 29 Welbeck Street, London, announces, "Thomas Woolner, Royal Academician, sculptor and poet, lived here, 1860–1892." Most passersby today are unlikely to have heard of this long-ago resident of the house that once stood on this spot (replaced in 1901 by the current structure), though he was well known in his time, not least as a founding member of the Pre-Raphaelite Brotherhood. On Friday, December 8, 1865, a distinguished party gathered here for dinner with Woolner, who had found commercial success chiefly as a sculptor of portraits of the famous men of the day, such as Alfred Tennyson, whom he had sculpted in 1856 and would again sculpt in 1873. Tennyson, in fact, was the evening's most eminent invitee, but also present were others Woolner sculpted: William Gladstone, whose portrait, done in clay in 1863, would be exhibited in stone in 1868, the year he first became prime minister; F. D. Maurice, the outspoken socialist theologian, whose portrait had been exhibited in 1861; the poet and critic Francis Palgrave, of whom Woolner had sculpted a medalion, also exhibited in 1861; and, finally, John Addington Symonds, MD, a respected physician from Bristol whose portrait-bust would be exhibited in the approaching new year.[2] Crucially for our story, Woolner had also urged the physician's son, also called John Addington Symonds, who lived not very far away, at 47 Norfolk Square, with his wife and newborn daughter, to join the party after dinner, at 9:30 p.m. The son, destined to become one of Victorian Britain's most prolific and wide-ranging authors, evidently contributed barely a word to the learned conversation, but he listened attentively, setting pen to paper back home that very night (or so he would later claim) to record all he remembered, which is what now allows us to reconstruct the scene.[3]

The main after-dinner amusement was provided by an ultimately successful attempt to persuade Tennyson to read a translation he had worked up of an episode from the eighteenth book of the *Iliad*. At this moment in Homer's narrative, Patroclus has been killed but his body still lies on the battlefield, desperately guarded by his fellow Greeks; Achilles' mother, Thetis, has commanded her son not to enter the fray until she returns with new armor for him to don; Iris, however, has just been sent by Hera to urge him to make some kind of appearance to rally the troops and so to save Patroclus' body from mutilation. Tennyson had translated the ensuing scene, as Achilles, accompanied and protected by Athena, makes his way to the edge of the battlefield and sends forth a shout that causes the terrified Trojans to turn and flee. He would later publish the translation as "Achilles Over the Trench," which first appeared on the first page of the August 1877 issue of *The Nineteenth Century*, a new magazine destined to exert significant influence over politics and art alike in Victorian Britain.[4] Before its publication, the translation was instead kept in a manuscript volume of other Homeric translations, now preserved at the Morgan Library in New York.[5]

In Symonds's account of the party, the volume of translations first appears in Woolner's hands, presumably having been brought by Tennyson himself that night or lent to Woolner by him on some earlier occasion. Woolner passes it along to Gladstone, who at first reads quietly, until Tennyson emerges from the dining room, from which the group is slowly migrating to the drawing room, in part to join the ladies, of whom, however, the account mentions only two: Woolner's wife Alice and her sister Fanny Waugh, nicknamed "the goddess" and engaged to the Pre-Raphaelite painter Holman Hunt, another of the male guests. Hunt's haunting posthumous portrait of his wife, who died in childbirth in Italy a year later, is now in the Toledo Museum of Art[6]; his statue of her adorns her tomb in Florence. Woolner himself had originally been in love with Fanny but married Alice instead; Hunt would later marry the youngest sister, Edith, to Woolner's fury and in contravention of what was then the law in Britain regarding incest.[7] Those earlier and later episodes are, strictly speaking, extraneous to the story I am now telling; nevertheless, they offer a peculiarly apt emblem of the way in which, in the world we have entered through the door of 29 Welbeck Street, people and things will continue to reveal themselves to be separated by surprisingly and even alarmingly few degrees of separation. This proximity, I might already say, exemplified by the endogamously exchanged desires of the Woolners, Hunts, and Waughs, is a sign that we are in the presence of something sufficiently self-contained and self-referential to be called a system. At the same time, Alice and Fanny themselves, in the drawing room, that is, in the room to which one "withdraws," including if one is a woman and not meant to participate in the conversations of gentlemen, reveal that even something as thoroughly systematized as a middle-class Victorian household is anything but a simple box, its property line neatly distinguishing between interior and exterior, like a moat around the castle that is a man's house. Inside Woolner's house, as in all the other houses that neatly line both sides of Welbeck Street, there was a drawing room, that is, a room that purported to be both outside and even deeper inside, a place not of inclusion, but of seclusion.

It is in this room that Woolner first asks Tennyson to read. Palgrave chimes in, "Come you! A shout in the trench!" Tennyson, visibly annoyed, refuses and yanks the volume from Gladstone's hands. Various attempts to sway him fail, and Tennyson diverts the conversation in order to expound his views on various other subjects, including God. Then, abruptly, Tennyson changes his mind about reading, and the entire party returns to the dining room, which we must assume that the house's other insider-outsiders, its servants, have cleared in the long interim, scurrying upstairs and downstairs and back again, mostly out of sight and out of mind. Tennyson begins in what Symonds characterizes as "a deep bass growl," and a miraculous piece of later evidence enables us to form a pretty good idea of what this sounded like. On May 15, 1890, two years before his death, Tennyson allowed himself to be recorded by an agent of Thomas Edison, sent to his house with a newly improved phonograph expressly for the purpose of capturing his voice. As several scholars have observed, Edison's urgent push to record Tennyson before his death was driven by more than the poet's global fame. Almost from the moment of the phonograph's invention, Tennyson's verses began to be re-read as having desiderated just such a technology, capable of capturing "the sound of a voice that is still," in the words of his "Break, Break, Break," itself frequently recorded in demonstrations of the new machine.[8]

Unsurprisingly, Tennyson in 1890 did not read "Achilles Over the Trench" or any of his other Homeric renderings. Conveniently for comparison, however, a similarly tumultuous battlefield was the setting of an original work he did read, namely, "The Charge of the Light Brigade," one of his most famous poems, written in 1854, just after the British military disaster it describes, at the Battle of Balaclava during the Crimean War.[9] Tennyson's delivery is startlingly bombastic, apparently seeking to activate poetic sound—including the poem's partly dactylic meter—as a distant and transformed but still unmistakable echo of the sounds of war: galloping horses, cannonfire, and the thud of falling bodies. A second recording captured him reading the "Bugle Song," a famous interlude in "The Princess." This time, the original take reportedly had to be abandoned when Tennyson's equally histrionic delivery of the words "Blow, bugle, blow" (which are followed in the line by "set the wild echoes flying") prompted his infant grandson to burst into laughter, soon echoed by Tennyson himself; the subsequent, surviving recording, alas, lacks the laughter of either. Just after the reading of the first poem and just before that of the second, Tennyson thanks the agent for demonstrating Edison's "miraculous invention." The two poems tell different stories, but the link between their soundscapes is there in the battle-bugle. A few months later, in fact, a recording would be made of the actual bugler of the Light Brigade, repeating the same blast he played at Balaclava; this and the Tennyson recordings would be used to raise money for the battle's surviving veterans, whose destitution had already been lamented a decade earlier by Rudyard Kipling in "The Last of the Light Brigade." If all this phonographic militarism momentarily surprises us now (though compare, of course, the still familiar role of war in film), it was very much part of the device's early history, as Friedrich Kittler has demonstrated in great detail. Under the circumstances, it is tempting to regard the grandson's laugh—as much an irruption of the sonic real, in Kittlerian terms, as is the recorded bugle blast—as an unwitting protest. In any case, its emitter would grow up to be thrice wounded in the First World War, in which conflict his two younger brothers, yet unborn in 1890, would perish. His autobiography, *From Verse to Worse*, is dedicated to his grandfather.[10]

In "Achilles Over the Trench," as in its Homeric source, war's sonic horrors are mostly concentrated into a single sound-object: namely, the hero's terrifying shout. For this Homer uses the verb αὔω, αὔειν, which iconically mimes a shout (and the open mouth that produces it) through unbroken vowel sounds, a feature conserved in the future and aorist by changing the initial diphthong to a disyllable, thus restoring the hiatus displaced by the sigma. Tennyson seemingly is trying to translate this effect. In theory the verses—whether Homer's or Tennyson's—endeavor not to transcribe but to describe that shout, mostly by indicating its effect on the Trojans. The text here enacts, in fact, a double silence, neither giving us the words he shouted nor confirming that the shout was, as seems more likely, wordless. According to the staccato long syllables of the simply worded Greek, the hero ἔνθα στὰς ἤϋσ'—"There standing, shouted," as Tennyson puts it. (In the Greek the final vowel is lost by elision to the ensuing description of the amplification of the shout's effect by Athena, who stands apart like a detached subwoofer.) In another sense, however, we *do* hear the unwritten, probably unwriteable shout, for it is embodied by the verses themselves as ensembles of acoustical values (such as those I have just begun to describe), especially when these are rendered in the "deep bass growl" of Tennyson's living voice, or in whatever voice we choose to imagine for the Homeric singer long before him, or even, plainly and simply, in the everyday voice in our own head as we read either version silently. As I have put it elsewhere, describing instead some noisy verses in Vergil to which we shall return later, it is difficult for a poem to sound like the sea but relatively easy for it to sound, like the sea, and it accordingly is the latter mechanism that usually links the sounds *in* to the sounds *of* poetry.[11] There is much more one could say about all this. Sarah Nooter, for example, has revealed how Homer's language likens Achilles' voice to the sound of the *salpinx* or "war trumpet"—an obvious comparandum, of course, to the Light Brigade's bugle.[12] And I myself can tell you first-hand that if a record collector stares long enough at this passage, the limit of sound and sense embodied by the wound-like trench at which Achilles stops to shout begins to look very much like a phonographic groove. But enough of all that: let us instead return to our eavesdropping.

To Symonds's partial dismay at the time, though not, apparently, to Tennyson's own, it is the audience—especially Gladstone—that winds up being the most vocal component of the ensuing performance, interrupting the poet constantly to query his rendering of this or that in the Greek. He is asked, for example, why he had translated *kallitriches*, here applied to horses, as "beauteous," thus losing the word's seemingly specific reference to their manes. He also is quizzed about what exactly Athena is described as doing to enhance Achilles' shout. (Tennyson says he is torn between imagining her shouting with him, adding her volume to his, or offering instead some kind of "echo," perhaps with the aid of her aegis.) But by far the longest and most contentious discussion, with Gladstone leading the opposing charge, regards the meaning of Athena's regular Homeric epithet, *glaukôpis*. Historians may remember Gladstone for his politics and his long run as prime minister, but classicists know him as the somewhat improbable author of an infamous bit of nineteenth-century neuroaesthetics. The ancient Greek vocabulary of color was often baffling to modern readers: how, for example, could Homer compare the color of the sea to that of wine? There could be only one satisfactory answer, according to Gladstone: the ancient Greeks were color-blind. The preposterousness of the idea hardly impeded its circulation; indeed, its virality has returned in the digital era, for it is again almost impossible to go to a dinner party—or even to a neighborhood bar—and admit one has read Homer without a stranger telling you that they have read on the Internet that the ancient Greeks couldn't see the color blue.

Tennyson had translated *glaukôpis* as "gray-eyed," by which, he explains, he really means "blue-eyed," following Shakespeare, who regularly calls blue eyes gray. Gladstone—

who, we pause to observe, never uses Shakespearean usage to argue that the English national bard was as color-blind as the ancient Greeks—here trots out his controversial theory, paraphrased by Symonds thus: "Homer knew nothing about colors: the human eye had not yet learned to distinguish colors." The epithet, Gladstone insists, should instead be translated "bright-eyed." Faulty as the reasoning behind it may be, Gladstone's translation was then and is still now the one endorsed by dictionaries like that of Liddell and Scott, which distinguishes between an early use of *glaukos* to mean "gleaming" from its "later" application to color. Newer understandings of the Greek language of color, let us note, mostly eschew diachronic explanations in favor of ones based on synchronic semantic "nodes" in which hue is only one of many points in a word's constellation of possible referents. Still, even a translator as recent (and rebellious) as Emily Wilson, rendering the same epithet in the other Homeric epic, mostly follows the dictionary (and Gladstone) here,[13] and with good reason: the most salient feature of Athena's eyes is the keenness of their laser-like vision, which Homer may well have understood along the lines of the ancient theory of extramission, in which sight is generated by rays sent forth by the eyes themselves.

Like the party's classically trained guests, I myself cannot stop digressing, it seems. So let me quickly bring this part of my story to a close. The lively reading and discussion of Tennyson's translation from Homer would have two concrete effects. First, when he finally got around to publishing "Achilles Over the Trench," Tennyson changed "gray-eyed" to "bright-eyed." (He also changed "beauteous" to "full-maned."[14]) Second, the soirée shaped Woolner's evolving plans to sculpt a triptych of reliefs of Homeric scenes to adorn the pedestal of his portrait-in-progress of Gladstone. The central relief, Woolner reveals in a letter to Palgrave a week before the dinner party, was originally to be a portrait of Homer, flanked by depictions of Achilles at the trench and the dragging of the body of Hector.[15] Tennyson, Woolner reports, was skeptical of the whole plan, which must have set the stage for the evening's reading and discussion, perhaps unbeknownst to the others (or at least to Symonds). In any case, Woolner persisted with a modified version of the plan. The result was a central relief of "Pallas and Achilles at the Trenches" (Figure 7), depicting the nude hero on the verge of emitting his famous shout, with the goddess at the ready behind him, holding up her aegis as a sounding board, flanked by two others on the pedestal's sides, showing "Thetis Praying to Zeus on Behalf of Achilles" and "Thetis Consoling Achilles."[16]

In her biography of her husband, Alice Woolner reports that the reliefs were "designed as a compliment to Mr. Gladstone's study and knowledge of Greek art," though Woolner himself, in the same letter to Palgrave, included by Alice in her biography, more accurately describes the compliment as one for Gladstone's prowess as a "commentator" on Greek poetry.[17] Alice does not take the opportunity to conjure the dinner party that surely lent the plan further shape and impetus, perhaps because she does not remember it, or perhaps because she had remained in the drawing room (or had gone to bed) when the gentlemen returned to the dining room for philological fisticuffs. But she does include a letter sent to her husband four days later by the Oxford printer Thomas Combe, expressing his envy for the "glorious evening you must have had with Gladstone," who

Figure 7 Thomas Woolner, sculptor. *Achilles Shouting from the Trenches, c.* 1868. Marble relief. 675 mm. London, Royal Academy of Arts, 03/1858. Image © Royal Academy of Arts, London. Photo: Paul Highnam.

"must indeed have been pleased to stay so late."[18] This is followed by a letter sent a few days later by Emily Tennyson, the poet's wife, thanking the couple for "all the enjoyment" they had given her husband during his stay in London.[19] Already at its first exhibition at the Royal Academy in 1868, the central relief of the pedestal was highly praised as one of Woolner's greatest works to date.[20] The ensemble was then set up, as planned, in the Bodleian Library at Oxford—an ironic home for such a mighty shout! (It later was moved to the Ashmolean Museum, and thence into storage.) Woolner would submit a copy of "Pallas and Achilles at the Trenches" as his "diploma work" for his election as Royal Academician in 1874, after which he could be styled "Thomas Woolner, RA," as he is on the plaque at 29 Welbeck Street.[21]

It all makes for a very pretty picture and a very tidy story. "This," we might well conclude, with a touch of Combe's envy at not having been there, "was Classics, once upon a Victorian time." Indeed, Woolner's party could easily have found a place among the other nostalgic vignettes of Richard Jenkyns's *The Victorians and Ancient Greece*. My story, however, is not yet finished.

A Hero Dies

On October 11, 1865, in Morant Bay, Jamaica, Black preacher Paul Bogle led a mostly impoverished group in a protest against worsening conditions and injustice at the hands of planters and the provincial government they largely controlled.[22] By the end of the day, the town's courthouse and police station had been burned to the ground, and two dozen people, including both protesters and their opponents, had been killed. In the days to follow, the protest spread through the region and took the form of an organized rebellion; indeed, though the interpretation of the evidence remains controversial, it seems that Bogle and others had been planning and training for some time. Famously chanting "colour for colour, skin for skin," the protestors called for solidarity against their oppressors. Nevertheless, the resulting battlelines of the "Morant Bay Rebellion," to use its customary name, were no simple black and white matter. On the one hand, many of the protestors directed their wrath equally at white and, in the colonial terminology of the day, "coloured" oppressors, that is, persons of mixed African and European descent. On the other hand, the outspoken businessman and politician George William Gordon, who was something of a muse to the movement and is remembered along with Bogle as one of modern Jamaica's founding heroes, had been born into slavery as the son of a Black mother and her Scottish enslaver, who freed him when he was ten. (Slavery in Jamaica was abolished by law in the 1830s, when Gordon was in his teens.) And if white commanders and mostly but not exclusively white troops were responsible for much of the violence with which the rebellion was suppressed, the final stage of the government's campaign was partly executed by one allied community of Maroons, reclusive descendants, in the case of Jamaica, of the enslaved populations left behind by the Spanish when they were defeated on the island by the British in 1655. Jamaican Maroons had already aided the British in the suppression of a widespread rebellion of still enslaved persons in the early 1830s. One of their white commanders then, James Fyfe, returned to lead them in 1865.

Governor John Eyre closely directed the provincial government's combined response, which lasted for more than a month. An estimated 500 Jamaicans were killed by the combined force, many of them plainly innocent even of the purported crime of protesting. Thousands more were savagely beaten, robbed of their property, with their homes burned to the ground—a fate that sometimes extended to entire villages. George Gordon was arrested, shipped to a part of the island that had been placed under martial law, given a perfunctory military trial, and hanged. The same was done to Paul Bogle, after his capture by Fyfe and the Maroons. Captives awaiting trial or summary punishment were forced to watch such executions and were beaten or shot if they looked away.

So savage was the government's response that it prompted widespread outrage in Britain. Gordon's self-education and resulting affluence and political career—as well as, one suspects, his relatively light skin—helped to make his execution a particular object of dismay, but the brutality of the whole campaign was decried. Abolitionists who had organized against British and American slavery reconvened, joining voices with others such as John Stuart Mill, to call for a thorough investigation. Governor Eyre was eventually recalled, and two unsuccessful attempts were made to try him in Britain for murder. Eyre, however, also found vocal supporters. These included military commanders such as the Earl of Cardigan, the Crimean War commander of the "Light Brigade" celebrated by Tennyson. (Another veteran of the charge, one Gordon Ramsay, later served in Jamaica under Eyre as Provost-Marshall at Morant Bay, where he committed a series of atrocities and was instrumental in Gordon's sham trial.) But the governor's most prominent defenders were literary men, who with others organized the "Eyre Defence Committee." Its members included Charles Kingsley, Thomas Carlyle, John Ruskin, Charles Dickens—and Tennyson himself.

With this we return to 29 Welbeck Street, London, and the soirée of December 8, 1865, not quite two months after the Morant Bay Rebellion began, with Eyre still in charge in Jamaica and his British defenders and detractors only beginning to organize themselves. In typical epic fashion, we earlier joined the party *in medias res* and must now rewind—or to use a relatively less anachronistic metaphor, move the phonographic needle backward—to an earlier part of the conversation. We cannot take the needle all the way to the start of the cylinder, since Symonds himself arrived after the discussion was well underway:

> When I arrived at Woolner's, the maid said she supposed I was "for the gentlemen." On my replying "yes," she showed me into the dining room, where they were finishing dessert. Woolner, sat, of course, at the bottom of the table, Tennyson on his left, my father on the right hand. Next Tennyson sat Gladstone, and Hunt next my father. I was seated in an armchair between Woolner and my father.
>
> The conversation continued. They were talking about the Jamaica business . . .[23]

Gladstone, Symonds tells us, "had been reading official papers on the business all morning" and was "bearing hard on Eyre," against Tennyson's objections, and "just after I had entered said with an expression of intense gravity, 'And that evidence wrung from a poor black boy with a revolver at his head!'"—probably a reference to evidence presented at Gordon's military trial. Symonds takes care to record not just the words but other aspects of the sound of Tennyson's crude reply:

> Tennyson did not argue. He kept asserting various prejudices and convictions. "We are too tender to savages; we are more tender to a black than to ourselves." "Niggers are tigers, niggers are tigers," in *obbligato, sotto voce*, to Gladstone's declamation.[24]

Connections between classical learning and racism have been, of course, objects of scholarly inquiry for some time now. The cursory reader of the more public parts of the resulting critique might be inclined to suppose that, regarding color, the essential point of contact is one constructed negatively, namely, "whiteness," tendentiously applied to ancient bodies made both of sculpted stone and of flesh and blood: on the one hand, there is racial and artistic "purity," coded as the absence of color (never mind that neither the whitest stone nor the whitest skin is truly colorless), and on the other, there is everything else. But the evening at Woolner's suggests that Victorian racists, such as Tennyson, were just as inclined to meditate on, and fume about, color as such, especially when it did not stick to its proper place, including but not only in dictionaries of Greek.

Some might object that this is only guilt by association. Topics at a party, they might observe, accumulate more or less randomly—or better still, the turn to Homer after Jamaica may well have been precisely an attempt to clear the air via an abrupt change of subject. But the link is there to hear in Tennyson's voice. It is not only that his muttered mantra makes him like a broken record *avant la lettre*. Symonds aims to record the sounds he heard by recourse to, instead, two musical terms. The second, *sotto voce*, "below the voice," seems at first to set up a contrast with the bombast of "Achilles Over the Trench" (and of the shout it versifies), which, again, we can probably imagine Tennyson reciting that evening with same drumbeat voice captured by the later phonographic recording of "The Charge of the Light Brigade." But the first term, *obbligato*, often used of a line of music that is meant to be heard on an equal footing with a primary melody to which it is only apparently secondary, marks music that must be played as written because its every aspect is essential and, therefore, "compulsory." Not even Gladstone's polished oratory, in other words, could drown out what was coming, ostensibly more quietly, from the lips of the vatically racist poet laureate. Tennyson's murmur, in fact, is a rhythmical one. And its rhythm is not any rhythm but the quantitative equivalent of the end of a line of qualitative dactylic hexameter, the verse-form, of course, of ancient epic. "Niggers are tigers, niggers are tigers," like Homer's oft-repeated *oinopa ponton, oinopa ponton*, as the "wine-dark sea" blends with the blood of the Atlantic slave trade and the brutality that endured in its wake, including—though hardly only—in Jamaica.

"For Caribbean man," observes Édouard Glissant, "the word is first and foremost sound."[25] He traces this to the rare, creolized communications between enslaver and enslaved and the more frequent obligation of the latter to silent obedience—regularly interrupted, however, by piercing bursts of wordless sound:

Since speech was forbidden, slaves camouflaged the word under the provocative intensity of the scream. No one could translate the meaning of what seemed to be nothing but a shout. It was taken to be nothing but the call of a wild animal. This is how the dispossessed man organized his speech by weaving it into the apparently meaningless texture of extreme noise.[26]

Riffing on this scream, "Creole organizes speech as a blast of sound." I do not say "riff" flippantly: Fred Moten quotes from the same pages of Glissant in "Resistance of the Object: Aunt Hester's Scream," the opening chapter of his *In the Break: The Aesthetics of the Black Radical Tradition*.[27] The "break" of Moten's book title is that of a jazz ensemble, designating a brief pause by the rhythm section at the start of extended improvisation by one or more melodic instruments, while the chapter's "scream" collectively names the "heart-rending shrieks" elicited from the victim of an especially brutal beating witnessed by the young Frederick Douglass, who would later look back on the event as marking his initiation into the full horror of his enslavement.[28] Gently critiquing Saidiya Hartman's principled refusal to reproduce Douglass's graphic description of the violence—among other things, she worries that its frequent citation anesthetizes responses—Moten concentrates on the scream itself, connecting it to Douglass's ensuing discussion of the music of the enslaved and so, more generally, to "the incorporation or recording of a sound figured as external both to music and to speech in black music and speech," which he follows onward not only to the improvisations of jazz but to the performance of Blackness itself (in all its multiplicity).[29]

Moten's titular "break" names an interruption of rhythm; Tennyson's "Break, Break, Break" instead echoes the repetitive, percussive force of the sea against the shore. Nevertheless, both attune their ears to, as the poem puts it, "the sound of a voice that is still." The fact that Moten's extra-notational Blackness thus participates in more general questions about the animation of poetry hardly banalizes his point. On the contrary, it invites a question in, as it were, the opposite direction: was a distinctively Black sound already at work that evening on Welbeck Street and, more generally, in the sonic imaginary, phonographic *avant la lettre*, of Britain's poet laureate? The question may seem far-fetched, but I am by no means the first to ask it. Tennyson's "Charge of the Light Brigade" was first published little more than a month after the Battle of Balaclava itself, in the December 9, 1854, issue of the *The Examiner*. A month later, it was picked up and reprinted in the January 12, 1855, issue of *Frederick Douglass's Paper*.[30] The republication is just one piece of evidence assembled by Daniel Hack in his revealing study of the poem's remarkable influence on abolitionist (and other Black radical) thought, which partly depended, as he explains, on a broader reading of the Crimean War itself as a sometimes David-and-Goliath battle against (Russian) autocracy. Hack, however, mostly misses the opportunity to consider the insistent sonority, not just of this poem, but also of others by Tennyson reprinted by Douglass, such as "Ring Out, Wild Bells," included in the paper's fourth issue, published August 21, 1851.[31] As Hack rightly notes, a line like "'Ring in redress to all mankind' holds clear appeal for a reform-minded newspaper—and indeed, the reprinting of the poem in the context provided by *FDP* has the effect of giving specific content to the poem's vague utopianism."[32] But in acoustical terms, Douglass's appropriation of the poem is more radical still, to the extent we imagine him hearing in it—or, perhaps it would be more accurate to say, in the voice in which he imagines its repurposed words being read— something analogous to the singing of the enslaved, to which, as Moten notes, Douglass's autobiography turns, tearfully, shortly after the beating of Aunt Hester.

In any case, it is in emphatically sonic terms that the question back to Tennyson was asked, in the very issue in which Douglass reprinted "The Charge of the Light Brigade." It is not Douglass who does the asking, but "Our New York Correspondent," James McCune Smith, under his regular *nom de plume*, "Communipaw," in an article that purports to relate a conversation between himself and "Fylbel," i.e., Philip A. Bell, another of the paper's contributors, in the lamplit interior of an elegant New York club, as they sip coffee while a hard rain falls outside.[33] Bell reads aloud the first two lines of Tennyson's new poem—"Half a league, half a league, / Half a league onward"—and asks if Smith agrees that it is "fine." Smith's assenting reply concentrates on the classicizing meter:

> Yes, it beats Virgil's *quatit ungula campum*; for we have not only the sound of the horses' feet, as they begin with a canter, but the rush into the gallop; and the poet has not only mastered the difficulty of repeating the same phrase in the same words, but actually triumphs, in the *cumulus* gained in the repetition, and bursting into the *praeruptus aquae mons*.

Smith had studied at the African Free School of Manhattan and then, denied admission to American universities because of his race, left for Scotland, where he received bachelor's, master's, and medical degrees at the University of Glasgow in the 1830s. In his reply to Bell, he deploys his formidable learning in order to craft a kind of sonic rebus out of fragmentary citations from Vergil's *Aeneid*. The first quoted phrase is from what is arguably the most famous onomatopoeic line in classical epic, as Vergil strings together five dactyls in a row in order to suggest the sound of a galloping horse: *quadrupedante putrem sonitu quatit ungula campum*, "galloping sound as the ground falls apart at the strike of the horse-hoof."[34] Tennyson thus echoes both British cavalry and Vergilian precedent. Bell's final quotation of *praeruptus aquae mons* more challengingly requires the reader to recognize that it is one of Vergil's rare endings of a line with a monosyllabic word, usually considered a fault but here generally regarded (rightly or wrongly) as serving a somewhat more abstractly onomatopoeic purpose, conjuring the crash of the "steep mountain of water" that falls upon Aeneas' capsizing ship (*cumulo*, "in a heap," transferred in Bell's comment to Tennyson's piling up of the repeated phrase "half a league").[35] Bell's implied point seems at least partly to be about the culminating partial stop on, paradoxically, the word "onward": the brigade's forward motion already seems as thwarted as that of Aeneas and his crew. It would be difficult to imagine a critical formalism more "radical," in the (apparently) low sense of the word.

The learned conversation's tone, however, was about to take a dramatic turn. Bell asks Smith for his artistic judgment on another excerpt from the poem, which he proceeds to read:

> Cannon to right of them,
> Cannon to left of them,
> Cannon in front of them
> Volleyed and thundered.

"Isn't that grand?" asks Bell, to which Smith replies by exclaiming "Flat burglary!" He then explains to his astonished friend, "It's a translation from the Congo, feebler than the original. Look in the *Revue des Deux Mondes*, Vol. 4th, page 1040, (I picked it up at Balliere's,) and you will find the Congo original, published four years ago, and as old as Africa: compare them." The article then prints both comparanda, labeled in all-capitals, "CONGO" and "TENNYSON." The former reads as follows:

Canga bafio te,
Canga moune de le,
Canga do ki la,
Canga li.

As Hack notes, Smith's charge is not that Tennyson has borrowed anything from his purported model's meaning but, rather, "that Tennyson has 'stolen' the chant as a formal construct—the anaphora, the stressed first syllable 'can,' the short line-length, and, roughly, the meter. This form itself, moreover, seems to have a content, and one that the chant more or less shares with Tennyson's poem as, before learning anything else about it," Bell correctly identifies it as a "war cry" and begs Smith to translate it. "Can't do it," replies Smith, explaining that he does not understand the words in the least, but he confirms, from his cited source, that it had been used to rouse enslaved masses in the Haitian Revolution at the end of the last century and that, even now, hearing it brings dread to overseers. Bell responds with such rhapsodic visions of a similar revolt in the American South that Smith must advise him to lower his voice. Swapping coffee cups for a chess board, they turn to more local and less consequential conflicts—still riffing, however, on Tennyson's poem.

Does Smith mean for his accusation to be taken seriously? Properly speaking, the article's demonstration of his critical virtuosity no more depends on the veracity of his claim than it does on definitive proof, which must forever be lacking, that Tennyson was thinking of Vergil when he set the brigade's charge in largely dactylic meter. So too does his polemical point arguably depend less on pinning a charge of plagiarism on Tennyson than it does simply on demonstrating that one of the most celebrated poems of the British poet laureate sounds very much like an African chant, regardless of the reasons why. Still, Tennyson did read (and even write) French, and it would not be particularly surprising if a periodical of circulation as wide as that of the *Revue des Deux Mondes* passed through his hands, if not at home, then in a library or club, attracting his attention to the magazine's serialized portrait of the Haitian emperor Faustin Soulouque, one installment of which is what Smith cites. Suggestively, Hallam Tennyson, the poet's son and biographer, immediately before describing the composition of "The Charge of the Light Brigade," relates that his parents, a few days before, had been reading Émile Silvestre's "account of the Bretons"—probably his *Les Derniers Bretons*—with particular attention to its depiction of the popular role of song in Brittany, even among attending physicians, which "struck my father," confirming some degree of ethnomusicological interest, albeit here directed much closer to home.[36] The younger Tennyson then turns to the hasty ("in a few minutes") first drafting of the poem, inspired, he reports, by an article in the London *Times*, not only through its reporting on the battle itself but by its use of the sentence "someone had blundered," which not only is imported into the poem but actually prompted, he claims, the poem's meter—which, by the way, complicates any assumption of a primarily Vergilian metrical model.[37] (Curiouser still is the fact that this exact sentence does not actually appear in the article in question, suggesting either that its source lay elsewhere or that the article's different but similar language rearranged itself into a metrical earworm in Tennyson's own head.) Finally, there is the fact that contemporaries often identified suspicious similarities between Tennyson's verses and those of others, forcing the poet to defend himself with rejoinders like this: "I will answer for it that no modern poet can write a single line but among the innumerable authors of the world you will somewhere find a striking parallelism. It is the unimaginative man who thinks everything borrowed."[38] Fair enough, but one cannot help noticing that Tennyson's "innumerable authors of the world" conjures something like the global phonosphere in and through which Smith has chosen to listen to him.

Once upon a time, in fact, Tennyson had directed his still unlettered ears toward an even more expansive soundscape, as he himself would later recall in a note to his son: "Before I could read, I was in the habit on a stormy day of spreading my arms to the wind, and crying out 'I hear a voice that's speaking in the wind,' and the words 'far, far away' had always a strange charm for me."[39] How, we might be inclined to wonder, did that open-armed little boy grow up to be the man we meet at Woolner's, fuming about rebellious Jamaicans and fickle dictionaries of Greek? Perhaps the metamorphosis is underway in the same note's very next sentence: "About ten or eleven Pope's *Homer's Iliad* became a favourite of mine and I wrote hundreds and hundreds of lines in the regular Popeian metre, nay could even improvise them . . ." By this device the same boy began to discipline not only his own voice, but that of the winds, not only like Homer and Pope, but like Vergil between them, in the very storm-scene that provides Smith with his second quoted phrase. Meter, in this regard, functions as the sonic equivalent of the visual imaginary, a realm bordered by words on one side and, on the other, by the unwriteable sounds heard in the wind's howl, a hero's scream, or a grandchild's laugh. This, for Tennyson, was the poet's workshop, and if he returned to it, day after day, with growing confidence, he nevertheless knew it remained a place where he risked being overwhelmed and overthrown.

It was into this realm of a thrilling, threatening sonic real that Blackness was now insinuating itself—and not only in the ears of Black readers and writers, singers and revolutionaries. For example, the French consul in Haiti, Maxime Raybaud, was the author, under the name Gustave d'Alaux, of the book consulted by Smith in its serialized form, which was far less sympathetic to the Haitian Revolution than its famously philhellene author was to the Greek War of Independence, in which he had fought. After quoting the African chant repurposed by the Haitians, he offers this condescending gloss: "I am ignorant whether I chance to speak, in these words, the language of Senegal or Yolof, of Fouli or Bambara, of Mandingo or Bouriquis, of Arada or Caplaou, of Ibos or Mokos, of

Congo or Mousombé; all that I can affirm is, that it is *negro*." What, however, of Aunt Hester's scream and all the other sounds of bondage and freedom (to use the title terms of Douglass's second autobiography) that Moten listens for and to "in the break"? To suggest that such are echoed by Tennyson's "shout in the trench" (as Palgrave calls the Achilles poem) is to join, at one's peril, a game started by Smith. One's odds are slightly improved by expanding the question's scope to include all the evening's guests. Douglass's two autobiographies to date had been international sensations, leading to two British speaking tours, one quite long, the other shorter, throughout which he was greeted by enthusiastic crowds; it seems unlikely that no one at Woolner's that night had read him, and it is impossible that any had not heard of him. Then there is the curious evidence of Woolner's

Figure 8 David Lucas, engraver, after a painting by Alexander Rippingale. *To the Friends of Negro Emancipation*. Mezzotint engraving. London: F. G. Moon, 1834. London, British Museum, 2010,7081.4512. Image © The Trustees of the British Museum.

relief, at least partly inspired by the evening's Homeric musings. The first thing one must say about its extravagantly muscular figure of Achilles is that the sculptor's model in this case was certainly not to be found among his dinner guests. If he drew from life, then perhaps his model was a boxer or boatman or some other member of London's vast underclass. Achilles' frontal pose, however, with his arm raised high, exhibits noteworthy formal similarities to the century's emblematic representations of the "freed slave," such as the 1834 print (after a painting) "To the Friends of Negro Emancipation" (Figure 8), issued to celebrate Britain's Slavery Abolition Act of the year before. Next to the print, Woolner's glistening relief starts to look just a bit like a classical whitewash.

My point, however, is one based neither on far-reaching *Quellenforschung* (with apologies to Smith) nor on a search for a Warburgian *Pathosformel* (by which the 1834 print and Woolner's relief would be taken as offering a pose universally recognized as, for example, release from constraint). My aim is instead to thicken the atmosphere of that evening at Woolner's with possible associations until the one point of curious contact we can confirm with certainty—the discussion's pivot from one kind of color to another— loses all semblance of arbitrariness. Like an animating (if somewhat malevolent) heart, it seems to provide both origin and destination to the party's varied thinking. We turn now to one final set of those thoughts, this time belonging to our informant—who that night kept them resolutely to himself.

A Hero Loves

Despite Symonds's evident disdain for Tennyson's "prejudices and convictions," it would not have been the "Jamaica business" that most captured his imagination as he listened in polite silence. Towering above the other topics was, surely, the figure of Achilles, around whom had already begun to coalesce his thoughts about ancient and modern same-sex desire, including in the poem that had formed part of the immorality charge that had brought him before an Oxford tribunal a few years before. (In the poem, he imagines future lovers who again will lead "Pure wedded lives of Achilleian honour."[40]) Tennyson's poem records a war-cry, but as Symonds would not have been inclined to forget, that cry echoed with the unspeakable anguish that was about to drive its source back into battle, intent on avenging the death of Patroclus, whose body still lay unburied. Though the subtlety has often been missed, Symonds turns to this famous pair not so much for Homeric precedent for same-sex desire per se as for a correction both to the conspicuous inequality of the pederastic couplings celebrated in later Greek and to the gendered logic of sexual "inversion": Achilles was a placeholder for what Symonds could not yet satisfactorily name.[41] Indeed, Symonds can be said to have shared Tennyson's frustration with dictionaries, albeit to different ends. In these very years, as it happens, the German sexologist Karl-Maria Kertbeny coined the word Symonds would be the first to import into English print, *homosexual*, which Symonds himself did not love but which was destined to stick, winning him a place, long afterwards, in the *Oxford English Dictionary.*

Nevertheless, if Achilles and love were front and center in Symonds's thoughts, the attendant discussion of Greek color-words was hardly background noise. Its stakes, however, were not fully revealed until, years later, Symonds returned lavishly to the question of color, Homeric and otherwise, partly motivated by his sojourns in Venice, where he had fallen in love with a gondolier whose eyes were the color of the lagoon, "as though the quintessential colour of Venetian waters were vitalized in them and fed from inner founts of passion."[42] Among the more prosaic consequences of Symonds's later chromatic obsessions was a brief essay on "Colour-Sense and Language," in which he takes direct if anonymous aim at Gladstone, twenty-five years after hearing Gladstone himself expound his theory of Greek color-blindness at Woolner's:

Our experience, however, must not make us draw a wrong conclusion from the poverty of language to express colour in earlier ages of civilisation. As it is, we have no proper nomenclature—only such as we pick up from commerce and the colour-men. The shifts we submit to in order to communicate sensations of colour ought rather to teach us that in the Homeric or other early ages colours were fully appreciated by the senses, but had not found their analogues in language.[43]

It is, of course, impossible to miss the parallel with the search for a suitable language for desires that still mostly went unnamed. Crucially, however, Symonds believed that neither problem could finally be solved solely by devising (or importing) "proper nomenclature." And so it is that a fundamental ineffability of color and desire alike drive the title essay of *In the Key of Blue*, which offers a medley of prose and poetry that attempts to capture the varied blues that clothed the city's male inhabitants and that blended them with their watery world. Symonds dressed and posed Augusto Zanon, a baggage carrier with whom he was infatuated, for most of the poetic vignettes, each of which was tagged as a "symphony" of two colors:

I crossed the Rialto, strolled through the Pescheria, and walked slowly along the Riva dell'Olio. At the very end, upon the barriers of the *traghetto*, under the flaring gas-lamp, Augusto was sitting gazing dreamily and tired across the Grand Canal. Scattered lights broke the surface of the water, and gondolas, like glow-worms, now and then moved silently upon that oily calm. Augusto was intensely blue, giving the single blot of colour on a ground of gloom. This suggested the first of my studies:

A symphony of black and blue—
Venice asleep, vast night, and you.

   . . .

How blue you were amid that black,
Lighting the wave, the ebon wrack!
The ivory pallor of your face
Gleamed from those glowing azures back

> *Against the golden gaslight; grapes*
> *Of dusky curls your brows embrace,*
> *And round you all the vast night gapes.*[44]

How far this night first seems from the one on Welbeck street, twenty-five years before! But peer more closely into the Venetian "gloom," and you may glimpse a ghost of that earlier occasion. For one thing, the pose of the classically named Augusto, gazing at the dark waters of the Grand Canal, reprises that of Achilles, staring out at the "wine-dark" sea. Then there is the fact that the colors paired in this opening "symphony"—black and blue—map the same chromatic and thematic range of the conversation at Woolner's, however innocent the meaning of black seems here. And can a pairing of "black and blue" ever really be innocent anyway? There is no reason to think that the pairing of Symonds and Zanon was itself ever physically violent, but it was predicated on an uncomfortable inequality of age (when they first met, Symonds was nearly 50 and Zanon, 17) and financial means. At the same time, the relationship caused Symonds pain he sometimes described in violent terms, including a presumably metaphorical "wound" inflicted by Zanon, which Symonds sought to assuage by turning to the same pastime that had generated Tennyson's verses on Achilles: that is, by translating from the Greek—in this case, from Bion's "Lament for Adonis," in which the beautiful youth's literal wound stains all around it with richly colored blood. The word-painting of "In the Key of Blue," which Symonds several times describes in the language of translation, extend the poet's work to include direct manipulation of the dress, pose, and setting of the body he depicts—unbruised, but made "black and blue" (and many colors besides) all the same.

But it is in the reported failure of this fashioning that the essay most fully exposes its haunted condition. After the final portrait, the author-narrator surveys his work with dismay:

> Were silence, then, not better than this speech?
> Words do no work of pencil, palette, brush,
> Words are designed to thrill the heart, or teach;
> Not to depict, not to revoke the blush
> Of dawn, or reincarnadine the flush
> Of sunset; break this wavering wand, and go
> Back to thy books, poor powerless Prospero.[45]

Shakespeare's Prospero could command even the winds, raising the storm that lends *The Tempest* both its title and its opening scene, which brings the magician's enemies to the shores of the exotic island on which he has been living in exile. Only one creature in his realm is not fully subject to his will: his resentful and rebellious servant Caliban, whose reluctant and partial obedience can only be achieved through the threat or actual infliction of physical punishment. Shakespeare fashions his name as an anagram of "cannibal" and bases him, and other elements of the setting, on recently published sensationalized accounts of colonial encounters in the "New World." He does not racialize him only as Native, however, for he also makes him the son of Sycorax, a North African witch. Shakespeare gives her "blue" eyes, which, as Leah Marcus shows at length, Victorian commentators and their successors turned philological backflips to explain away and so to homogenize her Blackness—even though, among other contradictions, they recognized Medea as her model.[46] Shakespeare interestingly does not tell us what color Caliban's eyes were, but he has Prospero address him as a generalized racial other whom he initially misrecognized as capable of civilization:

> A thing most brutish, I endowed thy purposes
> With words that made them known. But thy vile race,
> Though thou didst learn, had that in't which good natures
> Could not abide to be with . . .[47]

This reproach provides the negative image of Glissant's affirmation of the deployment by "Caribbean man" of "extreme noise" beyond language, mistaken by his enslavers (and later white listeners) for "the call of a wild animal." In fact, Caribbean writers in the second half of the last century famously embraced Caliban as a revolutionary archetype. "I know of no other metaphor, more expressive of our cultural situation, of our reality," wrote Roberto Fernández Retamar in 1971, responding, for example, to Aimé Césaire's rewriting of the play from a Caribbean perspective two years before.[48] Continuing, he asks, "what is our history, what is our culture, if not the history and culture of Caliban?"

Similar comparisons in Symonds's own day cut, predictably, in a rather different direction, most notoriously in Daniel Wilson's 1873 *Caliban: The Missing Link*, which speculated that Darwin's postulated transition from ape to man might still be discoverable in the nonwhite populations of this or that island.[49] At the very time that Symonds was penning his portraits in blue, a London production of *The Tempest* accordingly had its Caliban mime onstage the movements of monkeys. Of course, any identification of Zanon with Shakespeare's character, despite Venice's insular condition and the fact that Caliban too is made to carry luggage in the play, must overcome the problem of his "ivory pallor." The comparison arguably is more persuasive in the case of Zanon's Venetian predecessor, the swarthy gondolier Fusato, whom Symonds frequently describes in vaguely racial terms and whom he caused to be photographed, stripped to the waist, in order to capture his muscular physique, making of him something like a blue-eyed Caliban. Nevertheless, the frustration of Symonds-as-Prospero is said to be directed at neither of these nor even, properly speaking, at words and their inadequacies but, rather, at the unruly world those words fail to spellbind and tame. The real objects here, in other words, are Symonds's own unruly desires. That he often analogized these to a wolf waiting to pounce brings his metaphors in line with Tennyson's "tigers," Shakespeare's "thing most brutish," and even Wilson's "missing link"—especially if we think of both its apeman and Symonds's inner wolf as recalling the ancient monstrous hybrid of the werewolf. Of course, Symonds's ultimate goal was not only to humanize those desires but to emancipate them.

One could object that, in the end, Symonds thus fails to free himself from the metaphors of bondage that, years ago at Woolner's, had yoked black to blue, sound to fury. In his defense, one might counter that he thereby pursues the good queer strategy of embracing and upturning the very terms of oppression. But Symonds's project, like that of Smith and of the other thinkers briefly sampled here, offers something more radical, there to hear if we listen carefully. Consider, by way of final example (and last word), the line that got him into trouble already at Oxford, which is spoken by Hesperus, the evening star, to a shepherd:

> For this is virtue, when a friend with friend
> Linked in strong bonds of union, lets the years
> Flow over them unheeded, sees the flower
> Of boyhood perish, and man's strength appear,
> Yet alterns not, but grows in tenderness
> And mutual reverence and equal love;
> Till the grey-bearded village sires approve,
> Nodding their heads, and cry, the age of gold
> Comes round again when lovers thus can lead
> Pure wedded lives of Achilleian honour.

The natural way to read the final line is in the iambic pentameter of the rest—that is to say, in the metrical form that is said to correspond most closely to the natural rhythms of English speech: "Pure wédded líves of Áchilleían hónour." But change the accent of "Achilleian" to the second syllable, and the line can be re-read from the start as dactylic: "Púre wedded líves of Achílleian hónour." Let this contrivance be a caution against drawing the false lesson that queerness and blackness are essentially matters of matter or that the goal of radical justice is the eradication of form. Let us instead seek, as Symonds does here, the liberation of form itself from even the most seemingly natural of formalisms. And then, finally, let us seek a poetics of form and matter—a new, postcritical hylomorphism, let us call it—that escapes the language of discipline and domination once and for all.

Notes

1. This chapter offers a considerably expanded discussion of material far more briefly taken up in two chapters of my recent book, *The Passions of John Addington Symonds* (2022). My subtitle and key aspects of my approach borrow from Gilroy 1993. This essay has been improved by feedback from hosts and audiences on happy occasions at Oxford, Dartmouth, Chicago, and Yale. I would like to express my gratitude to them and to the editors of this volume.
2. On the sitters for and background of his works, see Woolner 1917.
3. Symonds 1893a, 32–7. Symonds describes the original account as belonging to a "diary," now lost, but the same can be found in a surviving letter nominally addressed to his sister Charlotte and dated the day of the party: see Symonds 1967, 1:591–8 (letter 451). As the

editors, Schueller and Peters, note, Symonds offers "to write down what happened at Woolner's that evening" in a letter to his friend Graham Dakyns dated December 27 (1: 603–4, letter 456), which suggests to them that the ostensibly earlier letter to his sister (and other presumed readers) has been backdated and that, if Symonds really did jot anything down that very evening, he did so in rougher form. The editors also provide the text of Woolner's invitation to the younger Symonds (1:597n1).

4. A. Tennyson 1877, 1–2.

5. A. Tennyson 1884.

6. William Holman Hunt, *Portrait of Fanny Waugh Hunt* (1866–8), oil on canvas, 104 x 73 cm, Toledo Museum of Art, 177.34, http://emuseum.toledomuseum.org/objects/55066/fanny-waugh-hunt

7. Holman-Hunt 1969.

8. On the phonographic anticipations of "Break, Break, Break," see Rubery 2014 and S. Butler 2015, 24–5. More generally, see Griffiths 2018.

9. Maxwell 1980, source also of the following details. These two first recordings were rediscovered in 1976; on other, later recordings of Tennyson, see C. Tennyson 1956. Some versions of the recordings variously available online seem to be the later ones; for the Steytler (the name of Edison's agent) recordings, see Paschen and Mosby 2001, disc 1 (of 3), tracks 3 and 4.

10. L. Tennyson 1933.

11. S. Butler 2018, 243.

12. Nooter 2019a, 240. See also Chapter 5, this volume.

13. E. Wilson (2018) offers some variation on the theme, sometimes with a "colloquial" touch, as notes Speliotis (2018).

14. On the author's further tinkering with the poem in proof, see P. G. Scott 1972, 38–9.

15. Woolner 1917, 268–9.

16. These are the titles given in the catalogue, *The Exhibition of the Royal Academy of Arts, 1868: The One Hundredth* (London 1868), 48.

17. Woolner 1917, 237, 269.

18. Woolner 1917, 269.

19. Woolner 1917, 269–70.

20. Rossetti and Swinburne 1868, 27, where Rossetti notes that "but for its small size, one would be minded to call it the finest thing Mr. Woolner has yet exhibited."

21. Woolner 1917, 238.

22. My summary of events is based mostly on Heuman 1994.

23. Symonds 1893a, 32.

24. Symonds 1893a, 32.

25. Glissant 1989, 123.

26. Glissant 1989, 123–4.

27. Moten 2003, 1–24. See also Chapter 15, this volume.

28. Douglass 1994, 18–20.

29. Douglass 1994, 6.

30. A. Tennyson 1855.

31. A. Tennyson 1851.

32. Hack 2016, 202.

33. J. M. Smith 1855.

34. Vergil, *Aeneid* 8.596. My awkward translation aims to replicate the meter.

35. Vergil, *Aeneid* 1.105.

36. H. Tennyson 1897, 1:381.

37. H. Tennyson 1897, 1:381.

38. A. Tennyson 1907, 1:361–2.

39. H. Tennyson 1897, 1:11.

40. Later published in Symonds 1880, 56.

41. S. Butler 2022, 99–125.

42. Symonds 2016, 514. On Symonds in Venice and the writing that was the result, see S. Butler 2022, 298–353.

43. Symonds 1890, 2:308. On the essay and its connection to Gladstone and others (including Symonds' sexologically minded interlocutors, some of whom found attractive a comparison, ultimately rejected by Symonds himself, of homosexuality to color-blindness), see Ribeyrol 2013, 153–9, and S. Butler 2022, 313–36.

44. Symonds 1893b, 5.

45. Symonds 1893b, 16.

46. Marcus 1996, 1–37.

47. Shakespeare, *The Tempest*, 1.2.360–3.

48. Retamar 1974, 24.

49. D. Wilson 1873.

CHAPTER 3
MIXED MEDIA: TWO BLACK ARTISTS AND THE ICONS OF CLASSICAL ANTIQUITY

Allannah Karas

From the moment, as it were, that Winckelmann passed on his famous claims about the superiority of whiteness in Greek sculpture, unpainted antiquities have exerted an immense influence on modern discourse, cultural imagination, and perceptions of value.[1] These colorless sculptures have not only become enmeshed within toxic pseudoscience around race and "whiteness,"[2] but they have also operated in and through what Monique Roelofs calls processes of "racialized aestheticization" and "aesthetic racialization."[3] Such processes, rooted in the Enlightenment, have mobilized classical aesthetic norms to create and enforce racial categories against Black people in general and Black artists in particular. Racist appropriations of Greco-Roman sculpture continue to challenge both Black and white artists seeking to engage with these pieces and the classical tradition[4] they embody in an intellectually honest, socially conscious, and nuanced way. Yet Black artists, when faced with the iconic sculptures of classical antiquity, not only experience ambivalence or "double-consciousness,"[5] but they also experience a frustrating professional dissonance. Due to aesthetic racialization, they may find that their training, creativity, and the need to eat come up against segregationist ideologies and unwritten rules around basic elements of their craft such as their choice of subjects and the pigmentation of their paint. To the Black artist, then, engagement with the classical subjects emerges as a practice both taboo and unsustainable.

Black and white artists have endeavored to remove the miasma from these sculptures, or somehow render these figures and the classical tradition they represent less noxious for their own artistic expression within an increasingly pluralistic society. While many in popular culture have advocated for destruction of the statues altogether, as if to cleanse the past through a modern *damnatio memoriae*, artists, instead, often tend to risk dirtying themselves and work with these objects for the sake of what Stephen Best calls "transgressive reversal,"[6] or, for "recovering a history, repairing a sense of damaged relation."[7] Still others use their art to provoke thought and new ways of relating with the past, an approach that corresponds with what Best describes as an "enhancing of the range of critical responses to aesthetic objects."[8] This latter approach resonates with the work of Emma Amos (1937–2020) and Robert (Bob) Louis Thompson (1937–1966), who persistently engaged with the vexed and racialized heritage of the classical tradition (as filtered through the European artistic tradition), while, at the same time, reveling in their "Blackness" and critiquing, or simply dismissing, the constrictive ideologies and practices that indiscriminately conflate "color," race, and the classics. This chapter explores two of their artworks and the ways in which Amos and Thompson disrupt and transcend the effects of aesthetic racialization (and racialized aestheticization) through mixing media, pigmentation, and styles with iconic sculptures from classical antiquity.

My analysis of Thompson's and Amos's artworks falls within the recent scholarly interest in the field of classical Africana or Black classicism, which examines the ways in which peoples of the African diaspora dialogue with, critique, rework, and provide new lenses with which to understand and relate with the ancient Mediterranean world and its continued influence. Classical reception by Black American artists has only recently begun to receive serious attention, but the ready accessibility of visual art allows for the work these pieces do to have a wide-ranging effect.[9] Through their art, Amos and Thompson showcase the generative admixture of ambivalence and responsiveness of Black Americans towards the classical tradition. At the same time, by provocatively resituating, coloring, and weaving iconic sculptures from Greco-Roman antiquity into their work, these artists model resilient and creative forms of resistance to the cultural toxicity and exclusivist artistic practices often bound up with these figures in their time.

This chapter has three sections. In the first, I introduce Amos and Thompson within their twentieth-century social and artistic contexts and with particular attention to the challenges they faced as Black artists interested in classical subjects. I then provide a close analysis of Emma Amos's *Measuring, Measuring* (1995), and Thompson's (1963) *Untitled* (*Augustus*), pieces that depict classical sculpture within a two-dimensional frame. Through a playful mixing of colors, material, images, and ideas in these works, I argue, Amos and Thompson, albeit in different ways, creatively integrate two worlds seemingly at odds while simultaneously offering perceptive metacritiques of the classical tradition and its implication with aesthetic racialization. In doing so, their work also models what Ruiz calls "a process or relational way of thinking" (2016, 236), one that combines playfulness, derision, appreciation, and grief in the enactment of artistic agency.

Amos, Thompson, and the Challenge of the Classics

Although both born in 1937 to middle-class Black families and raised in the segregated South, at first glance, Emma Amos and Bob Thompson seem an unlikely pair. Emma passed away in 2020 after a long career marked by outspoken feminist activism. By contrast, Thompson's politics hardly come out in his work, and he died from pulmonary edema in 1966, just a few years shy of key moments for the Civil Rights and Black Arts Movements. Despite these differences, both artists left behind bodies of work of considerable quality and quantity, Thompson completing nearly a thousand paintings before the age of thirty. Additionally, their lives as American artists followed similar paths in accord with the training and artistic fashion of their age: both began with abstract expressionism but ended up blending this style within more figurative work. And, while they do not seem to have met, they both lived and flourished in various communities of creatives and intellectuals in New York city from the 1960s on. Thompson worked and lived in Greenwich village among the Beat community and counted leading Black artists and, especially, jazz musicians such as Ornette Coleman and Charlie Haden, among his friends. Amos participated in vibrant intellectual collectives in New York such as *Spiral*, a community of Black artists led by Charles Alston and Romare Bearden, and the feminist art collectives *Heresies* and *Guerilla Girls*.

Furthermore, due to their higher education, time abroad, and expansive interests, both artists, while never negating their Blackness, frequently chose to work with classical themes and figures. Amos completed a degree in London where she studied painting, weaving, etching, and even stained glass. While mainly a painter, Thompson also traveled abroad to Europe where he visited museums and honed his craft in London, France, Spain, and Rome. All throughout, moreover, Amos and Thompson preserved beautifully capacious understandings of what it meant to be "Black." On this basis, they would daringly live and operate in Black, white, and interracial circles; they refused to flatten or, as Amos puts it, to "erase" themselves.[10] In words that could apply to both artists, Amos recounts: "I determined I was not going to do that [erase herself]. And so I began to paint the figure again in the early sixties, working in oils, and painting large standing women with multicolored limbs, one color here, another color there."[11] This expansive and assertive perspective on race and art, however, never fully assuaged the inevitable anxieties they experienced about their positionality and basic job security as Black artists in the twentieth-century art world.[12]

Emma and Thompson faced several challenges in this regard. Most American-based artists, Black and white, cut their teeth on sculptural models from ancient Greece and Rome. Paintings based on sculptural models or containing sculptures themselves occur frequently throughout the tradition of European art. Greco-Roman sculptures are brought into painting not only as models but also to express certain values and meaning, or to problematize classical icons and their continued value. Yet despite the longevity of this practice, Black artists have often been discouraged from building on their training and creating their own variations on the classical past. Thus, while it was a trend during the 1950s to return to the work of the "European Old Masters"[13] and their classical subjects (hence, the work of Picasso, Warhol, and others at the time), these subjects were often taboo for artists, such as Amos and Thompson, who happened to be Black.

Instead, the artistic intelligentsia explicitly and implicitly communicated, and perhaps still does, limiting expectations about what a Black artist is *supposed to* produce. Amos recounts in an interview with Isaak: "In the mid-eighties I noticed that curators from public institutions mostly chose to exhibit paintings of mine showing figures that could be identified as 'black.'" [14] As a result, she had to make a decision about her choice of subject, and in an interview with Courtney Martin she remembers thinking: "I said, 'Okay, I will also use the white body, but the paintings of mine that have a dark figure and another dark figure and a multicolored figure and a white figures will not get shown and they will not get purchased'—not that much of my work gets purchased."[15] But, regardless of the money, Amos asserted, "I was, and still am, rebelling against the expectation that a black woman does paintings only of and about black people."[16] Amos even put on an entire solo show, *Changing the Subject* (1994–1995), as a public critique of segregationist restrictions imposed by the art world of her time.[17]

Secondly, Black American artists also grapple with the multivalence and politicization of "color," the basic medium for their art. Black painters must confront the tragic reality that the intersection of their paint pigmentation and the pigmentation of their skin could pose obstacles to their artistic freedom and success. In an interview with Lucy Lippard, Amos comments:

> Every time I think about color it's a political statement. It would be a luxury to be white and never to think about it . . . We're always talking about color, but colors are also skin colors, and the term 'colored' itself— it all means something else to me. You have to choose, as a black artist, what to make your figures, which I'm very aware of when I paint.[18]

Thus, faced with supposedly "white" sculptures of antiquity, or the light-skinned depictions of many classical figures in Western European art, the Black artist must walk more carefully than most. Amos, however, resisted this artificially imposed compartmentalization by deliberately using a wide array of skin tones for her figures.[19] Thompson also, and even when riffing on the most venerable of Renaissance artists and classical myths, completely disregarded this restriction and painted the classics with a wild, almost psychedelic color palette. Against the ideological odds and even at the risk of unemployment, both Amos and Thompson chose to rework classical subjects with whichever colors they so wished, and in doing so, actualized their creative agency in intriguing and provocative ways.

Amos: *Measuring, Measuring*, 1995

In 1995, Emma Amos created a piece called *Measuring, Measuring* (Figure 9),[20] which incorporates a famous ancient Greek *kouros* (the Kritios boy) and a re-presentation of the Hellenistic sculpture Aphrodite of Melos (Venus de Milo).[21] Through her choice of subject matter in this and other works, Harris points out, Amos challenges "notions about what was permissible for Black artists to use as content for their paintings."[22] She also invites the viewer into a deeper dialogue about the icons themselves, and the racialized aesthetic that arises from them.

The Kritios boy, originally made in the early fifth century BCE, was found on the acropolis in Athens. Due to its proportionality, movement, and incarnation of both Greek idealism and the shift towards realism, this figure has become a standard in art and archaeology textbooks. Although only about 3.5 feet tall, the Kritios boy embodies, like Apollo Belvedere, Laocöon, and the Farnese Hercules, what Winckelmann describes as the idealized ("white") male standard of classical beauty, perfection, vitality, and strength.[23] Amos's work also engages with the *Torso of Venus* (c. 1918/1928)[24] sculpture by French artist Aristide Maillol (1861–1944), who in turn was referencing Venus de

Figure 9 Emma Amos (1937–2020), *Measuring, Measuring* (1995). Acrylic on linen canvas, photo transfers, and African strip woven borders with photography, 84 × 70 inches. Collection of the Birmingham Museum of Art. @ Artists Rights Society (ARS), NY.

Milo, an over-life size Hellenistic sculpture celebrated as "one of the three most famous female figures in the Louvre," along with the *Mona Lisa* and *The Winged Victory of Samothrace*.[25] Like the Kritios boy, this iconic figure also represents a transition from the Late Classical and Hellenistic Styles. Amos capitalizes on both the transitional nature of these figures and their iconic status to create the desired effect in her mixed media work, *Measuring, Measuring.*

Amos's piece presents three laser-transferred photographs side by side for the viewers' comparison: from left to right, a torso from the Venus de Milo, held up on a piece of paper by a gloved figure hidden except for its hat, a partially clothed Black woman against the backdrop of some indecipherable text, and, finally, the Kritios boy. The piece is divided into two halves: one with a Black background and the other red. Amos positions four hands, as markers of authorship, ownership, and agency, in each of the corners.[26] She paints the entire piece in acrylic paint on a linen canvas larger than the original sculptures and framed by Kente cloth and woven borders of African strip. Upon close examination, either side of the frame is bedecked with a series of legs that, Amos explains, "disrupt and measure the assumption that people know what they are looking at."[27] Sharon Patton writes: "She makes beautiful art, however, that art presents the unexpected. It elicits ambivalence, intellectual recognition, and denial."[28]

Amid this disruption, Amos weaves these iconic sculptures into her own work in order to provoke a conversation about what she calls "our still racially charged standards of beauty."[29] She also critiques them from a Black feminist perspective. Amos, however, does not destroy or dismiss these classical figures, but rather layers them with her own ideas, her own story, and her own mixed media.

Amos decenters the Kritios boy to make way for the Black female, and transfers to her body the tape measure typically used to showcase the "ideal" proportions of the Greek male. Although these figures are depicted in shades of black and white, closer consideration reveals a layering that playfully critiques our racialized perceptions of "color." On either side of the Black female, Amos depicts the supposedly "white" figures of the *kouros* and Venus. Yet, her Venus has already been layered by Maillol's reception and re-conception of her body as both darker and more voluptuous. Finally, Amos writes: "I sutured her lovely rounded thighs onto an image of an African woman,"[30] thereby superimposing the original Greek ideal of "white" female beauty onto the often-discarded, disregarded, and over-sexualized Black female body. She points out further, with provocative irony, that the models for those "repeated 'black' legs" were "actually photographs of my legs and those of two paid white models, all of us clad in black stockings."[31] With these literal and figurative layers and twists of artistic expression, Amos critiques the application of classical aesthetic norms to Black women, and exposes, in the words of L. E. Farrington, the "superficial or 'skin [stocking] deep' nature of assessments based on pigmentation."[32]

Amos also adds layers to the Kritios boy himself, or, more particularly, to his hair. In John Pedley's description, the Kritios's boy's "head has hair which radiates in thin strands from the crown and is rolled up over a fillet" in the Severe Style.[33] Amos herself asserts that she deliberately "touched up" his hair "to make it noticeable."[34] A closer look, indeed, reveals extra curl and definition to the *kouros*'s Severe Style coiffure. Is it even a little Afro? The story behind this detail is telling. When Amos was eleven years old, she took courses in oil painting at Morris Brown College in Atlanta. Around this time, she also attended the local grade school, where she first learned about ancient Greek sculptures and their original models.

About the *kouros*: As a child, I was taught by the educated black scholars who were relegated to teaching in the elementary and high schools of Atlanta's then-segregated school system. I learned that the Greeks, who eschewed manual labor, used slaves as models for their sculptures, which celebrated the beautiful bodies of the gods. I then equated all slaves with the black slaves of America, a few of whom I had been taken to visit when I was little. Though it may have been wrong to believe Ethiopians and West Africans were models for the treasured statues, I loved the thought.[35]

To her naïve and youthful imagination, there was never a separation between ideal "white" classical beauty and the beauty of her Black ancestors. In fact, to her child's mind, and perhaps also into adulthood (hence the *kouros*'s hair), they were one and the same, or at the very least, more intertwined than is often admitted. In an interview with bell hooks, Amos once said:

I don't think that the key for us in authenticating Blackness is to deny that we are fundamentally western and that we are influenced by Europe, but we are also influenced by the African diaspora, and the point is that we can lay claim to all of those multi-dimensional parts of ourselves and not that we have to flatten ourselves out one way or the other.[36]

As her "touching up" of the *kouros* reveals, Emma Amos never flattened herself. A staunch feminist, passionate artist, and confident Black woman, she leaned hard into multidimensionality by playing on, critiquing, and reworking even the most toxic white male icons of the classical tradition.

Her conceptual approach, therefore, naturally lent itself to what Phoebe Wolfskill has termed a uniquely "hybrid" artistic style, namely, "a mix of woven fabric with paint, abstraction and realism, and image and text."[37] In the 1960s Amos paid the bills by working as a designer in a carpet and rug manufacturing company. She also taught textile weaving in the Newark School of Fine and Industrial Arts in the 1970s, exhibited many mixed media artworks in the 1980s and, in the 1990s, even co-hosted a Boston TV series on craft called "Show of Hands." Her own weaving, therefore, looms large in her work, as well as textiles of African origin and significance such as Kente and Kanga cloth. In *Measuring, Measuring*, as in many of her works, by mixing media, Amos weaves the threads of the classical tradition within her own cloth, so to speak. "As such, Amos's art constitutes," Patton writes, "a form of resistance. She questions the validity of canonical traditions and institutions that for so long have been biased against the inclusion of women and artists of color, especially blacks."[38] At the same time, Amos does not negate its influence or even its aesthetic value, but instead "touches it up" and adds complex sutures and ironic new dimensions that allow her to exercise her own creative agency. In this way, she marks the classical tradition and its vexed history with her own hand: that of a Black person, an artist, an artisan, and a woman.

Thompson: *Untitled (Augustus)*, 1964

Bob Thompson engaged in artistic mixings of a slightly different sort but, with a daring and playful critique similar to that of his contemporary. As a painter, Thompson primarily mixed pigment: vibrant, jeweled tones and a spectrum of psychedelic hues. He mixed these colors, moreover, with classical forms and figures, many of them from scenes of Western European art. A small, *Untitled* painting from 1964, later given the name *Augustus* in a posthumous exhibition, forms the basis for my analysis in the remainder of this chapter. With this piece, Thompson, like Amos, performs what Alan Ruiz terms a "détournement"[39] of the classical tradition and, in this case, of the racialized aesthetics/ segregationist artistic attitudes that it has birthed. In this artwork, Thompson derides, intervenes, and presents his critique through mixing, adding layers, and repossessing an entire collection of classical sculptures and images from the Vatican Museum.

This collection of images, which functions as Thompson's canvas, comes from two illustrated pages from an American art publication, *Horizon: A Magazine of the Arts*. Thompson's choice of material for this piece underscores his insatiable obsession with creating, learning, and painting, using whatever material he had at hand, and taking inspiration from anything that struck him. Thompson often spent entire days and nights painting on a variety of materials: huge canvases were his preference, but he would also use concert programs, magazines, or pieces of cardboard. Trained at the Hite Art Institute at University of Louisville, and under the guidance of artists such as Jan Müller within the Provincetown artist community in Massachusetts, Thompson never stopped reading, seeking inspiration in the world around him, and improving his craft. In the case of *Untitled* (*Augustus*), he had been perusing an article on the Vatican collections. In his multiple trips to Europe (1961–3; 1965–6) he likely studied these images *in situ* as well.

In terms of the subject matter, Thompson habitually functioned with little to no concern about the aesthetic boundaries erected against Black artists. Gylbert Coker writes: "He was outrageous, not that his life-style was any different from other artists of the day, he was outrageous because he was a Black man who did not wait to be invited into the cultural circle of the world, he just went in."[40] He went where he found inspiration, which included everything from the jazz clubs of New York to the museums and churches of Europe, and he painted whatever he wished. His wife Carol Thompson points out how he was captivated by the classics of Western European art, like "Francisco de Goya, Nicolas Poussin, and Piero della Francesca."[41] Yet Thompson's attitude toward these artists was never one of inferiority, but of appreciation and confidence in his own, original, re-creations. He explains, in an interview with Jeanne Spiegel:

> I look at Poussin and he's got it all there. Why are all of these people running around trying to be original when they should just go ahead and be themselves and that's the originality of it all, just being yourself. Now you can't do anything. You can't draw a new form. The form has already been drawn. You see? . . . that total human figure almost encompasses every form there is. You know? . . . it hit me that

why don't I work with these things that are already there . . . because that is what I respond to most of all.[42]

Thompson began with what attracted him and ran with it, choosing to live and work as an engaged and free artistic intellectual, beyond racial and racist boundaries. Thompson carries this same bold confidence into his engagement with the classical sculptures depicted in *Horizon* magazine.

The original magazine article presents a montage of iconic classical pieces from the Vatican collection. Some of the most famous figures from Greco-Roman antiquity—the Cnidian Venus, Augustus of Prima Porta, Apollo Belvedere, the Discobolus of Myron and Laocöon—frame the collage.[43] The viewer's eyes move from the head of Venus at the top left across to the title "Antiquities from the Vatican Collections" to an Etruscan statue, Augustus, a black figure vase of Achilles and Ajax, Apollo, then down to a third-century Roman couple, an Egyptian statue of queen Arsinoe, and back via the Discobolus, part of a Roman sarcophagus, a Roman mosaic of Minerva, an Etruscan horse head, and the Hellenistic personification of the Nile river. The Laocöon is situated close to the center, near Augustus and two panels of image descriptions.

In his so-called *Augustus* image (Figure 10), Thompson makes several subversive and playful alterations to this collage, first and foremost in his application of color.

Figure 10 Bob Thompson (1937–66), *Untitled (Augustus)* (1963). Gouache on paper with printed image, 12¼ × 17¾ inches / 31.3 × 45.1 cm, signed. © Michael Rosenfeld Gallery LLC, New York, NY.

Thompson favored bold, jeweled tones in his work, and generally chose to use a vibrantly multicolored palette rather than identifiable skin tones or ideological "blackness" or "whiteness." In this way, Lowery Stokes Sims argues, Thompson "exploded habitual obsession about skin color by violating the naturalistic associations of color with pigmentation and suggestively de-privileging the component of color as it is associated with race."[44] In this work, Thompson imbues the first two thirds of the image with more vibrant hues. The latter third is a study of red and white contrasts: red for the "black figures" on the vase, the Egyptian Arsinoe, and the Roman male, and white for Apollo Belvedere, the Discobolus, and the Roman female. Looking from the right to left, however, the study of contrasts fades into the red or yellow of the figures on the left. Greens and blues fill in the background and some details of figures such as the Etruscan horse and the snake writhing around Laocöon and his sons. Finally, his own self-portrait, the most defined, interesting face in the painting, receives a veritable rainbow of pigmentation. With color, therefore, Thompson draws attention to the left hand portion of the painting, connected by Laocöon's artificially extended arms. The line of these yellow arms cross over the borders of the original composition and lead our eyes up to Augustus, thence to Venus' large and looming head, and finally back down to Thompson's self-portrait, framed by the smaller figures of the Nile beneath.

With a mix of appreciation and irreverence, Thompson "colors" this entire collection of classical figures, an act that likely has Winckelmann rolling in his grave. In adding this layer of paint, Thompson, like Amos's *Measuring, Measuring*, problematizes the supposed racialized "whiteness" of ancient sculptures, and the perceived one-dimensional nature of his own and others' "blackness." At the same time, he brings the "black and white" of the past into the living present and into his own style of abstract figurative expressionism. From these antiquities he creates perhaps more universal, monochrome figures differentiated, in a few cases, by their hair (e.g., with Venus, the Nile, or the horse on the bottom right). While he blots out the faces of the past, he preserves their original shapes and forms, which he then uses for his own symbolic expression.

Only the features of Venus, Augustus, Laocöon, and the Roman male remain vaguely visible, perhaps for the purpose of association with himself. Case in point, perhaps, is the figure of Augustus of Prima Porta,[45] the details of whose face and breastplate, those icons of Roman imperialism, he leaves mostly visible, albeit tinted with the yellowish hue of an old and faded photograph. To the right of Augustus' outstretched arm and just above his head, there is a thumbprint, presumably Thompson's. Whether imprinted intentionally or not, it begs association connection with Amos's hands and the claim to ownership, here upon the Roman emperor himself. Thompson, after all, uses the same color paint for Augustus and himself, or at least, half of his face. Even the shape of his head mirrors that of Augustus, and both face front, as if to confront the viewer with this comparison. Thompson thus sets himself with or against Augustus, and all that he represents, in what Robert O'Meally terms "antagonistic cooperation."[46] Through this principle of jazz, also applicable to visual representations, Black artists engage in provocative antiphonies with and against other artists, the bass line, and the audience.[47] Thompson performs this dance with Augustus, with the old European masters, and through them, with the classical tradition itself.

The tension of this approach is reflected visually by the figure of Laocöon.[48] His elongated arm stretches upwards, as if inflicting a blow to Augustus' stomach, but then ultimately leads the viewer's eye in a triangle through and beyond Augustus, to Venus, then to the Nile, and back to the artist himself. The longevity of Laocöon's fame as an icon of ancient art is perhaps unparalleled. Pliny himself claimed that this piece was "a work of art to be preferred before all other works of painting or sculpture" (*Natural Histories* 36.37).[49] And, in the eighteenth century, Winckelmann continued to wax lyrically on this famous Hellenistic piece, claiming it to be "the standard of the Roman artists, as well as ours."[50] Thompson, also, capitalizes on the Laocöon's energy and iconic status but harnesses it for his own artistic purposes. In Winckelmann's romanticizing description of the figure, "[t]he action of these muscles . . . is carried beyond truth to the limits of possibility; they lie like hills which are drawing themselves together—for the purpose of expressing the extremest exertion in anguish and resistance."[51] Thompson channels this anguished resistance within his own work;[52] and, by recoloring and repurposing this figure, Thompson too leans into "the limits of possibility" and creates a space for himself, a Black American artist, within the classical tradition. As Diana Tuite describes it: "he warps these received forms in ways that compound their ambiguity and permit them to double back on the United States, absorbing and implicating its particular legacies of injustice."[53]

Through his mix of classical sculpture with colored paint and his abstract expressionist style, Thompson ultimately redirects these figures and their tradition towards himself. The viewer is left pondering, not the old pieces, but Thompson's face. Not only it is the most multidimensional—not at all flattened—figure in the piece, but it is a composite of colors, as if he has internalized and now holds within himself the lights and shadows of the ancient world itself. Thompson situates his face in the quadrant not above Laocöon, not beneath Augustus' feet, but adjacent to the emperor, in the title space. A very close look, moreover, through the layers of paint, reveals the barely visible title "Antiquities" behind Thompson's forehead. Ever playful, Thompson admits that he has antiquities "on the brain." Yet, by shifting the focus of the montage and ensconcing himself firmly among these iconic images, now "colored," Thompson asserts his artistic agency and provokes reflection on the classics, "color", and our place with respect to both.

Conclusion: Beyond Palimpsest

In *Measuring, Measuring* (1995) and *Untitled* (*Augustus*) (1964), Emma Amos and Bob Thompson deliberately rework iconic "white" sculptures of classical antiquity: the Kritios Boy, Venus of Milo, Augustus of Prima Porta, Laocöon, and indeed the entire collection of Vatican antiquities. Their works, however, do not function, in the terms of Best, as a mere palimpsest, erasing the past to make room for the new. Nor do they seek to recover, repair, or reconstruct the classical tradition. Rather, through mixed media, playfully variegated coloration, and a sense of antagonistic irony, these artists ensconce these sculptures and their vexed history within their own aesthetic expression and social-cultural critique. They thus repurpose the classics to confront the contradictions inherent in the racist usurpation of aesthetics and racialized mobilization of the classical tradition itself. Their approach corresponds to what Dariek Scott describes as "a politics that does not organize itself around a stance of defense or aggression, [but] … that assimilates to itself racial identities and the history that makes them, knowing and naming the injustice of those identities and histories but choosing … to let them … flow through the self … and yet become transformed."[54] The resistance and disruption exhibited by these artists thus become acts of radical generosity. By mixing media and color with iconic forms and figures of antiquity, Thompson and Amos not only actualize their own agency but also break open the classical tradition for countless viewers and artists of all "colors" and for years to come.

Notes

1. C. West (1982, 52) identifies "the classical revival" of the Renaissance through the Enlightenment as one of the major historical processes "that circumscribed and determined the metaphors, notions, categories, and norms of modern discourse." This classical revival, he continues, "infuses Greek ocular metaphors and classical ideals of beauty, proportion, and moderation into the beginnings of modern discourse" (53).

2. C. West (1982, 54), for example, argues that Greek sculptural forms led to "the emergence of the idea of white supremacy," because, once they were idealized by Winckelmann and others, they became part of the "classical aesthetic and cultural norms," which, in turn, influenced supposedly scientific racial categorizations of peoples in the fields of natural history, phrenology, and physiognomy. For a commonly cited diagram that uses the head of Apollo Belvedere to evaluate the physiognomy of various ethnic groups, see Nott and Gliddon (1854, 458, Fig. 339–44) illustrated by Samuel Morton, MD.

3. Roelofs 2005, 83. While both West and Roelofs discuss these processes in analogous ways, C. West's (1982) analysis aims at reconstructing the origins of white supremacy and highlights how artistic norms have been implicated within scientific investigations as well. As a philosopher of aesthetics, however, Roelofs (2005, 84) sees these processes as operating within a "cultural system … [of] 'aesthetic relationality'" namely, "a dynamic network of aesthetically generated and aesthetically productive relationships that agents inhabit vis-à-vis one another and vis-à-vis artworks and other aesthetic objects and environments."

4. In this chapter, I use the term "classical tradition" very loosely to mean the body of visual and textual works and knowledge originating in Greece and Rome, which for centuries has influenced many cultures, particularly those connected with Western Europe.

5. DuBois 2018, 9.

6. Best 2018, 51. For artistic examples, see the work of Kara Walker or Robert Colescott.

7. Best 2018, 54. See the exhibit, *Chroma: Ancient Sculpture in Color*, on view from July 5, 2022–March 26, 2023, at the Metropolitan Museum of Art in New York. This exhibition raises awareness about the pigmentation that originally bedecked and gilded the supposedly "white" images of Greco-Roman Antiquity

8. Best 2018, 61. See Fred Wilson's exhibit *Wildfire Test Pit* (August 30, 2016–June 12, 2017) at the Allen Memorial Art Museum of Oberlin College, Ohio, which contrasted white and Black

sculptures while simultaneously commemorating the work of Mary Edmonia Lewis. Another example is that of his Yinka Shonibare, a British-Nigerian artist, who redesigns classical sculptures into colorful and provocative fiberglass replicas: e.g., *Farnese Hercules* (2018) and *Winged Victory of Samothrace* (2017).

9. See also Moyer, Lecznar, Morse 2020, 21, on "visual classicisms."

10. C. J. Martin 2012, 111. In this interview with Martin, Amos was specifically thinking about Romare Bearden. In her own words: "He could pass for white. He made his work as black as possible" (2012, 111). In an interview with Wilson and Hamalian, Thompson's friend Emilio Cruz described him as a Black man "totally intolerant of the notion of inferiority" (1985, 114).

11. C. J. Martin 2012, 111.

12. Works that seem to reveal some of these anxieties include Amos's *Tightrope* (1994) and Thompson's *Fearful Insider #2* (1958).

13. Although the term "old Masters" has vexed resonance given the context of slavery, I use the phrase because Thompson himself did, in reference to the Western European painters he studied. See Childs (2021, 68n1), who takes the same approach.

14. Amos 1999, 38. Further in this article, she confronts "curatorial and editorial definitions of 'black art' that both include and exclude works, thus continuing the segregation of images and artists" (1999, 38).

15. C. Martin 2012, 112. She also told bell hooks in an earlier interview, "They don't, even now, buy my pictures enough to pay the rent" (1993, 22).

16. Amos 1999, 38.

17. This exhibit, curated by Holly Block, was shown at Art in General in New York, and traveled to the Montclair Museum of Art in New Jersey. For more on Amos's work through this show, see S. L. Harris 2021, 33.

18. Amos in Lippard 1991, 15–16.

19. For more on Amos's perspectives on color, see S. L. Harris 2021, 25–6.

20. Sometime after this piece, Amos created a parallel work, *Models* (1995), acrylic with photo transfer on linen (with African fabric borders), 51 × 39 in (129.5 × 99.1 cm), Collection of the artist. While *Models* replaces the Venus image with a painting of Gaugin's Te Ha Amana, and hence has a slightly different valence, much of my argument applies to this image as well. Thus, I merely reference it here. One interesting difference lies in Amos's replacement of her hands with three *X*s beneath each figure. Amos writes: "The repeat of three *X*s, including my X-figure model, is the image with which I end this canvas. Here I am looking over my shoulder at the prejudices that would still my voice. I cross out my comments, my noticing, my daring to comment, as if to take my images back" (1999, 39). For more on these *X*s and their possible connection, also, to Malcolm X, see Patton 2002, 43.

21. Kritios boy: *c.* 480 BCE, Parian marble, 116.7 cm (45.9 in), Acropolis Museum 698; Aphrodite of Melos (Venus de Milo): *c.* 125–75 BCE, Parian marble, 2.04 m (6 ft 8 ¼ in), Louvre Museum, Paris, Ma 399 (LL 299).

22. S. L. Harris 2021, 33

23. Winckelmann 1972, 122–6.

24. Bronze, 155.3 × 47 × 38 cm (61 1/8 × 18 1/2 × 14 15/16 in), National Gallery of Art, Washington DC, 1984.27.1. On the connection between Amos's torso and this work of Maillol, see Wolfskill 2017, 60.

25. https://www.louvre.fr/en/explore/the-palace/ideal-greek-beauty, "Ideal Greek Beauty: Venus de Milo and the Galerie des Antiques" (accessed October 24, 2022).

26. On the symbolism of Amos's hands, see Farrington 2005, 162.

27. Amos 1999, 38.

28. Patton 2002, 47.

29. Amos 1999, 39.

30. Amos 1999, 38.

31. Amos 1999, 39.

32. Farrington 2005, 162.

33. Pedley 2012, 231.

34. Amos 1999, 38.

35. Amos 1999, 38–9.

36. Amos 1995, 45.

37. Wolfskill 2022, 127.

38. Patton 2002, 47.

39. Ruiz (2016, 234) describes "detournement" as "an effective critique, rather than reactionary practice, [which] can only take place through an intervention within the fixed institutions that we wish to change radically."

40. Coker 1978, 12.

41. Thompson 1999, 3. For more on Thompson and the old European Masters, see Childs 2021, 58–68.

42. Siegel 1967, 12.

43. https://archive.org/details/horizon0004unse_no3/page/46/mode/2up. Not only are these, perhaps, the most recognizable images for an American audience, but they are among the most discussed by Winckelmann in his essays on the superiority of classical sculpture (1972, 113–21).

44. Sims 2021, 141.

45. *Augustus of Prima Porta*, *c*. Tiberian age, Parian marble with traces of polychromy, 6 ft 10 in (2.08m), Vatican Museums, Vatican City, MV.2290.0.0

46. O' Meally 2007, 80.

47. O'Meally's use of the term comes within his analysis of how Romare Bearden in his *A Black Odyssey* (1977) series repositions Odysseus' enemies as, in fact, "partners in the creation of heroic action" (2007, 80). On this approach as participation in "antagonistic liberation," see Saul 2003, 158.

48. *Laocöon*, *c*. 40–20 BCE, Parian marble, 6 ft 10 in × 5 ft 4 in × 3 ft 8 in (208 cm × 163 cm × 112 cm), Vatican Museums, Vatican City, MV.1059.0.0.

49. *sicut in Laocoonte, qui est in Titi imperatoris domo, opus omnibus et picturae et statuariae artis praeferendum.*

50. See Winckelmann 1972, 61; see 72–3, for additional descriptions of Laocöon, and C. West 1982, 53–4, for further commentary on the influence of Winckelmann's views within the process of aesthetic racialization.

51. Winckelmann 1972, 123.

52. The shape of Laocöon's figure also brings to mind the *X*'s of Amos's *Models* (1995) referred to above.

53. Tuite 2021, 33.

54. Scott 2010, 145.

PART II
PROXIMATE FORMS

CHAPTER 4

TWO WAYS OF BEING ALONE: DUAL FORM IN SAPPHO FRAGMENT 168B

Alex Purves

And the left page nearly always has better words on it it seems.

Claire-Louise Bennett, Checkout 19

Should the interpretation of words in a poem be fixed or fluid? How much energy and commitment do we have to argue for one side or another in debates about meaning that are likely to remain unresolvable? How much do either/or and wrong/right matter, or can we be and have both? It is hard to fit either/or into the format of traditional literary criticism, especially into the structure of an essay, because writing takes its thread from the medium of a single, looping line. We are not well able to read in twos, and that means we are not well able to present an argument in twos either.

Except that classicists do sometimes read like this. Many readers are not entirely fluent in reading ancient languages, and so the practice of translating ("drawing across") may be one of reading sideways as well as down—across the page if with a facing page translation, or across the desk or screen to a lexicon or a commentary. For a beginning or intermediate student of ancient Greek or Latin, this horizontal style of reading may come more into play even than vertical reading, as the eyes travel right and left between words sentence, commentary, and lexicon, in a practice of pausing, checking, returning, rereading. In graduate school, I once was told that a good classicist could read the English on the left-hand page of the Loeb with one eye as she could simultaneously read the Greek or Latin with the other eye on the right (this was a joke, but it does speak to something about the way ancient texts are mediated).

There have been several creative experiments in criticism, theory, and fiction on the topic of reading in twos, especially playing with the printed form of the book. The ones that have mattered to me personally in writing this chapter have been Ali Smith's *How To Be Both* (2014), a novel whose form plays with reading from both front and back, Susan Foster's *Valuing Dance: Commodities and Gifts in Motion* (2019), which offers one chapter in which dance as gift and dance as commodity are presented in parallel arguments on the left and right hand sides of the page, respectively, and Claire-Louise Bennett's *Checkout 19* (2021), which draws attention to the differences between words on the left page and words on the right in the process of reading. For example, early on in her novel Bennett writes, on the left page:[1]

When we open a book our eyes nearly always go over to the left page. That's right— the left page, for reasons we have never previously reflected upon, has a much stronger pull on us than the right page. We always look down first of all at the right page. The right page first, that's right. But the words on the right page always seem much too close. Too close to each other and too close to our face. The words on the right page do indeed make us peculiarly aware of our face. Is it our face? Is it? Well? The words on the right seem far too eager, overbearing, and yes somewhat ingratiating in fact, and very soon our rattled eyes leave the right page in order to seek refuge in the left. We look down at the right page and up at the left page. We do actually. And we nearly always read the left page much more slowly than the right. There seems to be more time on the left page. Yes. Yes. Yes there does. On the left page there is more space it seems, on either side of the words, and above and below every sentence. And the left page nearly always has better words on it it seems. That's right—words like 'shone' and 'creature' and 'champagne' and 'ragged' and 'clump', for example.

Foster is likewise explicit about the difference in tone that paying attention to left page and right page affords her:

> In what follows two hypothetical domains of exchange in dance—commodity and gift—are presented as contrasting strongly with one another [on the right page and the left]. They are also portrayed as the starkest versions of what they might be and how they might function. By inhabiting each form of exchange separately and exploring its distinctiveness, I have found that its operations on any given instance of dance become more easily discernible. In an effort to highlight these differences I have slightly altered the prose style for each part so as to inflect it with the more anonymizing, uniforming capacity of commodification and the idiosyncratic unwieldiness of gift exchange.[2]

As she goes on to write, this set-up creates "a choreography of the page that . . . invites you to read back and forth between the domains."[3] In this chapter, I offer a similar experiment in form for an ancient Greek fragment.

Fragment 168b is a four-line fragment of seventeen words. It comes down to us without attribution in Hephaestion's abridged book on meter,[4] and most scholars—although not all— assign it to Sappho. Sometimes referred to as the "Midnight Poem,"[5] it recounts the experience of an individual sleeping or lying alone at night as the stars chart their course through the sky above. The fragment has typically attracted a doubled discourse, whether in relation to if it is by Sappho or Alcaeus (or someone else),[6] or whether it is good or bad.[7] Indeed, as Glenn Most has shown, Sappho's poetry has long attracted a discourse of duplication, as manifested especially in the contrasting identities (of poetess and prostitute) that have been attached to her by tradition.[8] But what interests me in particular in terms of the dual form I am investigating here concerns the interpretation of the Greek word *kateudô* (Aeolic κατεύδω, Attic καθεύδω), which appears in the last line of the fragment and can be interpreted both as "I sleep" and "I lie awake."

This chapter is an attempt to acknowledge the dual form of the poem's reception by keeping both sides of the divide, and both meanings of the word, in play, with the left pages offering a reading of *kateudô* meaning "I sleep" and the right pages a reading where it means "I like awake." I am interested—as Bennett explicates in the passage quoted above—in the way that such an organization might encourage the eyes reading the left page to also travel to the right, and vice versa (as well as up and down, as she underscores later in the passage). My hope is to draw attention to the central margin of this book as an area that can create an opening for a more fluid and freeform reading that exists in the critical half-light between being awake and asleep.[9] The placing of two different arguments side by side will also contribute, I hope, to the sense of unfinishedness that Sappho's ongoing experience of night engenders.

As my own attempt to write from both sides of an argument, this chapter also stands alongside other pieces I have written that analyze this fragment, but which do not present both sides of the argument in parallel.[10] It is my hope that this chapter can complement those due to its experimentation with form, offering an alternative point of view to those more traditional articles.

Although this chapter is structured around the binary of asleep/awake, I want finally to note the importance of the word *mona* ("alone") to this project, and the ways in which this word interferes with the dual nature of the chapter's form by asking what it means to be alone in a poem. The movement that I trace between one and two in the fragment, as between "I" and "you," will hopefully lead to points of insight and convergence between forms of criticism and forms of the lyric. Finally, *mona* looks back to my own writing of this piece during the first Covid lockdown, and the effect of that isolation on writing practices in general.

asleep

δέδυκε μὲν ἀ σελάννα
καὶ Πληΐαδες· μέσαι δὲ
νύκτες, παρὰ δ' ἔρχετ' ὥρα,
ἔγω δὲ μόνα κατεύδω.

The moon has gone down
As have the Pleiades. The nights are
At their middle – time is passing –
But I sleep, alone.

When we reach Sappho, asleep, at the end of this short fragment, her presence is marked as discordantly alone: ἔγω δὲ μόνα κατεύδω ("but I sleep, alone"). Each of the four words in the last line quietly breaks the rhythm and tone, for although there are modulations in verb and tense in the preceding lines (the moon and Pleiades "have gone down," the nights "[are] at their middle," time "is passing"), the poem's first three verses draw the night into a single orbit and temporal sweep. Something about Sappho's "I," though, is asynchronous with that movement, accentuated by the transition from third- to first-person voice as we reach the end of the sentence and stanza. The poem's unusual movement between singular and plural (both "the nights (*nuktes*) are at their middle" and "the time (*ôra*) is passing" are unusual collocations), eventually settles on the insistent singularity of the final *mona*.

Sappho's "I" marks this scene as different from the extended and exclusive use of the third-person voice in Alcman 89, the famous "Sleep of Nature" poem (Alcman 89 PMG):

εὕδουσι δ' ὀρέων κορυφαί τε καὶ φάραγγες
πρώονές τε καὶ χαράδραι
φῦλά τ' ἑρπέτ' ὅσα τρέφει μέλαινα γαῖα
θῆρές τ' ὀρεσκῷοι καὶ γένος μελισσᾶν
καὶ κνώδαλ' ἐν βένθεσσι προφυρέας ἁλός·
εὕδουσι δ' οἰωνῶν φῦλα τανυπτερύγων.

The peaks and ravines of the mountains sleep,
And the headlands and the streams,
And the tribes of creatures as many as the black earth rears
And the beasts who dwell in the mountains and the race of bees
And the beings in the depths of the purple sea,
And the tribes of long-winged birds sleep too.

In Alcman's poem, the night coordinates harmoniously with the poem's subjects to create a synchronic effect, undisturbed by the human perception of time. εὕδουσι ("they sleep") unites a number of different natural entities, from mountain peaks and streams to sheep, sea creatures, and birds.[11] In Sappho the situation is different. The *egô de* of the fragment's

awake

δέδυκε μὲν ἀ σελάννα
καὶ Πληΐαδες· μέσαι δὲ
νύκτες, παρὰ δ' ἔρχετ' ὤρα,
ἔγω δὲ μόνα κατεύδω.

The moon has gone down
And the Pleiades. The nights are
At their middle, the hours go by,
And I lie alone.

Awake at midnight, Sappho lies alone while the rest of the world sleeps and night moves through its natural course. The present tense of her final declaration (ἔγω δὲ μόνα κατεύδω) holds her within the space of what is often referred to as the lyric present: a tense that has the ability to float free from the actual moment of enunciation, to extend here into an iterative sense ("every night") or into an attenuated stretch of the present that has the benefits of being elusive and imprecise. The temporal sense of *kateudô* is then as broad as the night-sky—a pervasive present tense that resists anchoring in time or space, so that the lying might be occurring "now" but it might also be occurring at any time, including the time at which you are reading this.

And yet, it is hard not to hear a complaint here about the speaker's bondage to time. Sappho's insomnia makes her aware of the night's passing to which she should if she were sleeping be oblivious.[30] Each stage of the night moves, dragging her with it against her will, so that she is forced to engage with time, to stare it in the face and try to measure her sleepless self against it.

It is likely that fragment 168b is a complete poem, as Diskin Clay argues, because there is little place for it to go after the fourth line except back again to the start.[31] We might think of this in terms of Roland Barthes's "scenography of waiting" where the I who waits has no sense of proportions. "I am waiting, and everything around my waiting is stricken with unreality."[32] The world of stars and sky is both outside her but also within, the "sublunary world … beneath the lids,"[33] a darkness and sinking (δύω) that sleep promises but also holds back from her. With the cadence and rhythm of the poem (like a lullaby), we move back and forth between the biological cycle of Sappho's body and the cosmic cycle of the night, so that the difference between them (as with the difference between falling asleep and being asleep) becomes almost imperceptible.

The *de* of the final line then not only whispers back to the insomniac the *de* of the poem's first word (*de-duke*); it also draws into its orbit the string of *de*'s that have come before (μέσαι δὲ / … παρὰ δ'. … / ἔγω δὲ … 2–4). These *de*'s act like clouds or foam—wisps that join one thought to the next as the mind drifts into sleep (*and … and … and I …*). As the poem falls on us, and on Sappho, it brings the sleep of night with it. In the second line we learn that stars have sunk with the moon and surround it, but the moon (*men a selanna*) is nonetheless formally alone in the first line just as "I" am (*mona*) in the last. The chiasmus between verses 1 and 4 is held together not only by the threads of *de*

asleep

last line sets us apart from nighttime's smooth rhythm, ending with a verb that is sonically consistent with the preceding verses (note the repeated consonants and reshuffling of letters in *deduke . . . nuktes . . . kateudô*), yet semantically off-kilter; the "I" is marked as different in its actions and its state to the preceding lines. Sappho is playing with an aesthetic that even as it summons time, seems to remain outside it.

Where Alcman in Fragment 89 creates a connective, cumulative movement through all the elements of the poem by his use of words meaning "and"—

. . .δέ . . . τε καί . . .
. . .τε καί . . .
. . .τε . . .
. . .τε . . .
. . .καί . . .
καί . . .
. . .δέ . . .

in Sappho 168b the speaker's separation from the world and its natural elements is nuanced through the responsive movement of

. . .μέν . . .
καί . . .δέ
. . .δέ . . .
. . .δέ . . .[12]

Structurally, the poem can be understood as a preparatory *men* followed by two connectives *de*'s and then a final adversative one.[13] In Alcman, the connective particles bind together each element through the soft fabric of sleep, and in Sappho they almost promise to do the same, with the regular breath and rhythm of the night's cycle responding line by line.

But if Alcman's line-endings coincide with the putting to bed of each subject, the *de* in the last line of Sappho 168b creates a shift in tone, from "and" to "but" (compare lyric's use of the priamel "but I," most famous from Sappho 16.3).[14] In addition, the *de* at line-end in verse 2[15] signals differently the merging properties of sleep, so that night's middle erodes any clear separation of categories.[16] As Paula Reiner and David Kovacs have argued, "the enjambment μέσαι δὲ/ νύκτες is highly unusual for the style" of folk song or *carmina popularia* (to which 168b has been both compared and attributed), where "we would expect each colon . . . to be self-contained."[17] The fact that the line-ending *de* bridges a concept across the verse break indicates a complexity of structure and tone—a circling and troubling of the sleeping subject around the lines of the poem, a restlessness or achronicity that throws the form of the poem slightly off balance.

After tracing for her audience the actions of the moon's descent and time's passage, by ending with *kateudô* Sappho leaves the reader or listener suspended in an ongoing present, almost as if she is still now sleeping, since this is how the fragment closes: I sleep.

awake

but also by the anagrammatic resemblance of *deduke* and *kateudô,* the poem's first and last words. Like the moon, we might say that Sappho is willing herself to sink down (*kata*) into sleep, to join the full (*pleô*) world of the Pleiades and the plural "middles of nights" waiting beneath her eyelids:

δέδυκε μὲν ἀ σελάννα
καὶ Πληΐαδες· μέσαι δὲ
νύκτες, παρὰ δ' ἔρχετ' ὤρα,
ἔγω δὲ μόνα κατεύδω.

This falling down into sleep through the verses of the poem is mirrored, as the underlining of syllables here makes clear, with a lengthening of *e* to *ô* right before the turn into the final line: ὤρα/, ἔγω . . . κατεύδω, as if Sappho were falling too.[34]

And yet Sappho's *mona* interrupts the notion of a smooth passage between her body and the sky because it explicitly separates her from sleep's canopy of night, leaving her alone in contrast to the moon, which is surrounded by the stars that have sunk with it (δέδυκε μὲν ἀ σελάννα/ καὶ Πληΐαδες). The spectral presence of the absent other for whom Sappho waits alone draws *mona* into a negative relationality[35] (unlike the *men a,* which connects). The gap after *kateudô* at the poem's end would thereby imply waiting . . . for a fifth line that will, like line 2, usher in a *kai* (*kai Pleiades*). The fragment does not fulfill that arrival, but instead lies suspended in the bracket between a return to the poem's beginning (the repetition of insomnia) and a return to sleep.

The rhythm of that return is both implied by the reduplicated form of *duô,* with which the poem begins, and broken by the *de* that follows *egô* at the poem's end. *Deduke* sets the poem off in the perfect tense: the moon has sunk, denoting an open present, stretching from the past through the point of now and beyond. The cadence of the fragment, moreover, suggests a perfect circle between this *de-,* as I have proposed, and the particles (*de*) of lines 2, 3, and 4. Except that, if the poem is a fall into a sleep, then it is also a complaint about still being awake. The *de* of the last line jerks the poem back to consciousness with a word that cannot decide between "and" and "but." The interruption of the "I" pulls the poem back into shape, preventing it from collapsing into the formlessness of sleep.

Here is where form, or formalism, is not quite radical enough. The form of the poem is constructed through a refusal to slacken or fall apart. As Susan Wolfson explains in the introduction to *Reading for Form* (2006), where she offers a reading of the thirteenth stanza of Matthew Prior's *The Dove,* formalism depends on structure and "press" (such as the press of letters and sounds running from "*storm* across *horn* to reach its rhyme in *form*"):

> Have you observ'd a sitting hare,
> Listening, and fearful of the storm
> Of horns and hounds, clap back her ear,
> Afraid to keep, or leave her form?

asleep

Or rather: I sleep alone, and, as you hear this, I am again sleeping alone—this is where I exist, held in limbo by my own line of verse. The moon, stars, and night may pass through time (*deduke, parerchetai*) but I do not, caught in the negative relationality of waiting, of being alone. Even though I have achieved with this line a kind of timelessness, I am also either too early or too late—as the *mona* indicates, in sleeping I have somehow missed you (whether you are my lover or my audience).[18]

It now becomes clear that sleep is interfering in an interesting way with the speaking voice of the poet.[19] The fragment's last two words are of course impossible—Sappho is neither alone nor asleep, for she speaks to us. The poem's explicit denial of its performative context even as it points to its own voice emphatically (*egô de*) is doubled by the speaker's denial of doing anything at all. During this special, extended duration of the night Sappho first bears witness to the passage of time and then explicitly claims that she has *not* borne witness, since she is asleep. The force of the last line is especially strange, because it inserts Sappho into a scene within which she does not appear to play a role. We end up in a space of deflection or negation that is defined, in part, by the difficulties and paradoxes of speaking in the present tense.[20] This difficulty applies differently to both sleep and poetry, but in ways that can be productively compared.

The problem of the fragment's last line could be solved by pointing to aspect: if the speaker intends "but I, every night, sleep alone" the utterance need not be tied to the actual *now* of being asleep. This reading is hard to square, however, with the temporal markers in the lines above: *deduke, mesai, parerchetai,* and *ôra.*[21] Why so much insistence on trying to pinpoint a precise moment in time—"the middles of the night"—if Sappho does not intend to point to *now* at all? If the *now* through which the mountains, dales, and animals sleep in Alcman 89 is homogeneous and inclusive, in fragment 168b, the sleeper's *now* speaks to an experience of alienation from the world and even from time itself. My now, Sappho seems to be saying, is different from your now.[22] While the rest of the world appears to move as one, I am stuck here, alone, in a different register of time.

In the first verse of Alcman 3 PMG, the present-tense voice of the poem's speaker is complicated by sleep in a different but applicable way (3–7):

> ἰθύ]ω δ' ἀκούσαι
> παρσενηΐ]ας οπος
> πρὸς αἰ]θέρα καλὸν ὑμνιοισᾶν μέλος   5
>   ].οι
> ὕπνον ἀ]πὸ γλεφάρων σκεδ[α]σεῖ γλυκύν

> I [am eager] to hear
> the [maiden] voice
> of girls singing a beautiful melody [to the heavens] ...   5
> [it?]
> will scatter sweet [sleep] from my eyes

awake

The stanza, as Wolfson puts it, "plays a game of keep and leave: the *a*-rhyme cued by *hare* hits the atonal, splayed lettering of *her ear*."[36] It is explicit about the game it is playing with "form"—a word that refers to the hare's seat or bed as well as the shape of a poem, resulting in what Wolfson calls a "satire of form-addiction" among poets and, especially, critics.[37] The stanza makes explicit that there is no form without holding, without some kind of return or game at the end: a remembering of who or what the subject of the poem is. Similarly, even though so many poems and songs take the form of lullabies, that lulling must also be controlled in order to work. The fragment, like all of Sappho's lyric, has a careful metrical pattern, and was indeed transmitted through Hephaestion's *Handbook on Meters*.[38] Sleep, on the other hand, *can only work* once form has fallen away and everything has gone slack, including forms of attention, which is why Sappho's *egô de,* even as it tries to submerge itself beneath the press of rhyme, repletion, and long vowels, cannot help but jolt Sappho (and the poem) back awake.

Every sleeper must consent to a feeling of falling—what Jean-Luc Nancy calls sleep's "most common and well-defined aspect"[39]—and it is that sinking, drowsiness, slackening, descent (*deduke*) that occurs *right before* sleep that is our only marker of its existence. Thus sleep, as he writes, is always antecedental ("sleep is itself a force that precedes itself and that carries its power forward into its action")[40]: we never know it, we never know ourselves in it, we can only anticipate it. In sleep, according to Nancy, "I myself become indistinct from the world . . . A simultaneity of what is one's own and not one's own occurs as this distinction falls away."[41] Fragment 168b can be read as a descent into precisely such an indistinction, until the "I" trips Sappho back awake and reminds her that she is an individual—apart, alone, and alert. The final *de* of the fragment, then, does not just hover indeterminately between *and* and *but*; it also marks the poem's voicing of *now*—a pulling back into "real time" at precisely the moment when the poem had almost fallen out of it.[42]

Nancy's "antecedence of sleep"—the fall before the event—pairs with the perfect tense of *deduke* to suggest that Sappho's position, alone and awake at the end of the poem, is bracketed, on the one hand, by a moment that the poem has just missed but whose effects linger on (the moon and stars' descent), and, on the other, by a moment whose effects draw her to it but at which she has not yet arrived (the fall of sleep). The "and/but/now I lie alone" of the last line thereby draws us all the more urgently into the fragment's present moment, even as we—like the insomniac—may find it difficult to accurately count or gauge that time.

Sappho's *kateudô* must then mean "I lie," despite the more common meaning of the verb as "I sleep" towards which the fragment wills its way. This unforeclosed meaning of the term ("I lie; I almost sleep") compares with the similarly strained or unrealized use of *koimaomai* ("I fall asleep, go to bed, lie down") in the Watchman's speech in Aeschylus' *Agamemnon* (1–4):

Θεοὺς μὲν αἰτῶ τῶνδ' ἀπαλλαγὴν πόνων,
φρουρᾶς ἐτείας μῆκος, ἣν κοιμώμενος

asleep

Like the speaker in Sappho 168b, the sleeping narrator's relation to time in these lines sets her apart from the world around her. The singer, who goes on to describe herself as a dancer in the chorus, imagines being awakened by—and then running to join—the song and dance that she is already participating in ("[the girls' singing] leads me to go to the assembly, / where I shall rapidly shake my yellow hair . . . / soft feet . . ." 7–10). Later in the poem, after a lacuna of 50 lines, sleep recurs in the phrase "with limb-loosening desire (λυσιμελεῖ τε πόσῳ) . . . / [the chorus leader] looks [at me?] more meltingly than sleep or death (τακερώτερα/ δ' ὕπνω καὶ σανάτω ποτιδέρκεται)," 61–2), suggesting a swirling together of sleep, desire, and song; as if the desire of the girl is imaginatively recast within the structure of the poem as the experience of sleeping.

Despite the fact that this is a choral song, the poem zeroes in on the singularity of the singer, whose wish to hear the maiden chorus belies the fact that she is a member of the very same group. This projected aloneness merges with the melting that is akin to sleep and destabilizes her presence in her description of the song's performance ("But Astymeloisa makes no answer to me" 64). Through sleep, the present tense of the singing moment is thus turned into a kind of negative or doubled space via the speaker's own denial of her part in it, even as she performs it.

The singers of both Sappho 168b and Alcman 3 gain access to this sense of being alone in, or cast out of, time through a stop gap (or to borrow from Roland Barthes, as I will suggest later, an airlock) that is created through the strange affinities of sleep and song. Other lyric poets speak through the barrier of sleep but in the opposite direction, when they attempt to comprehend or pierce the sleeper's obliviousness (as with Danae to the sleeping Perseus in Simonides 543 PMG).[23] But in these two fragments the first-person voice that issues from within the sleep-cocoon briefly articulates an elusive perspective on self and time. Sleep forces a different kind of subjectivity on me. The "I sleep" could refer to a lifetime ("I always sleep alone") or it could refer to a single moment in time, the moment of lyric enunciation. Is Sappho's "I sleep" an expression of her frustration at being caught in duration, or is it an escape from duration? Does *mona* invite the listener to share in this time (we might consider Mark Payne here on "the coming together of the time of the poem and the time of the reader [as] the essence of the lyric encounter"[24]) or does it exclude us from it?

What is clear is that as soon as we speak (or write) the "I" in poetry we set it apart from ourselves—it becomes a kind of double of the self that is not unlike the double "I" that we experience when dreaming. As Maurice Blanchot has put it, "[b]etween the one who sleeps and the one who is the subject of the dream's plot, there is a fissure, the hint of an interval, and a difference of structure."[25] This doubled "I" that is created between the sleeping and the dreaming self replicates, in this case, the doubled "I" of the one who performs and the one who inhabits that "I" through the experience of reading.[26] To be alone (*mona*) in sleep is then to be separated not only from one's lover but also from oneself. If lyric poetry is, according to one reading, "the speech of the self to the self," then here even that transaction is impossible across the sleep-divide.[27]

awake

στέγαις Ἀτρειδῶν ἄγκαθεν, κυνὸς δίκην,
ἄστρων κάτοιδα νυκτέρων ὁμήγυριν . . .

I ask the gods to give me release from these sorrows,
from my long year on watch, in which I, lying down
on the roof of the House of Atreus on my elbows, like a dog,
have watched the constellation of nighttime stars . . .

In this speech, the Watchman fights sleep as Sappho draws it to her; both are caught in the complaint that emerges from sleep's exclusion, and for both the words they use to describe lying down hover on the edge of the vocabulary of sleep. The Watchman's speech also opens and closes with the word *apallagê* ("release, deliverance"), specifically "release from suffering" (*apallagê[n] ponôn* 1, 20); for both him and the speaker of Sappho's poem, this release can be paired with the dissolution of sleep and the falling away of the "I" that accompanies it. Never mind the fact that the Watchman sings (*aeidein*) or hums (*minuresthai*) as a *defense* against sleep (ὅταν δ' ἀείδειν ἢ μινύρεσθαι δοκῶ,/ ὕπνου τόδ' ἀντίμολπον ἐντέμνων ἄκος 16–17),[43] while Sappho's song, inversely, draws us and her into sleep's orbit; for both, their songs' formal and semantic properties are maintained by being held just on the other side of the sleep that invites them.

To "lie down" in Greek poetics is not just to lie asleep or awake, of course, but also to enter into the realm of Sleep's brother, Death.[44] In fragment 55, Sappho abuses another woman by telling her that, in the future, "you will lie there dead and unremembered" (κατθάνοισα δὲ κείσῃ οὐδέ ποτα μναμοσύνα σέθεν/ ἔσσετ' 1–2). The *kateudô* of fragment 168b could be said to cross over into the epitaphic realm too. Consider, for example, the stele of Mensitheos (probably from the first half of the fifth century), which begins χαίρετε τοὶ παριόντες, ἐγὼ δὲ θάνον κατάκειμαι ("Greetings you who pass by! I lie down here dead . . .").[45] This solves in a sense the puzzle of why Sappho would use a verb that properly means "sleep" (*kateudô*) instead of one that properly means "lie" or "lie awake." To write "lie alone" perhaps brings this short poem too close to the loneliness of death, whereas what the "I" is expressing here is precisely the frustrations of being alive; of feeling too vivid, too alert, too out of place with time.[46]

While the "I" of the epitaph is constructed in an imagined relationship of reciprocity—always inviting a response from its future reader as he or she passes by this spot, *here*—there is no place in this fragment that Sappho lies except alone and there is no opportunity in the dead of night for anyone to answer her. To that extent, like the *egô de* in fr. 16 ("Some say x, some say y, *but I say . . .*,"), the *egô de* of 168b is disobedient to the norms and conventions of the world around it. Compare [Simonides]' epigram on the Spartan dead at Thermopylae:

Ὦ ξεῖν', ἀγγέλλειν Λακεδαιμονίοις ὅτι τῇδε
κείμεθα, τοῖς κείνων ῥήμασι πειθόμενοι.

asleep

Barthes suggests that the suspended time of sleep functions "like an airlock, not perhaps between two worlds (dream/awake) but between two bodies."[28] That separation creates a form of soliloquizing that is born from dreaming alone rather than sleeping together (*à deux*).[29]

Perhaps then to be "alone" in 168b does not just mean "being apart from you," but more fundamentally being one who operates alone in the universe: Sappho alone, of all the elements in the poem, is sleeping. Unlike Alcman 89, here the stars, moon, and hours are seen performing their natural roles, moving, or having just finished moving, through the sky. Only Sappho is passive, doing nothing, caught in the strange isolation of poetry and sleep.

awake

Stranger, tell the Spartans that here we lie,
Obedient to their laws.

If sleeping and death are forms of obedience to the laws of nature as well as life, then Sappho's presence as someone who is still awake (even if unwillingly) stands as a form of rebellion. Wilamowitz read the speaker of fragment 168b's disobedience in moral terms, claiming that it was intolerable to imagine Sappho lying in bed "with the door open," in what he claimed was the pose of waiting for a lover. For Denys Page, it is the dialect of the fragment as it is handed down to us in Hephaestion that is disobedient—since the language is not properly Aeolic, that is good enough reason for striking it from the canon of Sappho (modern editors convert it to Aeolic spelling).[47]

But the real disobedience of the fragment, I think, is its insomnia—its refusal to sleep as the world turns and its radical proclamation (whether complaint or celebration) of its own condition of being alone. The fourth line of 168b zeroes in most acutely on what it means to use the first-person voice in poetry, to place it on the page (so to speak) and simply leave it there, without anyone to talk to except the listener, who has yet to wake up and hear it.

Conclusion

As soon as Sappho registers an "I" in fr. 168b, she must also register a "you"—the audience member or reader whom she insists is absent. The space of that lag between "I" and "you," as between "and" and "but" or "awake" and "asleep," draws the form of the poem to our attention: holding us in the ongoing present of its composition and structure. The word *kateudô* speaks to Sappho's interrupting, lingering presence in the world, even as it makes it impossible for us to fully know or find her.

Holding open both sides of the page and reading them together requires a special kind of vigilance, a wide-awakeness that cannot lose itself in the solipsism of a single train of thought. And yet reading both sides of the page at once also lures the eyes towards the blank space in the middle, lulling the reader to sleep, through the incoherence of a world seen in double. The contours of this short fragment are bound by the small scene of Sappho's *kateudô* over a single night or many, threaded together by the fragment's encrypted *de* (*and? but? now?*) that lulls through repetition as it also snaps us back to attention. Whatever this little word really means here, it is also important to hold onto its immateriality; its "nothingness" as an inflective particle towards which Sappho's *egô* looks forward, in the fall into and away from sleep.[48]

Notes

1. Bennett 2021, 4

2. Foster 2019, 51.

3. See also Derrida 2021 (discussed by Telò in this volume), which is written in two columns—one in the style of Hegel and the other in the style of Genet.

4. Many have suggested that the poem arises from the tradition of folksong. One of the problems with the fragment is that it was transmitted by Hephaestion in his abridged treatment on Greek meter (*Enchiridion* 11.6) not in the Aeolic dialect (he also preserved it as a distich). Editors, following Theodor Bergk, "correct" the poem by printing it in Aeolic dialect and as four lines.

5. As here: https://en.wikipedia.org/wiki/Midnight_poem.

6. Page (1955, 1962, 1968) rejected Sapphic authorship, an idea that perhaps originated in a footnote of *Isyllos von Epidaurus* (Wilamowitz 1886, 129n7), as noted in Clay 1970, 120–1. Voigt (1971) restored it, with editors such as Campbell (1982) following suit (Jenkyns 1982, 77–9 provides further arguments against). The case is still open; the fragment is transmitted by Hephaestion without attribution, but alongside three or four fragments of Sappho. The meter is otherwise unknown in Sappho and Alcaeus, but has parallels in other Aeolic verse.

7. Clay calls it "one of the loveliest of all Greek lyrics" (1970, 119); Wilamowitz (1886) deemed it morally wrong and incompatible with the figure of Sappho; see Clay 1970, 121, and Reiner and Kovacs 1993, 150.

8. Most 1995.

9. As in the Italian word *dormiveglia,* the state of being half-asleep or half-awake. Thank you to Mario Telò for this reference.

10. Purves forthcoming; Purves and Wohl forthcoming.

11. On the strangeness of sleeping mountains, see Budelmann 2013.

12. Compare Sappho 31, where there are barely any particles in the first two stanzas, but as her body breaks down we have "*alla . . . men, de, de, de, de, de, de, de*" in the third and fourth stanzas.

13. The moon has gone down (δέδυκε μὲν [PREPARATORY *men*]) / so (*kai*) have the Pleiades. It is the middle (CONNECTIVE *de*) / of the night, time is passing by (CONNECTIVE *de*), / but I (ADVERSATIVE *de*) sleep alone.

14. Reiner and Kovacs 1993, 155.

15. It is somewhat unusual for *de* to appear at the end of a line of verse; it happens only three other times in Sappho's extant poetry (23.9; 31.13; 39.1; see following note).

16. A similar use of eroding line-end *de* can be found in Sappho 31.13, also within a sequence of *de*'s: τρόμος δὲ/ παῖσαν ἄγρει, "trembling seizes all of me". For erosion of categories within the sky, see fr.1.

17. Reiner and Kovacs 1993, 147.

18. Contrast *Odyssey* 23.241–6, where Athena draws out the night so that Penelope and Odysseus can enjoy the extended time together. On the state of being alone in antiquity, see also Matuszewski 2022.

19. See further Purves and Wohl, forthcoming.

20. As also by the philosophical problem of sleep. Cf. Wohl 2020.

21. The correct translation of *ôra* (hour, season, time?) is disputed here. Some have suggested that it means that "the bloom of (my) youth is passing"; see Reiner and Kovacks 1993, 146–7.

22. Purves and Wohl, forthcoming.

23. See Rosenmeyer 1991, and Purves and Wohl, forthcoming.

24. Payne 2018, 259.

25. Blanchot 1997, 141.

26. As Svenbro (1993) has argued for Sappho 31, the "I" of that poem may be understood to address, in jealousy, a future pairing of poem ("you") and reader ("he") from which the performer will necessarily remain absent and excluded; see Tamás 2021, 23–4.

27. Burt 2016, 433.

28. Barthes 2005, 37.

29. Ferrari (2010, 139–41) contrasts the two forms of sleep.

30. Blanchot 1982, 264: "Night, the essence of night, does not let us sleep."

31. Clay 1970, 126. Cf. Tomás 2021, 21 (in relation to a different poem): "Can a text that plays on its own unfinishedness still be called 'unfinished'?"

32. Barthes 1978, 37–8.

33. Nancy 2009, 248.

34. Technically a "heavying" rather than a lengthening. ε is the most frequently occurring vowel in the fragment (11x), followed by α (8x), ω (3x), υ (2x) and o, ι, η (1x). Diphthongs are infrequent: αι (2x); ευ (1x).

35. Especially if we follow the etymological connection between *mona* and *menô*, "I wait."

36. Wolfson 2006, 4.

37. Culler 2015, 133–4: "[I]n lyric greater importance falls on the various kinds of equivalence, of brief metrical units, lines, and stanzas, but also of the sound patterning of rhyme, alliteration, and assonance and the possible semantic relationships such patterning brings."

38. In this sense form overlaps with technique. Culler 2015, 6: "Poetics . . . does not attempt to find a meaning but to understand the techniques that make meaning possible."

39. Nancy 2009, 4.

40. Nancy 2009, 3.

41. Nancy 2009, 7.

42. On "real time" in lyric, see Culler 2015, 36.

43. Literally: "Whenever I think to sing or hum to myself, / cutting this remedy in as a sounding in place of sleep."

44. Cf. Wohl 2020.

45. Cf. Simonides 35 = *A.P.*13.4 Ἀργεῖος Δάναδις σταδιόδρομος ἐνθάδε κεῖται (1); 36 = *A.P.*13.26; 37 = *A.P.*7.348; 78 = *A.P.* 7.254b (. . . ἐνθάδε κεῖμαι 1).

46. Emmanuel Levinas calls insomnia "a supervaluing of presence, which is without escape routes or subterfuge" (2000, 207).

47. Clay 1970, 121–3.

48. I am grateful to Ella Haselswerdt, Sarah Nooter, Seth Schein, and Mario Telò for advice on this chapter. Special thanks go to Susan Foster, whose recent book, as noted, provided the inspiration for its format and who has patiently discussed these ideas with me over several walks in the Hollywood Hills.

CHAPTER 5
ARISTOPHANES AND THE FLYING SOUND
Sarah Nooter

Let us conceive of a sound-object:[1] it need not be just one sound or syllable; rather it is an *it* not because it is a single thing, but because it is repeatable. In being repeated, it becomes recognizably something. It is not a word, and never becomes one, seemingly never having been invested with the intention of its speaker (or writer or singer) to have discursive content. But it can be recalled or forgotten; it can be pronounced correctly or painfully mangled; and though it means nothing, it accrues meaning like the fuzz gathered by static electricity. It is as if the meaning were collecting around it, not emanating from it, as if meaning could simply envelop it. And, yet, the meaning that gathers, envelope-like, around the sound is not singular, not still, not solid, but is rather fluid, mobile, in motion, in flight: it is first one meaning, and then another; it is in one position as regards language, and then in another. Even as the sound flies through waves in the air, so does its meaning flit from mode to mode.[2]

What might I mean by all of this? First of all, let me establish that what I mean by "mean" is the standard dictionary definition, i.e., "intend to convey, indicate, or refer to (a particular thing or notion); signify."[3] That is: a word, through its referential content, signifies or refers to something else, something beyond the sound that it is. But these sound-*objects* that I was just describing are not words. So let us take an example—in fact, the example that will form the heart of this chapter. Aristophanes' magnificent avian chorus from his comedy *Birds* sing two lyric stanzas (740–51, 769–83) in the midst of their parabasis. These two stanzas offer a sound-object such as I have been describing, which is *tiotiotiotinx*. They sing this sound-object eight times throughout these stanzas. Additionally, twice, they sing a distended version of it, which is this: *totototototototototinx*.

Since the two stanzas work in responsion to one another, sharing the same metrical pattern and presumably the same melody and even dance-steps with one another, the second set of sounds comes in a predictable form, rather as an extended echo. The sound-objects in the antistrophe, then, do not merely respond metrically to the strophe, as the other lines of the antistrophe do. They also repeat sound for sound, like the chorus in a modern-day pop song, or like the word-end in a rhyme. Yet, though the sound is itself the same each time, its meaning—the meaning that envelopes it—is constantly moving: it is first an onomatopoeic interjection, then an iconic illustration, then seemingly both at once but within a more distanced fictional frame, until finally it is transformed into a transformative, theriomorphosizing, divine exclamation. It travels, too, from the singer's mouth, to the locale of his nightingale partner, who resides in a thicket, to the banks of the river Hebrus, to Olympus and finally to a windless sky filled with awe-struck gods. And yet it never itself directly *means*, it only *is* and *does*.

In this chapter, I explore the affectual implications of such a sound-object, slowing down to illustrate each of the points I have just made about the flights of *tiotiotiotinx*. I attempt to interrogate the workings of this sound-object, making use of some theory on this topic, including that which explores onomatopoeia, which might at first seem to describe the whole phenomenon we find here. But I find that onomatopoeia, as a frame of reference, is simply too limiting. In restricting the scope of sound-objects to that which is imitative, as if there is inevitably a "real" sound to which it may or may not relate felicitously, onomatopoeia is not capacious enough to unpack the work done by sound-objects. I suggest rather that more is gained from exploring and comparing the extensions and distention of meanings found in the sound poetry of Tracie Morris, whose performances of the criss-crossing of words and sounds might be said to mobilize many meanings without strictly *meaning* them. Thus, sound-objects push the listener to radically renegotiate the activities of both hearing sounds and making meaning. If this can be understood through the lens that we are calling "radical formalism," it is because approaching the contours of sound-meeting-meaning suggests infinite possibilities in the present—however ancient the work, and however not-yet-imagined the work—for the creation of new realities, a literary space that Kevin Quashie has described as "subjunctivity ... the animating of being through the expressiveness of might-be."[4] In hearing sounds as *might-be*, as animate, the living work of meaning also comes alive.

The *Birds* and the Entrance of Sound

I begin with a little contextualizing. In Aristophanes' *Birds*, the protagonist Peisetairus and his sidekick Euelpides have left Athens in search of a more peaceful city, or as Euelpides puts it, "an unbusy place" (*topon apragmona* 44). The two heroes, however, instead find themselves founding, or perhaps colonizing, a sort of avian paradise that they dub "Cloudcuckooland" (*Nephelokokkugia*), explicitly transforming a so-called *polos* (179), meaning sphere or vault of the heavens, into a *polis* (173), a city-state much like the Athens they left behind.[5] To effect this transformation, they must first persuade a Hoopoe, who was formerly the human Tereus, to help them, and so it is Tereus that our two main characters are searching for when we meet them at the start of the play, under the guidance of two birds that they purchased in the marketplace.

I want to pause on the opening lines of the play, because of the particular emphasis we find here on the question of how sounds might mean or not mean.[6] This is such a live question for the beginning of the *Birds* that it is actually impossible to tell from our evidence now what the first utterance of the play would have been in its early performances. Here is the text (1–2):

ΕΥΕΛΠΙΔΗΣ. Ὀρθὴν κελεύεις, ᾗ τὸ δένδρον φαίνεται;
ΠΕΙΣΕΤΑΙΡΟΣ. διαρραγείης· ἥδε δ' αὖ κρώζει "πάλιν"

Euelpides: Do you bid [me] on the straight [way], on which the tree appears?
Peisetairus: May you burst apart! This one again croaks "back."[7]

So what is just happening here? It appears that by the time Euelpides has spoken, one or two birds have just emitted a noise. (If so, did the audience here this sound? And how was it created? We do not know.) Euelpides and then Peisetairus, in response to what they have heard or seen from their birds, try to pick apart whether the sounds from the birds signify, or *mean* anything within the framework of directionality. As the men try to decipher the meanings of the birds' sounds, and then decide that the sounds mean nothing, and that thus they are lost, "wandering and up and down" (3), they demonstrate a fact about uttered sounds in general, and about meaning and intentionality: the first trick is to decipher whether any referential meaning is intended at all. For sounds must be located within conventions of language and communication to *mean* in the first place. In this case, the whole theatrical project of having the stage-set mean anything other than a bunch of planks on the Southern slope of the Acropolis seemingly depends upon whether these presumed bird-sounds—that may or may not have actually been heard in the theater through some aural device—indicate anything at all.

As I said, our heroes are trying to find a path to another, more peaceful, town, but they soon decide instead that they will stay where they are and create place and meaning anew. If we doubt the analogy being drawn here between the bird sounds that may or may not mean, and the capacity of human language and exchange to make meaning, then we need only read a little further to Euelpides' dismissive description of Athens. He says (39–41):

οἱ μὲν γὰρ οὖν τέττιγες ἕνα μῆν' ἢ δύο
ἐπὶ τῶν κραδῶν ᾄδουσ', Ἀθηναῖοι δ' ἀεὶ
ἐπὶ τῶν δικῶν ᾄδουσι πάντα τὸν βίον

For the cicadas for their part for just a month or two
from the branches sing, but the Athenians always
from the law-courts sing, all their lives.

Here we have, on the one hand, a standard jibe at Athens, one so familiar to students of Aristophanes that it hardly registers: Athenians are litigious. But the form of the joke is interesting in a few ways: 1. the people of Athens are compared to insects as if they too are a form of animal 2. the Athenians are compared to cicadas, which we know to be highly symbolic animal for its metapoetic, vocal quality—or so it appears in Homer, possibly by allusion in the *Homeric Hymn to Aphrodite* and Sappho, in Aesop, in another play by Aristophanes, and then again later in Plato's *Phaedrus* and the prologue of Callimachus' *Aetia*.[8] The cicadas are creatures whose existence is defined almost exclusively by their voice. Indeed to refer to the voices of the cicadas is usually to suggest that the utterance in question is otherwise evacuated of meaning; the cicadas utter *only* voice, and nothing more.[9] Here as usual the cicadas sing, and so too do the Athenians. According to Euelpides, there are really just two differences between cicadas and Athens, and this is point number 3. First, there is a difference of temporality: the cicadas are insects of the natural order and, as such, are seasonal. They sing only for one or two months out of the year. But Athenians, cultured all out of nature, never stop singing, like machines on automatic forever. Finally, point 4: the joke echoes, or even rhymes, if in a frontal sense, with the first halves of two lines distinguished by only a single syllable (40–1):

> ἐπὶ τῶν κραδῶν ᾄδουσ᾽, Ἀθηναῖοι δ᾽ ἀεὶ
> ἐπὶ τῶν δικῶν ᾄδουσι πάντα τὸν βίον.

Why the soundplay? Or, rather, what is its effect? Presumably the dissolution of the words into repeating sounds echoes the vocal repetitions of the cicadas, and the even more relentless—because never-ending—vocal repetitions of the Athenians. It is not just that the soundplay means that the words do what they describe but also that the speech of Euelpides himself is shown to dissolve into repeating sounds. Aristophanes' plays often include in the prologue mini-meditations on matters that relate, slantwise, to the rest of the play. So it is here, where questions of sound, meaning, and ontology all come into play, if very briefly: the birds who appear before the first lines pose the question of when sounds *start* to have meaning; the cicadas and litigious Athenians implicitly pose the question of when vocalizations *stop* meaning anything referentially but instead come to mean only as sound-objects. In this case, there is still meaning, of course; it is simply sourced elsewhere than from referential content. We will return to this point.

Back to the plot: Peisetairus and Euelpides find the Hoopoe, the once human Tereus, decide to found a city in the clouds, and convince the Hoopoe to call forth a large swath of birds so that they can convince them too. The birds who appear, twenty-four in all, ultimately constitute the chorus of the play. But, before that, the Hoopoe sings to the nightingale who is, in accordance with the mythological tradition, Procne his estranged wife. This solo passage, which is in anapests, acts as a sort of preamble to her summoning of the chorus of birds.[10] It was likely accompanied throughout (like most choral song) by the *aulos*, the instrument whose song turns out to constitute the voice of the nightingale (209–24):

> Επ. ἄγε, σύννομέ μοι, παῦσαι μὲν ὕπνου,
> λῦσον δὲ νόμους ἱερῶν ὕμνων,
> οὓς διὰ θείου στόματος θρηνεῖς
> τὸν ἐμὸν καὶ σὸν πολύδακρυν Ἴτυν,
> ἐλελιζομένης δ᾽ ἱεροῖς μέλεσιν
> γένυος ξουθῆς.
> καθαρὰ χωρεῖ διὰ φυλλοκόμου
> μίλακος ἠχὼ πρὸς Διὸς ἕδρας,
> ἵν᾽ ὁ χρυσοκόμας Φοῖβος ἀκούων,
> τοῖς σοῖς ἐλέγοις ἀντιψάλλων
> ἐλεφαντόδετον φόρμιγγα, θεῶν
> ἵστησι χορούς· διὰ δ᾽ ἀθανάτων

στομάτων χωρεῖ ξύμφωνος ὁμοῦ
θεία μακάρων ὀλολυγή.

<αὐλεῖ>

Ευ. ὦ Ζεῦ βασιλεῦ, τοῦ φθέγματος τοὐρνιθίου·
οἷον κατεμελίτωσε τὴν λόχμην ὅλην.

Hoopoe: Come, my companion, cease from sleep,
release the tunes of sacred songs
with which, with your divine mouth, you mourn
much wept-for Itys, my son and yours,
trilling with sacred songs
from your tawny jaw.
Clear comes the sound through the leafy
yew-tree at the seat of Zeus,
where golden-haired Phoebus, hearing,
strumming to your elegies
his ivory inlaid lyre, puts in place
the choral dances of the gods. From their immortal
blessed mouths comes harmonious, and all at once,
divine ululation.

[the *aulos* is played]

Euelpides: O king Zeus, the voice of this bird!
How it fills the whole thicket with sweetness!

This passage is itself a remarkable document on the reach of meanings in music in classical Greece, and particularly illustrates what we may think of as a trajectory, or path, of song: for the song—not the one sung by the Hoopoe, but rather the one summoned— is first located as originating in the mouth and jaw of the nightingale and then shifts places to a new source: the yew trees and seat of Zeus. The situated origins of song, then, are both embodied orality and the gods: once the song has reached the gods, it is echoed by Apollo on his lyre, who then constitutes a harmonious chorus of gods, who apparently—and strangely—sing an *ololugmos*, an otherwise very human cry that accompanies sacrifices and victories, as well as lamentations.[11] As the nightingale's song, which is the *aulos'* song here, is imagined in song as summoning a chorus of gods, so does it also literally summon the chorus of birds that is the play's own chorus—who will soon "become" gods, incidentally—so that the imagined space of song harmonizes with the actual, embodied, and rather grand space of the stage. The song of the chorus too, as we will see, will reach back upwards and outwards to the divine, suggesting a cosmic, reverberating alignment through sound between these different modes and realms.

The Sound-Object: *Tiotiotiotinx*

So on to our passages, and our sound-objects. The stanzas that I will examine are the fourth and sixth parts of the play's rather spectacular (first) parabasis. The parabasis is a portion of Old Comedy where the chorus usually address the audience at length as spokespeople for the poet—often in the first person singular, stepping out of their dramatic role.[12] What is most unusual here is that the chorus maintain their dramatic characterizations as birds for the entirety of this parabasis, and address the contemporary Athenian audience only in a manner that follows upon the plot: that is, they try to convince them to accept themselves as birds in place of the Olympian gods. The play, first performed in 414 BCE, happens to be our last extant comedy to include a full-blown parabasis—and it goes out with a bang. It stretches on for 125 lines and has seven parts, which run the metrical gamut. The fourth and sixth sections are a strophe and responding antistrophe, lyric passages on the topic of bird song. These two stanzas, which are sung in a mix of mostly dactyls and trochees, are my focus. Here is the strophe (740–51):

Μοῦσα λοχμαία,
τιοτιοτιοτιοτίγξ,
ποικίλη, μεθ' ἧς ἐγὼ νά-
παισί <τε καὶ> κορυφαῖς ἐν ὀρείαις,
τιοτιοτιοτιοτίγξ,
ἱζόμενος μελίας ἔπι φυλλοκόμου,
τιοτιοτιοτιοτίγξ,
δι' ἐμῆς γένυος ξουθῆς μελέων
Πανὶ νόμους ἱεροὺς ἀναφαίνω
σεμνά τε Μητρὶ χορεύματ' ὀρεία,
τοτοτοτοτοτοτοτοτοτίγξ,
ἔνθεν ὡσπερεὶ μέλιττα
Φρύνιχος ἀμβροσίων μελέων ἀπεβόσκετο καρπὸν ἀεὶ
φέρων γλυκεῖαν ᾠδάν,
τιοτιοτιοτίγξ

Muse of the thicket,
tiotiotiotinx
speckled, with whom I, in the glens
and on the peaks of mountains,
tiotiotiotinx
sitting in the leafy-haired ash tree,
tiotiotiotinx,
through my tawny jaw singing,
I reveal the sacred songs for Pan
and the holy choral dances for the mountain Mother,
totototototototototinx,
whence like a bee

> Phrynicus feeds on the fruit of our ever ambrosial melodies,
> bearing back the sweet song,
> *tiotiotiotinx.*

The song is persistently placed in a landscape: it starts in glens, peaks, and a leafy ash tree, and moves from there.[13] The birds that sing lead us to the bird who acts as their muse—probably the nightingale once again—whose songs lead to Pan, the "mountain Mother" Cybele, and, as the mention of the playwright Phrynicus reveals, back to Athens and the music of the tragic stage.[14] Whereas the song of the nightingale was heard before as an untranscribed and vocally unrepeatable tune played an *aulos*, now its song seems to edge its way into vocality, and through it into a mode of language by way of *tiotiotiotinx.* What is this *tiotiotiotinx*?[15] At first, it seems merely to be a kind of interruption or interlude in the sentence that starts the strophe, like a *doo-wop doo-wop* or a *sh-boom*:[16]

> Muse of the thicket,
> *tiotiotiotinx*
> speckled, with whom I, in the glens
> and on the peaks of mountains,
> *tiotiotiotinx*
> sitting in the leafy-haired ash tree . . .

But then, unlike in the song "*Sh-boom*," the mode of *tiotiotiotinx* starts to change, and to move from rather simply interrupting the lyrical sentence to melting into its syntax:

> *tiotiotiotinx,*
>
> through my tawny jaw singing

Note how gradually this happens: after two *sh-boom*-like instances of *tiotiotiotinx*, the third case appears to be used also as a lyrical interlude—until after it is sung, when we learn that the *tiotiotiotinx* is actually the object of the participle "singing" (μελέων), and that the one singing it is not actually the "muse in the thicket" being described, but is rather the choral voice itself, since the lyrics say that the singing is happening through "*my* tawny jaw."

The *tiotiotiotinx* in this instance might be said, then, to hover between what I am calling a *sh-boom* and something more like quotation, which I illustrate with reference to Van Morrison's song "Brown-eyed girl,"[17] particularly this part: "do you remember when we used to sing, *sha la la la la la la la la li la ti da* . . . just like that." When Van Morrison uses the nonsensical phrase "*sha la la la*," he is (perhaps facetiously) suggesting that this phrase—and *exactly* that one (hence "just like that")—is a true transcript of past songs and, as such, transports him and his listeners to a lost memory. The bird chorus, however, does something more ambitious: they convert what was just a sound (a *sh-boom*) into what is now a quote or excerpt of song (a *sha la la la*), although one that is self-referential—i.e., "and here's the song I'm singing right now: it's *la la la.*" But then they keep going and the mode of the sound-object changes again. The fourth usage takes the *tiotiotiotinx* to yet another level as it is transformed into something much more lofty, namely "a sacred song for Pan" that is accompanied by a "holy choral dance for the mountain Mother." Moreover, the sound itself has changed, though not so much that it is not recognizable as a version of the sound *tiotiotiotinx* that we have been hearing; now it is *totototototototototinx*, a sort of extenuated, enthused version of the sound-object, its length and hurried repeatability growing commensurately with its consequence as a holy song dedicated to divinities. The sound is then heard a fifth time here:

> whence like a bee
> Phrynicus feeds on the fruit of our ever ambrosial melodies,
> bearing back the sweet song,
> *tiotiotiotinx.*

Note that our *tiotiotiotinx* has changed its mode again: now having acquired the signifying function of standing in for a particular "sweet song" (or *glukeian aoidan*), it has become also a metaphorically embodied object, one both invested with physical, gustatory properties—since it is appropriately sweet for the "bee" that is Phrynicus—and one that is also endlessly elastic, from our present chorus to Phrynicus' song, from the mountains where Pan and the Cybele reside to Athens, presumably, where Phrynicus' songs resounded on the stage. This *tiotiotiotinx*, then, has charted two kinds of movement simultaneously: one is imaginary, spatial movement. It sends the song of the Chorus to the mountains and summons it back to Athens. The other kind of movement is a flight through different modes of meaning: as this pattern of syllables becomes ever more familiar, its role as a sound-object changes, gathering signifying capabilities as it goes.

Let us move to the antistrophe, which comes after some trochaic lines addressed by the birds to the audience. This matching antistrophe is the final part of the parabasis. Here song becomes an even more ambitious marker of immanent, unlimited space (769–83):

> τοιάδε κύκνοι,
> τιοτιοτιοτιοτίγξ,
> συμμιγῆ βοὴν ὁμοῦ πτε-
> ροῖσι κρέκοντες ἴαχον Ἀπόλλω,
> τιοτιοτιοτιοτίγξ,
> ὄχθῳ ἐφεζόμενοι παρ' Ἕβρον ποταμόν,
> τιοτιοτιοτιοτίγξ,
> διὰ δ' αἰθέριον νέφος ἦλθε βοά·
> πτῆξε δὲ ποικίλα φῦλα τὰ θηρῶν,
> κύματά τ' ἔσβεσε νήνεμος αἴθρη,
> τοτοτοτοτοτοτοτοτοτοτίγξ·

πᾶς δ' ἐπεκτύπησ' Ὄλυμπος·
εἷλε δὲ θάμβος ἄνακτας· Ὀλυμπιάδες δὲ μέλος Χάριτες
Μοῦσαί τ' ἐπωλόλυξαν,
τιοτιοτιοτίγξ

Such [songs] do the swans
tiotiotiotinx
in a mingled shout cry out, while
striking the air with their wings, for Apollo,
tiotiotiotinx
sitting on the banks by the river Hebrus,
tiotiotiotinx,
and through the airy cloud comes their shout.
It strikes fear into the varied tribes of beasts,
a windless sky quenches the waves,
totototototototototinx.
All of Olympus resounds.
Wonder takes hold of its lords. And the Olympian Graces
and the Muses ululate back the song,
tiotiotiotinx.

By now the *tiotiotiotinx* has attained an iconic and syntactical status—that is, it is no longer just an interrupting *sh-boom*. It is instead likely the object of "cry out" (*iachon*) and appositive to "such things" (*toiade*), which probably means "such songs," and is perhaps also appositive to "a mingled shout" (*summigê boên*), though this phrase could also be being used here in respect to the songs. The *tiotiotiotinx* in any case is apparently located elsewhere, specifically on the banks of the Hebrus river in Thrace. So the *tiotiotiotinx* is not the song of the choral singers anymore, or the nightingale, or of Phrynicus, but is now the song of swans, accompanied by the beating of their wings and sung evidently for the sake of Apollo, which is a traditional activity for swans, as we see in *Homeric Hymn 21 to Apollo*.[18] And yet the grammar still leaves room for ambiguity. The deictic *toiade* ("such things") tends to refer to the utterance, story, or song that is about to be pronounced by a speaker. Is the deictic here referring then to the chorus's own song, or suggesting that the chorus's song is a perfect echo of the swan's song? In any case, the mode of our *tiotiotiotinx* shifts again in the lines following:

tiotiotiotinx
sitting on the banks by the river Hebrus,
tiotiotiotinx,
and through the airy cloud comes their shout.

By the time we have racked up another two repetitions of *tiotiotiotinx*, the sound-object has combined the two modal aspects that we heard in the strophe: it is still a

Van-Morrison-esque *sha la la la*, but it is also once again a *sh-boom*, supplying an echo in the background to a piece of the sentence. And then, as in the strophe, there comes a sonic expansion:

> It strikes fear into the varied tribes of beasts,
> a windless sky quenches the waves,
> *totototototototototinx*.
> All of Olympus resounds.
> Wonder takes hold of its lords

The sound *tiotiotiotinx* once again expands to become its longer, even more rapidly repetitive version *tototototototototototinx*, and the imagined spatial frame also reaches sonically outward to the widest scope imaginable in Greek terms, as all varieties of beasts hear it and feel afraid, and the skies and waters echo, and "all of Olympus resounds."[19] Indeed, its lords—the gods—are filled with wonder at this sound. The sound-object, then, potently reenters the narrative: the *tototototototototinx* is identified as the very sound that reverberates around Olympus and stuns the gods. It is both the name of the event and the event itself, which, then, redoubles again, as the final instance of *tiotiotiotinx* is heard:

> And the Olympian Graces
> and the Muses ululate back the song,
> *tiotiotiotinx*.

We have returned, ring-composition-like, to the Muse at the beginning of the strophe, only that Muse, who seemed to be the auletic nightingale (or perhaps the nightingalic *aulos*), has now transmuted into the whole set of divine Muses, joined by their cousins the Olympian Graces. We have also returned, in a sense, to the crowning moment of the Hoopoe's song that he sang earlier for the nightingale, in which he pictured Apollo starting up choral dances and all the gods joining in divine ululation—a cry, as noted above, that is not otherwise something gods do. Nor is it a verbal action that tends to imply a melodic tune, as this one (with its object "song") does. It is, in general, a human sound, usually a female one, or sometimes a bestial one. But according to the tenets of *this* sound-object, ululation is in fact a divine, melodic sound too, sung by gods, echoed across the skies, flying off to the farthest limits of the imagined universe, over land, sky, and waves, and back again to this stage. This sound-object has done all of this while also traveling again in through different modes: it started this antistrophe as a combination of title and excerpt, skidded along again as a refrain or interlude, and then turned back resoundingly to pure quotation. Perhaps all of this sonic interfacing with Olympic realms does in fact make the birds more believable as gods.

It is worth noting that Aristophanes plays a similar sonic game with comparable rules when he has his chorus of frogs, in the *Frogs*, pronounce their famous *brekekekex koax koax*. In similar fashion, this series of syllables gets repeated eleven times total, always in song, and then is eventually referred to, shorthand, by the character Dionysus as "the *koax*" with an article and everything. I have written about that one already, noting that,

> Dionysus transforms and domesticates the nonlexical sound "*koax*" into a word, *koax*, that metonymically represents the whole song and sound, indeed the whole existence, of the frogs. In effect, he turns the nonlinguistic sound of "*koax*" into a perfectly semantically acceptable noun: voice, in his vocalization, becomes language.[20]

Returning to the phenomenon now, I think my formulation was too simplistic. There is no instance at which the frogs' *brekekekekex*, or indeed the birds' *tiotiotiotinx*, ever performs the specific task that language is supposed to perform; neither one ever refers to or signifies something else. Nor, however, are they ever completely beyond the bounds of the meaning-creation work of language, for their acts of flitting in and out of referential sense is never actually non-linguistic. What we find is just one way that language functions: language can be non-referential, and meaningless in this respect, and yet it can remain communicative by virtue of its movement through time—injecting itself as a sonically capacious pause within a syntactical stream from which it gathers an inverted meaning. Through its further gathering of associations with the words surrounding it, it picks up other elements of meaning, like so much semantic lint.

Is It Just Onomatopoeia?

At this point, I turn to a seminal article by literary critic Derek Attridge on the topic of onomatopoeia. I do so in light of a reasonable question about these sound-objects, namely can this whole phenomenon just be wrapped up in a bow of the device that is onomatopoeia, which is merely the work of language imitating its referent through sound or, by the dictionary definition, "the formation of a word from a sound associated with what is named"?[21] According to this definition, the word *cuckoo* is meant to resemble the sound that a cuckoo bird makes, the word *buzz* is supposed to sound like the noise of bees, the word *hum* should sound like what happens when we make noise through our closed lips, and so on. And of course the *tiotiotiotinx* sound like the frogs' *brekekekekex*, is clearly a noise that is meant to be recognizably imitative of animal sounds, echoing earlier sounds made by the Hoopoe and the bird chorus when they first communicate with one another. Let us examine that scene briefly before we look to the argument of Attridge.

Recall that the nightingale was summoned by the Hoopoe to call the birds who will constitute the chorus. So, in response to this call, the music of the *aulos* apparently begins, and along with it, the Hoopoe himself sings a song of summons presumably in harmony or in tune at least with the auletic nightingale. Here is his whole song (227–62):

Hoopoe: *epopopoi popopopoi popoi,*
iô iô come [*itô*] come come come,

> let any of my fellow feathered friends come,
> whoever of you graze
> in the well-seeded fields of farmers,
> the myriad tribes of barley-eaters
> and races of seed-gatherers, swiftly flying,
> letting flow your soft cry.
> And all of you who often in the furrow
> twitter around the land so gently
> with your delightful voice,
> *tio tio tio tio tio tio tio tio.*
> And those of you who in gardens and shoots
> of ivy make your way,
> and you who in the mountains feed on wild olive-berries and arbutus fruit,
> make your way, in flight, to my call,
> *trioto trioto totobrix.*
> And you who gulp down the sharp-mouthed mosquitos
> in the hollows of the marshes, and you who inhabit
> the dewy places of the earth and the lovely meadow
> of Marathon, and the speckled-
> winged bird, the godwit, godwit.
> And the tribes of you who fly with the halcyons
> over the rising swell of the sea,
> come here to learn the news,
> for all of the tribes of long-throated birds
> are gathering here.
> For a certain shrewd old man has come,
> new-fangled in his thinking,
> embarking on new-fangled deeds.
> But come to these words, all of you,
> hither, hither, hither, hither,
> *torotorotorotorotix*
> *kikkabau kikkabau*
> *torotorotorotorolililix.*

I do not have space here to work through this passage, but one may observe the several repeated passages of apparent onomatopoeic versions of bird-sounds, or at least of heavily repeating sounds. Note that the first run is a play on the Hoopoe's own name (which is considered an onomatopoeic word itself),[22] and the second run is a riff on the word *itô* ("let him come"),[23] while the third and fourth lines of more *tau*-heavy sounds are evidently quotes: one (*tio tio tio*)[24] seems to give an example of the twittering of the birds in the furrow and the other (*trioto trioto totobrix*) is an icon for the Hoopoe's own song. The final three lines of various repeating sounds echo and follow the repeating word *deuro* out of language and back into nonsensical sound, the route through which bird-sound actually entered at the start of this song. It is notable too that the metrical shifting we find here is unique in extant comedy.[25]

The birds then arrive on stage in fits and starts, with one showing up and uttering a *torotix, torotix* (267), but the others remaining silent until the whole chorus of twenty-four birds have gathered. When they have finally all arrived on stage, they, or their leader, address the Hoopoe as follows (310, 314–15):

ΧΟ. ποποποποποποπο ποῦ μ᾽ ὅς ἐκάλεσε . . .
τιτιτιτιτιτιτιτι τίνα λόγον ἄρα ποτὲ
πρὸς ἐμὲ φίλον ἔχων;

Chorus: Popopopopopopopo where [*pou*] is he who has called me?
Titititititititi what [*tina*] dear word then
do you have for me?

Here the apparent bird sounds *popopo* and *tititi* resolve into actual Greek words (*pou* for "where" and *tina* for "what"). As I have discussed elsewhere, this shifting between sound and sense demonstrates the bird chorus' in-between state as animals who been taught to speak Greek, though imperfectly, by the once-human Hoopoe.[26] These passages, then, play largely with the question of language versus sound, and the ambiguous ontology that accompanies this distinction. It is this part of the play that most begs the question of whether the real issue here is onomatopoeia.

In an article called "Language as Imitation: Jakobson, Joyce, and the Art of Onomatopoeia," Derek Attridge aims his sights on claims to "specify some feature that can be said to constitute the distinctiveness of poetic language."[27] He frames as seemingly contradictory two accounts of poetic language in accordance with the famous pairing of sound and sense. The great Russian Formalist Roman Jakobson has asserted that "poeticity is present" when "the word is felt as a word and not a mere representation of the object being named,"[28] meaning, when one hears in the words their own "weight and value," as he puts it, or sonic effects or sound patterns, and these qualities are not fully subordinated to the referential work of representation. But, on the other hand, in poetry, "the sound must seem an echo to the sense," as Alexander Pope tells us in his poem "Sound and Sense," and so does the poet and thinker Paul Valéry, and so does Jakobson elsewhere.[29] Thus we have two stories here about the sound and material of words in poetry: "according to one," writes Attridge, "speech-sounds draw attention to themselves and their configuration, independently of their referential function; according to the other, [speech-sounds] tend to disappear in an enhanced experience of referentiality."[30] Attridge attempts to square this circle—maintaining that poetry can combine both an "intensified referentiality" through the workings of sound and sense and offer a "heightened awareness of the aural qualities of language" by taking a close look at the "concept of art as *imitation*"[31] and looking specifically at the workings of onomatopoeia in some lines from the novel *Ulysses* by James Joyce.

Attridge focuses particularly on a non-verbal kind of onomatopoeia: "the use of the phonetic characteristics of the language to imitate a sound without any attempt to produce recognizable verbal structures, even those of traditional 'onomatopoeic' words," a mode he calls "*nonlexical onomatopoeia*," crediting this type with the "naked ambition to mimic the sounds of the real world."[32] In this formulation of nonlexical onomatopoeia, and its naked ambitions toward mimicry, we find the applicability of our Aristophanic sounds. One thing that all lexicographers, textual critics, and literary scholars seem to agree on, after all, is that the sounds *tiotiotiotinx* and the rest are a straight-up, uncomplicated, naked mimicry of bird sounds. How they *get* to seem so clearly linked to the sounds made by birds is another matter however. Attridge goes on to show how certain strings of letters in Joyce's work—*Prrprr./ Fff. Oo. Rrpr./Kran, kran, kran./ Krandlkrankran./Karaaaaaa./Pprrpffrrppfff. —*have the effect in context (where they are interlaced with sentences) of seeming to offer up the sounds of a fart and a tram passing, but to do so strictly because of immediate context of these strings of letters and also because of a much broader context, namely "the reader's prior familiarity with rules of graphology and phonology."[33] In other words, as a reader or listener, one only understands how to understand a string of letters that do not add up to a word because one has learned to "override the normal procedures of language comprehension whereby the sound functions"[34] to communicate sense. So the punchline, then, is that nonlexical onomatopoeia is just another linguistic convention.

When then is the point of either nonlexical onomatopoeia or of Attridge's argument about it? Part of what Attridge is aiming to do is to show how very far from actual imitation just about any instance of onomatopoeia really is. And it is probably not news to anyone that the "bow wow" and "woof woof" we in English suggest for the noise of a dog is no closer really than the suggestion in Spanish that a dog says "guau guau." Indeed, if a twenty-first-century Anglophone told her neighbors that she had heard the lovely sound of the birds singing *tiotiotiotinx*, they would probably give her a very strange look, which they would not do if she said something like, "I heard a bird singing *chirp chirp*." Our onomatopoeic sounds are built by conventions more than they act as accurate aural representations.[35] Several scholars have made this very point about Aristophanes' animal sounds, both those of his birds and frogs, namely that they follow ancient Greek conventions of nonsense. Here, for example, is Kenneth Dover making sense of the frogs' nonsensical *brekekekex*:

> Why βρ-, and why –ξ at the end? The latter seems to be a Greek spelling convention for the representation of sounds; so –τοροτίξ and –λιλιλίξ in bird-song (*Av.* 260, 262), παππάξ for farting (*Nu.* 390), and exclamations in –άξ (cf. 63). Initial βρ appears in many Greek words denoting the production of sound, e.g. βρέμειν, βρυχᾶσθαι, βρωμᾶσθαι, and even in the baby-word βρῦ, "drink," although the combination of initial stop and fricative is notoriously difficult for infants to pronounce. Βρεκεκεκέξ seems thus to embody two non-representational conventions.[36]

According to linguistic theorist Nikolai Trubetzkoy's *Principles of Phonology*, "[p]honemes that ... occur in interjections, onomatopoeic expressions, and in commands or calls directed toward animals . . . form a special part of the vocabulary, for which the ordinary phonological system is not valid."[37] That is to say that language sets aside certain sounds meant to act as imitative or ejaculative or just *other* than the regular, referential run of linguistic phonemes. As Attridge puts it, the only time that onomatopoeia is truly successfully mimetic is when it is imitating the human voice, which "written language, in a sense, does all the time."[38]

But if the nonlexical onomatopoeic versions of farts and bird sounds are not really imitating the actual sounds of farts and bird sounds, then what are they doing? Why do James Joyce and Aristophanes make use of them instead of just essentially saying, "then they made bird sounds." (One might object in the case of Aristophanes that there were no stage directions for ancient Greek drama, but actually a sonic stage direction does occur in Aeschylus' *Eumenides*, when the still sleeping chorus of Furies is said to make a *mu* sound.[39]) Attridge concludes that nonlexical onomatopoeia is potent as poetic language, because we notice it and, in noticing it, we become aware too of "the momentary and surprising *reciprocal* relationship between phonetic and semantic properties, a mutual reinforcement which intensifies *both* aspects of language."[40] "All speech," Attridge reminds us, "involves muscular movements in the oral cavity, rhythmic contractions of the diaphragm, the tensing and relaxing of the larynx, the sensations of changing pitch and volume, the passage of air over the surfaces of the speech organs, and so on." What the use of *Pffff*'s and *tiotiotiotinx*'s achieves is not *more* physicality or materiality in sound. That's not really possible, since every vocalization really has the same amount of sound. What these trilling sound-objects rather do is draw our attention to the medium of vocalized language that stands "*between* us and direct experience itself," bringing a kind of vivacity or intensity to our experience of this medium. In this way, Attridge declares, "onomatopoeia becomes a model for all poetic language."[41]

Much as I admire Attridge's article, I think that his account, and really the whole framework of onomatopoeia, falls short for *tiotiotiotinx*. This is because even to assert that the function of onomatopoeia is *not* to imitate is to still limit our lens to one which merely sees the sound-object as fulfilling, or not fulfilling, its duty to the rather hegemonic rule of referentiality in language. What I want to suggest about sound-objects, as I have called them, is that they invite us to consider whole realms of meaning and meaning-creation that have, in some ways, less to do with their being sounds, and more to do with their being objects moving through time, accruing meaning, changing, returning, and becoming legible, multifarious, and intricately expressive—all apart, really, from the issue of whether they signify or not, and whether they imitate or not.

Beyond Imitation

As I come to the close of this chapter, I want to refer to one more example of how sounds, and sound-objects, might mean, not because this example presents a perfect parallel for what Aristophanes is doing with his *tiotiotiotinx* (and I have found no such parallel), but because I think it shows how very many possible routes there really are through sound to making meaning. I refer to an example of a sound-poem by the contemporary poet Tracie Morris, which works in the tradition of a genre fittingly called "sound poetry." This one is called "Slave Sho to Video aka Black but Beautiful."[42] The poem does not exist in written form; it is strictly an oral performance, though of course any listener is welcome to attempt to transcribe it. I offer a few lines here, as transcribed by the critic Christine Hume in what she calls a "typographic rendering, albeit provisional":

> Ain't she beautiful / She too black / She too beautiful / boot-booty-ful / she too black / aint she aint she boo-boo-beauty-ful ain't she / she ain't beautiful she too black / too too beautiful tutu tu-tu / beautiful / she ain't ain't she she ain't ain't she she ain't / is she ain't she beautiful / e-sh-she too black too beautiful ain't she / she ain't she ain't / anxy she too black / too beautiful too b-b-beautiful butt-beautiful butt booty full booty too black[43]

Hume's attempt captures some of Morris's layered ambiguities and resonances, but any "typographical rendering" requires one to nail down a number of polysemous sounds and potential sentences into particular words and sentences—that is, to shut down meanings that are gestured at here, but not committed to singularly.[44] As one description of this poem puts it, "Morris has the capacity to turn negatives into positives without leaving behind the aurality of the negative."[45] In fact, the brilliance of Morris's sound poems may lie in how they move into and through and past a great number of meanings without committing to, or leaving behind, any of them. Thus Hume has written of Morris's poems more generally,

> Usually Morris's sound pieces begin with an illocutionary performative that quickly gets restless and distends—amending and appending itself—into a theatrical parade of mobile meanings that leaves behind any empirical descriptives or expository elaborations ... Morris releases the physicality of words, plays with sonic associations, and funnels the referential residue of language into more visceral, more estranging and ethical functions.[46]

In view of Morris's making meaning more mobile, I invite my reader, as a listener of Aristophanes' sound-object *tiotiotiotinx*, to think of this sound-object too as making meaning more restless, more mobile, and indeed more flighty. So let us circle back to our sound-objects one last time. Here again are the two passages in play, strophe and antistrophe (740–51, 769–83):

> Muse of the thicket,
> *tiotiotiotinx*
> speckled, with whom I, in the glens
> and on the peaks of mountains,
> *tiotiotiotinx*
> sitting in the leafy-haired ash tree,

tiotiotiotinx,
through my tawny jaw singing,
I reveal the sacred songs for Pan
and the holy choral dances for the mountain Mother,
totototototototototinx,
whence like a bee
Phrynicus feeds on the fruit of our ever ambrosial melodies,
bearing back the sweet song,
tiotiotiotinx.

Such [songs] do the swans
tiotiotiotinx
in a mingled shout cry out, while
striking the air with their wings, for Apollo,
tiotiotiotinx
sitting on the banks by the river Hebrus,
tiotiotiotinx,
and through the airy cloud comes their shout.
It strikes fear into the varied tribes of beasts,
a windless sky quenches the waves,
totototototototototinx.
All of Olympus resounds.
Wonder takes hold of its lords. And the Olympian Graces
and the Muses ululate back the song,
tiotiotiotinx.

Let us remember that the passages end with the wonder (*thambos*) of the gods and then the uniquely ululating cry of the Graces and Muses in return, a cry that turns out to be none other than our sound-object *tiotiotiotinx*. Hearing it, we seem to be told, we are in fact hearing the most acute, even redoubled version, of divine song—the more so as the birds cap their argument that they are themselves divine, and so too is their song.

In the spirit of both Derek Attridge's and Tracie Morris's explorations of sounds, which however do not forsake words, I close this chapter by noting that the sound *tiotiotiotinx* and its distended version *totototototototototinx* are really not so deeply encrusted in the conventions of sonic nonsense that they do not offer echoes of actual, known words: *tio*, after all, is almost a perfect homophone for *tiô* —meaning "I honor." The sound *toto* is not very far off from *tote*—meaning "at that time" or "then." And *tinx* is not so distant from the phoneme at the root of *tiktô* —"bring forth, bear, or beget." Aristophanes' supposedly conventional nonsense sounds that, as far as we know, were coined by him, encase within them hints of honor, memory, and creation. I would never claim that his sound-objects *mean* any of these things, but I am happy to suggest that they shoot right through these meanings and fly off in search of something far more strange.

Notes

1. I am using the phrase "sound-object" in a way not wholly related to Pierre Schaeffer's "*objets sonores*" (1966), a concept intended to present sounds as "discrete and multifaceted phenomena rather than as carriers of meaning or as effects bound to sources and causes" (Steintrager and Chow 2019, 8).

2. I find here some resonance with Kevin Quashie's description of what he calls "the first-person essay," describing it as "volatile embodiment; an instantiation and incantation, a magic thing where words are substance and are capable of making substance; a corpus of transformation or crossing" (2021, 72). While the scale of an essay and a sound-object are different, the "volatile embodiment" suggested by Quashie seems well positioned to show the animation of both.

3. https://languages.oup.com/google-dictionary-en/ (accessed October 12, 2022).

4. Quashie 2021, 61, and see his comments on "the text as an object of animacy that invites encounter" (69).

5. As per Mahoney 2007, 271: "Cloud-cuckoo-land is Athens with feathers." There are numerous studies on the founding of "Cloudcuckooland," the question of to what degree it is to be understood as a fantastic utopia versus a rebooting of Athens, and how the portrayal of its foundation relates to foundational myths more generally. See Whitman 1964; Dover 1972, 30–41; B. Zimmerman 1983; Bowie 1993, 151–77; Konstan 1990 and 1997; and Slater 1997. Cf. Payne 2010, 92, on the *polos/polis* pun, and Telò 2020a, 219–20, on how "[t]his simple exchange of vowels, which entails a closing of the mouth, has to be materially shored up through the construction of a wall."

6. Cf. Gelzer (1996, 196–7) focuses on how gradually information is disseminated to the audience in the opening lines of the play, inviting a particularly acute form of what I might call "listening" from them: "The way in which information, essential for understanding the comedy, is revealed step by step compels the audience to concentrate on virtually every word which is said, and creates a readiness to follow, almost without knowing it, Aristophanes' train of thought—and this readiness is then the basic means by which the audience is drawn into Aristophanes' comic inventions." Slater (1997, 75) notes that "the original production could easily have extended this into a long silent sequence of physical comedy." Silence too is a tool in Aristophanes' toolbox of sounds. Cf. Payne 2010, 89–90, on the opening lines of the play on how "human characters" come to adopt "a form of utterance that mixes articulate speech with nonverbal indication," a form that "works wonders." As he states, "Peisetairus and Euelpides must learn new sounds to enter a new territory."

7. Translations are my own.

8. Homer, *Iliad* 3.150–2; *Homeric Hymn to Aphrodite* 5.237–8; Sappho, "Tithonus Poem" 11–12; Aesop, *Fables* 185; Aristophanes, *Peace* 1159–60; Plato, *Phaedrus* 230b–c; and Callimachus, *Aetia* 1.29–34.

9. See LeVen 2018, 216–19, and Nooter 2020.

10. Dunbar (1998, 151) points out that an anapestic preamble of this kind, "leading into his lyric invocation of the birds has its closest parallels in the anapaestic laments followed by chorus-entry in Sophocles' *Electra* and Euripides' *Hekabe* and *Troades*." So, among other implications, we can imagine a rhythmic triggering of paratragic associations, which is matched as well in the seemingly tragic subject matter of mourning for Itys. See Telò 2020a, 221–2, on Tereus' performance as occluding Procne's, thus echoing the violence of their mythic past, and as "practic[ing] a deliberate metrical normalization" of the virtuosic expression we would expect from the song of the nightingale, a "kind of mutilation."

11. See Nooter 2017, 286–8, which offers a list of usages. The one exception to its use as a non-divine cry comes in the *Homeric Hymn to Apollo* 3.119, when Apollo elicits the *ololugmê* from goddesses at his birth.

12. Cf. Whitman 1964, 186. See Biles 2011, 12–55, on the literary history of the parabasis in the tradition of poetic competition and on the comic parabasis as "serv[ing] a deeply embedded function not just of poetic performance but of agonistic performance generally in Greek society" (15). See Mahoney 2007, 272, on the birds' "displace[ment of] the voice of the poet from its conventional spot in the parabasis."

13. See the rapturous description of this passage (and its antistrophe) in Whitman 1964, 185: "Here a majestic, pervasive harmony arises from the peaceful trills and twitterings of the thicket." See Pozzi 1985–6, 125, on the "pastoral-lyric" motif in both of these passages, and in the portrayal of Tereus and the nightingale more generally.

14. Parker (1997, 320) speculates that "[t]he mention of Phrynicus tempts one to wonder whether a metrical or musical debt is being acknowledged."

15. It is to be noted that the *tiotiotiotinx* also raises a different kind of epistemological problem by being metrically difficult to categorize. There is also disagreement among the manuscripts among the correct number of *tio*'s in various lines, and similar divergences in the matter of *totototototototototinx*. See Dunbar 1998, 313–16. For my interpretation, a certain consistency is assumed, but the actual number of iterations within each repeated phrase is not a critical matter.

16. https://www.youtube.com/watch?v=SBgQezOF8kY (accessed October 12, 2022).

17. https://www.youtube.com/watch?v=kqXSBe-qMGo (accessed October 12, 2022).

18. Cf. also Euripides, *Heracles* 692, *Ion* 161–9, *Electra* 151, and *Iphigenia among the Taurians* 1104.

19. See Holmes 2019, 33–5, on how the birds' songs reflect their "special relationship with the gods" that is "mirrored" in the harmony of their own singing.

20. Nooter 2017, 40.

21. https://languages.oup.com/google-dictionary-en/ (accessed October 12, 2022).

22. Payne (2013, 47–8) links the name of the Hoopoe, when pronounced here and elsewhere in the play (56–60), to the cries of the hero Philoctetes in pain in Sophocles' *Philoctetes*, and speculates that the Hoopoe's song articulates a "relationship between lifestyle and phoneme inventory . . . such that the audience perceives a fit between certain sound clusters in their own language and certain kinds of nonhuman lives" (48).

23. Cf. Payne 2010, 93, and Telò 2020a, 223, on the echoing of the name of the mourned-for Itys in these syllables.

24. Parker (1997, 297) notes that "[t]wittering, especially at moments of emotion, is mimicked by resolution."

25. As per Parker 1997, 297: "In *Birds*, Aristophanes seems to have set out to dazzle his audience with a display of metrical and musical virtuosity . . . the chief metrical characteristic of the play is diversity: every major type of metre found in Attic drama is represented, with, in addition, some rarities . . . The first song of the play, the Hoopoe's solo (229ff.), sets the tone: that song in itself includes every type of metre except choriambic." Further detail on the Hoopoe's song is found at Parker 1997, 302–3. Parker also lists our two lyric passages (737ff. = 769ff.) under the heading of "virtuoso compositions," and discusses them in detail at 318–21. Cf. Dale 1969, 136: "The music (and solo-dance?) much have been punctuated by the oddest pauses and unexpected turns."

26. Nooter 2017, 35–7.

27. Attridge 1984, 1116. Of course, much more has been written on onomatopoeia since this article. Sasamoto (2019) contains a recent bibliography of theoretical studies of the topic.

28. Jakobson 1981, 750, quoted in Attridge 1984, 1116–17.

29. Valéry 1957, 210–11, and Jakobson 1960.

30. Attridge 1984, 1118.

31. Attridge 1984, 1118.

32. Attridge 1984, 1120.

33. Attridge 1984, 1122.

34. Attridge 1984, 1124.

35. When I presented this paper in Chicago, Shane Butler challenged this view, noting that it is indeed possible to represent the sounds of birds and other animals, if one has pitch and rhythm at one's disposal. I do find this position somewhat convincing. It is perhaps *written* onomatopoeia that is the more ineffective form of representation and thus the more mired in/ as convention. Maybe oral onomatopoeia stands a chance.

36. Dover 1997, 119.

37. Trubetzkoy 1969, 208.

38. Attridge 1984, 1128.

39. Cf. *Eumenides* 117–26 and Nooter 2017, 261–5.

40. Attridge 1984, 1131. [Italics are in the original.]

41. Attridge 1984, 1134. [Italics are in the original.]

42. https://media.sas.upenn.edu/pennsound/authors/Morris/Morris-Tracie_From-Slave-Sho-to-Video-aka-Black-but-Beautiful_2002.mp3 (accessed October 12, 2022).

43. Hume 2006, 425.

44. As Hume 2006, 425, puts it: "Once beached on the page, the words flatten and forget their flexibility . . . The sounds are full of decisions that one need not make while listening . . . In addition, many of the sounds hover between two words in their actual articulation, so that a composite listening is the only accurate experience."

45. https://jacket2.org/podcasts/too-beautiful-poemtalk-108 (accessed October 12, 2022).

46. Hume 2006, 417.

CHAPTER 6
WHAT THOU ART WE KNOW NOT: PINDAR AND ROMANTICISM

Tom Phillips

The central concern of this chapter is the capacity of poetic form to enact and enable distinct apprehensions of the world. The chief objects of these apprehensions are experiential domains as they disclose themselves to authors and readers, and the manifestation of those authors and readers as intersubjective relations to the worlds in which they emerge. Consideration of the latter process enables a scrutiny of interactions between poems and their social worlds in which the workings of form are the primary means by which poetry makes available and sustains the attitudes and sensibilities that ground the ethical comportment that it aims to occasion. Attending to such workings requires an account of form that is alert to its power to make as well as to reflect, to project experiences that are its own preserve, and that can only come about through its particular ministrations.

My conceptual claims are exemplified and tested in readings of two passages from poems by Pindar and Shelley. By juxtaposing these passages, and considering their parallel means, I pursue a method that is relatively unconcerned with contextualizing the texts against the social backgrounds and historical processes that shaped their production. The justification for this method is not, needless to say, that specific historical and cultural contexts are unimportant. Rather, it is that the comparative gesture foregrounds effects and implications that are not well grasped by versions of historicist hermeneutics that have predominated in the recent study of ancient Greek lyric. I also aim to illuminate the poems' transcontextual appeal, and to suggest that Pindar should matter to us today as much as, for example, Shelley does, and for similar reasons. Pursuing this approach also draws attention to some blindspots in modern Pindaric criticism, and helps to articulate alternatives that can pay different, and differently productive, attention to the miracle of Pindar's poetic creativity.

Causal Form

Pindarists of the last century have written with great richness and insight about the epinicians' rhetorical structures and their relations to a social world of performance, ritual, and politics. But because of some of their cardinal assumptions and frameworks, these modes of reading have tended to be less adept in canvassing the range of means by which poetic form can give rise to feeling, reflection, and self-consciousness. The fundamental reason for this is a tendency to conceive poetic form as resultative, the outcome of prior intentions or structures that are regarded, in different ways and in differing degrees, as determining form's ontic character. It follows that the operations of form are subordinated to and dictated by these exteriorities; the capacity of form itself to act causally, to affect and reshape the attitudes and outlooks of its readers, is constrained in proportion to that subordination. When epinician is conceived as rhetoric, interpretation is oriented towards elucidating how the poem discharges the obligations and fulfils the aims which, conceived as independent generic principles, limit what the poetry can be validly understood as saying. Closely related is the tendency to conceive the epinicians as defined and regulated by their execution of a social function. By exploring how the epinicians participated in the social life of communities, critics who have employed the methods of cultural poetics have considerably expanded our sense of what the poems can do. Yet however variously and creatively the poems are read as enacting such functions, the move of making social context determinate creates a hierarchy in which elements of the poetry that cannot be assigned or understood in terms of a social function are either not grasped at all or relegated to triviality.[1] Such frameworks inevitably narrow the range of thought that epinician is capable of occasioning.

A helpful alternative to such resultative conceptions is provided by the project of conceptualizing poetic form as affordance. As Caroline Levine points out when discussing the use of the term "to describe the potential uses or actions latent in materials or designs," such an approach is concerned with elements of form that bring about encounters specific to artworks:

> [I]t allows us to grasp both the specificity and the generality of forms – both the particular constraints and possibilities that different forms afford, and the fact that those patterns and arrangements carry their affordances with them as they move across time and space.[2]

The ways in which forms open out in the world and create effects when their "possibilities" are taken up, Levine suggests, matter as much as the objective, generic, and material properties in which those "possibilities" originate. Three implications of this position are of particular moment for my arguments. The first is that poetry's affordances demand a capacious sensitivity, which we might term a phenomenology of form, because they arise from a wide range of semantic (diction, metaphor, intertextuality) and sensuous (rhythm, rhyme, temporal articulation) phenomena, and from interactions between them. The second is that such interactions can produce what Elizabeth Anker and Rita Felski call "specific configurations of perception and experience that resist translation into the norms or calculus of political strategy."[3] This is because poetry's "configurations" can be other than those habitually experienced, and can therefore project readers into previously unavailable or unrecognized apprehensions of the world,[4] or indeed articulate experiential domains and possibilities that emerge singularly in the poem. Third, because of the continuities between its "configurations" and those experienced elsewhere,[5] poetic form gives rise to relational encounters,[6] in which our internalizations of the poem's configuration of its subjects become the grounds for the forms of personhood that we might adopt.

The comparative alignment of Romanticism and ancient Greek poetry gives to the phenomenology of form I pursue an historical dimension that is both diagnostic and creative, because the features of Romantic poetry that have been least well grasped by Pindarists are those in which its handling of form is most complex, and therefore suggest points at which our responsiveness to Pindar's poetics might be most productively heightened. Both Shelley and Pindar share a concern with subjective expression as a figuration of possible communality. In both poets' work, such expression arises as much from the minutiae of diction, syntax, rhythm, and rhyme as from larger rhetorical structures. The extent to which the critical tradition has looked elsewhere in its accounts of ancient lyric poetics is illustrated in an aside by Reviel Netz, which reveals the salient contours of the opposition between Romanticism and the song culture of archaic and classical Greece, as it is often propounded or assumed:

> The romantic image of the author is based on the author's craftsmanship of his own body of works, which are fictional, hence idiosyncratic to him. To be fully appreciated as an author, you must stand apart, solipistically, in your realm. Ancient literary works were not like that; they concerned the shared world of myth and history, and they were much less central to the identity of the author. The author did not stand apart but was appreciated socially, as a member of a group of authors. He was vividly present, through the power of words to evoke the vividness of imagined encounter.[7]

While heuristically useful, the contrasts recorded here also disguise important continuities. The opposition between the "fictional" works taken to characterize Romantic poetics and the "shared world of myth and history" drawn on by Pindar and others downplays the fact that much Romantic poetry is not straightforwardly "fictional," because it too appeals to "shared" traditions and makes claims about the real world that are designed to be taken seriously. Just as importantly, the dichotomy obscures the extent to which both types of poetry attempt to invent or reconfigure relations to the world, rather than being predominantly characterized by manufacture of "idiosyncratic" fictions, or by recourse to "shared" exteriorities that subsist securely independent of their realizations in poems. Equally, the notion that the "romantic image of the author" entails a figure who "stand[s] apart, solipsistically" oversimplifies the Romantic poets' self-figuration, and indeed their social conduct and literary reception. And as much as the Romantics explore the possibilities of shared life, so Pindar "stands apart," and can be "appreciated" for a thinking given purchase by being enacted in "idiosyncratic" language, not only as a social agent in a group of authors.[8]

The concepts that Netz documents have a long and richly stimulating critical history. One especially influential antecedent of "the romantic image of the author" is Hegel's discussion of lyric subjectivity, according to which the lyric poet "must be independent by being in himself an enclosed inner world from which all the dependence and mere caprice of prose has been stripped away." Such independence emerges under particular historical conditions:

> [T]he times most favourable to lyric are those which have achieved a more or less completed organization of human relationships, because only in those times has the individual person become self-reflective in contrast to the external world, and, reflected out of it, achieved in his inner life an independent entirety of feeling and thinking. For in lyric both form and content are provided precisely not by the external world or by individual action but by the poet himself in his own personal character.[9]

Pindar exemplifies this individualization. Although occasional, his odes are grounded in the poet's mood, from which arise "considerations" such as "admonition, consolation, exaltation" that structure the poem as a whole. Such considerations, in Hegel's view, "belong solely to the poet as the composer of his poems," and dictate his treatment of his subject.[10] The emphasis on the author realized as a subjective "entirety" is a useful counterweight to predominant tendencies in Pindaric criticism to collapse authorial idiom into social function, because treating "form and content" as products of "character" opens the way to seeing the granular complexities of form as reflecting a proportionately complex orientation in the world.

For all their emphasis on subjective autonomy, the terms in which Hegel theorizes the poet's emergence as "an independent entirety" also point towards the transferability of this self-realization. When considering Pindar's use of "admonition, consolation, exaltation," he finds the poems unified by perlocutionary structures in which an addressee is encouraged to adopt an attitude towards reality exemplified by the speaker's stance. What ensures the odes' status as subjective expression is therefore based on the possibility of a conversation, the efficacy of which in turn rests on the presupposition that poet and reader share frameworks of experience and conceptualization that the poem's idiomatic "form and content" might inflect. When elaborating the poetic means by which such transferability is effected, and in order to account both for the possibility that the poem might misfire and the reality that its effects are dependent on readerly involvement, I substitute for Hegel's claim that lyric's subjective projections must "possess a universal validity" the proposition that such projections create a transcontextual appeal.[11] In accordance with the conception of form as affordance outlined above, this formulation puts more emphasis on the causal flipside of Hegel's resultative concern with form as the product of character, namely that the poem potentiates an encounter that is opened up for and in subjective life.

Considering the stimulations and shortcomings of Hegel's account foregrounds the extent to which the simplified versions of "Romantic" authorship recurrent in Pindaric criticism, offered as a foil to the versions of Pindar's poetics that critics wish to advance, have hamstrung such criticism's ability to conceptualize adequately the relations that arise in epinician between form and subjectivity. A telling example is Elroy Bundy's rebuttal of the notion that Pindar's "transitions are abrupt":

All this is extremely adroit and hardly the production of a poet whose bursts of inspiration carry him beyond the bounds of sense and relevance. At every point he is in perfect control, and if this is typical of the Theban eagle, our estimate of his irrelevant outbursts and violent transitions (as of much else) must be revised.[12]

What enables the poetry to be read as the result of such "control" is a narrowing of its affordances to the execution of an encomiastic task.[13] The possibility that the poetry might expand our understanding of what "sense" and "relevance" consist of, and that one agent of such expansion might be the emotive effects created by "violent transitions," is foreclosed by limited versions of those concepts being presupposed, separate from their poetic enactment, as determinative parameters for interpretation. Likewise, what might be conceived as generatively idiomatic movements of thought are instead described in the ironized language of an overused, imprecise critical idiom ("bursts of inspiration" ... "outbursts"). By implicitly denying interpretive validity to such language and its antecedents, Bundy substitutes an intentionality of "perfect control" for the more varied mental landscapes countenanced by Hegel and explored in Romantic poetry, and hence reduces the range of interiorities that form might reflect.[14] With the same gesture, he sunders Pindar from a Romantic poetics of "inspiration" by making him belong to a different compositional mode, rendering moot the possibility that the two types of poetry might be illuminatingly juxtaposed. Gray's canonical figuring of Pindar, evoked by the "Theban eagle,"[15] is accordingly recast as an exemplarily unproductive misreading.

If Bundy underestimates the range of experience that poetic form can evoke and open up, we find in another treatment of Pindaric parataxis an underestimation of the relationship between authorial idiom and interpretive community. Discussing the movement in *Nemean* 5 from the half-told tale of the death of Phocus to Pindar's comparison of himself to an athlete ready to jump, to "eagles fly[ing] beyond the sea" (18–21), Lewis Farnell asks why "Pindar bring[s] us up to the very brink of the story and then recoil[s] from it." The question cannot be answered:

> [W]e are dealing with the most wayward and capricious of poets, and we cannot hope to account for all the flittings of his fancy ... He redeems himself by some great phrases, suggesting the flight of the "Theban eagle," before he returns to the Aiakidai.[16]

Farnell traces the utterance as an event in the poet's mental life. The poem's subjects and phrasing result from the unpredictably fluctuating processes of attention by which "fancy" executes what Dryden describes as "the variation, deriving, or moulding of [a] thought, as the judgment represents it as proper to the subject."[17] As "flitting" is transformed into the elevated purposiveness of "flight," Farnell, by contrast with Bundy, makes use of Gray's "Theban eagle" metaphor to register affective value. The type of "great phrases" exemplified by "and eagles leap beyond the sea" (*Nemean Odes* 5.21) give rise to the metaphor not only because of their subject matter, but because they correlate with the poet's intensified experience of his subject. On the other hand, the Hegelian derivation of poetic form from the poet's interior life serves to posit poetic subjectivity as a bar to understanding, an unknowably distant alterity that defies critical "account[ing]." While we might marvel at the poet's dazzlingly "wayward" self-assertion, the interiorities from which it proceeds are not conceived here as capable of informing readers' own thinking.

In my reading of *Nemean Odes* 5.19–21, I argue that Pindar's parataxis should not be seen either, in Farnell's terms, only as a capricious flaunting of subjective freedom, nor, as in Bundy, as testifying to a readily paraphrasable set of meanings. Instead, such parataxis should be read as combining with metaphor, intertextuality, and rhythmical articulation to engender an arrangement of reality specific to it, and thereby to create a correspondingly specific incitement to shared self-understanding. Before examining this passage, I turn from the theorization of poetic subjectivity to its instantiation in Shelley's "To a Sky-lark." This poem's use of sensuous form to capture elements of experience that are not readily denoted, and its projection of communal experience, parallel Pindar's workings in ways that are the more stimulating for their relative obliquity.

The Flight of the Sky-Lark

Critics have frequently probed the ways in which "To a Sky-lark" explores the possibility of mimetic alignment between its speaker and its subject through its apostrophes, questions, and comparisons. Characteristic in its concern with subjective self-expression is Michael O'Neill's conclusion that what drives Shelley's "desire to know the secret of the bird's 'clear keen joyaunce'" is the prospect of being able to compose "poems that would both solve and escape the contradictions of the human condition."[18] Yet concomitant with the "desire" to articulate a response to a particular experience that is also a means of confronting "the contradictions of the human condition" is a less remarked feature of the poem's organization, namely its use of the first person plural to stage an incipiently communal attitude to the events and elicitations it documents.

The first person plural emerges for the first time at line 25 ("Until we hardly see—we feel that it is there") and recurs frequently. Sometimes, as in the reference to "we mortals" (84) who "look before and after / And pine for what is not" (86–7), it encompasses humanity as a whole. Elsewhere, as when the exclamation "What thou art we know not" leads directly to the orienting question "What is most like thee?" (31–2), from which the comparisons of 36–60 unfold, the relation between speaker and group seems more immediate. Here, the question and its responses address the wondering incomprehension that the speaker recognizes as characterizing the shared experience brought about by the sky-lark's effusions. Similarly, when "Teach us, Sprite or Bird / What sweet thoughts are thine" (61–2) is followed quickly by "I have never heard / Praise of love or wine" (63–4), it is if the speaker turns briefly aside to a group of fellow listeners who, although they remain unspecified, are also open to being borne into an intensified imaginative life by what they hear.

These passages enact an unobtrusive but persistent concern with the juncture between individual and communal listening, a juncture that is also visible in Mary Shelley's biographical account of the poem's origin, which invites us to imagine Shelley, Mary herself, and perhaps others, walking in the countryside near Livorno during the "spring" of 1820:

> In the spring we spent a week or two near Leghorn, borrowing the house of some friends, who were absent on a journey to England.—It was on a beautiful summer evening, while wandering among the lanes, whose myrtle hedges were the bowers of the fire-flies, that we heard the carolling of the sky-lark, which inspired one of the most beautiful of his poems.[19]

In this narrative, the sky-lark's song finds the walkers listening together ("we heard"). In an act that is minimally interpretive, insofar as it discloses birdsong as a meaningful event, they apprehend sound assuming a form lightly inflected by associations of human joy and celebration ("carolling"). As well as locating the poem's beginnings in exterior places and events, therefore, Mary's aetiology anticipates the poem's desire to interpret and analogize the sky-lark's song. More importantly for my reading, her story is faithful to the poem's structuring of a response to the sky-lark in the plural.

The contours of such response become evident when the first person plural first comes into view (16–25):

> The pale purple even
>   Melts around thy flight;
> Like a star of Heaven
>   In the broad daylight
> Thou art unseen, but yet I hear thy shrill delight,   20
>
> Keen as are the arrows
>   Of that silver sphere
> Whose intense lamp narrows
>   In the white dawn clear,
> Until we hardly see — we feel that it is there.

With the final line of this passage, a "we" emerges abruptly, unprepared for, interrupting what had been an apparently private communion between the speaker and his experience, impelled by perceptions apparently exclusive to him ("I hear your sweet delight").[20] This sudden awareness of communality occurs simultaneously with a shift from sensory to a more subtle, partly disembodied apprehension ("Until we hardly see — we feel . . ."),[21] suggesting that such heightening impels a turn to the others with whom it is shared.

The implicit, almost inadvertent emergence of plural relationhood that Shelley stages can be contrasted with the extensive and explicitly dialogic treatment of a similar experience in Coleridge's "The Nightingale."[22] The combination of narrative and conversational structure is announced at the outset ("Come, we will rest on this old mossy bridge" 4). When the speaker directs and anticipates his companions' feelings, he does so by assuming the existence of a shared sensibility (8–11):

> and though the stars be dim
> Yet let us think upon the vernal showers
> That gladden the green earth, and we shall find
> A pleasure in the dimness of the stars.

The capacity to partake in a subtly discriminating experience is the product of the same common history that grounds the poem's central move, the rejection of the cliché of the nightingale as mourner ("My Friend, and thou, our Sister! we have learnt / A different lore: we may not thus profane / Nature's sweet voices ..." 40–2) in favor of an attention that lingers on the nightingales' movements and sounds. In the opening stanzas of "To a Sky-lark," the absence of any specification or description of the group's members or history, and the absence of a narrative structure in which present sensibility is dependent on communal recollection, work to a different end. These absences allow the grouping denoted by "we" to manifest itself solely as an effect of the perceptions for which it is the vehicle, and presents readers with a tantalizing picture of subjectivity being shaped purely by experience, free from prior determinations.

Whereas Coleridge draws on the resources of argument and meditation, Shelley achieves a more oblique, compressed formalization of communal experience, in which the clarified and heightened perception of the sky-lark's presence is projected by the interaction between metaphor and rhyme. Thus, when "arrows" is met by "narrows," the diminution of force registered in the displacement of metaphor by metonym, "arrows" by "lamp," is translated into harmony. As the feminine rhyme combines with the long second vowels of its paired elements, a drawn out sonic coalescence substitutes for diminished perception by extending the moment in which what becomes memory lingers. The rhyme of "sphere" with "clear" likewise resists complete transition, as recurrent sound enacts the apparition of recollected moonlight in the "white dawn," and allows the shape and definition of the former to be felt in the sound of the latter. That resonant interaction gives way to the awkwardness of the half-rhyme of "clear" with "there," which intimates the failure of demonstrative perception, as the mismatched rustle of sound analogizes the failure to fill a "there" with the full clarity of what is not quite perceived. Simultaneously, however, the rhyme charges "there" with a significance and sensory weight that enables "we feel" to be apprehended more fully. As these interactions unfold, rhyme establishes itself as an alternative sensory modality, which both reflects experience and invents its own processual knowledge.

The cumulative effect of these rhymes gives form to the process described in "we feel that it is there." What is formalized and opened up to readerly scrutiny here is what might otherwise slip into evanescence, the feelings and tentative apprehensions that organize shared sensibility, and that undergird the decisive identity of idiomatic and communal feeling at 66–70:

> Chorus Hymeneal
>   Or triumphal chaunt
> Matched with thine, would be all
>   But an empty vaunt,
> A thing wherein we feel there is some hidden want.

Here, the speaker's attitude to previous poetry is transferred to the community that the poem is inventing. Like the process of apprehension in "we feel that it is there," the "hidden want" detected in such poetry is made more substantial by Shelley's formal adumbrations of what a fully attentive relation to the sky-lark entails. His poem might afford readers only imaginative trajectories and imperfect analogies, rather than a mimetic plenitude that can be adequately "[m]atched" with the bird's "clear keen joyance." But by making readers into vehicles for such trajectories, the poem "enlarge[s] the circumference of the imagination," as Shelley puts it in *A Defence of Poetry*. It does so by "mak[ing] familiar objects be as if they were not familiar," charging arrows and lamps and moonlight with an unfamiliar significance derived from the relations into which they enter through the poem's arrangements. Just as importantly, however, it enables "the apprehension of that which has not appeared to the senses,"[23] namely the phenomena that arise in and through the poem's formal constellations. Such additions to our imaginative resources are proportionate to the "want" that "we feel" in poetry, which we now perceive with a critically sharpened eye.

These passages exemplify the "art" by which "thought [is] recreated into feeling or self-consciousness into a more communal power of vision," which Geoffrey Hartman identifies as common to a Romantic poetics of expressivity and Modernism's theorization of poetry as "impersonal." But the poem's "power of vision," on my reading, is not only a force of intellection in which ideas (the sky-lark's "joyance," art's insufficiency) are manifested with special clarity. It is not only a bounded totality that results from experience or reflection being "recreated" into a self-complete form, but a set of affordances that interacts with and opens out into readers' own perceptions and understanding. Their power derives in part from their inciting readers to reflect on the incomplete, elusively ongoing emergence of a "communal power of vision" in the poem's opening stanzas. When opening ourselves up to the effects of Shelley's formalization of this emergence, we become subjects of the relations to the world that undergird the poem's imagined community.

The Theban Eagle

"To a Sky-lark" might seem an unpropitious starting point for a comparison of Shelley and Pindar. Shelley admired Pindar's poetry, and drew frequently on it during his years of mature composition, but he appears to hint at 66–70 that his epinicians, as the preeminent representative of the "triumphal chaunt," are among those productions of human culture that comparison with the sky-lark relegates to an object-like inertness. Nevertheless, there are numerous points in the poem at which we might detect Pindaric influence. Shelley's tracing of the sky-lark's flight ("Higher still and higher / From the earth thou springest / Like a cloud of fire; / The blue deep thou wingest" 6–9) might suggest an evocation of Pindar's avian imagery and its successors,[24] combined with a deliberately Pindaric abruptness of transition.[25] The sky-lark as "Like an unbodied joy whose race is just begun" (15) recalls and transforms the image of the poet poised, athlete-like, on the brink of his "race" in *Nemean Odes* 5.20 ("I have in my knees a light spring"). Here, the intertextual transubstantiation of a bodily "spring" into an "unbodied joy" contributes to what Judith Chernaik describes as the poem's central recognition, that "the highest certainty is not of the eye, but of the 'feeling.'"[26] Rather than pursuing these effects, however, I want to suggest that the effects that I have examined in "To a Sky-lark" can be helpful in sensitizing us to more oblique similarities between the poets' manufacture of communal subjectivity.

Pausing between his curtailed intimation of Phocus' death and the account of the Muses' song at the wedding of Peleus and Thetis, Pindar reflects on the task of celebrating Pytheas, his victory, and his ancestors, with a series of metaphors that has been variously understood as suggesting his joy in his commission, the rhetorical efficacy of his language, and the beguiling subtlety of the story of attempted deception that is about to unfold (*Nemean Odes* 5.19–21):[27]

> εἰ δ' ὄλβον ἢ χειρῶν βίαν ἢ σιδαρίταν ἐπαινῆ-
>   σαι πόλεμον δεδόκηται, μακρά μοι
> αὐτόθεν ἅλμαθ' ὑποσκά-
>   πτοι τις· ἔχω γονάτων ὁρμὰν ἐλαφράν·
> καὶ πέραν πόντοιο πάλλοντ' αἰετοί.

If it has been decided to praise wealth or strength of hands or iron-clad war, let someone dig out for me, from here, a long jumping-pit. I have in my knees a light spring, and eagles leap beyond the sea.

What has been less well grasped, however, is the combination of paratactic structure and handling of temporality that makes the passage's incitement to thought distinctive.[28]

Parataxis intensifies and causal relations are correspondingly more weakly specified as the sentence unfolds. The syntax of a conditional followed by a wish (*ei . . . dedokêtai . . . huposkaptoi*) grounds present utterance in a past event. Then, although asyndetic, *echô gonatôn horman elaphran* is readily understood as giving the reason why the "jumping-pit" should be dug. But as the sentence reaches its climax, *kai . . . aietoi* combines bare syntactical addition with an imagistic shift that puts more pressure on readers' construal of its relation to the preceding clause. If parataxis withholds a transparent causal sequence, it simultaneously urges readers to work harder in attending to what Abraham Cowley called "the almost Invisible connections" at work in Pindar's syntax, which here are constituted by the figurative movement from digging to the tensed, expectant body, to the eagles' leaping flight. When tracing this progression, readers are led through images of ascendingly light, impulsive motility, a cumulative trajectory up and away from the earth.

Just as importantly, the lines draw together a range of temporal relations. They voice an orientation shaped by past events (*dedokêtai*), and anticipate a bounded, short-range future that is on the verge of beginning (*huposkaptoi*) but will extend itself through "long" (*makra*) spaces which, in the metaphor's two-way domain, hint at a narrative time of as yet uncertain scope and duration. They grasp at a sensation-laden, person-specific present (*echô*), which is juxtaposed with an apparently timeless, exterior world of recurring actions (*pallont' aietoi*). They constitute a terse yet synoptic picture of the ways in which it is possible for human beings to be implicated in time, articulating personhood as an arrangement of "temporal dimensions [that] hold open the horizons on which entities may manifest themselves in determinate ways."[29]

Such bold juxtapositions might be felt as almost disorienting. If parataxis in narrative can create the impression of a world in which events unfold with fluent regularity and in which causal sequences are assumed in proportion to their transparency, its use here works quite differently. Showing the intensity with which the mind can be immersed in the present, and the swiftness with which it leaps almost despite itself into recollection and anticipation, diction and syntax bring into the foreground of readers' attention the jostling temporal relations that are always at work, more and less clearly apprehended, in human experience. But as parataxis pulls apart the temporal segments created by each syntactic unit, it creates gaps for the mind to traverse, and thus draws on the imagination's power to grasp the configurations that it evolves. As much as the lines impel an intensified consciousness of sublime distances and suprahuman agency (*peran pontoio*),[30] they also induce wonder at the world of inner experience that they fashion and hold open for our contemplation. My readings trace the shaping of such effects in the passage's figurative arc and the individual phrases of which it is composed. What they will highlight is the process by which an idiomatic regulation of time articulates an appeal to transpersonal understanding.

A concern with shared subjectivity is evident in the coordination of the passage's first two verbs, the senses and functions of which are strongly contrasted. By using *dedokêtai* without an indirect object, Pindar intensifies the verb's impersonal force, its sanction so thoroughly diffused that the means by which it is purveyed recede into insignificance.[31] An impersonal, completed past event is immediately juxtaposed with an open-ended, incomplete future action for which an individual is the vehicle. With *huposkaptoi*, Pindar appeals to an anonymous listener (*tis*) on the basis of an assumed trust and shared commitment to the task at hand. The metaphor suggests that, just as the digger understands the likely length of the leap and will dig in a manner fitted to it, so the *tis* grasps the poem's purposes in advance. The appeal therefore orients the poem towards the kind of receptive listening the results of which are enacted in a performance, whether choral or monodic. The abrupt move from one verb to another accentuates their different temporal registers.

In the next phrase, attention shifts to time as experienced through the body. As Alex Purves has pointed out, the phrase *echô gonatôn horman elaphran* "places [Pindar] in the role of the athletic victor,"[32] such that his imagination resonates in sympathy with the body on the cusp of competitive endeavor.[33] Again, a particular temporal experience takes shape through Pindar's unfamiliar use of familiar terms. The word *hormê* is only once the direct object of *echô* in previous literature,[34] and the slight strangeness of the verbal arrangement highlights the subtlety of what it attempts to capture. Diction here both enacts and is inflected by the experience of potentiality; "having" or "checking" occasions an awareness that the *hormê* is "light," both in the sense of having its own, autonomously welling momentum and of working against and intensifying the restraining action of *echô*. Sensation slips away from and spreads the action of *echô* across the body, so that the lines' only present tense verb describes a presence that is both spatially dispersed and elongated in time. The metonymic *horman elaphran* shows affinity with the athlete extending itself into how time manifests itself as feeling; as the present is sensed as a mutually amplifying interaction of "checking" and "lightness," it is drawn out into a duration that testifies that fidelity to athletic success has become part of how the speaker senses time passing.

From the immediacy of the sensing body, the poem's gaze moves suddenly with *kai peran pontoio pallont' aietoi* into the far reaches of the earth. Because the eagle is a figure for poetry elsewhere in Pindar, their soaring into untrammeled distance here has often been understood as a celebration of the poet's competence to fulfil his encomiastic task and his pleasure in doing so.[35] But the line also contributes to the passage's concern with enacting an orientation in time, and fashions this orientation into specific affects and perceptions. Whereas *echô … horman elaphran* creates a distinctively sensed present through the verbal interaction within a phrase, Pindar makes the "eagles … leap" in language defamiliarized by its departure from established patterns of reference.

Homeric usage reflects the fact that eagles usually fly alone;[36] the plural here is therefore most naturally taken as iterative, a telescoped reference to multiple solo flights. More distinctive still is *pallonto*, which is used here for the first time of eagles, and which produces a "leap" that outdoes Homer in boldness of diction. The middle form is applied by Homer to more contained movements: closest to Pindar's phrasing is Andromache's description of her heart "leaping to her mouth" (*palletai êtor ana stoma*, *Iliad* 22.452). As it launches the eagles into unbounded spaces, substituting the "leap" of flight for the short-range "leap" of the heart within the body or the "brandishing" of the spear about to fly, the intertextual aspect of the phrase enacts the eagles' freedom from human limitations, showing their flight untrammeled by the associations of anguished fear or incipient threat that shadow the verb's Homeric contexts.

This effect is strengthened and lent a temporal dimension by what might be described as a situational intertextuality, created by the manner in which Pindar's *pallonto* departs from the distinct narrative grammar that characterizes many Homeric uses of *pallô*. When lots or spears are shaken in Homer, or when a heart "leaps" in fear, the actions proceed from defined customs or normative calculations, and drive the narrative forward by precipitating specific consequences: a lot will nominate one man to fight or compete; a spear poised in challenge will provoke an enemy or stir friends to fresh exertion; Andromache's fear results from a perception and leads directly to an action. Standing out by contrast against this associative background, Pindar's eagles "leap" in a language that enacts their suprahuman agency. Their flight is uncircumscribed by motivation or plot, and their action reaches into spaces and future time uncharted by calculation. Fittingly, therefore, the sentence's climactic destination is emblematic of its subtle temporal facture. While *aietoi* condenses the times in which multiple flights will occur into the moment of the present utterance, *pallonto* pulls the present apart by making it the domain of an indefinitely extended event that escapes regulation in narrative.

In the movement from the speaker's "knees" to the eagles' leap, then, Pindar juxtaposes two strikingly differentiated formalizations of presence. The immediate, localized tensing of the human body, grasped empathetically, gives way to a flight that can only be apprehended at a distance by a focalization that emphasizes the movement's almost object-like alienness (*pallonto*). The former manifests itself through its internal segmentation, as the interwoven sensations of spontaneous momentum and conscious gathering intensify each other; the latter is simultaneously timeless, something that has and will continue to occur, and a continuous, unbounded vector. Several commentators have noted that *horman elaphran* and *pallonto* invite readers to connect the movements they suggest: as Charles Segal puts it, "the athlete's spring . . . expands to a bolder figure."[37] Simultaneously, however, the lines' differing presentations of time strengthen the separative force of their paratactic arrangement, and foreground the imaginative exertion entailed in traversing the distance between the limbs' expectancy and the eagles' flight.

Rhythmical structure also helps to hold the lines apart. Two distinct rhythmical profiles are set against each other, as a light, primarily dactylic emphasis (D – D – e –) gives way to a heavier epitritic movement (E – e):

— ◡ ◡ — ◡ ◡ — —

αὐτόθεν ἅλμαθ᾽ ὑποσκά-

  — ◡ ◡ — ◡ ◡ — — — ◡ — —

πτοι τις· ἔχω γονάτων ὁρμὰν ἐλαφράν·

— ◡ — — — ◡ — — — ◡ —

καὶ πέραν πόντοιο πάλλοντ᾽ αἰετοί.

The lines afford different possibilities for vocal comportment to express affinity to the subjects at hand. The predominating light syllables in *autothen … gonatôn* lend themselves to a delivery in which vocal momentum realizes the excited anticipations of the sensing body, while the weightier measure of *kai … aietoi*, in tension with the swiftness it frames, suggests the senses of the human onlooker arrested in prolonged contemplation.[38] Yet whatever expressive force is enacted in the voice or sensed by a reader, the rhythmical shift acts here as a kind of punctuation, intimating a separation between the two lines' referential domains.

Rhythmical articulation, metaphor (*pallonto*), the paratactic break between limbs and flight, and the different experiences of presence opened up in the two lines therefore combine to emphasize the gap that separates the speaker from the eagles. Simultaneously, the means of bridging this gap, however provisionally, are made available in the affordances of poetic form. The jolting leap of the transition from the "light spring" to flight itself produces a formalized version of such elevation, an adumbration in diction, rhythm, and syntax of what the contours of such flight would feel like when they seize the body. The cumulative force of these concatenated, interacting separations strengthens the imaginative movement that traverses them. The extraordinary relations that Pindar's language documents are thus echoed in the mental striving that the task of being adequately responsive to them entails.

Parataxis adumbrates a temporal dispersal, the dizzying juxtapositions of impersonal past, intimate sensation, and indeterminate future, that might appear to threaten a putatively coherent self. Simultaneously, however, paratactic organization precipitates the co-ordination of images, feelings, and associations, and occasions the perceptual leap that bears us away as our gazes strain after the eagles' flight. The distances of "beyond the sea" induce the kind of cosmic spectatorship, which in Longinus' account is brought about when sublime writing handles what human nature is most drawn to, "the extraordinary and great and beautiful" (*to peritton . . . kai mega kai kalon* 35.3). But if the lines alight on such phenomena in the exterior world, they also come close to enacting what Hegel sees the lyric poet's emergence as "a subjectively complete world" in which "[the] man becomes a work of art himself."[39] Construing an arrangement of ideas that only come into being through their action, they prompt a reflective self-awareness of our own internalized consciousness of sublime matter, and of the temporal and affective relations that we are capable of grasping synoptically. We grasp these not just as sources of an exhilarating emotional impulsion, but as a meaningful coherence that both testifies to and challenges our powers of comprehension. The result is that human thinking itself, the subject's own overlapping, intersecting temporal relations with the world and others, becomes a source of "that which is great and more divine than ourselves" (*tou megalou kai hôs pros hêmas daimoniôterou* 35.2).

Ethics and Exaltation

Despite their generic and contextual differences, "To a Sky-lark" and *Nemean* 5 approximate each other in their handling of the relationship between form and subjectivity. Shelley's use of metaphor and rhyme to make substantial the fleeting emergence of a shared response to the sky-lark's song, and Pindar's combination of parataxis, metaphor, and rhythm, are alike in formalizing the idiomatic apprehensions of the speaker as an appeal to readerly understanding. Both make sensibility, the sensuously realized apprehension of the world that form reflects and affords, the ground of a subjectivity in which readers might share. Both poets assert self-consciousness in conjunction with a recognition of the self as relational.

In order to underscore what is distinctive about Pindar's configuring of the lyric speaker's relations to others, I turn back to Hegel's account of lyric, two elements of which are particularly important here. The first is the claim that the lyric poet's orientation is constituted by a tension between "subjective freedom" and "the topic which is trying to master it." For Hegel, the relationship between the poet's free assertion of himself as a distinctive person and the material that he internalizes as the basis of this assertion is the source of the "digressions" and "sudden transitions" that characterize lyric, and Pindar's epinicians in particular. The second is that Hegel sees lyric as articulating a developmental movement from an unproductive immersion in feeling to a "self-expression . . . [which] grasps and expresses in the form of self-conscious insights and ideas what formerly was only felt."[40]

Both of these claims illuminate the appeal created by the lines under discussion. The first makes sense of the authorial self-assertion that is salient from the opening lines of *Nemean* 5, in which the celebrated opposition between static statues and mobile song (*ouk andriantopoios eim'*, "I am not a maker of statues" 1–2), and the command issued to the "sweet song" to "go" on its travels from Aegina (*glukei' aoida, / steich' ap' Aiginas* 2–3) present the poem as the product of a designing intelligence. What occurs in *Nemean Odes* 5.19–21, however, is less a "struggle" between "subjective freedom" and a material recalcitrant to poetic "mastery," than the process through which the speaker shows himself as emerging into relations with the other phenomena by which his world is peopled: most obviously, the athlete, his victory, the others with whom he celebrates; more subtly, poetic traditions and the experience of time. In these lines, therefore, the speaker's self-positing as a subjectively distinct crystallization of these phenomena manifests itself as an affordance for relational thought.

The second of Hegel's claims helps to clarify what this relational thought involves. The bodily echo of athletic endeavor ("I have in my knees a light spring") intimates a sympathetic identification of speaker with athlete, but also expands our sense of what Pytheas' successes might mean to us. We are induced to relate to him not just as someone to be admired for his prowess, but as someone whose achievements have enabled us to enter into the experience of time that the poem affords.[41] The wish ("let someone dig") draws us into the assurance the speaker feels when sensing the proximity of others who grasp that experience intuitively. The eagles' leap likewise links readers to others who share in the experience of being left behind by a flight at which they can only marvel. For all that these lines heighten awareness of the gap between the exterior world and the domains of inner experience into which that world can be transformed through the agency of the poem, they, like Shelley's apprehension of the sky-lark, chart less a movement from "feeling" to "insights and ideas" than an intensified sense of the relations to others that inform our capacities for self-consciousness.

It is from this sense that the passage's ethical claims arise. Both poets rise to the challenge of articulating the kind of ethical comportment that Anahid Nersessian describes as "address[ed] . . . to the hypothetical being over and above the actual one, to the form of a life and not to a reference point tethered to some specific living thing." Such addresses are therefore constitutively futural: "what we call ethics is just an exaltation aimed at preserving the future as a *there* for someone else."[42] Pindar and Shelley alike work towards producing such a "hypothetical being," the personhood that would be the reflex of their poems' "exaltations." When the first person plural first occurs in "To a Sky-lark," less a defined group than an orientation towards a possible experience, it adumbrates a "hypothetical being" that is offered as an alternative to anguished sense of insufficiency that besets the human condition elsewhere ("We look before and after / And pine for what is not" 86–7). Pindar's display of paratactic and metaphorical virtuosity in *Nemean* 5 likewise creates a set of relations that exalt the reader who might become "the new subject made possible by the event" that they constitute.[43]

Both poems, in other words, seek to "preserve the future as a *there*" for others by crafting experiential possibilities that might inform such a future, and by urging reflection on the means by which these might be sustained. Rather than expressing a subjective stance that precedes them, they both afford, or at least seek to afford, a subjectivity contingent upon the range of expressions of which lyric is capable. Both experiment with ways of relating to the world and to others that combine an assertion of the individuated self as a distinct locus of experience with an eschewal of claims to epistemic mastery, or to a hierarchy in which the poet's self-complete subjectivity achieves exemplary predominance.[44] Their formal configurations realize poetry's aspiration to remake the worlds we inhabit.

Notes

1. See e.g., Kurke 1991, 1 for the programmatic claim that "[j]ust as genre depends upon performance, poetics depends upon the broader social context, for given its setting, we must believe that such poetry fulfilled a *social* function."

2. Levine 2015, 6.

3. Anker and Felski 2017, 17.

4. "Apprehension" as a distinct mode of thought is usefully discussed by R. Wilson (2013, 13–18).

5. For which see Levine 2015, 11–12; for a critique of Levine, see Introduction; for discussion specific to early Greek poetry, see Budelmann and Phillips 2018, 11–13.

6. See Rimell's chapter; see also the Introduction.

7. Netz 2020, 173.

8. See, e.g., *Olympians* 1.114–16 and *Pythians* 4. 298–9.

9. Quotations taken from Hegel 1975, 1115 and 1123. See Culler 2015, 99–101, for further discussion.

10. Hegel 1975, 1115 and 1120.

11. Hegel 1975, 1111.

12. Bundy 1986, 2 and 14.

13. For a critique of this move, its influence on later Pindarists, and its consequences, see Hamilton 2003, 85–7.

14. Exemplified by his celebrated claim that "there is no passage [sc. of the epinicians] that is not in its primary intent encomiastic—that is, designed to enhance the glory of a particular

patron": Bundy 1986, 3. Here, "intention," realized transparently in "desig[n]" and inferred in the process of critical "catalogu[ing]," is what causes "conventions" to have the qualities that "control" the poetry's effects.

15. "The Progress of Poesy: A Pindaric Ode," line 115.

16. Farnell 1930, 2.188.

17. Quoted at Bullitt and Jackson Bate 1945, 10. Farnell is doubtless drawing here on *Pythians* 10.53–4.

18. O'Neill 1989, 121.

19. Mary's recollections are chronologically inexact: the Shelleys stayed with John and Maria Gisborne from 15th June to 4th August 1820; "To a Sky-lark" was composed in late June or early July: see *LAEP* III, 468.

20. Pyle (2014, 323) comments that "[i]t is not so much the disjunction of sight and feeling that is a surprise here but the sudden turn to the plural."

21. For discussion of this perceptual shift, see Chernaik 1972, 127–8.

22. This poem is also relevant to Mary's autobiographical account: by supplying the details of group experience that the poem leaves unmentioned, her emphasis on the group encounter assimilates "To a Sky-lark" to the "conversation poem."

23. Pyle 2014, 320.

24. The "blue deep" nods to Gray's "azure deep of air" ("The Progress of Poesy: A Pindaric Ode," line 117).

25. For which see Chernaik 1972, 125.

26. Chernaik 1972, 127.

27. Rhetoric: Pfeijffer 1999, 134; Segal 1974, 403; Burnett 2005, 69–70; intimation of interpretive complexity and assertion of the poem's transcendence of immediate context: Fearn 2017, 39.

28. See however the tersely suggestive account of Nersessian (2020, 25–6).

29. M. Zimmerman 2006, 296.

30. On the Pindaric sublime see e.g., Porter 2016, 350–6.

31. This is one of only two uses by Pindar of the impersonal construction, and the only one without the indirect object; cf. *Isthmian Odes* 8.59.

32. Purves 2019, 98.

33. An additional effect of the language is to create an association between the athlete's poised body and the physical comportment of both a chorus and a monodic performer, whose movements resonate with recollections of the athlete's. The potential for dance movements to register this recollection makes the connection more direct in the former case.

34. Cf. *Homeric Hymn to Demeter* 382, but here the sense of the verb is "arrest" (*hippôn athanatôn out' akries eschethon hormên*).

35. See e.g. Pfeijffer 1999, 134.

36. The only exception to solo flight in Homer is the dual at *Odyssey* 2.146. Indeed, *Nemean Odes* 5.21 is the first instance of *aietos* as a plural subject in Greek literature. On flight, see also Rankine's and Nooter's chapters.

37. Segal 1974, 403. Cf. also Bury 1898, 92, who comments that *pallonto* "smooths the transition from the leaper to the eagle, as it might apply to either."

38. For similar connections between sense and rhythm elsewhere in Pindar, see Phillips 2018, 81–7.

39. Hegel 1975, 1120.

40. Hegel 1975, 1142 and 1112.

41. A particular version of the "fidelity," which Payne (2018, 265–9) sees as enacted in epinician.

42. Nersessian 2020, 54. Cf. the discussion of Pindar's "future-oriented" ethics in Payne 2006.

43. Badiou 2013, 48.

44. For similar complication of (the desire for) interpretive mastery elsewhere in Pindar, see Fearn (2017, 98–104), discussing *Nemean Odes* 8.1–5.

CHAPTER 7
"I'M SORRY ABOUT THE POEM": *NARCISSI* AND INCOMMENSURABILITY IN JAMAICA KINCAID'S *LUCY*
Ren Ellis Neyra

A Prelude

"I did not know what these flowers were, and so it was a mystery to me why I wanted to kill them."[1] These words should echo across how this chapter pursues a reading of Jamaica Kincaid's 1990 novel *Lucy*. In several scenes, the novel arranges a seeming repudiation of poetry—particularly British Romanticism—while using figural and rhetorical structures that one associates with poetry and poetics, i.e., prosopopoeia, effacement, catachresis, and disfiguration. As one perhaps can deduce even from the line that opens this paragraph, the novel does not convey *physis* into felicitous *poiesis* or phenomenal encounter into linguistic representation so that subjective disturbance then eventuates recovery, promises vitality, and/or reincarnates the self-stabilized subject.[2] Rather, poetry's appearance through its evoked and described effacement and disfiguration—and specifically one of William Wordsworth's poems—conveys destructiveness and incommensurability.

Lucy begins and ends with the theme of *hospitality*, and configures questions of how it signifies, and does not, relationality. The specific anti-Black damage of hospitality is on frequent, if sometimes subtle, display. *Lucy* positions its titular character on the wavering arc of the *Künstlerroman* to stage scenes, especially its (in)famous "daffodils scene," that do not yield what we may call *Bildung*-humanism. Between its opening and closing configuration of hospitality, one can read the novel for how it evokes the trope of the lyric "I" errantly moving across a landscape, listening and looking for sensory encounters. However, as I have suggested already, sensory disturbance in *Lucy*, rather than eventuating stability, will show the impossibility of such and of relation where certain assumptions are made to readily cure linguistic misalignment with perception, and vice versa.

The novel unfolds, notably, from the Black Caribbean point of view of Lucy, a "visitor" to the United States, and not from the point of view of someone else *on* her although inevitably she must deal with how her appearance seems to appear particularly in "mixed company." Beginning in the darkness of a cold, January night, Lucy will quickly move into a pale-yellow, still-cold sunny morning. Lucy is not mere *cogitatum* among *cogito*, but she sometimes functions as *sheer* object.[3] This may be, in part, because her Afro-Caribbeanness and Queens English signify differently to white North Americanness than African Americanness and American English. This does not imply that she appears some other way than by the Manichean, heliotropic, Christianizing metaphors inextricable from the historical yet anti-genealogical production of "the blackened position," from what Jacques Derrida calls the "founding photological metaphor of Western philosophy as metaphysics," of light/dark, revelation/concealment, whiteness/blackness, good/evil, *homo sapiens*/the fallen, etc.[4] On the contrary, readers can trace throughout the novel how she seems to challenge, and sometimes rhetorically toys with, the perception of those around her. *What comes at her*, Lucy can sometimes repel, often linguistically; and there are projections launched that she constitutively cannot repel, including linguistically, from the "blackened position"—language, in other words, is operative in what magnetizes toward her. And that does not make what magnetizes predictable in terms of *how* it will take on momentum, that is, how the language of Western metaphysics will violate. The way that I am introducing her in these sentences is also to say that sometimes she is *overloaded* with the signification of "history"—and on the scenes that will be close-read here, history manifests *via* the poetic, where the poetic is also traumatic. It is so, I argue, because it operates in a catachrestic chain whereby colonialism is *not said. Compacted* into and effaced by the word "poem" are many words that remain unsaid by Lucy; in their remaining unsaid, they raise questions of the (un)representability of her experience of the "life-world" in the milieu of assumed equitable relationality. "Having" a history does not protect Lucy from being de-historicized, misread, and mistreated, in other words. "Historiality," in Gayatri Spivak's words, "is not changed into genealogy."[5] Her *past* (which does not exist "behind" or apart from her experience of time) and the stability of a *heritage* are not the same. "What a history you have," says her white employer to her at one point.[6] To whom she replies, "You are welcome to it if you like."[7] The pathetic surprise at the other's account of her trauma that sustains a statement like, "What a history you have," does not become aggressive on the scene of its utterance, but it foreshadows a scene that, in the name of *care*, is aggressive, where what becomes clear is that *history has Lucy*. The cartographic, cultural, and linguistic coordinates that represent Lucy's difference have the rug ripped out from under them by ontological and ontic force more than once, in narrative moments in which her suffering, what brings her pain, is not just made illegible to the white other, unrepresentable in the "living present" that they seem to share, but hastily crowded-out of the delays of representation for an affective order to be "restored"—a domestic affective order through which she sees almost immediately. The white, bourgeois female subject who hosts her would sound something along the lines of: *I will grant that you signify in a signifying chain that is partly beyond me, and I will still try to interject myself there, so that what is beyond me there may be controlled for me to enjoy the stability of my disorder.*

With that said, what unfolds here is a close reading of the aforementioned "daffodils scene" from Chapter 2 of the novel. The scene configures a catachrestic chain where to say "daffodils" is to say poetry, which is to (un)say colonialism. On the "daffodils scene," a signifier known only as a signifier—daffodils—materializes to Lucy's horror, who had not known its phenomenal, material form. Whereupon she encounters it, and is told, *Look, this is it!*, where *it is a them—many, many of them—speech* vanishes, and she wishes to do what she has *attempted to do* to the poetic system in which *they* had hitherto dwelled in her mind: destroy them—and destroy *it*. The seeming referent and its materiality, in other words, does not come with stability—*it* is immediately destabilized and destabilizing of Lucy's perception and grasp on language. She immediately recognizes that she does not know the time of what she beholds and feels compelled to kill *this* which she cannot name—knowing, as she does, that *it* belongs to a system that conceives of her and hers as that which can never be killed enough. With that said, the provisional stakes of my argument in this chapter are simple: reading *Lucy* conveys that relationality is not a given or necessarily a good.

Luc[ifer] Josephine Potter

The first time the character Lucy asks her mother why she named her thusly, her mother does not reply.[8] Lucy is maybe nine years old when she asks this question, so the year of this scene of power play over naming could be circa 1958 in what the reader assumes is Antigua. "Lucy," Lucy thinks, has no substance, no heft, no liked-by-her literary source, unlike the names she prefers, Charlotte, Emily, Jane, even Enid. When Lucy asks this question again, her mother is pregnant with a pregnancy she does not want, with her fourth and last child, who will be another boy, another boy whose needs, education, and well-being are prioritized over Lucy's—who is not only a girl, but specifically the first and only girl after whom males trail, a particularly onerous positioning in the misogynistic structure of some Caribbean households. Watching her mother, studying her, even, while she is tired, standing over a bowl of fresh fish, and working to prepare dinner, Lucy poses the question of her name again.

> [U]nder her breath she said, "I named you after Satan himself. Lucy, short for Lucifer. What a botheration from the moment you were conceived." "I"—says Lucy— "not only heard it quite clearly when she said it but I heard the words before they came out of her mouth. And yet I said, "What did you say?" But she wouldn't repeat it; she only said, "Why do you torment me so?" and wouldn't speak to me anymore. In the minute or so it took for all this to transpire, I went from feeling burdened and old and tired to feeling light, new, clean. I was transformed from failure to triumph. When I was quite young and just being taught to read, the books I was taught to read from were the Bible, *Paradise Lost*, and some plays by William Shakespeare, and from time to time I had been made to memorize parts of *Paradise Lost*. The stories of the fallen were well known to me, but I had not known that my own situation could even distantly be related to them. Lucy, a girl's name for Lucifer. That my mother would have found me devil-like did not surprise me, for I often thought of her as god-like, and are not the children of gods devils?[9]

Whether what her mother says is "true" or not is not what matters to Lucy, whose name, per this tale, is both a truncation and a catachresis. Lucy as a character, after all, is the embodiment of "a statement of distrust."[10] Lucy experiments with truth and falsity all the time; she is—or, she calls herself—"two-faced," and she distrusts. Suspicion is her "permanent hypothesis."[11] The figure of Lucifer as insult does not occur to her, either. Lucy's "What did you say?" is not marked with having taken offense, or a wish to have been named, given her particular literary imagination, say, for Wordsworth's "Lucy poems." Rather, she anticipates her mother's utterance, and is nominally reborn by it, going from "burdened and old and tired" to "light, new, clean," so unburdened that she has dispensed with the clunky repetition of the inclusive conjunction "and and and." What the text elaborates after the mother's account of her daughter's name, or the re-naming of her Lucifer, in terms of the reading-history of the titular character, is that she apprehends not just the signified but what is possible, what may be innovated through this name: severance. What I would emphasize is that established here is her "relation" to "the fallen." To the children of gods, devils, to be sure, but who else and what else is operative in the categorization of "the fallen"? In a text about an Afro-Caribbean child of "the letter," of the written word, of a mother who is an avid and engrossed reader, of the British literary tradition's regulatory and white supremacist function in its colonies? Of a teenager who will not answer her mother's mailed letters once she is working as an *au pair* in the United States, yet wears them on her person, in her brassiere, folded, unopened against her skin?

What if, after Cecilio Cooper's argument about fallenness and Blackness, this gendering, "Lucy, a girl's name for Lucifer," retraces that: A. the Luciferian fall *pre-dates* the "Adamic fall," i.e., is reconfigured and reproductively punishingly re-gendered by Eve's fall; and B. that Lucifer's fall—one impelled by a sin in language, no less—figures the vertically and temporally *unending*, abyssal fallenness of (anti)Blackness?[12] Cooper theorizes the Abrahamic and especially the Christian tradition's fetishization of the uterus as the "reproductive locus" that involves both a romance with the project of Being (onto-metaphysics) via sexual differentiation *and* a sadistic relationship to the punishability of those assigned female at birth who are metonymized by the uterus, the site of "feminine dysfunction." For Cooper's argument, this is a dysfunction *blackened* since "time immemorial" by the story of the Luciferian fall and the collapsing of darkness and Blackness that exceeds exact historical representation and also precedes the Adamic, i.e., Eve's, fall. The Luciferian fall, again, is reconfigured in the Edenic scene of expulsion and changed embodiment, after which "propagation" occurs via "interactions between wombs, hormones, genitals, zygotes, and gonads," an "ensemble of corporeal characteristics."[13] "The contours of the sex-gender binary as we know it," argues Cooper, "only crystallize against a pre-existing primal and incorporeal backdrop of blackness as asexual and chaotic (re)production manifest . . . [B]lackness as darkness' quintessence is the ante-binaristic milieu from which all subsequent modes of differentiation—sexual or otherwise—are accomplished. The violence that ensues from classifying life into genres—which is again to say genders—must first disembark from blackness as the launchpad for viability in the universe.'"[14] I evoke Cooper's deconstructive, demonological reading of the Luciferian fall and the abyssal, incorporeal, chaotic conception of Blackness that predates the Adamic fall for two relevant reasons. One, it returns us, in the inverse, to

Moses' narration of God's statement, "Let there be *light,*" and to light as the first spoken predicate,[15] light that can only be light out of its emergent juxtaposition with darkness, which is also sometimes a juxtaposition (theologically) with *nothingness.* Two, Cooper's shift, let's say, of one imagined order of the relationship between gendering and the long story of biological and epidermal racialization presents the difficulty of locating a "thereness" of Blackness not only in space (although the essay does do this in its readings of cosmology, theology, and the Black chthonic), but also in the discourses of (historical and literary) representation. Western historiography and representation chart themselves precisely along the coordinates grounded by onto-metaphysics.[16] What I would underscore here is that Cooper's argument positions the punishment of sexual difference as subsequent to the collapse of the significations of fallenness with darkness and darkness with Blackness.[17]

In a text enacting a figural matricide (as well as a kind of literary patricide), Lucy's re-positioning through this story of "the origin" of her name as "the fallen" binds her to her mother, and binds her to being at odds with her, which also gives her a way to navigate perceptual disturbances in language and in the world: not by ameliorating them, but by drawing de-sedimenting attention to assumptions of commonality (of kinship, of tradition, of affect, of mediation) that do violence. This will have specific implications as she enters the world of "mixed company," that is, a world in intimate proximity with US American whites, where proximity will frequently be confused for shared meaning, shared feeling, shared expression. We may read Lucifer as a framework for thought and speech in the novel, and not only as a nominalization. For Satan's "sin" is in speech itself, and long before the temptation of Eve—since "time immemorial," that is, at the limits of empirical history's representational capacity and forever in tension with the first spoken and recorded predicate. If Lucy is a way of *saying* Lucifer, then how Lucy *lucifers* returns us to the misalignments of language and perception. Lucifer as Lucy's way in the world—a way not made uncomfortable by generating obstacles to facile relation—also yields another approach to reading the novel's reconfiguration of the dynamic of Echo and Narcissus, between *narcissi* and Lucy.

"I wished that I had an enormous scythe . . ."

I was torn between the title of this chapter being what it now is and "When a lyric is not there to be read," for it is built out of rereading a scene that evokes and disfigures a specific lyric poem, one that is incidentally never properly named or presented on the pages of the novel. The reader knows of it via its effacement. Additionally, the trope of *wandering* that I invoked at the beginning is disfigured on this scene. "Behind the lyric wandering, there is a Greek journey, an erased and reinterpreted odyssey. But Ulysses' journey is also the journey of the deceiver or the traitor. And lyricism is then called to return to the place of the lie or of the original treason by which meaning exists, the meaning that sings itself."[18] So goes part of Jacques Rancière's story of lyric poetry in *The Flesh of Words,* a story that fixes the meanings of the metaphorical, epic transports of "freedom" into lyric poetry in a sequence of "already traced" European and Mediterranean poles in the West's mythopoetics of itself—enclosed by metaphysics.[19] Behind William Wordsworth's encounter with "a host, of golden daffodils," argues Rancière, is the (supposedly) solitary walker's poetic reinterpretation of "liberty" and the French Revolution. Of "America," meaning also in the context the Caribbean, Hortense Spillers writes, "It is as if the Word, for Europe, engenders flesh."[20] Here, the relationship between "word" and "flesh"—and body—is not treated as the stuff of utopian sensory and political experiments. "The lie" that the trope of the wandering lyric "I" returns "us" to is not the rights of Man, nor the idea of an "original" and fixedly meaningful treason in language that points to the eventual triumph of a proletarian revolution, but the lie of the *commensurability* between "abyss" and subjective alienation, between "Blackening" and exploitation. In her dynamic with Mariah, Lucy conveys their incommensurable positions in history. And we may read the novel's dissemination of incommensurability between their positions in scenes where it disfigures evocations of an "I" on the predetermined path of humanistic errancy. In the writing of this chapter, my meditation became less about lyric per se, or the question of lyric reading posed in the aborted title (which would have been an obvious echo of sometimes divergent approaches to lyric poetry in the work of Paul de Man, Jonathan Culler, and Virginia Jackson), and more about reading the novel's configuration of disdain for *narcissi* in the infamous "daffodils scene" and a suspension of commonality.

To say *narcissi* is to say daffodils—the bulbs that give early spring buttercup-shaped flowers. And it is to (not) say Narcissus, Echo, as well as Wordsworth and British Romantic poetry. This concatenation also becomes a metaphor for the British colonial subjectivizing procedures that Lucy by definition cannot merely avow, but rather, in the "something" of it that she forcibly *inherits,* necessarily deconstructs. Her forced returns to this tradition, in other words, could be made in service of further solidifying it, but can be read for how they reveal at least one layer of its procedures of sedimentation so as to draw out their possible de-sedimentation. Lucy's disdain for daffodils is configured via a false "injury" of her white, liberal-subject employer, Mariah, precisely because Lucy, the *au pair,* is expected by Mariah's use of language and emotion to function as Narcissus' Echo, and she does not. She quickly inverts the trope of Echo and functions as Narcissus, and then as the Grim Reaper, Death's collector. The "daffodils scene" disturbs Mariah's imagined-to-be-given paradigm of relation, and subsequent passages in the novel further suspend relation. Instead, the daffodils metaphorize how disturbance and misperception are at the heart of representation itself, as they are of subjectivity, including that which is operative in the colonial auto-affective procedures that (violently) stabilize the circular reproduction of self-sameness, selfhood, i.e., *ipseity*. Disturbance haunts the gap between mental and emotional processes and language. Disturbance haunts the phenomenological struggle with immediacy and authenticity of expression as presence (which lyric poetry has sometimes been made into a symbol of) and the delays of language, of difference. Perception, meaning-making, nonsense, and historicity fray from the disturbed forces inherent to representation. Since the long, violent, and strange biologization of Race since at least the fifteenth century, these disturbed forces' *appearances* are more acute where there is the sure-fire *anaphylaxis* of the "epidermal-racial[ization]" of already-disturbed representation.[21] As I have written about elsewhere, cries may configure the anaphylaxis, and so might other figures, including ones that do not move discernably "outward."[22]

Let us close-read the evoked "daffodils scene," when Mariah, the attempted supplemental white mother-employer of Lucy—Lucy who wants no mother but her Black mother, and distance from her mother, at that, and her nucleate domestic role as eldest daughter in a family of several, younger male children—takes her to see *gardened* swaths of her (Mariah's) favorite flower. We read from Lucy's perspective:

> I did not know what these flowers were, and so it was a mystery to me why I wanted to kill them. Just like that. I wanted to kill them. I wished that I had an enormous scythe; I would just walk down the path, dragging it alongside me, and I would cut these flowers down at the place there they emerged from the ground. Mariah said, "These are daffodils. I'm sorry about the poem, but I'm hoping you'll find them lovely all the same." There was such joy in her voice as she said this, such a music, how could I explain to her the feeling I had about daffodils—that it wasn't exactly daffodils, but that they would do as well as anything else? Where should I start? Over here or over there? Anywhere would be good enough, but my heart and my thoughts were racing so that every time I tried to talk I stammered and by accident bit my own tongue. Mariah, mistaking what was happening to me for joy at seeing the daffodils for the first time, reached out to hug me, but I moved away, and in doing that I seemed to get my voice back.[23]

The fantasy of *flos-icide* occurs before Lucy *knows* that the flowers that she is seeing *are* the phenomenon that corresponds to the word that she apprehended as a child going to British-Commonwealth-era school in mid-twentieth-century Antigua. She wants to kill them, that is, before she is cognizant that these are hosts of *that* flower.

Lucy's emotional response to the encounter is anger, and not an anger that inclines her to look harder but that sends her reeling and stammering to speak. Mariah misreads Lucy's stammer (which happens in the place of outward "expressiveness" and cognitive clarity), her bitten tongue, the tongue she used to recite the unnamed-but-alluded-to Wordsworth poem before an audience as a child—a story, note, that she has told Mariah prior to this scene, and as a memory of a trauma. Mariah, however, commands a specific emotional response from Lucy—one in the vein of what Rei Terada calls "the expressive hypothesis"—that Lucy will not give. Mariah misreads Lucy as "Echo" who will bounce back *her feelings for* the daffodils to her, such that Mariah perhaps imagines herself not even as Narcissus, but as Ovid. Lucy does not and, further, refuses Mariah's embrace of comfort for the emotion she cannot read properly on Lucy's face. Lucy refuses any fellow feeling. I must underscore that Lucy is expected to emote—to be moved—in language along whitened lines of expression. And she does not. As we proceed, we will read how misnaming and disfiguration function in the representations of how she does not.

In *Feeling in Theory: Emotion After the "Death of the Subject,"* Terada writes of her conceptualization of the term I used above, the "expressive hypothesis":

> Although people rarely advocate expression as such, however, current discussions of emotion are ubiquitously expressive. The purpose of expression tropes is to extrapolate a human subject circularly from the phenomenon of emotion. The claim that emotion requires a subject—thus we can see we're subjects, since we have emotions—creates the illusion of subjectivity rather than showing evidence of it. This sleight of mind, in which "expression" serves as the distracting handkerchief, strikes me as self-serving. It is this relatively large complex of circularity, naturalization, and inversion which I refer to as the *expressive hypothesis.* To object to the expressive hypothesis or any other mechanism of the ideology of emotion is not to discredit emotion, but to extricate it from expedient mythologies."[24]

Prior to this passage, Terada has already traced how the etymology of emotion, *e + movere,* is read to show "something lifted from a depth to a surface."[25] A "lif[t]" "expedite[d]" by "[v]ocal and facial diaphaneity" which bears "illusionistic witness" of "the subject."[26] This emotional "lift" from depth to surface retraces the *de profundis* conception of creation and matter, rather than its more materially unwieldy foe, *creatio ex nihilo.*[27] In other words, the standard expectation of emotionality is both that it moves outward and that the outwardness bears the discernible resemblance of an irrepressible *immediacy* of feeling about *an X* that, in its "depth," is authentic, *true,* nay, "poetic." Its surfacing is part of the conservation of the matter of subjective coherence.

The scene that I cited at length above, and am reading through Mariah's expectation of a specific "auto-affective" and circular expressive procedure, is not the *first* daffodils scene, but the *third.* Some ten pages earlier in the novel, so, not at that encounter with the "real" daffodils, but with Mariah's suggestion of going to see them, Lucy describes herself as "two-faced" and recounts her first encounter with "daffodils." She does so in conjunction with what, after Paul de Man, I read as her disfiguration of Wordsworth's poem, "I Wandered Lonely as a Cloud."[28] The encounter with the real daffodils is *horrible* because of their colonial, linguistically and metaphorically regulatory signification. One could point out here that the graphemic, *i.e.,* writing, precedes experience, and/or "the essence" of the daffodil *is haunted by* its mediation and representation (or vice versa), or even that the daffodils *mean* mediation. But I want to emphasize these two thoughts in this reading: 1. Lucy, the teenager working as an *au pair* (that term, *au pair,* is supposed to mean, *on equal terms,* so we are using it in quotations) is not gentle with not only her employer Mariah's feelings about daffodils but also Mariah's "auto-affective" and audio-phonic[29] expectations that Lucy will express and emote according to *her* wishes about seeing the *real* flowers, *en masse,* at that, and that the seeing of the real flowers will magically undo the colonial damage of which they are synecdochal; and 2. Her refusal to express and emote as Mariah expects only comes after the memory of having memorized the poem and recited it perfectly.

As a child, Lucy recited what the reader assumes from contextual clues is "I Wandered Lonely as a Cloud." She remembers having hated the poem, *and* having hated the auditorium of parents', teachers', and her fellow pupils' approving reactions to her public performance of it. But she did not say, upon first, second, or who knows how many readings prior to the recitation, Fuck this poem, fuck this man Wordsworth, and fuck this performance. No, she memorized the poem, recited it stirringly, apparently, at Queen Victoria's Girls' School, and is heartily congratulated with applause and "an enthusiasm that surprised" her.[30] After which she notes that she is "two-faced." "I was then at the height of my two-facedness: that is, outside I seemed one way, inside I was another; outside false, inside true. And so I made pleasant little noises that showed both modesty and appreciation, but inside I was making a vow to erase from my mind, line by line, every word of that poem."[31] One does not read the trope here of colonization having some "upside," some silver subjective lining, like the humanistic arc whereby the structurally tortured good student who flails nevertheless *becomes* a good person. Having "good" grammar and stirring proper public emotion does not make Lucy into a subject with "integrity," or who expresses emotions as expected. Her "internalization" of the poem rather undoes the subjective presumptions of her memorization of it. She is not an obedient citizen or dutiful daughter of the supposed history of "liberty" that is the backdrop to Wordsworth's sensory encounters with "nature"/"daffodils," but rather "two-faced," "false," and distrustful.

Perhaps some of this explains why "Wordsworth" is never named in *Lucy*; "I Wandered Lonely as a Cloud" is never properly named; the signifiers of Romantic Poetry and British colonial education, none of that is named as such on the pages of the novel, neither in "outward" dialogue nor in the interior account of Lucy's memory of public recitation of that poem—or some poem that one imagines is that poem.[32] The violence that is claimed is that of rote memorization involving a signifier related to a phenomenon that Lucy has not seen. The tension between her two faces configures the tension of outside and inside, expressed and un-expressed. Her two-facedness also generates the disfiguration of the Wordsworth poem in that it is only *there* in the novel through the effacement of saying colonialism which is, instead, articulated through the words, *the poem* and *daffodils.* Additionally, the hyper-*personifying* of Lucy as having two faces is not *humanizing,* but vexing.[33] A *face* does not ensure humanization, nor does humanization auto-immunize the Blackened against anti-Blackness. It is obvious that one should read the daffodils encounter in some connection with the account of the memory of the daffodils poem recitation scene. And I would re-direct us to the scene that recalls Lucy's mother's claim that she named her for Lucifer, which is also to say, Satan, a noun that was first a verb in Hebrew—meaning, *stands in your way,* or *blocks the way of.*[34] Out of Lucy's "two-faced" (and "fork-tongued"?) mouth, the encounter with *daffodils* enacts not a self-fulfilled expression but an effacement, if not defacement, that situates *the poem* in a *catachrestic chain* with *colonialism, slavery, Blackening*—words present in their pointed absence. Mariah, in any case, does not *listen* to what Lucy is saying (and un-saying). Recall that "What a history you have" is how she responds to seeing Lucy react "negatively" to the mere suggestion of seeing daffodils, and, one assumes, then sets about sublimating Lucy's cautionary tale. "I'm sorry about the poem," is how she echoes herself with a difference once standing in the botanical garden field of daffodils, "but I'm hoping you'll find them lovely all the same."[35] For Mariah really believes that the real daffodils will heal Lucy from her (un)real history, which is also to say, will release her, Mariah, from complicity in the violent history of the West, its metaphysics and mythopoetics. She thinks that there will be a remedy in the *immediacy* and *reality* (hers) of the "beauty" of the flowers. She thinks this, in part, because she does not apprehend even something as banal as *to say colonial history is to say trauma*, much less that there is no *remediation* for the violent anti-genealogy of *political and metaphysical Blackening*.

Some pages later, Mariah has taken Lucy and her daughters, the girls in Lucy's charge, *sans* husband Lewis, out to the family's country estate. There, in another moment of tension, Mariah will say to Lucy that "I was looking forward to telling you that I have Indian blood, that the reason I'm so good at catching fish and hunting birds and roasting corn ... is that I have Indian blood."[36] Lucy "ruins" this for Mariah, too, asking in reply, "How do you get to be the sort of victor who can claim to be the vanquished also"?[37] She undoes her racial fable, which I argue is perhaps less immediately discernibly grounded in a fundamental anti-Blackness. Mariah's self-representation and play with "Indian blood" fictionally metonymizes her imagined relationship to land and, let's say, "activities" that are seeming extensions of her natal and aboriginal emergence from that land (i.e., fishing, hunting, corn-roasting). As benign as Mariah's articulation of herself as "Indian" might seem, this tropological collapsing of the Indian into land (in the Americas) can be traced to, at least, the mid-sixteenth-century Spanish Enlightenment debates at Valladolid around the enslave-ability, capacity to reason, and the justification or lack of justification for going to war against (the catachresis that is) the "Indians" of the New World. Such a debate, as Frank Wilderson III has shown, did not take place with regards to the African. What historian María Elena Martínez has shown at great length was crucial to that violent utopian argument of anthropomorphizing New World land as Indian and juridically humanizing the Indian as land-steward in need of proper, Petrine Christian patrons is the "natal alienation," Blackening, emptying of capacity to reason, and irredeemable en-fleshment of the enslaved of African descent.[38] One may accuse me here, because her name is Mariah and not María, of attempting to make a transnational or trans-linguistic "Indian." Rather, I draw from Martínez to observe that Lucy, whose mother is from Dominica and is of Carib and African descent, has a history but that it is not synonymous with a "genealogy." Semantically and in Mariah's experience of the "life-world," Lucy would serve the self-satisfied function of relation that thrives-off of the dispossessions of the Blackened other; it is this that Lucy points to and refuses to then *comfort* Mariah about, which is the perverse expectation.

On their train ride out to the inherited country estate, Mariah laments the loss of marshes in that region due to development and pollution. She gestures, also, to the fields of high grasses blowing in the breeze. Lucy does not understand Mariah's affect about either the loss or the plenitude (or the notion of loss preceded by a notion of plenitude as a "personal" matter). She sees these fields and thinks, what a relief that she is not the one who must labor to clear them.[39] Mariah sees them and rehearses a liberal rhetoric that re-colonizes "nature" in the lament of the "loss" of "nature" as she has known it. Pathos, again, marks the affective-ontic framework of whiteness. To vitalize herself, Mariah renders herself elusively part "Indian," and un-ironically implies that Lucy is not and cannot be "part Indian," and that she, as one perceivably Black, *is not* of the land—that land or any land. While Mariah is incurious about Lucy's actual Carib ancestry, Lucy is figuratively important to Mariah's compulsion to insert herself and her conception of loss into the imagined place of the losses of the other, which is a mode of evacuating them of their history.

I would emphasize for the purposes of our reading that Mariah again seeks Echo in reply to her claim of "Indian blood." This "Indian blood" country estate scene is an encore with a difference of the botanical garden daffodils scene which was an encore of the scene of Lucy recounting to Mariah the (supplemental) "primal" poetry scene of trauma. Repeatedly, the auto-affection of one character installs the expectation of the other character's spoken, verbatim repetition of what she (the One) feels about phenomena and the world. And I wonder, by now and by way of Lucifer as a framework that *gets in the way of*, about Echo, not as another way to say relation, but rather as relation's stammering *suspension*, if not its rupture and severance. Which follows on my reading of Lucy's "What did you say?" to her mother, not as marking disorientation given an overload of meanings, but rather as enacting a blockage of any redemptive aspiration for herself, a blockage that opens her paradoxical "relation" to "the fallen," which may be another way to say *incommensurability*.

Echo as echoing relation's *rupture* rather than serving as its notary elucidates something that Frank Wilderson III's second chapter in *Red, White, and Black*, called "The Narcissistic Slave," argues via Frantz Fanon and in contention with Jacques Lacan. I will be unforgivably brief with this summary. Wilderson builds on Lacan's insight that "alienation [is] the structuring modality of subjectivity,"[40] and goes on to theorize *the incommensurability*, we might also say the incommunicability—the un-commerce—between the subject underwritten by its alienation (i.e., the Human/White/junior partners of white civil society) and "the Blackened position." (Note that he does not write Blackened *subject* position there.) Alienation "is a grammar underwriting all manner of relationality," Wilderson writes, "whether narcissistic (egoic, empty speech) or liberated (full speech). But it is not a grammar that underwrites, much less explains, the absence of relationality."[41] Whereas alienation gives some nonBlack subject positions gendered nuance, gets some nonBlack subject positions lauded, laid, published—in what Gayatri Spivak calls "the multiculturalist masquerade of the privileged as the disenfranchised, or their liberator,"[42] and in what Wilderson calls "a multicultural paradigm that takes an interest in an insufficiently critical comparative analysis … in pursuit of a coalition politics … which, by its very nature, crowds out and forecloses the Slave's grammar of suffering,"[43] and it—the grammar of alienation's relationality—may speak the difference of contingent violence, however it forecloses accounts of how to think about the Blackened position produced through the gratuitous violence of "fungibility," not that of exploitation. It does not push our thinking about what to do with ground not habitable or held in common in the world.

Such ground readily brings us back to the "daffodils scene" anew, in which Lucy's stammer gives way to her speech as a Black Narcissus, which here is also to say, the Grim Reaper, Death's collector. In passages that we now apprehend as enacting a suspension of relation, or pointing to how it was always already impossible outside of an imaginary, romanticized, fantasy realm, not only with Mariah, but also with the Romantic tradition and Wordsworth's "host, of daffodils," a metaphor for a certain poetic and colonial subjectivizing procedure that Lucy does not take to mean what it has been read to mean (i.e., eventual and whitened freedom), Lucy shuts down the false comfort (for some) of proximity. She does not speak a faux-liberated rhetoric. The ground slips out from under Mariah's expectations of the givenness of relation, world, perceptual and historical compatibility, communicability of shared affect, and affective solidarity. Lucy's strange and inhospitable inheritance of *narcissi* through her English colonial education is not a metaphor for relationality, but for haunting.

After Mariah says that stuff about "Indian blood" to Lucy, Lucy asks rhetorically and devastatingly, and in accord with Spivak's and Wilderson's language above, "How do you get to be the sort of victor who can claim to be the vanquished also"?[44] Mariah looks at Lucy for comfort from Lucy's words, "as if asking for relief, and I looked back, my face and my eyes hard; no matter what, I would not give it. I said, 'All along I have been wondering how you got to be the way you are."[45] This is where I read *Lucy* as offering a foreclosure of the emotional and linguistic assumptions of relation, where relation is not about the other and hospitality toward their difference, but in service of the violent and highly genealogized reproduction of self-sameness.

Conclusion

After Lucy tells Mariah of the first encounter with daffodils—i.e., with the poem, the event of public performance, and the rage of attempted erasure after the disturbing success of the recitation—she remembers having a recurrent nightmare of being engulfed by piles of daffodils. The nightmare reoccurs and morphs into a dream about cowboys chasing her down to kill her. These engulfing nightmares return us to the thematic of fallenness, and to the ethical and political insufficiency of the discourse of relation in configurations of anti-Blackness.

This chapter has been interested in reading Lucy's desire to kill *the host*, and, necessarily, its system of representation, out of a sensory encounter with the signifier, *daffodils*, as it is interested in the fact that neither Wordsworth's name nor "I Wandered Lonely as a Cloud" are uttered, and yet are disfigured. Is this a variation on what Terada has asserted about lyric, "If 'lyric' is a concept that will help us think, it's because it helps us think something besides lyric"?[46] The erased lyric poem helps us think the daffodils in a catachrestic chain that *lucifers*—blocks—the fellow feeling for which they were supposed to stand in.

Notes

1. Kincaid 1990, 29.

2. On *prosopopoeia*, see De Man 1986 (ch. 3), Chase 1986, and Terada 2001.

3. Terada 2009, 21.

4. See Sexton 2016, 5, and Derrida 1978, 27.

5. Spivak 1999, 430–1.

6. Kincaid 1990, 19.

7. Kincaid 1990, 19.

8. Kincaid 1990, 152.

9. Kincaid 1990, 152–3.

10. The full sentence from which I purloin is: "A statement of distrust is neither true or false: it is rather in the nature of a permanent hypothesis" (De Man 1979, 150).

11. De Man 1979, 150, and Terada 2009, 57.

12. Cooper 2022.

13. Cooper 2022.

14. Cooper 2022.

15. De Man 1983.

16. I am expediting insights, and a project, in some cases, of other scholars, regarding the relationship between history, narration, historicity, and onto-metaphysics. The list could be longer, but must include select works by: Edmund Husserl, Jacques Derrida, Ronald Mendoza de Jesús, Gayatri Chakravorty Spivak, Hayden White, and Ethan Kleinberg.

17. I would consider Cooper's argument regarding the "ante-binary" with Derrida's *Geschlecht* (2020) and several of Calvin Warren's essays on ontology, what he calls "onticide," and sexuality elsewhere: see Warren 2018.

18. Rancière 2004, 14.

19. Rancière 2004, 17.

20. Spillers 2003, 321.

21. See Wilderson III 2010 and Martínez 2004 and 2008. Regarding the "epidermal racial" schema, see Fanon 1952, 223, and 1967, 204.

22. Neyra 2020.

23. Kincaid 1990, 29–30.

24. Terada 2009, 11.

25. Terada 2009, 11.

26. Terada 2009, 13.

27. Cooper 2022.

28. Wordsworth 1807. Accessed via: https://www.poetryfoundation.org/poems/45521/i-wandered-lonely-as-a-cloud

29. Derrida 1976, 165–7.

30. Kincaid 1990, 18.

31. Kincaid 1990, 18.

32. In the recently published interview that she gave to Darryl Pinckney, Kincaid states that she has planted some twenty thousand (!) daffodils in her Vermont garden, and that she "suppose[s]" they are her "reconciliation with Wordsworth" (Kincaid 2022, 168). She also uses the metaphor of "road to Damascus" with reference to Wordsworth in that interview (179), which also takes up the idiom of literary heritage and genealogy. As I. Smith (2002) writes, Kincaid (a famous gardener) has also interviewed or said on the record that she dislikes daffodils. I do not take her first-person and not fictionalized word—in this interview or others, or in articles printed in the *New Yorker*, say—as "authentic" and/or in place of what I read in the novel. If anything, I find the resistances between these different articulations (about daffodils and/as Wordsworth) amusing, and only further motivating of my close readings.

33. León 2021, 64, and De Man 1978.

34. Thanks to my colleague at Wesleyan, Yaniv Feller, for this relay regarding the verb, and to the faculty fellows and student fellows of the Spring 2022 Wesleyan Center for the Humanities cohort for critical feedback on a talk related to this paper.

35. Kincaid 1990, 29–30.

36. Kincaid 1990, 40 and 41.

37. Kincaid 1990, 41.

38. See Martínez 2004 and 2008. I am torn between writing en-fleshment and something like en-bodiment here, but must take this up elsewhere.

39. Kincaid 1990, 33.

40. Wilderson III 2010, 73.

41. Wilderson III 2010, 73.

42. Spivak 1999, 176.

43. Wilderson III 2010, 57.

44. Kincaid 1990, 41.

45. Kincaid 1990, 41.

46. Terada 2008, 196.

PART III
FORMS (UN)BECOMING

CHAPTER 8
HERACLITUS STUTTERED
Victoria Wohl

We only live, only suspire
Consumed by either fire or fire.

T. S. Eliot, Little Gidding IV

Before it came to denote the universe, the word *kosmos* denoted adornment or an orderly arrangement. Heraclitus may have been the first to use the word in the sense of a world order, and his work shows an exceptionally tight connection between the aesthetic and the cosmological.[1] For Heraclitus the universe has a beautiful structure, one he self-consciously reproduces in the formal structure of his aphorisms. His term for both structures is *logos*, and the agreement (*homologia*) between his *logos* and the cosmic *logos* is one of the main aims and stakes of his philosophy. Both text and universe are characterized by exceptional symmetry, wholeness, and coherence, a unified metaphysical structure in which "all things are one" (B50). But every so often we find a rupture in this unity, a stutter in Heraclitus' *logos*. My chapter examines one such moment and traces its implications for Heraclitus' *kosmos* and for the history of philosophy more broadly.

My focus is the endlessly intriguing fragment B52:

αἰὼν παῖς ἐστι παίζων, πεσσεύων· παιδὸς ἡ βασιληίη.

Aiôn pais esti paizôn, pesseuôn; paidos hê basilêiê.
A lifetime is a child playing, playing checkers. The sovereignty belongs to the child.[2]

If ever Gilles Deleuze's adage that "the aphorism is interpretation and the art of interpreting" was true, it is true of this aphorism.[3] Nietzsche, who returned to this fragment again and again throughout his work, focuses on the first half of the sentence. Purely intuitive and hostile to reason, his Heraclitus was a poet of flux who "altogether denied being."[4] Emphasizing the ludic (*paizôn*), he takes the playing child to figure an immanent creative impulse of pure becoming: "as children and artists play, so plays the ever-living fire. It constructs and destroys, all in innocence. Such is the game that the aeon plays with itself."[5] Thus Nietzsche ignores the verb *pesseuôn*, transforming the game of checkers into the building and destroying of sandcastles, the cosmic play of coming-to-be and passing-away.[6]

While Nietzsche emphasizes *paizôn* and the creative/destructive force of becoming, Charles Kahn, Heraclitus' greatest modern reader, focuses on *pesseuôn*, the orderly rule-bound game. In the alternating moves of this game he sees a reference to the regular measures of the cosmos as it moves in its endless cycle of elemental transformation and the sequential kindling and quenching of the cosmic fire (B30).[7] In this reading, the second participle overwrites or corrects the first: behind or beyond mere child's-play, Kahn's philosopher sees the coherent and orderly structure of reality, the *kosmos* of the cosmos. The dynamics of the fragment thus reiterate not only the underlying structure of the universe but, as we will see, the process by which we come to comprehend it, that is, philosophy itself.

My interest is less in the ludic, random *paizôn* or the orderly, structured *pesseuôn* than in the stutter between them. This fragment's asyndetic syntax sets the two participles in a disjunctive conjunction that forbids us from privileging one over the other. On the one hand, this stutter is not mere baby-talk, a superfluous repetition (as Nietzsche's omission of *pesseuôn* might suggest). Leaving aside the exceptional care and artistry of Heraclitus' language in general, *pesseuôn* is required to produce the formal symmetry of the fragment (ABCCBA) and forms the hinge between two seven-syllable isocola. On the other hand, the stutter is not merely a self-correction, for if *pesseuôn* overwrites *paizôn* it does not fully erase it and *paizôn* is repeated in *paidos* (to which it is etymologically related) and in the alliterative play of plosives that continue right to the end of the line. Both participles are necessary and together— asyntactically juxtaposed, connected and separated by a mere breath—they produce a momentary hesitation in the tight chiasmus of this aphorism, a repetition-with-difference that makes it impossible to decide between *paizôn* and *pesseuôn*, random play and orderly structure.

How are we to understand this strange micro-phenomenon of form? In his essay "He Stuttered," Gilles Deleuze examines the stutter not as an accident of speech but as a particular mode of language, "a syntax in the process of becoming, a creation of syntax that gives birth to a foreign language within language, a grammar of disequilibrium."[8] Through its formal disruption and the threat of nonsense it introduces, stuttering releases a deterritorializing force within language and the possibility for new reterritorializations: the stutterer "carves out a nonpreexistent foreign language within his own language," and in this way not only stutters himself, but "makes the language as such stutter."[9] In the asyndeton of B52, I propose, we hear a stutter not only in Heraclitus' language (*logos*) but in the very structure of reality (*logos*) he propounds. This stutter deterritorializes Heraclitus' philosophy, disrupting the cohesion and regularity of his physical and metaphysical universe. It also deterritorializes a certain narrative of the history of philosophy, which imagines it as a maturation from error to truth. At the same time, however, in the rupture it creates, the stutter holds open a space for human life—*aiôn*— that is repeatedly closed in Heraclitus' metaphysics. It preserves that life as something unassimilable within philosophy but also generative of philosophy. In the stutter, Deleuze writes, "language in its entirety reaches the limit that marks its outside and makes it confront silence."[10] The stutter in B52 marks the limit of Heraclitus' philosophical language and suggests that the silence it confronts at that limit is the *aiôn* itself.

*   *   *

Heraclitus' *Peri Physeôs* presents both a physical and a metaphysical order of exceptional unity, coherence, and balance, physics and metaphysics being closely intermeshed for this philosopher. His fragments describe the cosmos as a cycle of physical transformation:

πυρὸς τροπαὶ πρῶτον θάλασσα, θαλάσσης δὲ τὸ μὲν ἥμισυ γῆ, τὸ δὲ ἥμισυ πρηστήρ ... <γῆ> θάλασσα διαχέεται, καὶ μετρέεται εἰς τὸν αὐτὸν λόγον, ὀκοῖος πρόσθεν ἦν ἢ γενέσθαι γῆ. (B31)

Turnings of fire: first sea, but of sea half is earth, half lightning-storm ... As earth sea is poured out, and it measures up (*metreetai*) to the same amount (*ton auton logon*) as it was before becoming earth.

This perpetual becoming does not mean that Heraclitus "altogether denied being," as Nietzsche claimed, nor is his cycle of transformation a multidirectional flux that erases all fixed identity or meaning, as Plato imagined.[11] The process follows a regular order and rhythm and "measures (*metreetai*) up to the same amount (*logon*)." Always changing but always returning to the same point, the "turnings of fire" form a circle of which, as Heraclitus says in another fragment, "the beginning and end are in common" (*xunon* B103).

This dynamic symmetry is reiterated in the formal structure of Heraclitus' aphorisms (B30):

κόσμον τόνδε, τὸν αὐτὸν ἀπάντων, οὔτε τις θεῶν οὔτε ἀνθρώπων ἐποίησεν, ἀλλ᾽ ἦν ἀεὶ καὶ ἔστιν καὶ ἔσται πῦρ ἀείζωον, ἁπτόμενον μέτρα καὶ ἀποσβεννύμενον μέτρα.

This cosmos, the same of all, no god nor man created, but it always (*aei*) was and is and will be fire ever-living (*aeizôon*), kindled in measure (*metra*) and extinguished in measure (*metra*).

"The same of all" (*ton auton hapantôn*) throughout the regular alternations (*metra*) of its kindling and extinguishing, this "ever-living" fire enacts change within sameness. We can feel the symmetry of the elemental transformation in the symmetry of the fragment, with its isometric antithesis (*oute tis theôn oute anthrôpôn*), tricolon polyptoton (*all' ên aei kai estin kai estai*), and balanced repetitions (*haptomenon metra kai aposbennumenon metra*). The fragment formally enacts the *kosmos* it describes. The eternal circling of cosmic transformation—fire-water-earth-water-fire—is also enacted in the chiastic structure that characterizes so many of Heraclitus' aphorisms, like B88 "these things, changing, are those and those, changing again, are these" (*tade gar metapesonta ekeina esti k'akeina palin metapesonta tauta*) or B10 "from all one and from one all" (*ek pantôn hen kai ex henos panta*).[12]

Heraclitus' formal symmetry is often understood as an artful mimesis: Heraclitus self-consciously makes form imitate content. But this understanding imports a dichotomy between ontic original and expressive copy alien to Heraclitus' thought. For him, language does not re-present reality as a second-order mimesis. Instead it shares in and therefore directly manifests reality's basic structure. This is suggested by Heraclitus' ambiguous use of *logos*. The term is introduced in the first lines of the first fragment:

τοῦ δὲ λόγου τοῦδ' ἐόντος ἀεὶ ἀξύνετοι γίνονται ἄνθρωποι καὶ πρόσθεν ἢ ἀκοῦσαι καὶ ἀκούσαντες τὸ πρῶτον· γινομένων γὰρ πάντων κατὰ τὸν λόγον τόνδε ἀπείροισιν ἐοίκασι, πειρώμενοι καὶ ἐπέων καὶ ἔργων τοιούτων, ὁκοίων ἐγὼ διηγεῦμαι κατὰ φύσιν διαιρέων ἕκαστον καὶ φράζων ὅκως ἔχει. τοὺς δὲ ἄλλους ἀνθρώπους λανθάνει ὁκόσα ἐγερθέντες ποιοῦσιν, ὅκωπερ ὁκόσα εὕδοντες ἐπιλανθάνονται.

Of this *logos* that is always (*aei*) mortals are uncomprehending (*axunetoi*), both before they have heard it and when they have first heard it. Though all things come about in accordance with this *logos* they are like people without experience even when they experience such words and deeds as I expound, distinguishing each thing according to its nature and saying how it is. But other men are not aware of what they do when they are awake, just as they forget what they do when asleep.

Appearing at the opening of Heraclitus' book as a kind of authorial *sphragis*, "this *logos*" seems to refer to the work we are about to read, the "words and deeds" the philosopher will expound.[13] But in its eternal being (*eontos aei*) this *logos* also signifies the fundamental order of the physical and metaphysical universe of which Heraclitus' own *logos* will be an account, what he calls in B2 "the common *logos*" (*xunos logos*: *xun-* is a variant of *sun-*). Heraclitus' project is to align these two *logoi*: conveying cosmic truths to uncomprehending (*axunetoi*) mortals, he will bring their comprehension (*xunesis*) together with the common (*xunos*) *logos*, on the assumption that "to think (*phroneein*) is common (*xunon*) to all" (B113). This *homologia*—this unison of human and cosmic *logos*—is Heraclitus' definition of wisdom (*to sophon*): "Having listened not to me but to the *logos*, it is wise (*sophon*) to agree (*homologein*) that all things are one" (B50).

Kahn's reading of B52 annexes that fragment to Heraclitus' vision of cosmic and aesthetic order and reenacts the drive toward *xunesis* of the *xunos logos* that motivates his philosophical discourse. *Pesseuôn*, for Kahn, is a correction of *paizôn*: what initially seemed like random child's play is gradually understood to be the eternal order of the cosmos, an order expressed semantically by the image of the board game and instantiated syntactically in the tightly woven chiasmus of the aphorism as a whole. In this reading, the trope of self-correction, epanorthosis, masquerades as an admission of error but is in fact a proclamation of mastery. Indeed, it stages the attainment of that philosophical mastery in its linear movement from mere *doxa*, via riddling paradox, to orthodoxy. Children are exemplars of ignorance elsewhere in Heraclitus: mortal opinions (*anthrôpina doxasmata*) are compared to "children's toys" (*paidôn athurmata* B70), and to accept things at face value is to take them "as children from parents" (*paidas tokeônôn* B74).[14] B52's self-conscious shift from childish ignorance (*pais paizôn*) to insight into the fundamental order of reality (*pesseuôn*) would seem to enact the philosophical process of comprehension, *xunesis*, the end of which is a philosophical mastery figured as sovereignty, *basilêiê*.[15] The child becomes a man and a king.

This narrative of rectification, maturation, and mastery is appealing, perhaps especially for a philosopher. But the form of the fragment disrupts this teleological narrative, for as I suggested earlier, the repetition of *pais* in *paidos* means that *pesseuôn* does not completely overwrite *paizôn* and the child never matures into adulthood. In fact, we might say that the correction (*paizôn > pesseuôn*) is itself corrected in the royal reassertion of the child (*pesseuôn > paidos basilêiê*). Moreover, if *pesseuôn* represents the ultimate comprehension (*xunesis*), the communion with the common *logos* that is the culmination of Heraclitus' teaching, it is noteworthy that this philosophically freighted word is framed by asyndeton on both sides, marked in the modern text by the comma and interpunct. Punctuation was rare in archaic Greek orthography and it is likely that the participle would have originally been separated from the surrounding words, if at all, only by a space.[16] The punctuation marks, probably added to the text of Hippolytus in which the fragment is quoted in the Middle Ages, formalize that space but do not bridge it. In this sense, they function like dashes, which, as Theodor Adorno writes, "capture both connection and detachment": "in the dash, thought becomes aware of its fragmentary character."[17] Adorno's comments have been developed by Rebecca Comay and Frank Ruda in their brilliant study of Hegel's dashes. A mark of both interruption and continuity, its syntax inherently ambiguous and under-determined, the dash, they observe, "induces a moment of essential uncertainty in reading." It is the orthographic mark of the stutter.[18]

The punctuation in B52 acts as a conceptual dash inscribing an ambiguous asyndeton within Heraclitus' text and thought around the word *pesseuôn*. Now, asyndeton is not uncommon in Heraclitus. It occurs in particular in lists of unconnected opposites in fragments that express the fundamental unity of those opposites, such as B10: "Conjunctions (*sunapsies*): wholes and not wholes, converging diverging, consonant dissonant, and from all one and from one all" (B10).[19] In these fragments, the asyndetic juxtaposition of opposites forms a microcosmic parallel to Heraclitus' book as a whole, which seems to have been composed not as a continuous stream of prose but as a series of disconnected aphorisms tightly interlaced through verbal, structural, and imagistic resonances, making the whole book an example of Heraclitus' central thesis that "all things are one" (B50).[20] But *paizôn* and *pesseuôn*, *pesseuôn* and *paidos* are not clearly opposites in the way consonant and dissonant are, nor are they unified through an overarching "conjunction" (*sunapsis*). The asyndeton between them thus suggests not an antithesis synthesized into cosmic *xunesis* but instead a rupture within Heraclitus' unified cosmos, a slight "dash" preventing the closure and coherence required to constitute it *as* a cosmos.

This dash "induces a moment of essential uncertainty," both epistemological and ontological, within Heraclitus' *xunos logos*. The asyndeton between *paizôn* and *pesseuôn* marks the rift between human understanding and metaphysical reality. B1 suggests that this rift is unbridgeable: "Of this *logos* that is always mortals are uncomprehending" (*tou de logou toud' eontos aei axunetoi ginontai anthrôpoi*). As Aristotle noted, the ambiguous placement of *aei* leaves it unclear whether it is the *logos* that is eternal or the ignorance of mortals or both.[21] This ambiguous *aei* eternalizes the schism between *axunetoi anthrôpoi* and the *xunos logos*, but it also sutures the two in a way that promises a possible overcoming of that schism, and the final lines of the fragment hold out hope that

Heraclitus' words may wake his listeners from the slumber of ignorance. B52, by contrast, offers no bridge between human understanding and the cosmic order. Instead its asyndeton holds them in a tense proximity that will never yield to synthesis or *xunesis*. Moreover, the asyndeton marks the limit of Heraclitus' unifying project in ontological terms too, for how can the *logos* be truly common if it does not include the understanding of mortals? Human *axunesia* risks negating (*a–*) the *xunon*, creating a break in the circle whose beginning and end are in common (*xunon*, B103). The asyndetic syntax of B52 thus holds open a gap not only between human comprehension and metaphysical reality but also within that reality itself. An interval of unassimilable difference, the stutter between the participles introduces a foreign element into Heraclitus' exquisitely synthetic universe, an element that resists the cosmic arithmetic by which "all things are one" (B50). It is not just Heraclitus' *logos* that stutters but the cosmic *logos* itself.

"It's easy to stammer," note Deleuze and Guattari, "but making language itself stammer is a different affair; it involves placing all linguistic, and even nonlinguistic, elements in variation, both variables of expression and variables of content."[22] Variables of expression: the fragment disorders the ubiquitous form of the chiasmus, that linguistic manifestation of cosmic balance. Formally B52 is a chiasmus (ABCC'B'A'), but its syntactical chain is broken by the two asyndeta. Moreover, the formal repetitions of the chiasmus belie semantic difference. In most of Heraclitus' chiastic aphorisms form and meaning are closely aligned: in the ABB'A' structure of a phrase like "from all one and from one all" (*ek pantôn hen kai ex henos panta*, B10), A = A' and B = B'.[23] In B52's chiasmus, by contrast, *paizôn* (C) returns in the different form of *pesseuôn* (C') and *aiôn* (A) in the unrelated form of *basilêiê* (A'). The structural symmetry of the fragment does not change the fact that semantically C ≠ C' and A ≠ A'.[24]

Variables of content: the stutter of B52 disrupts the very concept of *basileia* that is, on Kahn's reading, the aphorism's point. What is the nature of this sovereignty? The only other occurrence of *basileus* comes in B53:

Πόλεμος πάντων μὲν πατήρ ἐστι, πάντων δὲ βασιλεύς, καὶ τοὺς μὲν θεοὺς ἔδειξε τοὺς δὲ ἀνθρώπους, τοὺς μὲν δούλους ἐποίησε τοὺς δὲ ἐλευθέρους.

War is father of all and king of all, and he has revealed some as gods and some as men, he has made some slaves and some free.

This fragment organizes the entire cosmos in a totalizing structure of opposition mirrored in the almost-oppressive symmetry of the fragment, with its triple *men-de* construction. *Polemos* is one name for the singular principle that organizes Heraclitus' cosmos, also known as thunderbolt (B64), fire or gold (B90), the god (B67), *to sophon* or Zeus (B32, cf. B41). This sovereign principle unites opposites and in this way ensures the coherence of the cosmos, the truth that "all things are one" (B50). Thus at B67 "the god is day night, winter summer, war peace, satiety starvation." The standard reading of B52 would seem to reaffirm this unitary metaphysics. Its game of *pessoi* imposes the structured oppositions—the *men/de* of winner and loser—revealed by the father and king of all, War. We take the "king piece" when we recognize *aiôn* as another name for "the one."[25] To win the cosmic game is to accede to this metaphysical sovereignty.

But the sovereignty in B52 belongs not to "the father of all," as in B53, but to the child. The child's victory in the game dethrones the father-king and interjects an element of chance into his hierarchical universe.[26] The child's unstructured play bears the possibility not merely of reversing the binarism of divine and human, slave and free revealed by Polemos but of eliminating that dyadic structure entirely. The child's *paizôn* follows a different logic than the game of Polemos. It neither reveals hierarchical binaries nor unifies opposites into a sovereign singularity. Its sovereignty does not fit easily into Heraclitus' metaphysical politics. Heraclitus' stutter thus deterritorializes both his philosophical content and its formal expression. It introduces an ambiguous dash in his coherent and unitary cosmos, a break in the circle, and an element of unassimilable difference within its eternal repetition of "the same *logos*" (*ton auton logon*, B31).

B52 names this unassimilable element *aiôn*. *Aiôn* denotes a lifespan, a period of vitality that ends in death. Although it was related to *aei* and later became synonymous with it, *aiôn* denotes a temporality quite distinct from *aei*'s eternity: it is the duration of a human life seen from the perspective of its end.[27] In Heraclitus, this brief moment is absorbed into the eternity of the cosmic cycle in a way that risks ellipsing human life altogether. Upon death the soul is drawn into the elemental cycle of transformation: "For souls (*psuchai*) it is death to become water, for water it is death to become earth; from earth water is born, from water soul (*psuchê*)" (B36). In early Greek, *psuchê*—the vital force of a life—is a near-synonym of *aiôn*.[28] A physical substance associated with fire and air, the *psuchê* that animates us during life is for Heraclitus exhaled at death and joins the revolution of the elements; our individual lives (*psuchai*) are thus transformed into a singular material element (*psuchê*). The momentary spark of our life is absorbed in the end into the eternal cosmic fire.[29]

Through this conflagration we become immortal, as Heraclitus suggests in B29:

αἱρεῦνται γὰρ ἓν ἀντὶ ἁπάντων οἱ ἄριστοι, κλέος ἀέναον θνητῶν· οἱ δὲ πολλοὶ κεκόρηνται ὅκωσπερ κτήνεα.

The best men choose one thing in exchange for everything: glory ever-flowing (*aenaon*) among men. But the many are sated like cattle.

Kahn reads this fragment as an allusion to Achilles' choice in the *Iliad* between undying *kleos* ("glory") and a long but finite life.[30] Heraclitus integrates this theme into his cosmology: the adjective *aenaon* ("ever-flowing") connects *kleos* to the "ever-living" (*aeizôon*) fire of B30 and the *logos* that exists *aei* of B1. Through this echo, *kleos aenaon* connects the mortal *aiôn*—a brief life ending in death—to the *aei* of the cosmic cycle. In making this choice of "one thing in exchange for everything," "the best men" exercise a philosophical *prohairesis* that aligns with the principle of cosmic sovereignty, the union of all things under one, as in B90's "exchange of all things for fire and fire for all things." Choosing their unity with this union, they enact a *xunesis* that will be their ever-living glory.

But this union comes at a high price, for one of the things given up in this exchange is the human experience of life, which is reduced in B29 to the brute satiety of the herd. What it means to trade all things for one is limned in fragment B88:

ταὐτό τ' ἔνι ζῶν καὶ τεθνηκὸς καὶ [τὸ] ἐγρηγορὸς καὶ καθεῦδον καὶ νέον καὶ γηραιόν· τάδε γὰρ μεταπεσόντα ἐκεῖνά ἐστι κἀκεῖνα πάλιν μεταπεσόντα ταῦτα.

The same (*t'auto*) within: living and being dead and being awake and sleeping and young and old. For these things, changing (*metapesonta*), are those and those, changing (*metapesonta*) again, are these.[31]

The first sentence measures out the finite arc of a human lifespan. The leisurely polysyndeton (and … and … and) counts off the sequential moments and experiences that make up an individual *aiôn*. But "the same within" erases these distinctions and compresses the human narrative into an atemporal simultaneity of "the same" (*t'auto*). That unity is eternalized in the chiasmus of the second sentence. Kahn connects *metapesonta* in this fragment to the game of *pessoi* in B52: the game is, on his view, precisely this orderly transformation of the elements.[32] This fragment thus provides the template for his teleological reading of B52 and also enacts its consequences through its formal structure: youth and old age, life and death are collapsed in the sovereignty of the same, our lived *aiôn* obliterated in the endless circling of the cosmic chiasmus.

In this process death becomes an eternal life, but by the same token, life—the individual *aiôn*—becomes a kind of death, as fragment B62 spells out:

ἀθάνατοι θνητοί, θνητοὶ ἀθάνατοι, ζῶντες τὸν ἐκείνων θάνατον, τὸν δὲ ἐκείνων βίον τεθνεῶτες.
Immortals mortals, mortals immortals, living the others' death, dying the others' life.

In this supremely mysterious fragment, the chiasmus implodes, voiding the difference between life and death, mortals and immortals. The sequence of living and dying recalls the cosmic cycle, which is described in B36 as a cycle of material birth and death. But this aphorism, like B88, collapses those sequential states into a single static condition, a condition that (in the absence of a finite verb) is interminable. In its asyndetic juxtaposition of opposites, the signifiers that define human existence lose their meaning: mortals and immortals alike are robbed of their proper being as each lives/dies the death/life of the other. Death is gone but so too is the *aiôn*, the concept of human existence as a duration of life punctuated by death. We may become immortal in the blaze of cosmic eternity, but we lose our lives in the fire.

This is the ambiguous glory "the best men" gain in the exchange of all things for one. Alongside *kleos*, the other traditional means of posthumous survival and symbolic immortality for ancient Greeks was reproduction. Heraclitus turns reproduction, too, into a choice of death, as Clement observes:

Ἡ. γοῦν κακίζων φαίνεται τὴν γένεσιν, ἐπειδὰν φῇ· γενόμενοι ζώειν ἐθέλουσι μόρους τ᾽ ἔχειν, [μᾶλλον δὲ ἀναπαύεσθαι], καὶ παῖδας καταλείπουσι μόρους γενέσθαι. (B20)

Heraclitus reproaches generation when he says "once born, they want to live and to have their destiny (*moroi*), [or rather, to pause] and they leave behind them children to be their doom (*moroi*)."

In the desire for children, the life-instinct becomes a death-wish. The chiastic structure of the fragment connects it to the cosmic cycle and the eternal kindling and quenching of its ever-living fire. But reproduction does not give the individual a share in that cosmic eternity. Instead, the aphorism's play on the double meaning of *moros* figures reproduction as a cycle of doom, as the morbidity of generation (*morous genesthai*) obliterates not just the hope for immortality, but even the modest desire to live out one's allotted lifespan (*morous t'echein*).[33] The cycle of reproduction, like the cosmic cycle, reiterates sameness, but in the form not of life but of death: in the fragment's punning and ring composition, destiny (*moros*) returns as doom (*moros*) and birth (*genomenoi*) generates death (*morous genesthai*). The child figures that morbid vision.[34]

This brings us back to B52 and the child *aiôn*. B52's juxtaposition of *paizôn* and *pesseuôn* would seem to present the two alternative forms of immortality, the dead-end of the reproductive cycle and the immortal glory of communion with the cosmic cycle, and to enact a shift from the one to the other.[35] The fragment itself seems to enact the *prohairesis* of "all things for one" as our brief and terminal *aiôn*—as ephemeral as youth itself—is exchanged for the sovereign immortality won through participation in the cosmic game. But again that asyndetic pause between *paizôn* and *pesseuôn* should give us pause. It interposes something that refuses to be assimilated to the cosmic fire. We could call that something a death-drive or a life-instinct or simply, as Clement does in quoting B20, a "pause": "once born, they want to live and to have their destiny or rather," he interjects, "to pause, and they leave behind them children to be their doom."[36] Life, the life-instinct (*zôein ethelousi*), is a mere pause between doom and doom. Clement's interpolation intuits the place of human life in Heraclitus' cosmos: a momentary interval, a brief dash, in the eternal revolution of the cosmos.

What Clement articulates expressly, B52 enacts in its stutter. Its asyndetic break reclaims the "pause" that is human life. If, as T. S. Eliot says, "we only live, only suspire, consumed by either fire or fire," the asyndeton is the fragile moment of that suspiration.[37] The stutter's "grammar of equilibrium" reterritorializes both reproduction as a cycle of doom and the glorious immortality of our cosmic conflagration. It not only preserves a breathing-space within these hermetic circles of the same but proclaims the temporary sovereignty of human life in its difference from the cosmic cycle. In this way it posits the *aiôn*—human life—as a "foreign" element in Heraclitus' physics and metaphysics, the one thing that resists its eternal symmetry, that refuses to be exchanged for fire.

This foreign element reterritorializes not only Heraclitus' philosophy but the history of philosophy of which it is a part. I suggested earlier that Kahn's reading of *paizôn, pesseuôn* as an epanorthosis turns fragment B52 into a performance of philosophical enlightenment: it enacts the movement from erroneous *doxa*—the *doxasmata* that Heraclitus compares to children's toys (B70)—to the orthodoxy of wisdom and the philosopher as the sovereign subject of knowledge. In this way, as we have seen, the fragment achieves the implicit promise of the opening sentence of Heraclitus' book, by means of his own *logos* to bring *axunetoi* mortals to comprehension of and communion with the *xunos logos*. This pedagogical fantasy is expressed in Heraclitus' own authorial voice in B50:

οὐκ ἐμοῦ, ἀλλὰ τοῦ λόγου ἀκούσαντας ὁμολογεῖν σοφόν ἐστιν ἓν πάντα εἶναι.

Having listened not to me but to the *logos*, it is wise (*sophon*) to agree (*homologein*) that all things are one.

Wisdom is the *homologia* that marks humans' ultimate concurrence or harmony with the *logos* in the truth that all things are one. The aphorism is performative inasmuch as comprehending its meaning enacts that meaning, uniting the wise reader with a *sophia* that is itself unitary ("the wise is one," *hen to sophon*, B32, B41).

But the very aphorism that epitomizes that wisdom also contradicts it, for there is one thing that fails to join in the *homologia* of wisdom, the speaker himself (*emou*). Even as it articulates the wisdom of unity, B50 sounds a dissonance between Heraclitus' *logos* and the cosmic *logos*, reopening the very gap that Heraclitus' philosophy (from B1 on) attempts to close. Perhaps the antithesis "not to me but to the *logos*" circumvents that gap by simply circumventing Heraclitus' words to offer unmediated access to metaphysical reality. But this move merely compounds the aphorism's ironies. On the one hand, the instruction is impossible. The command to ignore Heraclitus is Heraclitus' own utterance; the accord of wisdom thus becomes a liar's paradox: to listen to the *logos* not Heraclitus is also to listen to Heraclitus not the *logos*. On the other hand, if it were possible to separate Heraclitus' *logos* from the eternal *logos* it would negate the wisdom that *logos* offers, the *homologia* that all things are one. In the ironic tension between the performative and the propositional, Heraclitus himself stutters in relation to his own most basic philosophical principles. Speaking "like a foreigner in the language in which he expresses himself," Heraclitus opens a schism between the philosophical *egô* and his theory.[38] That breach cannot be repaired by epanorthosis because it marks an interval not only between the speaker and his *logos* but within that very *logos*. The philosopher is himself the foreign element within his philosophical theory: he is the asyndeton.

This reading of B50 suggests that the irreducible interval between *paizôn* and *pesseuôn*, between human life and cosmic order, is not a failure to be overcome or corrected by philosophy but in fact is constitutive of philosophy. In *Metaphysics* I, Aristotle offers a brief genealogy of philosophy from its earliest beginnings in the empirical study of physical nature. As philosophy matures, it will take on its highest object—metaphysics—and also find its proper form. But "the earliest philosophy stammers (*psellizomenêi*) about everything, since it was young and just beginning."[39] The verb *psellizesthai*, which may be onomatopoeic, denotes a speech impediment associated with the language and play of children.[40] This philosophical phylogeny would seem to be recapitulated in the ontogeny of B52, as the stammering, playing child matures into a player—and victor—in the game of metaphysics. The fragment thus encapsulates the entire early history of philosophy, as Aristotle tells it.

And yet, as we have seen repeatedly, the structure of the fragment refuses this teleological trajectory. The stammer of philosophical baby-talk is not overcome but instead replicated in the stammering of the fragment as a whole: *pai-pai-pai*. In the line's complex repetitions, even *basilêiê* might be seen not as a sovereign victory over immature error but as a final stutter, softened and elongated, of the fragment's sonic reiteration of *pa, s,* and *ai*.[41] Read as a stutter rather than a correction, *paizôn pesseuôn* produces a radically different history of philosophy, a narrative not of the progressive evolution from ignorance to mastery, but of a persistent and generative hesitation between metaphysics and mere child's-play, between philosophical speech and random stammering, even between sense and nonsense—an uncertainty strongly felt in this fragment that so stubbornly resists clear interpretation.[42] The stutter of the playing child represents the history of philosophy not as a smooth developmental maturation or paternal lineage but as a process of discontinuity. In it philosophy, as Deleuze says, comes up against its limit and confronts silence. For Heraclitus, I have suggested, that silence at the edge of philosophical speech is human life. *Aiôn* cannot be spoken, it can only be stuttered. But that stuttering marks the first faltering baby-steps of philosophy.

Notes

1. On *kosmos* in ancient thought see Horky 2019 and on Heraclitus' use of the word, Kahn 1960, 224–7, and Schofield 2019, 70–2.

2. All fragments are cited from Diels and Kranz 1951. This fragment is quoted in Hippolytus' *Refutations* (9.9.4) along with many other passages chosen to illustrate Heraclitus' theory, as Hippolytus understands it. I follow Kahn (1983), Sassi (2018, 102), and others in assuming that Heraclitus' text was disseminated in writing, not orally based on the complex structure of fragments like B1 and B5 and the tradition that he deposited his book in the temple of Artemis (Diogenes Laertius 9.6). I agree with Deichgräber (1963, 5–13), however, that the text was meant to be read aloud and more than once.

3. Deleuze 2006, 31. See Wohlfart 1991, 124–49, for a history of interpretations of B52.

4. Nietzsche 1962, 51–2.

5. Nietzsche 1962, 62. On Nietzsche and Heraclitus, see Hershbell and Nimis 1979; Porter 2000, 250–1; Przybyslawski 2002; and Meyer 2014, esp. 34–74; on this fragment in particular, see the exhaustive study of Wohlfart 1991.

6. Nietzsche 1962, 62: "Transforming itself into water and earth, it builds towers of sand like a child at the seashore, piles them up and tramples them down." The simile of children making and destroying sand castles is found at *Iliad* 15.361–4 where it illustrates the ease with which Apollo destroys the Achaean wall. Nietzsche followed Bernays in connecting Heraclitus' fragment to that passage and transforming Heraclitus' rule-bound game into random and arbitrary play: see Wohlfart 1991, 94–101 and 132–3. Ellis (2021, 53–9) explores the fragment's antinomy from a Deleuzian and Bergsonian perspective, echoing in their terms Nietzsche's interpretation of the child as "a form of creative distribution that precedes the subsequent stratifications and limitations imposed by the state-organized board" (55n51).

7. Kahn 1979, 227–9. Cf. Plato, *Laws* 903c5 for the creator of the cosmos as a *pessoi*-player. *Pessoi* was a generic name for board games. Kurke (1999, 263–4), drawing on Kahn, believes this fragment refers specifically to the game of *pente grammai*, in which the two players vied to move the "king" piece from the "holy line" that divided the board. She thinks the game also involved dice, more like backgammon than modern checkers.

8. Deleuze 1997, 112 and 107. Cf. Deleuze and Guattari 1987, 100. Deleuze does not specify how he understands the stutter, whether as the repetition of a sound or a silence around certain sounds. The medical definition of stuttering encompasses a variety of symptoms that impede the normal fluency of speech. For the ancient understanding of stuttering, see below, note 40.

9. Deleuze 1997, 107. Albrecht-Crane (2011) offers a clear and accessible treatment of Deleuze's concept of the stutter. See also Gaudlitz 2010.

10. Deleuze 1997, 113.

11. Plato, *Cratylus* 402a, 411b–c, 439c–440d; cf. Aristotle, *Metaphysics* 1010a7–12 and 1078b12–17. Nietzsche too, however, stresses the symmetry of Heraclitus' universe: for the "contuitive god" there is no disequilibrium or injustice, only a balanced order of creation and destruction, like the child Aion building and destroying sandcastles (Nietzsche 1962, 61–2). Fragment B52 thus illustrates "law in becoming" (68): "what wonderful order, regularity and certainty manifested themselves in all coming-to-be" (71).

12. Cf. the final sentence of B1 and B21, B25, B26, B36, B90, B126.

13. Sextus Empiricus tells us this was the opening passage: *Against the Mathematicians* 7.132–3; cf. Aristotle, *Rhetoric* 1407b15–16. Sextus also quotes B2, which he says came shortly after B1. Otherwise the order of the fragments in Diels-Kranz's edition is pointedly arbitrary, alphabetical by source author.

14. Thus "a man is called infantile (*nêpios*) by a divinity, just as a child (*pais*) is by a man" (B79). Ellis (2021, 49–52) notes the unusual frequency of children in the fragments of Heraclitus. Focusing on B56, in which children stump Homer with the riddle of the lice, he proposes that children at play access a Deleuzian form of intuition through an embodied, multiple, and rhizomatic way of thinking.

15. This trajectory is replicated in Diogenes Laertius' biographical report that Heraclitus "was remarkable from childhood, and when he was young he used to say he knew nothing, but when he became an adult he claimed he knew everything" (9.5). Heraclitus himself was supposedly of royal lineage but he was said to have renounced the kingship to his brother (9.6).

16. Dilcher (1995, 137–8) believes that Heraclitus did use the interpunct to mark "an imperceptible transition from one assertion to the next … an uninterrupted flow of ideas which inherently belong together" (138). If that is true, Heraclitus expresses this connection through a grammar of literal disconnection: the interpunct—a non-signifying dot—replaces any connective particle and calls attention to its absence. Thus the mark seems rather to confirm the "general impression" Dilcher identifies "of disparateness … almost complete lack

of explicit interconnections between various sayings and parts of the doctrine" (134). On the conventions of punctuation in ancient texts, see Pfeiffer 1968, 179, and Renehan 1969, 75–6.

17. Adorno 1991, 95 and 93.

18. Comay and Ruda 2018, esp. 53–61. The quotation is on p. 7; cf. 55. They compare the dash to a stutter at Comay and Ruda 2018, 80, 108; cf. 94–9 on the comma, with reference to Deleuze's "He Stuttered." Their explication of the dash's uncertainty in Hegel's text resonates closely with my reading of Heraclitus: "This uncertainty connects to the most intractable questions of the whole Hegelian enterprise: totality and closure; continuity and transition; development and progress; identity and difference; beginnings and ends" (7).

19. *Sunapsies hola kai ouch'hola, sumpheromenon diapheromenon, sunaidon diaidon, kai ek pantôn hen kai ex henos panta*. The reading *sunapsies* is disputed, and some editors read *sullapsies* ("graspings"). Cf. B60, B62, B67, B111, B126. Lilja (1968, 93 and 97) identifies asyndeton as the most conspicuous feature of Heraclitus' sentence structure, noting that almost half of his main sentences are unconnected. Other examples of sentence-medial asyndeton she cites are B28, B55, B58.

20. Kahn 1979, 90. The assumption that Heraclitus wrote in aphorisms is based on the lack of connective particles in the extant fragments and on his ancient reputation for "brevity" (Diogenes Laertius 9.7). Demetrius, *On Style* 191–2 condemns the obscurity produced "when the whole is asyndetic and dispersed" (*to de asundeton kai dialelumenon holon*); Theophrastus' diagnosis of "melancholia" (i.e., inconsistency) may speak to the same qualities (Diogenes Laertius 9.6).

21. Aristotle, *Rhetoric* 1407b11–18.

22. Deleuze and Guattari 1987, 98.

23. Another clear example is B90: "All things are exchange for fire and fire for all things, just as goods for gold and gold for goods" (πυρός τε ἀνταμοιβὴ τὰ πάντα καὶ πῦρ ἁπάντων ὅκωσπερ χρυσοῦ χρήματα καὶ χρημάτων χρυσός). Throughout the exchanges of this double chiasmus, gold and fire remain the same.

24. Vieira (2013) labels this structure, in which the first and last term are related but in tension, "bow composition" and sees it as a mimetic description of the union of opposites within a cosmic process that he takes to be rectilinear and reciprocal rather than circular. The equation of *aiôn* with *basilêiê* strains this structure.

25. Kahn 1979, 228: "It is obvious why the player possesses 'kingship', since the game is a cosmic one, and the player must be lord of the universe . . . The games played by Lifetime and by War have the same structure. Just as the bow, whose work is death, is named 'life' (*bios*), so the king of conflict and destruction can be called 'life-time' (*aiôn*)." Contrast Nietzsche 1962, 55: there is no winner; sovereignty is the everlasting strife of opposites. Kurke (1999, 260–70) explicates the political associations of *pessoi*, based in part on this fragment. Cf. B33: "law is also to obey the will of one."

26. Kahn (1979, 228–9) notes this possibility but presents it merely as "a paradoxical counterpart" to the wisdom of the cosmic principle. Diogenes Laertius (9.23) recounts that when the Ephesians asked Heraclitus to establish laws for them he refused to do so. He withdrew into the temple of Artemis and "played knucklebones with the children," replying to the Ephesians, "is it not better to do this than to engage in politics with you?" There the game— played in the temple where Heraclitus was said to have deposited his book (Diogenes Laertius 9.6)—is a clear displacement of politics.

27. Aristotle, *On the Sky* 279a24–6: its *aiôn* "is the end (*telos*) encompassing the time of the life (*zôês chronon*) of each creature, which nothing can exceed in accordance with nature." Keizer (2000) tracks the evolution of *aiôn*'s meaning from "life-span" (in Homer) to "the whole of

time" (in the fifth century) to the infinite time of the universe. Deleuze's conception of Aiôn as the empty or virtual non-present of the event, influenced by Stoicism, is hard to square with Heraclitus' usage (Deleuze 1990, 62–5 and 162–8, with a veiled allusion to Heraclitus at 164). Wohlfart (1991, 33–55) provides a detailed discussion of the meaning of the word in this fragment: he argues that we should hear *aei* (eternity as eternal recurrence) in *aiôn* (51); see also Couloubaritsis 1989, insisting on the link to both time and vitality.

28. Chantraine 1968, 1294–5; Rohde 1925, 3–54; and Snell 1953, 8–17. Homer links *psuchê* and *aiôn* at *Iliad* 9.408–15 and 16.453.

29. Cf. B118 "the dry soul is a spark (*augê*), wisest and best." (The text is uncertain, however.) On the material composition of Heraclitus' soul, see Betegh 2013.

30. Kahn 1979, 233–4. Cf. B24, B53 on death in battle.

31. The opening as Diels prints it is probably corrupt, and scholars are divided on how to understand τ' ἔνι. Laks and Most 2016 (D68) print γ' ἔνι and translate "there is the same within": see Laks 2015, 43. They attribute the second clause (*tade gar metapesonta ekeina esti k̓akeina palin metapesonta tauta*) to Ps.-Plutarch, who quotes the fragment. But the same pattern of paradoxical unity of opposites followed by chiasmus is also found in B10, B62, and B67, and I am inclined to think it is original. Bollack and Wismann (1972, 261) offer a subtle analysis of the temporality of the fragment, and Deichgräber (1963, 31–3) parses its meter, remarking on the structural similarity to B10 (35).

32. Kahn 1979, 227.

33. Ellis (2021, 49) rightly notes "the feeling of enclosure, or entrapment, within this fragment," produced by the repeated forms of *gignomai*.

34. Edelman (2004) calls this "the Ponzi scheme of reproductive futurism" (4). In B52, the child represents not the fantasy of futurism (a future wholeness of the self with itself and of revealed meaning) but the queer death drive Edelman invokes to resist it. Heraclitus' child is itself queer.

35. The alternative may be posed as such in the punning of B25: "greater deaths (*moroi*) are allotted greater destinies (*moiras*)" (*moroi gar mezones mezonas moiras lanchanousi*).

36. *Mallon de anapauesthai* is presumably Clement's interjection, but note the suggestive parallel at B84a: *metaballon anapauetai*.

37. Eliot's asyndetic repetition-with-difference can be read as a stutter. The thematics of the line (and the poem) are close to Heraclitus', especially if we remember the Greek association of the *psuchê* with animating breath (evident in B12). The striking archaism "suspire" figures life as breath, its double sibilants forcing the reader to breathe. This verb is what makes "live" rhyme with "fire," but also represents one last gasp of breath before total consumption. The *Four Quartets* begins with two epigraphs in untranslated Greek from Heraclitus—τοῦ λόγου δ' ἐόντος ξυνοῦ ζώουσιν οἱ πολλοὶ ὡς ἰδίαν ἔχοντες φρόνησιν (B2) and ὁδὸς ἄνω κάτω μία καὶ ὡυτή (B60)—and engages with his thought and themes throughout.

38. Deleuze 1997, 107: "It is no longer the character who stutters in speech; it is the writer who becomes *a stutterer in language*. He makes the language as such stutter" (original emphasis). In this fragment, character and writer alike stutter over articulation of the fundamental *homologia*.

39. Aristotle, *Metaphysics* 1.9.993a.15–16. Cf. *Metaphysics* 1.4.985a4–7 of Empedocles: if one pays attention to his meaning and "not to what he says stammering" (*ha psellizetai legôn*), one can see that his Love and Strife are actually efficient causes. To the unsympathetic listener, all philosophy is childish stammering. Thus Callicles in Plato's *Gorgias*: "I feel the same towards those who philosophize as toward those who stammer and play (*tous psellizomenous kai*

paizontas). When I see a child, for whom it is proper to speak in this way, stammering and playing, I am delighted ... but when I hear a man stammering or see him playing, it seems to me ludicrous and unmanly and deserving of a beating" (Plato, *Gorgias* 485b).

40. Scholiasts on Aeschylus, *Prometheus Bound* 816 explain the word *psellos* as "from the metaphor of stammering children." See further Aristotle, *Problems* 902b16–29, on the speech impediments of children. There he explains *psellotês* as a kind of hiccup or interval in speech, the omission of a letter or syllable, and differentiates it from *traulizein* (lisping or the inability to pronounce a certain letter) and *ischnophônein* (which is his word for what we usually think of as stuttering). Cf. Aristotle, *De Audibilibus* 804b26–39. But a scholiast on *Odyssey* 6.57 seems to understand *psellos* as a form of reduplication: he identifies "*pappa*" (father) as "a stammering voice" (*psellizomenê esti tis phônê*). Compare Jakobson (1962), for whom (in a teleology that goes back to Aristotle) the reduplication of syllables in *mama* and *papa* marks a first step in the move from random babbling to recognizable words (*phônê* to *logos*): see S. Butler 2015.

41. *P/b: aiôn p̱ais esti p̱aizôn, p̱esseuôn; p̱aidos hê ḇasilêiê. S: aiên pais̱ es̱ti paizôn, pes̱seuôn; paidos̱ hê bas̱ilêiê. Ai: a̱iôn pa̱is esti pa̱izôn, pesseuôn; pa̱idos hê basiḻêiê* (the eta is a lengthened epsilon not alpha, but it is unlikely that this difference was marked in spoken Greek).

42. Cf. Comay and Ruda 2018, 55–9: stumbling over the "speculative punctuation" of the dash, we are forced to reread, and that rereading is the essence of philosophy; philosophy "teaches us to stumble" (58).

CHAPTER 9
ELECTRA, AGAIN
Sarah Olsen

Electra is one of Greek tragedy's most oft-repeated heroines. A major character in four surviving plays (Aeschylus' *Libation-Bearers*; Sophocles' *Electra*; Euripides' *Electra* and *Orestes*), a significant figure for several others (Aeschylus' *Agamemnon* and *Eumenides*; Euripides' *Iphigenia among the Taurians*), and restaged time and again across the last two millennia of dramatic productions and adaptations, Electra is likely to be a familiar figure to anyone with even a passing interest in ancient Greek myth, drama, and performance.[1] My title thus nods to the weariness with which a reader (or a critic) might approach this character and her associated plays: Electra, *again*?

And indeed, at the outset of Sophocles' *Electra*, the titular character herself seems exhausted. She performs her characteristic mourning, refusing to "leave off [her] laments and miserable cries" (104), yet she also acknowledges her physical and emotional weariness, her inability to "bear [her] grief alone any longer" (119–20).[2] Later in the play, Sophocles nods to the tiresome persistence of Electra's lamentation, as Orestes tells her to "leave off [her] superfluous words" (*ta men perisseuonta tôn logôn aphes* 1288) in order to allow the murder of Aegisthus to proceed.[3] In this chapter, I aim to reflect upon the excessive and repetitive qualities of Electra's speech as they emerge at the outset of Sophocles' *Electra*. I will begin by discussing some of the literary effects (and affects) associated with the repetition of words, phrases, themes, and structures, especially as theorized by scholars associated with the "turn" (or "return") "to form" evident in the last decade of literary criticism. I will then explore the poetics of repetition in Electra's opening lament (86–120), considering how repetition both exhausts and excites its performers and audiences. By way of conclusion, I will compare Sophocles' poetic strategies with the dramatic use of repetition in the work of the modern playwright Suzan-Lori Parks, in order to advance our understanding of repetition as a generative force in the ongoing production and reimagination of Greek tragedy.

Theorizing Repetition

Attention to repetition is essential to all kinds of formalist criticism: consonance, assonance, metrical feet, rhyme schemes, and ring composition are but a handful of the terms and conceptual frameworks invoked by New Critics and radical formalists alike.[4] Literary repetition is likewise associated with a wide range of effects: emphasis, an underscoring of affinity, the creation of textual structure through rhyme or refrain, the construction (and deconstruction) of time and tempo. In its ability to call attention to variations upon a form or a theme, repetition is a crucial strategy for reconciling tradition and innovation. Greek tragedy is a genre responsive to the traditional analysis of repetition and innovation, and it has also been well-served by theoretical accounts of repetition from a diverse array of perspectives: psychoanalytic, deconstructive, formalist, and historicist.[5] Instead of surveying the vast bibliography on this subject, I would like to focus on a specific point of tension in the conceptualization of repetition: its relationship to both exhaustion and creation. The critical claims discussed in this section will then provide a framework for exploring the poetic and performative significance of repetition in Electra's lament.

Shlomith Rimmon-Kenan argues that "constructive repetition emphasizes difference, destructive repetition emphasizes sameness (i.e., to repeat successfully is not to repeat)."[6] Creative repetition, in other words, relies on some degree of variation—repetition that produces only sameness is dull, tedious, or unproductive. Rimmon-Kenan's observation is grounded in a Freudian distinction between pleasurable and productive (or "constructive") repetition, and that which, through its "over-sameness," contributes to a death-driven inertia.[7] For both Jacques Derrida and Gilles Deleuze, repetition provides a crucial entry-point to the discussion of difference and sameness more broadly.[8]

Responding to this critical tradition, Namwali Serpell observes that "[w]hile repetition's most common affective features—boredom, enthrallment, ecstatic joy—have wildly different connotations when it comes to pleasure and intensity, they all tend toward a dissolution of the boundaries and agency of the ethical subject."[9] Serpell proposes that the distinction between constructive, optimistic repetition (that which leads to innovation and improvement) and destructive repetition (a static excess of similitude) is, in fact, a paradox: "these versions of repetition may be two sides of the same coin."[10] Focusing on late twentieth- and early twenty-first-century American novels, Serpell reveals how the repetition of words, themes, actions, and textual structures can enthrall, bore, shock, and unsettle, generating modes of uncertainty that pose various ethical challenges.[11] Her reading of Tom McCarthy's *Remainder*, for example, explores how repetition lulls the reader into a "quasi-hynotic state," thereby drawing them into "the murderous narrator's orbit," while also offering the "escape hatch" of laughter, through which sameness can come undone.[12]

Caroline Levine likewise attends to the unsettling power of repetition, observing that legal, musical, and poetic rhythms "depend not only on repetition but also on difference—variations and departures that repeat past patterns, but never perfectly."[13] While Levine's attention to the difference inherent to repetition recalls Rimmon-Kenan (along with Deleuze and Derrida), she is distinctively optimistic about the potential of a "canny formalism" capable of achieving politically progressive ends through a strategic balancing of "tradition and innovation, repetitions and ruptures."[14] Levine argues, for example, that in Elizabeth Barrett Browning's poem *The Young Queen*, "[b]oth the poem and the state are composed of rhythmic repetitions and sudden breaks," yet neither literary nor institutional structures achieve an easy primacy.[15] Attending to thematic and poetic repetition, she insists, "leads not to equilibrium but to collision, superimposition, even mind-boggling disarray."[16] Serpell, responding to this reading, adds that "repetition and difference do not just describe form, they also condition our experience of form in time." She urges us, therefore, to attend even more closely to the weirdness, the tension, and the instability created by the experience of repetition as a temporal phenomenon.[17]

Mario Telò explores how the "frustration and pleasure of endless repetition" permeate Greek tragedy and, like several of the critics mentioned above, he attends to the dynamic interplay of boredom and intensity, destruction and reproduction, sameness and difference.[18] Analyzing a choral ode in Euripides' *Phoenician Women*, for example, he reveals how sonic repetition and doubling contribute to a sense of both "insistent energy" and "depleting saturation," an obsessive return to the themes of fratricide and incestuous intimacy echoed on the level of language, in a way that both "excites and exhausts."[19] In his readings of Sophocles' and Euripides' plays about the house of Oedipus, Telò highlights tragedy's ability to "[draw] its readers or viewers toward endlessly iterated stories and heaps of harrowing affect," to extend "a masochistic experience of repetition and deferral." He thus offers a psychoanalytically inflected account of the genre's particular investment in repetition.[20]

Another way to think about the issues of sameness and difference raised by repetition is to consider how repetitive literary forms may represent both disintegration and proliferation. Serpell, we may recall, sees a profound "dissolution" of the self as the unifying feature of repetition's diverse affective powers.[21] From a slightly different angle, Deleuze's discussion of the Cartesian Cogito (*cogito, ergo sum*, "I think, therefore I am") emphasizes the fractures in force and meaning between the repeated first-person forms of the phrase.[22] The mythic figure of Echo, whose physical body wastes away until she is nothing more than pure, repeated sound (itself dissipating over time), offers a potent image of such destructive repetition.[23] Yet the myth of Echo and Narcissus is also a valuable site for scholars seeking to highlight the creative or generative force of repetition.[24] Repetition, reproduction, replication: these terms describe how letters, words, and structures proliferate—appearing not once, perhaps not merely twice, but again and again across a poem, page, or performance. Proliferation (rooted in Latin *proles*, "offspring," and *fero*, "to bear") is a way of describing repetition that underscores such procreative potential. As Telò demonstrates, Euripides' *Medea* makes particularly effective use of such repetition: in Medea's recounting of her past services to Jason (cf. 475–82), the proliferation of sigmas (*s*-sounds) enacts a "repetitious circularity," while simultaneously highlighting the failure of "self-identical repetition" and "perfect reproduction."[25]

The theorists I have cited thus far engage with very different texts and contexts, and they discuss "repetition" in a wide variety of guises: from the micro-level repetition of a Greek prefix to the citation of an artistic tradition writ large. But they share a sense that repetition is at once exhausting and generative. Literary repetition can create a sense of boredom, sameness, and oppressive immutability, even as it also calls attention to the significance of subtle variations and shifts, through which new possibilities and formal shapes emerge. Keeping these dynamics in mind, I would like to now explore how Sophocles' *Electra* uses repetition on a micro-scale (anaphora; the repetition of a single word) to generate a model for tragedy as an art of repetition.

Electra in Pieces

Electra begins her lament by addressing the "light" (*phaos* 86) and the "air" (*aêr* 87), reminding them that (88–90):

πολλὰς μὲν θρήνων ᾠδάς,
πολλὰς δ' ἀντήρεις ἦσθου
στέρνων πλαγὰς αἱμασσομένων,

Many are the songs of lamentation, and
many are the blows you have perceived,
against my bloodied breast.

The anaphoric repetition of "many" (*pollas*), twice positioned at the beginning of a line, underscores the repetitive quality of Electra's mourning. The "songs" (*ôidas*) and the "blows" (*plagas*) are not merely (grammatically) plural, but multiple, "many," and her description of them enacts the experience of witnessing the same performance, the same actions, again and again (*pollas, pollas*).

On one level, the lines beginning with "many" (*pollas* 88 and 89) form a clear visual unit (for a reader encountering this text in writing), as well as a sonic one (for a listener or viewer of the text in performance); this effect is enhanced by the metrically distinctive quality of lines 88–9, wherein the lament's anapestic rhythm exhibits a set of lyric features.[26] Yet this sense of coherence is complicated by the flow of the words themselves. Electra's description of her "breast" or "chest," "bloodied" by her self-inflicted "blows" (*sternôn plagas haimassomenôn*) is found on line 90, extending the reference initiated by *pollas* on line 89. The image of the bloodied breast is a conventional one within ancient Greek lamentation.[27] Yet I would like to suggest that it figures Electra herself as undone, somatically, by her mourning: her blood leaks out from her body, surpassing its bounds through the violent repetition of self-harm as an expression of grief. This image is echoed by the structure of the lines themselves, in which the description of Electra's body spills out, beyond the neat couplet created through the anaphoric repetition of *pollas*. Recalling the theoretical work described above, we might see these lines as a site in which poetic structure underscores the dramatic theme of repetition as destruction of the (embodied) self.

A similar collocation of sonic repetition and somatic rupture occurs when Electra turns to the object of her mourning: her father, Agamemnon. Electra cries "how often I lament my unfortunate / father" (*hosa ton dustênon emon thrênô / pater'* 94–5). As Nancy Worman observes, these lines situate Electra in a "syntactic embrace" with her father, as the references to Agamemnon (*ton dustênon, patera*) encircle the references to Electra herself (*emon, thrênô*).[28] The phrase "I lament my unfortunate" [father] also contains a striking number of *-on* and *-ên* sounds (**ton** *dus**tênon** e**mon** thr**ênô***). The interweaving of Electra and Agamemnon that occurs on the level of syntax is thus further intensified by the repetition of sound, which lends this line another layer of coherence. Yet again, the phrase continues beyond these apparent bounds: the word "father" (*patera*) is separated from its article (*ton*) and adjectives (*emon dustênon*) by enjambment: it sits alone on the following line (95). This effectively prefigures the description of Agamemnon's death, which occurs a few lines later, as Electra emphasizes how Aegisthus and Clytemnestra "split his head with a bloody ax" (*schizousi kara phoniôi pelekei* 99). While Electra elsewhere narrates Agamemnon's life and death in the aorist (*exenisen* 96; *thanontos* 102), figuring the events referenced as occurring once and in the past, she employs a present-tense verb to describe the "splitting" (*schizousi* 99) of her father's head. This shift in tense highlights the enduring presence of this action in Electra's imagination—as well as the mythic and dramatic imagination that animates this play. Agamemnon's life is, paradoxically, always and repeatedly ending, his death enacted again and again through Electra's recollection of it here as well as the reperformance and retelling of it more broadly.[29]

The violent schism of Agamemnon's body is quite different from the repetitive battering implied by Electra's bloody breast. Yet these two images exhibit similar formal and thematic effects. In both cases, we can identity structural units reinforced through repetition: the use of anaphora and metrical rhythm to mark off lines 88–9 as a kind of "couplet," and the use of word order and sonic repetition (*-on/-ên*) to form Electra's "syntactic embrace" of her father at lines 94–5. It is the words and phrases that spill beyond the bounds of these units, however, that prove particularly revealing: Electra's "bloodied breast" (*sternôn ... haimassomenôn*) at line 90, and the description of Agamemnon as "father" (*patera*) at line 95, separated from the rest of the "embrace" by a line break and its lack of a vowel + *nu* (n-sound). Both of these instances of excess or spillover call attention to the bodies enacted or imagined on stage, and especially, the forms of violence they have suffered. The paradoxical present-tense of *schizousi* (99) captures the dramatic significance of this tension between poetic representation and embodied experience: through the performance of tragedy, a violent action (the splitting of a skull by an ax) that should only be able to happen once does, in fact, happen over and over again. Just as Electra is always lamenting, Agamemnon is always dying. At the same time, a play varies each time it is produced —its repetition is part of a process of reinvention, transformation, and innovation.[30] The sense of immutability and endurance implied by a text (which may be highlighted through the use of repetitive structures) is always potentially exceeded, expanded, or complicated by the body (or bodies) that perform it.

Electra's use of the keyword *phonos* (murder, slaughter, blood, gore), and its adjective, *phonios* (bloody, deadly) likewise highlights how repetition and transformation interact. She first explains that "bloody (*phoinios*) Ares did not receive [Agamemnon] as a guest" (96) at Troy—that is, he did not die in war. She then describes how Clytemnestra and Aegisthus "split [Agamemnon's] head with a bloody (*phoniôi*) ax" (99). Finally, near the end of her lament, she calls upon a series of deities to help in her avenging the "murder (*phonon*) of her father" (116). These three moments sketch out a timeline for the life and death of Agamemnon, and underscore how repetitive violence functions as the engine of the broader mythic and dramatic narrative. Agamemnon's participation in the Trojan war, the realm of the "bloody" (*phoinios*) war-god, creates the conditions (his absence, the death of Iphigenia) that lead directly to his murder, conducted with a "bloody" (*phoniôi*) ax, at the hands of his wife and her lover. When his children set out to avenge his "murder" (*phonon*), they instigate a further wave of bloody slaughter.[31]

Each appearance of *phonos/phonios/phoinios* in this passage, however, is also distinct in grammatical form: nominative singular adjective (*phoinios*), dative singular adjective (*phoniôi*), and accusative singular noun (*phonon*). In addition, the first adjectival use (*phoinios* 96) features a lengthening of the initial syllable (*phoi-* for *pho-*), a variant of the word used to fit metrical demands. The use of this word, over the course of Electra's lament, thus exemplifies how a word can both repeat and mutate in response to meter, syntax, and context. The intonation of an actor's speech and the movement of their body, of course, offer further ways in which the same word could be framed and expressed anew. The repetition of deadly violence (*phonos*) is central to this play and the mythic cycle in which it is embedded. Yet the transformations of *phonos* across this passage are emblematic of how repetition is not necessarily static: the permutation of violence, its enactment by distinct characters and in distinct forms, drives the dramatic narrative.[32]

The energizing force of repetition becomes even more prominent near the end of Electra's lament, when she again employs anaphora in her appeals to the gods for aid (110–17):

> ὦ δῶμ᾿ Ἅιδου καὶ Περσεφόνης,
> ὦ χθόνι᾿ Ἑρμῆ καὶ πότνι᾿ Ἀρά,
> σεμναί τε θεῶν παῖδες Ἐρινύες,
> αἳ τοὺς ἀδίκως θνήσκοντας ὁρᾶθ᾿,
> αἳ τοὺς εὐνὰς ὑποκλεπτομένους,
> ἔλθετ᾿, ἀρήξατε, τείσασθε πατρὸς
> φόνον ἡμετέρου,
> καί μοι τὸν ἐμὸν πέμψατ᾿ ἀδελφόν.

> O halls of Hades and Persephone,
> O Hermes of the underworld and lady Curse,
> and Erinyes, solemn children of the gods,
> you who look upon those who die unjustly,
> you who [look upon] those secretly dishonoring marriage beds
> come, help, avenge
> the murder of our father,
> and send my brother to me.

Electra's repetitions, as in the case of *pollas* ("many") above, underscore the multiplicity of figures addressed. She begins by addressing two deities (Hades and Persephone), united within their "halls" (*dôma*), then adds two more: Hermes and a feminine personification of "Curse" or "Vow"—but now, each figure receives a distinct descriptive addition (*chthonie*, "of the Underworld;" "*potnia*," "lady" or "mistress"). The vocative form of address repeats ("o," "o"), but the gods pile up: Hades, Persephone, Hermes, Curse. Her turn to the Erinyes, goddesses of vengeance, extends this divine accumulation beyond the bounds of the two anaphoric lines (110–11). While Electra continues to employ the vocative, the plural "Erinyes," with their expanded descriptive tag ("solemn children of the gods"), crowd out the prefatory "o" employed in the preceding lines. Electra repeats the process of invocation throughout these three lines (110–12), yet the effect of that repetition, the proliferation of deities and their descriptions, also means that she cannot continue to precisely reproduce the same vocative structure.

Electra returns to the device of anaphoric repetition in the lines that follow, however, as she expands even further upon the Erinyes. Using a pair of relative clauses ("[you] who," *hai*, 113, 114) to address the Erinyes as those who "look upon" (*horath'* 113) the victims and the perpetrators of unjust violence and violation, she also continues her emphatic use of plural forms. She gestures not to singular or individually identified figures (e.g., Agamemnon, Clytemnestra, Aegisthus), but to "those" (*tous* 113 and 114) who both suffer and enact such crimes more generally. The abundance of plural forms, underscored by repeated endings (*-ai, -as, -ous*), makes these lines feel increasingly crowded or congested.

Electra's repetitive and cumulative process of invocation, at this point in her lament, may be read as a kind of "revving up," a gathering of forces required for the action to come. Her two pairs of anaphoric lines (110, 111; 113, 114), bridged by the expanded invocation of the Erinyes (112), culminate with a line addressed, presumably, to the whole series of deities invoked ("come, help, avenge [my/our] father," *elthet', arêxate, teisasthe patros* 115). This line forms a tricolon crescendo, in which the three verbal phrases in the Greek gradually expand (*elthet'* = two syllables, with elision; *arêxate* = four syllables; *teisasthe patros* = five syllables, across two words). The intensifying effect of such a sequence corresponds well with the energy accumulated over the course of the preceding lines through the steady expansion of divine forces. On the one hand, the repetitive quality of Electra's cries would seem to enact, once again, her exhausting process of continual lamentation, through which, as we have seen, her own body is beginning to leak blood. At the same time, her repetitions are now interwoven with forms of expansion and accumulation that confound the forces of precise formal replication.

The growing intensity of Electra's invocations bring us to the arrival of her brother, Orestes. I say "arrival," yet of course, for the audience, Orestes has already appeared: the prologue of this play features a dialogue between Orestes and his tutor, who, along with Pylades, choose to withdraw when they hear Electra's cries (cf. 82–5). While Electra believes herself to be alone, perhaps enacting a plea for the aid of her brother that she has futilely repeated many times before, readers and viewers alike know that Orestes will soon reappear. This knowledge lends additional weight to Electra's reference to "our" (*hêmeterou* 116) "father" (*patros* 115): the first-person plural form here contrasts with her earlier, first-person singular reference to Agamemnon as "my" (*emon* 94) "father" (*patera* 95). While Greek poetry often uses the first-person plural for singular (and vice-versa), this particular variation underscores Electra's shift away from her lonely plight and towards a plaintive cry for help from others. When she proceeds to demand that these deities "send my brother to me" (*mon ton emon pempsat' adelphon* 117), she clarifies the other person who might be embedded within the collective "our" (*hêmeterou*)—her brother, a person with whom she shares a father. Since we know that Orestes will eventually reappear on stage and come to Electra's aid, the cumulative force of her invocations might be seen as producing that presence, building intensity that points forward to the return of her brother.

As I discussed above, Electra intertwines herself with Agamemnon through the syntactic structure of her words: "the unfortunate man, my, I lament, father" (*ton dustênon emon thrênô / pater'* 94–5). She repeats this kind of verbal entanglement when she subsequently refers to Orestes: "to me, the [man], my, you send, brother" (*moi ton emon pempsat' adelphon* 117). Her "syntactic embrace"[33] of her father transforms into a structurally similar "embrace" of her brother. This shift in object reflects Electra's important shift in orientation: she still laments for her father, but she also longs for the arrival of her brother, and looks forward to the possibility of vengeful action (cf. 115). In a similar way, Electra initially stresses how she alone mourns for Agamemnon, lamenting that "no pity" (*oudeis ... oiktos* 100) is "born" (*pheretai* 101) for her father "by anyone else, apart from me" (*ap'allês / ê 'mou* 100–1). Yet she concludes her lament with a powerful refusal of that lonely mourning, declaring that "no longer do I alone (*mounê*) have the power to bear / the counterweight burden of grief" (119–20). At the moment when Electra delivers these lines, she is alone (*mounê*) on stage, yet the audience is keenly aware that this play is driven by the arrival of Orestes—by a transformative shift in Electra's lonely state.[34] The interplay of repetition and variation embedded within Electra's lament prefigures the action to come.

In essence, I have been suggesting that Electra's oscillation between repetition and transformation, exhaustion and intensity, replication and proliferation, may be understood in metatheatrical terms. When Sophocles put Electra on stage, he entered into a dramatic tradition in which specific figures and forms were already being repeated—and Electra, in her various dramatic guises, has been repeated many times since the fifth century BCE. But encoded within Electra's lament, her first contribution to the Sophoclean play, we can already find a poetics of dramatic repetition. Nightly lamentation exhausts Electra, even to the point of bodily dissolution, while the repetitive quality of her words might induce a similar effect in her audience. Electra's plaintive imagination and the tragic stage align as a space in which Agamemnon's death can, horrifically, occur over and over again. Yet Electra's repetitions are also remarkably generative: her different uses of the keyword *phonos* (blood, slaughter) underscore how this mythic cycle moves through various permutations of violence, and the cumulative energy of her vocative cries propels the drama forward. As I noted at the outset, Electra is a mythic figure prone to proliferation—to repeating herself within and beyond the bounds of a given play. This lament, scripted for her by Sophocles, demonstrates the fertility of repetition for both Electra and Greek tragedy more broadly.

Electra, Again (and again, and again)

Suzan-Lori Parks's *365 Days/365 Plays* (2006) exposes the power of structured repetition in the composition, production, and experience of drama. The result of Parks's commitment to writing a play every day for a calendar year (from Nov. 13, 2002 to Nov. 12, 2003), this collection was presented through readings at the Public Theater (NYC) in August and September 2006, as well as a coordinated festival running from November 2006 to November 2007.[35] The plays vary in theme and content, while their formal and stylistic commonalities are underscored by Parks's presentation of them, in the published version of the collection, through a consistent set of formatting choices.[36] In an analysis of *365 Days/365 Plays* and its original production, Rebecca Ann Rugg notes the "steady beat" of the plays' composition, the repetitive temporal rhythm of daily writing through which they were produced, and contrasts this with the nonlinear or "manifold" temporality evident throughout the work: "stories and characters loop around and circle back, themes carry forward and reverse themselves."[37] Repetition, whether in the form of Parks's own writing practice or in the performer or audience member's experience of repeated components, proves to be a rich, complex, and generative dramatic force.[38]

Greek tragedy, along with many other influences and inspirations, surfaces at various points in Parks's work, but it is perhaps most explicitly invoked by the play composed on April 2, 2003, entitled "Greek Tragedy & Jerry Springer."[39] Any number of ancient Greek mythic families could surely be richly parodied through the medium of modern daytime television, and Parks gestures to this by including Tantalus, Oedipus, and Cassandra among her characters. But within this brief (half-page; eleven lines; two stage directions) play, the house of Atreus features most prominently. After Clytemnestra justifies her decision to murder her husband, the "Host" chimes in to say "Yr children have a different take on that." Clytemnestra expresses surprise, and the Host continues, "Come on in, kids. Folks meet—Clytemnestra's kids," after which the play concludes with a stage direction: "The Kids rush at Clytemnestra and fight with their mama."

By putting Clytemnestra, Agamemnon, Electra, and Orestes on *Jerry Springer*, a television show immediately associated with predictable and repetitive spectacles of familial drama, Parks demonstrates just how quickly and succinctly a modern playwright can evoke the core elements of this ancient myth.[40] But within this short, spare play, the repetition of the word "kids" across the final few lines is particularly striking. Electra and Orestes (or Chrysothemis, or Iphigenia) are not named, although an audience familiar with the plays and myths to which Parks alludes could imaginatively fill them in. In the text, however, they are reduced to the vague collective "kids," which picks up on the frequent description of Electra and Orestes in Greek tragedy as "the children" (*paides, tekna*) but translates it into casual, English form. As we also saw in Sophocles' scripting of Electra's lament, the repetition of a plural word ("kids") intensifies the sense of accumulation and crowding. There are already several characters on stage —we now imagine more (and more: kids, kids, kids). For readers especially, the repetition might feel a bit tedious: we are told twice by the same character that the kids are about to enter, then informed again by a stage direction.

The repetition of the word "kids" also adds a drumbeat to the final spoken line, punctuating the Host's words: "Come on in, **kids**. Folks meet—Clytemnestra's **kids**," but the word is then transformed in the stage directions (which are presented in a distinct font, as well): "The Kids" (now capitalized) become the subject of the action. Assuming that the stage direction is not read aloud in performance, the production of this play would feature just two verbal repetitions of the word "kids," followed by the physical appearance of actors representing "The Kids." As with Sophocles' use of the word *phonos*, repetition coincides with formal variation. And just as Electra's invocations prepare the way for the appearance of Orestes, the Host's verbal repetition (kids, kids) points toward the imminent presence of The Kids.

In Parks's *Greek Tragedy & Jerry Springer*, the repetition of "kids" both closes out the drama, placed emphatically at the end of the Host's phrases, and also gestures to the open-ended quality of action with which the play "concludes" (how long should "The Kids" and "their mama" fight? How and when will it stop?). In this sense, the micro-repetition of this single word, within one brief play among many, is emblematic of the role of constancy and creativity in Parks's broader project, which also includes "The 3 Constants"—three additional plays, added after the initial year of writing, which are to be incorporated whenever portions of *365 Days/365 Plays* are performed.[41] These plays were meant to give the diverse performers and audiences of the 2006–7 festival "something in common," yet their stage directions and temporalities are radically open-ended.[42] The term "constant" implies consistency, repetition, replication, yet Parks's composition of these three additional plays (e.g., a stage direction: "The sound of wind or whales forever") ensures variation and difference in performance.[43] Rugg connects the "radical inclusion" central to Parks's *365 Days/365 Plays* project with Parks's quasi-spiritual approach to composition, as emblematized by her ritualistic practice of daily play-writing.[44] In essence, the scripts of these brief plays skillfully encode both their own repetition (their constant or consistent elements) and insistent invitations to creative permutation.

Parks's bold dramaturgical experiment, diffused across the country in performance and open, even "rhizomatic," in structure, could certainly be contrasted with Greek tragedy as a bounded and organized form.[45] Yet as we have seen, Sophocles and Parks employ strikingly similar strategies of repetition on a micro-scale—a poetic technique that bridges these very different forms of drama. I would thus like to suggest that the two playwrights can help us think about how Greek tragedy operates as an art of repetition. Just as Electra laments again, the ancient and modern artists of "Greek tragedy" return again to the same stories, characters, forms, and settings. The proliferation of productions of a specific play or playwright at a given historical moment can be described and accounted for in fairly specific terms, of course, but I am speaking here of the genre's tendency to proliferate in general: to invite reproductions, reperformances, retellings. In both Electra's lament and Parks's "kids," we can see how a repeated word (form, play) can move and mutate, simultaneously exhausting and inexhaustible in its expressions of meaning and affect. These poetic strategies resonate, on a micro-scale, with the broader theoretical accounts of repetition discussed at the outset of this chapter. Parks's plays are also examples of the ongoing reenactment of Greek tragic figures and cycles, which are recognizable in even the sparest of sketches in part because they have been repeated so many times, and in so many ways, since the fifth century BCE. An actor, audience member, or critic might reasonably feel exhausted (both bored and depleted) by the reappearance of Greek tragedy: Electra, *again*? Yet Parks and the many other contemporary artists and playwrights restaging and reimagining Greek tragedy today reveal that yes, Electra (and Antigone, and Orestes), again (and again, and again) can still energize and excite us.

Notes

1. Cf. Dunn 1996; Foley 2014, 239–48; Andújar 2015; and M. Powers 2018, 51–88.

2. I have used Lloyd-Jones and Wilson 1990 for the text of Sophocles' *Electra*.

3. On the particularly repetitive and persistent qualities of Electra's lamentation in this play, see Kitzinger 1991, 204–307; Nooter 2012, 101–9; Worman 2021, 236. On lament and repetition in tragedy, see also Loraux 1998, 98; Suter 2003; Phillips 2015; Weiss 2017. Alexiou (2002) traces the importance of verbal, sonic, and structural repetition to Greek ritual lament more broadly. The essays in Beck 2021 offer a range of perspectives on repetition in Greek and Roman literature, with particular attention to Homeric poetry.

4. See the Introduction.

5. Cf., e.g., Easterling 1973; Pickering 2000; Konstantinou 2015; Wohl 2015, 30–4 and 110–31; and Telò 2020b.

6. Rimmon-Kenan 1980, 153.

7. Rimmon-Kenan 1980, 154–5. Cf. Freud 1920, 11–16.

8. See Deleuze 1994 and Derrida 1996, both discussed in relation to tragic aesthetics by Telò (2020b, 13–17 and 29). See also Geue's chapter in this volume.

9. Serpell 2014, 193.

10. Serpell 2014, 193.

11. Serpell 2014, 191–2.

12. Serpell 2014, 194. See further Serpell 2014, 230–67.

13. Levine 2015, 68. For a reading of similar dynamics in Alice Oswald's repetitions of Homeric similes in in her poem *Memorial*, see Minchin 2021.

14. Levine 2015, 73.

15. Levine 2015, 79. See further Levine 2015, 73–81. See Macpherson 2017 for a critique of Levine's reading.

16. Levine 2015, 80.

17. Serpell 2017, 1236.

18. Telò 2020b, 26.

19. Telò 2020b, 84–5.

20. Telò 2020b, 87–8.

21. Serpell 2014, 193.

22. Deleuze 1994, 85–91, 110, 169–70.

23. See Ovid, *Metamorphoses* 3.339–508 for the most influential ancient recounting of this myth.

24. Cf. Derrida 2005, xi–xii; S. Butler 2018; and Telò 2020b, 141–3. See also Neyra's chapter in this book.

25. Telò 2020b, 99.

26. Finglass 2007, 118: "these four lines all have contracted bicipitia throughout . . . and lack word-division between the metra, with the overlap in three of four cases consisting of a full long syllable."

27. Cf. Homer, *Iliad* 19.282–300; Aeschylus, *Libation Bearers* 423–8; and Euripides, *Trojan Women* 793–5. This motif is discussed in comparative contexts by Alexiou (2002), and further tragic parallels are noted by Finglass (2007, 125).

28. Worman 2021, 237. Worman (2021) further demonstrates how this blurring of the boundaries of the body, or attention to the "edges of the human," is a crucial feature of Greek tragedy more broadly.

29. As Nooter (2012, 105) observes, Electra's "lamentation has been designed to extend the progressive present tense of her father's death." Cf. also Sze 2019, 78, on the impact of repetition in and for Anne Carson's poetic "book in box," *Nox*, which draws upon the Roman poet Catullus in crafting an elegy for the author's brother, Michael: "the more *Nox* is replicated, the more Catullus is translated, the more we grieve with Carson, the more Michael lives."

30. As Duncan (2005) demonstrates, attention to the mutability and adaptability of Sophocles' *Electra* is evident already in antiquity. The power of repetition (in terms of reperformance, reenactment, and "restored behavior") is, of course, a major theme in performance studies more broadly: cf. Schechner 1981.

31. Cf. Sophocles, *Electra* 1422, wherein the chorus describes how Orestes and Pylades emerge, after killing Clytemnestra, with "bloody (*phoinia*) hands."

32. See also Nooter 2012, 108, on Electra's use of the verb *êchô* ("sound," "cry," "echo") to describe her repeated cries of mourning, in a way that implies "endurance and ability to amplify." As Shane Butler pointed out to me, the sonic similarity between *phonos* (slaughter, violence) and *phônê* (sound, voice) further underscores the relationship between the enactment of violence and its representation in the form of dramatic speech; see further S. Butler 2015, 133, on how "tragedy attracts its audience not so much with living voices as with reanimated ones."

33. Worman 2021, 237.

34. In terms of the stagecraft of the ancient play, it is fairly clear that Orestes, Pylades, and the tutor depart before Electra arrives to deliver her lament (Jebb 1924, 19, and Finglass 2007, 117), and the choral *parodos* (entrance song) occurs immediately after (Finglass 2007, 140).

35. Parks (2006) provides text and production history; see also Rugg 2009. On Parks's engagement with Greek and Roman antiquity in a different context, see Derbew 2019.

36. Parks 2006, ix.

37. Rugg 2009, 76.

38. Cf. also Rugg 2008.

39. Parks 2006, 167 (all subsequent quotes are from this page).

40. For media studies analyses of Springer and related forms of daytime television, see Grabe 2002, Epstein and Steinberg 2003, and Lunt and Stenner 2005.

41. Parks 2006, x.

42. Rugg 2008, 55–6.

43. Parks 2006, x; cf. Rugg 2008, 56.

44. Rugg 2008.

45. Rugg 2008, 74. Rugg also situates Parks's project in an anti-Aristotelian tradition (2008, 74); cf. Telò 2020b for an anti-Aristotelian reading of Greek tragedy itself.

CHAPTER 10
A POETICS OF IMPERCEPTIBILITY IN STATIUS' *THEBAID*

Efrossini Spentzou

Statius' *Thebaid* is a poem trapped in past stories and texts. A reference to Thebes' inherited guilt opens the narrative (1.2), and reflections of it are scattered in the opening books of the epic.[1] The ghost of the dead Oedipus (cipher of the epic poet) demands of his Muse cipher, the Fury Tisiphone, not inspiration but rather that his two sons, already arrogant kings, should fight to the death, puppets in the hands of a Fury and a curse, both of which drive this inexorable story. Thebes' evil past pollutes the text from its opening, hardening characters, setting rigid boundaries between protagonists and communities and severely limiting the scope of epic action. Unloved, even despised, the characters are caged within the juggernaut of Oedipus' machinations and Jupiter's ire. In this polarized narrative structure, the female voice appears aligned programmatically with a trespassing of boundaries and is marginalized by male authority already before the first book is over. First comes Tisiphone, a kind of wet nurse for Oedipus and the inspiration behind his enjoyment of his mother (1.60–2), closely followed by the snake girl-woman (1.596–626) unleashed on the ancestors of the current Argives by Apollo in a misogynistic episode focusing on her mutilation and maiming, while a tamed Medusa is carved on the libation cup Adrastus uses during the commemorative festival in honor of Apollo.[2]

Yet, neither powerful nor loathed, nor, as we will see, marginal, a different female intervention/voice emerges through non-spaces of affect, eluding the signifiers that support epic hierarchies and divisions. Unforeseen and *out of reach*, these emergences weave a poetics of imperceptibility that loosens the rigid fabric of the text and tilts the story out of balance. Throughout, this essay on moments of representational crisis for the epic edifice has been enriched by insights from contemporary critical thinking on the trappings of representation and identity politics, explicitly acknowledged at particular instances of generative synergy.

Girls, Interrupted

The first encounter in the narrative present of the plot takes place in a space marked by patriarchal prestige. Rejected by their cities, Tydeus and Polynices have bickered at the gates of Argos. They are then welcomed inside the Palace by Adrastus. Transitioning from physical and political wildernesses they are met by spectacular signs of order: altars, luxurious bedspreads, gilded lanterns, baskets heaped with bread, opulence, and a king confident of his ability to rule, proudly beaming from high up on his throne (1.525).[3] But the text has already introduced doubt, centered on the king's daughters (1.390–4):

> Rex ibi tranquille, medio de limite vitae
> in senium vergens, populos Adrastus habebat,
> dives avis et utroque Iovem de sanguine ducens,
> hic sexus melioris inops, sed prole virebat
> feminea, gemino natarum pignore fultus.

> The King here [in Argos], passing from life's midpoint
> towards old age, ruled his people peacefully;
> rich in ancestors and tracing his line from either side of Jove,
> he lacked male offspring—but he flourished in female heirs
> supported by a twin pledge of loyalty from his daughters.

The problem concerns what the daughters lacked: masculinity (obviously), and the ability to perpetuate the line of succession. The absence of a male heir jeopardizes the security of the kingdom and this care gnaws at Adrastus; what is one to do with two unmarried girls (1.392–400)? The text singles out this worry as a notable affliction on the serene governance of the king, whose line is traced back all the way to Jove (1.392). Yet, although the girls are in need of husbands, they also strengthen, support, and enable their father to flourish.

The girls have a muddling effect on the thoughts of their father, and this confusion is duplicated later on when they are ushered onto the stage at the official reception of Tydaeus and Polynices in Argos. The setting is meticulously rendered to reproduce kinaesthetically an assertion of hierarchy and identity. Adrastus as a resplendent master, propped up by proud cushions (1.525–6), oversees proceedings. He is the wise king who has achieved peace, with his two new allies (and prospective grooms) symmetrically flanking him, in a picture of harmony and order. Adrastus' authority is extended through his dealings with the trusted nurse[4] of his daughters, who assumes the role of the representative of state watching over their pathway to acceptability. The text dwells on the girls' obedience and highlights the powers of surveillance that keep the girls *in their place*, protected and entrapped within their private chambers, emphatically not a public space; they emerge from a secret chamber (*arcano thalamo*), we are told (1.534). That is, the girls are kept from the public gaze until they emerge under controlled circumstances, establishing a script of the supervised gaze and of hidden imperceptibility. The care, discipline, and surveillance of the young females works as a representation of gendered hierarchies and familial order. Nevertheless, as we are about to see, behind these performances of surveillance there lies a parallel concern with the potential for failure: of the line, of the kingdom, of the supervisory structures, and of the epic narrative itself.

When the two girls are put on display for the men, they are "a wonder to see" (*mirabile visu* 1.534), a pleasing and tightly controlled spectacle that promotes masculine authority and leads to Tydeus and Polynices cementing their alliance with Adrastus through marriage. Their passivity as objects of the gaze and their shy and blushing demeanors are, however, undermined by a reference to the virgin goddesses (1.535–6), "Athena rattling with armor and quiver-wearing Diana" (*Pallados armisonae pharetrataeque . . . Dianae*), who are, however, notable for their indomitable independence and fierce, even violent, self-reliance. The text emphasizes the tear in the girls' passive representations through denial; they lack the terror the goddesses inspire (*terrore minus* 1.536), it hastens to add. And yet the tear re-opens with the same association in Book 2 right at the moment of their marriage, a rather dissonant context for a comparison of the princesses again to the "armed and stern," emphatically virginal goddesses (2.236–8).

Deiphobe and Argia are suspended between contradictory images of power and dutifulness, a worrisome form of ambient subjunctivity,[5] a mix of obedience, uncertainty, desire, and possibility that challenges easy understanding. They are both hidden and displayed. They are powerful supports for their father, and at the same time sources of weakness and worry. They have agency in support of their father, but they perform only under surveillance and supervision. Exposed to voyeurism in the public domain, they also elude scrutiny of the private chamber. But why would the text surround the girls with this representational ambivalence?

In her consideration of the relationship between visibility and representational economies, Peggy Phelan muses on the ways mimetic correspondence is employed by those holding power:

> Mimetic representation requires that the writer/ speaker employs pronouns, invents characters, records conversations, examines the words and images of others, so that the spectator can secure a coherent belief in self-authority, assurance, presence. Memory. Sight. Love.[6]

This trap of visibility is clear when the maidens are inspected by their prospective grooms. Looking keenly and absorbing every detail provides the patriarchal viewers with reassurance that the girls are beautiful and tame. But the text stumbles. There is an excess of representation that questions the authority of this vision. The sisters are not really the goddesses, but once linked with them they are not just blushing girls either; they become both modest and indomitable. They reside in more than one signifier with the potential to undermine representation. This potential of the girl, the danger that she might sidestep her script, evade her surveillance and slip out of her representational role, generates concern about the effectiveness of this powerful gaze of appraisal, especially given the familiar reversal of the power dynamics of the gaze in Diana's mythologies, perhaps referenced in 2.240 *si fas oculis* ("if your eyes had leave [to gaze]"). The power to gaze upon the girls is a concession to the men, but the power dynamics are such that the girls-goddesses might intervene, and that they might, as they show later in the narrative, be much more than mere objects of desire and status. The spectators cannot completely capture them, however hard and long they look at them, unable to decide who is the prettiest and forced to admit that each can carry the other's insignia with equal grace (2.240–3). With the two blended beyond recognition,[7] affective traces of their presence linger in the narrative.

This episode is not the only time the narrative fails to pin an identity on a girl in Book 1. A festival for Apollo takes place the day after Tydaeus' and Polynices' arrival. For the sake of the newcomers, the narrative relates the myth: Apollo visited Crotopus, a previous Argean king, and raped Crotopus' daughter. The resultant child was abandoned and the daughter was savagely punished by her father. Apollo reacted by releasing on Argos a snake-woman. She was killed by Coroebus leading to Apollo afflicting the region with plague before the reconciliation of the Argives and the god (1.562–666). The gendered violence of this story is lost in the commemoration, as solemn feasts and placating practices bind the community together and vouchsafe the position of the king, while Phoebus takes pleasure in the ritual and thus continues to confer his favor upon the Argians (1.666–8).

Hidden from view during the ritual is Crotopus' unnamed daughter. But the text had made space for her before (1.571–4):

Huic primis et pubem ineuntibus annis
mira decore pios servabat nata penates
intemerata toris. Felix, si Delia numquam
furta nec occultum Phoebo sociasset amorem.
Namque passa deum Nemeaei ad fluminis undam

[His] daughter, in early puberty and an amazing beauty,
spotless in bed, kept a pious home; a happy creature,
had she never shared secret trysts and hidden love with Phoebus.
For she endured the god by the waters of Nemea's stream

At first sight, the text controls the maiden. The girl is undefiled (sexually and morally), maintaining, and destined for, a pious home. She is also *mira*, wondrous to the eye. In other words, once again a scopic economy seeks to place and restrain the girl within familiar moral economies and gender disciplines. But the girl's pathway towards meeting the expectations placed upon her, respectable marriage and children, is not complete. Her transitional status in the above lines is striking: on the cusp of adulthood, and yet to achieve adult identity and status. She is thus, ultimately, an unknown quantity, as befits a character who eludes a name. Any doubt faintly flickering in these lines is substantiated by what comes next. Divine, masculine power takes her from the pathway on which patriarchal authority had placed her. The girl suffers the force of the god in an unmistakeable reference to rape, but in the previous line the text also deviated into elegiac mannerisms that point to "secret trysts" and "hidden love" (1.573).

The commemorative narration tries to tag the event within secure representational structures, but the text remains uncomfortable for both modern and ancient readers. These formulations co-opt oppression with agency, rape, and seduction. Did she ever enjoy a stolen love with the god, disregarding parental authority? She hides the result of her rape with a shepherd in the forest (1.579–81), as she has presumably hidden the pregnancy. This princess of Argos is neither closely watched nor had her appearances scripted under the royal eye. Consequently, she is indeed spotless (*intemerata*), virginal and unmarked, and eluding putative surveillance attempts, apart from those of the god. The text suspects her, even blames her for her own rape, but also opts to omit her, unable to tame her and rather insecure of its ability to control her. Her identity emerges in a failure of the narrative to identify and name her, for she is a girl trapped—and free—in her in-between status and her place in the wilderness. As Phelan puts it, "[u]nmarked is a configuration of subjectivity which exceeds, even while it informs, both the gaze and language."[8]

When news that her boy was devoured by rabid dogs reaches her, the girl's grief overwhelms the text as "she fills the house with wild shrieks" (*ipsa ultro saevis plangoribus amens tecta replet* 1.592), a radical performance, and a break from language that resists commodification. The breach with the patriarchal code is explicit: once she has heard of the cruel death of her baby (1.591), "father, modesty, and fear lose their grip on her" (*pulsi ex animo genitorque pudorque et metus*). Emotion and the trauma of devastating loss tear a hole in the false representation of the girl, breaking with her fixed (but unreal) position in the familial narrative, and leading her own unmoved father to condemn her to death in an effort to re-establish masculine control. Unsurprisingly, then, her explosive grief does not inform the official narrative and the practices of commemoration. As Phelan submits,

> The "hole in the signifier," "the Real-impossible" which is unsayable, unseeable, and therefore resistant to representation, is ignored in the full fling forward into representation.[9]

The out-of-wedlock girl-woman-mother is indeed ignored by, and is a nuisance for, rituals "in the full fling forward into representation." The Argive rituals are in the business of closing down contested spaces in favor of shared, communal, uncomplicated ones. But as Phelan warns, "[t]he danger of taking all on representation is that one gains only re-presentation."[10] Re-presentation—repetition—dulls the senses and social memory every year the rituals are performed in Argos. But the unnamed daughter of Crotopus, unsayable and unseeable, escapes repetition and co-option into the cultural prerogatives of the city, a reflection and a trace of Argia-Diana and Deiphobe-Athena (or is it the other way round?). Inhabiting "unmarked realms of affect, [the girls] remain partially glimpsed ghosts,"[11] disrupting the masculine logic of this divided and divisive epic.[12]

Girl Co-opted—not

Three winters (and three books) later, the men of the epic are on the move. Motivated by the sorrows of his son-in-law and the entreaties of Argia, his daughter, Adrastus gives in, albeit reluctantly (4.40–1),[13] to the quintessential epic demand: the leading of men to war. The soldiers burn with eagerness for an epic narrative here summed up in rather unsavory terms: rage, burn, ravage (4.648–9). But towards the end of Book 4, the narrative enters a prolonged delay (*morae* 4.650), a narrative as well as a literal aberration (*medius. . . euntibus error* 4.650).

The enemy in this section is inhuman and inhumane. A drought has afflicted Nemea as Phoebus has ordered the springs of all Argive rivers to withdraw their water. Excruciating thirst undermines the Argives' heroic representation rendering them "too weak to carry their shields or their tight breastplates" (*nec ardentes clipeos vectare nec artos / thoracum nexus* 4.730–1). When Adrastus attempts to fulfil his leader's duties, thirst garbles his words, reducing him to stuttering (*anhelitus ardens / verba rapit* 4.765–6).[14] A leader lost in the woods, away from his ancestral palace and cut off from places of belonging, *fails to make sense,* as a leader and as an epic hero too.

The outlook is dire when a sudden encounter pulls the army from the jaws of death-by-thirst. Meandering aimlessly in the Nemean forest, Adrastus and his men stumble upon a woman for whom the text struggles to form a coherent representation (4.743–5): "her hair was neglected and her clothes poor; yet marks of regality were on her face and a sense of honor not drowned by misfortune" (*neglecta comam nec dives amictu, / regales tamen ore notae, nec mersus acerbis / exstat honos*). As the text attempts but fails to "mark" Hypsipyle, Adrastus' male gaze is rendered, in the words of Kevin Quashie exploring Black feminist literature, "bewildered … taken out of [his] sense of common sense … lured into the wild,"[15] and he addresses the stranger with a mix of admiration, suspicion and disdain (4.764–66): "Nothing is too shameful or too humble for men in such plight; it is you we implore now instead of the winds or Jupiter, the rain giver" (*nihil hac in sorte pudendum, / nil humile est; tu nunc ventis pluvioque rogaris / pro Iove*).

Discomforted by his inability to determine the woman's position, Adrastus will resort to another trope; he allocates her divine heritage, thus explaining away his difficulty to grasp her social identity, and proceeds to offer animal sacrifices and to mark the area with an altar (4.763–4). Unlike the daughter of Crotopus in Book 1, who was excluded from the ritual performances of state-making, this woman is expected to be co-opted into ritual and thereby to support Adrastus' temporarily jeopardized authority. After all, both forgetting and ritual remembrances are reactions of defensive regimes towards women who elude definition.

Dominated by half uttered contradictions, the woman's first response provides only scant further elucidation of her identity (4.769–73):

Diva quidem vobis, etsi caelestis origo est,
unde ego? Mortales utinam haud transgressa fuissem
luctibus! Altricem mandati cernitis orbam
pignoris; at nostris an quis sinus uberaque ulla,
scit deus, et nobis regnum tamen et pater ingens

How can I be a goddess to you—though I am of divine origin.
But I wish my sorrows had not transgressed the mortal sphere.
A foster mother, you see, with a commissioned charge, herself bereaved.
God knows if there was ever a lap or breast for mine.
Nevertheless, I once had a kingdom and a mighty father.

The impermanence of the woman's position is the overpowering impression of this condensed "career" review. She is a temporary mother, having also been an "interrupted" mother before (now deprived of her children, who may or may not be alive), a king's daughter, but also a queen with her own kingdom. She has divine origins but a low-class current position. In a way resonating with Crotopus' daughter, the most salient feature of her short speech is emotion-as-identity, experienced not as what she is, might have been or might have done, but as what she feels (which is the deepest sorrow) and *this sorrow* is worthy of a god, a statement that confounds Adrastus' attempts at reaching recognition.

Soon after, the stranger picks up yet another role: that of the army's leader guiding the distressed Argives to Langia river in the hope that some water remains nearest to its source. But even then, the text fails to cover the cracks in the logic of the episode. The moment the Argives reach the water is likened to a proper battle: "You'd think armies clashed in war, that a formal battle raged next to the flood" (4.821–2). But this is no ordinary or coordinated battle as everyone plunges into the stream, keeping no rank or order (4.809–11). Leading some, in amidst some others, and following behind yet other groups, the stranger's position continuously flows, unpinned and unfixable, in this charge (4.805–6): "some surrounded, some in a tight crowd followed, some hastened before their guide" (*pars cingunt, pars arta plebe sequuntur / praecelerantque ducem*). Thirst and this woman dissolve many familiar hierarchies of the military and epic landscape, depriving it of conventional modes of leadership and drivers of action.

Deflecting the Gaze: Hypsipyle's Crystalline Wor(l)d

By the start of Book 5, restored to health, the Argives are getting ready to depart. Surrounded by a ring of chieftains and leaning on a spear offered by Polynices, Adrastus is once more a powerful signifier of respected, ancestral authority (5.17–19). This is the opportunity for the narrative to domesticate the elusive stranger. "The soldiers turned their wholehearted attention to her and they all craved to know everything about her" (5.40–2); they need "full representation" so that they can co-opt her within their systems of understanding, leading to Hyspipyle's uninterrupted first-person account (5.49–498), during which the epic text slows down and zooms in, drawn into a formal mode of hyper-granularity, mesmerized by the challenge posed by this absurdly ambivalent figure.[16] But as the immediate settings recede from view, other times and spaces become dominant, deflecting the soldiers' hungry male gaze away from her present, precarious self.

Hypsipyle first takes her audience back to Lemnos and her life as the king's daughter. The Lemnian men linger in the beds of the women in mainland Thrace, as their wives gaze longingly across the coast, elegiac incarnations that recall Ovid's collection of the *Heroides*. After four years of waiting in vain, sorrow turns to anger. One of the older women, Polyxo, incites wrath in all the others, at which point Hypsipyle juxtaposes her carefree life as a girl (5.81). She is the unmarked figure, separate from her immediate environment, free from concerns and from responsibility. And yet, rather paradoxically, when Polyxo urges the women to the temple of the Goddess Athena Pallas, Hypsipyle is part of "the disorderly mob that rushes to pack the place" (5.101–2). Being with them, party to the lethal plan they have hatched, makes her one of them. Polyxo also counts her as one of them, and eager to fix her position in the narrative she leaves a dagger for Hypsipyle on her mattress covering (5.140). But Hypsipyle is not a married woman, and her unfettered, virginal trajectory undermines Polyxo's attempt to integrate her within her territory.

Her ill-defined status as a girl-woman means that Hypsipyle is unburdened by social positioning and the collective demands that are being played out in Polyxo's conspiracy. She is not bound to experience her identity as one of the wives of Lemnos. Not yet assigned a role either by society or by the text, which way will she turn? Co-opted by the women, she witnesses their secret preparations that will lead to the murders of the males returning from Thrace; but, does she see herself in the enraged women? Her recollections form a fusion of images that resist decipherment: is hers a complicit or a disapproving narrative gaze? She is proud and potentially complicit when she admires Polyxo "for daring to speak in the midst of them all" (*et medio sic ausa profari* 5.103). Yet, at some point, she ceases to be complicit and feels like "a deer encircled by savage wolves, lacking any strength in her sensitive heart and meager confidence in the speed of her feet" (*qualis cum cerva cruentis / circumventa lupis, nullum cui pectore molli / robur et in volucri tenuis fiducia cursu* 5.165–7). But can we pinpoint this moment in her narrative? Can we tell apart a complicit narrative gaze from an indifferent or a disapproving one? And more to the point, can she? As the last simile suggests, she does not believe she can completely remove herself from the fury that she flees from and to which she is also drawn. Powered by an irreducible multiplicity, her narrative denies her audience certainty.

She enjoys the confidence of the emotionally drained women, and yet she is not one herself; she is omnipresent but keeps her distance, her narrative holding together sheets of the past and the present in a mess of complicity and impotence. So, her account both suggests and does not suggest that she can be one of them, as chaotic and powerful images roll into each other halting any attempt at fixing them. But is it possible that actually she *is* one of them? The answer, when it comes, stuns even her. When she sees Alcimede carrying her own father's head, the realization hits hard: "These could be my Thoas and my own detestable hand, I thought" (5.240). But of course, lest we forget, in reality it isn't. At this moment of unexpected and deflected (non)recognition, Hypsipyle reaches imperceptibility; she is not what she is seen to be and what she really is cannot be seen. Her character is continuously de-formed and created afresh, in a tension between virtual identities. Thus, she is both a parricide and not a parricide. She controls and delivers her narrative of identity, but within that narrative her identity is never moored and thus never singular. In the trauma of Lemnos, Hypsipyle's subject position as a girl never develops into that of a woman and her pathways are not fixed; similarly, it seems that the tension is not between real and virtual identities, but between sequences of virtual identities that remain within her narrative, and hence blend with each other and cannot be distinguished and captured.

Gilles Deleuze's work on the absurdities of post-1945 experimental cinema includes a concept that resonates with the difficulties the text of the *Thebaid* appears to face when trying to incorporate Hypsipyle. This is the time-image, also referred to as a crystal image in his writings. Working through Bergson's philosophical musings on the abyss of time, and the inevitable blend of past and present, actual and virtual within it, Deleuze foregrounds the power of this blended, mutual image to subvert dominant regimes of patriarchy by undermining what he calls an "organic" understanding of the world, an understanding that assumes a reality pre-existing to its description, which he finds multiply problematic and dependent on mainstream authority.

> The crystalline description stands for its object, replaces it, both creates and erases it . . . and constantly gives way to other descriptions which contradict, displace, or modify the preceding ones. It is now the description itself which constitutes the sole decomposed and multiplied object.[17]

Actual and virtual, real and imaginary, are indistinguishable in the crystalline description that the narrative adopts in its engagement with Hypsipyle. Her flow of images produces chaotic and creative descriptions promoting a world that, at the same time, she is at pains to stop from becoming reality. The male gaze of Adrastus and his men is refracted and weakened in their vain attempt to follow Hypsipyle in a world where, as Deleuze reflects, "immediate and direct confrontations take place between the past and the future, the inside and the outside, at a distance impossible to determine and independent from any fixed point."[18]

Retreating into imperceptibility, Hypsipyle thus inhabits the realm of the unforeseen and the unpredictable. And in a further and sudden breach, she breaks away from the murderous landscape that has tried to co-opt her.[19] Marching into her father's bedroom, she snatches him away from the city that is now governed by death, entrusting him to the sea as instructed by her grandfather Thyoneus (5.266–95). After his departure in the hull of a boat, the girl returns to the city and finally gets co-opted by it, as she feigns a funeral pyre for her dead father and is then made the new queen of the land. But the scopic pleasure is averted and the understanding that Adrastus' men yearn for is still unattainable, as virtual and actual remain in a messy entanglement within it, undermining any secure predictions of what is to come. Hypsipyle needs a convincing funeral procession to establish a narrative that would save her from death. A real throne (and her safety) depends on a virtual death masquerading as real, and the throne needs to remain virtual (even if masked as real) for the father's death to be averted. Scopic domination is dismantled as Hypsipyle's crystalline image is dissolved in the irreconcilable layers of her existence: a king's princess daughter as a queen inheriting due to the fictitious death of her father. She gains a throne based on a lie, but a lie invented to enable an act of piety, leader and hostage of the Lemnian women at once.

Is Hypsipyle a savior or a failure? The question will become more poignant and complicated when, as Book 5 draws to a close, Opheltes, the baby she was appointed to nurse in Nemea, dies neglected by her in the course of her long narrative delay.[20] Scholarly consensus, unconvinced and even distrustful at times, places her in the margins of the narrative.[21] Approaching Hypsipyle with references to the Kristevan chora of female writing and the concomitant abjection associated with motherhood, Antony Augoustakis is first drawn to the authorial space she carves out with her feminine/maternal intervention. However, he also notes Hypsipyle's inability to graduate from the semiotic to the symbolic, which leads to her inevitable excision by the text:

> Hypsipyle indulges in this chora of rewriting by fashioning her story in epic and elegiac terms, but is inevitably confronted by the perils of having entered the world of heroic poetry, where (m)otherhood is threatened by obliteration.[22]

Indeed, the text moves swiftly to foreclose any lingering doubt immediately after the end of her long narrative. Calling her a Lemnian exile (*Lemnias exul* 5. 499), it keeps her at a double distance that underscores her exclusion. Straight after that Hypsipyle mourns the death of Opheltes with a mother's vehement grief, and yet she does not belong to Opheltes, just as Opheltes does not belong to her. Similarly, at the moment of reunion with her own long-missing sons, the text expresses deep joy but cuts her off before she can speak: "shocked by such a gift, she collapses, eyes wet with different tears" (5.727–8). Even when she did speak about her sons earlier on, devoid of any agency, her words alluded to rape. It is "a harsh guest and a ravished bed" that she remembers (5.463–4).

But Hypsipyle does not belong to a single place or a single role for any length of time. The potential of motherhood to settle her image and organize a liminal position for her ultimately fails. Her acting as a mother is also incompatible with her leader's role getting the Argives to water and safety. Her role as a queen is made impossible by her daughter's role, and the other way round. A maiden-mother, free from the stronghold of identities organized and distributed by those in power around her, Hypsipyle exposes the precarity and limitations of female identity politics amidst the Lemnian women, whether in the city of Lycurgus, or inside the Argive army. Hypsipyle acts out roles, without ever embodying those roles, always becoming-Hypsipyle, but always never quite becoming Hypsipyle and thus retaining that critical imperceptibility, a courier of energy and a trace of affect that cannot be anticipated or predicted but can be deeply felt. It is telling that for all his contempt of her, Lycurgus (the king of Nemea and father of baby Opheltes) admits to Adrastus in disbelief tinted by irony that he does not have control over her (5.686–87). She is a slave, but she is also, incompatibly, the epic guest of honor, reciting her back story in a distortion of one of the most typical hospitality scenes expected in an epic: distrusted by all, belonging to none, understood by nobody.

A Line of Flight to Freedom: Argia

My approach to girlhood in the *Thebaid* has been enriched by an engagement with the figure of becoming-woman in Gilles Deleuze's corpus of work. This figure has received much attention by those interested in forging new avenues for a feminism beyond identity politics.[23] In critiquing the oppression of lack inherent within the Oedipal mode of identity, Deleuze looks up to the "girl" as a figure and a gesture of anticipation and escape from the centers of authority in a powerfully alluring world where difference is immanent and continuously evolving. As Deleuze and Guattari put it in *A Thousand Plateaus*:

> Doubtless, the girl becomes a woman in the molar or organic sense. But conversely, becoming-woman or the molecular woman is the girl herself. The girl is defined by a relation of movement and rest, speed and slowness ... She is an abstract line, or a line of flight. Thus, girls do not belong to an age, group, sex, order or kingdom: they slip in everywhere, between orders, acts, ages, sexes: they produce n molecular sexes in the line of flight in relation to the dualism machines they cross right through ... The girl is like the block of becoming that remains contemporaneous to each opposable term, man, woman, child, adult. It is not the girl who becomes woman; it is becoming-woman that produces the universal girl.[24]

Thinking with the girl-as-a-line-of-flight away from the normative codes that constitute the subject allows for the impact to emerge of Argia in Book 12 as a semiotic flow in the narrative that slips through cracks and unsettles the signifying dualism of dominance versus marginality. In this book the narrative marches at pace towards resolution. One king (Creon) meets defeat and another king (Theseus) is inserted as a signifier of a new and healthier order, as a courier of an era of peace and clemency for Thebes (and potentially Rome as well)[25]. In this final section I focus on an episode that moves the narrative away from these locations of power and cannot be co-opted into any of the ritual closures in the text, such as funerals, supplications, a duel, and the final victory of Theseus over the decaying regime.

The start of Book 12 finds Argia amidst the group of the Argive women heading to Thebes to plea with Kreon for their men's bodies.[26] On the way, they meet a surviving soldier, Ornytus, who manages to plant doubt in their hearts regarding their ability to execute the task they have undertaken, and in so doing re-affirms the authorial and authoritative structures that limit the women's options: they can return to Lerna and mourn their dead with empty tombs, new Andromaches signifying the marginality of their grief, or they can turn to Theseus of Athens, pleading with what he claims to be his illuminated authority (12.159–66). The women struggle with this inadequate choice of options (12.174–6). Dissent and dissatisfaction block their plan, trapping them within spaces that are not interested in recognizing them, let alone representing them.

The impasse is blown apart by Argia's deterritorialized line of flight away from the entrapments of location, which keep her in a woman's submissive role. In an interlude, similar, though much shorter, to the one led by Hypsipyle in Books 4 to 6, Argia hijacks the plot, pulling it away from its newly established twin pillars (Creon or Theseus). The epic narrative again adopts a tight focus on her and yet it struggles to articulate her new incarnation and her plan, though trying not to lose sight of her (12.178–82):

> Hic non femineae subitum virtutis amorem
> colligit Argia, sexuque immane relicto
> tractat opus: placet . . .
> comminus infandi leges accedere regni,
> quo Rhodopes non ulla nurus nec alumna nivosi
> Phasidis innuptis vallata cohortibus iret.

> Now Argia conceives a sudden passion of unfeminine strength
> and, abandoning her gender, pursues an immense plan.
> She decides to oppose the laws of that abominable kingdom
> where no maiden from Rhodope, no child reared on snowy Phasis
> surrounded by virgin ranks would go.

Freed from the hegemonic code on appropriate feminine behavior, as the text admits, Argia ventures into a realm that not even mode-defying Amazons would dare enter. The narrative knows she deviates but can neither name nor encompass her flight. It simply follows her through the watchful eyes of old Menoetes, the "supervisor attached to her in childhood to guard her virginity" (*virginei custos monitorque pudoris* 12. 205), a signifier of the guardian role of the state over her. Menoetes is still by her side, but Argia, no longer a maiden, is now married and widowed to Polynices; and she has just transgressed the limitations associated with the married women and widows she has left behind. Feared and desired by all as she now is (12.280–1), she outpaces and shames the narrative's male representative who "feels embarrassed for being slower and admires the strong step of his infirm ward" (12.237–8). The elderly guardian also laments the chilly shadows that swallow up the light of her torch and the numerous times the flames desert her in her arduous journey through the mountain (12.240–2). But she does not seem to care. The narrative also notices the hidden ditches, the wild beasts and the lairs infested with creatures both huge and hideous (12.234–6). But she transverses untroubled and with ease (*secura* 12.235) as if lifted out of her surroundings, losing contact or connection with the world around her. She fails to notice the fading of the light and the plunging of darkness and carries on her journey regardless: an accelerating line of flight defying normative structures.[27]

Through the eyes and misgivings of Menoetes,[28] the text and the authorities that engendered it worry about the loss of supervision as Argia is plunged into darkness, made invisible and imperceptible by those tasked with her surveillance. And with good reason. Exploring the energy underpinning Deleuze's concept of becoming-woman, of the girl as a line of flight, Dorothea Olkowski concentrates on its indifference to differentiation from a regime of the One and the Self-Male-Same. As she puts it:

> "Becoming," for Deleuze and Guattari, is not a metaphor, not a matter of acting like something or imitating something; it is a *deter-ritorialization*, which involves more than simply undermining or doing away with hierarchy. To deterritorialize is to turn toward "lines of flight" so as to dismantle the subject, disorganize the body, or even to destabilize the state.[29]

A thoroughly destabilizing event, indeed, takes place in the no-man's-land outside Thebes once Argia finally locates her dead husband's body. Holding it tight, she lets her grief pour freely until another shadow interrupts her lament (12.349). The text names this shadow immediately; she is Antigone, Polynices' sister and another girl held captive by the watchful eyes of power (12.351-52). But once the two figures meet over the dead body, the narrative gradually moves away from the oppressive need for recognition and control. To start with, Antigone insists on discovering who the hooded figure over her brother's body is (12.362–7). But Argia manages to release them both from the need to control—and thus also their susceptibility to be controlled—by a plea to an affective mode of being as the only worthwhile one (12.375–8):

> Si tu quoque dura Creontis
> iussa times, possum tibi me confisa fateri.
> si misera es—certe lacrimas lamentaque cerno—
> iunge, age, iunge fidem.

> If you also fear Creon's harsh commands
> then I can reveal myself to you.
> If you are in distress—and I certainly discern tears and lament—
> come, join me in trust ...

Bypassing antagonism and the hostility of recognition, Argia invites Antigone to a co-witnessing of pain that takes each one of them out of herself and towards the other. Absorbed by the force of affect,[30] Antigone also starts speaking in a concordant mode beyond the reach of the authority that had kept her hostage in her room until recently. She sees herself disappearing in the body of her brother ("mine are the limbs you hold, mine the corpse you grieve for" 12.383), "her sisterly devotion fading" (12.384–5), folded inside the intensity of Argia's conjugal love that brought the Argian woman to Thebes before Antigone had the chance to escape her prison. In turn, Argia willingly weakens the widow's identity ("I was a lesser care and easily relinquished" 12.397), which she offers when speaking of the affections of the dead warrior in front of them.

A surprising (even random, as Antigone admits: *pro fors ignara* 12.382) encounter is enabled here that resists, through ignoring, dominant modes of perception in Argos as well as in Thebes. Withdrawing from epic sight, the women construct an idiom that functions undisturbed by the binary structures that the violence of those in power has established in the rest of the narrative. Abandoning any demand for cognition, they share touch and tears and the very body of the man responsible for their worlds kept apart. And then they start listening and talking about the evil events, but as witnesses. Each one is determined to construct their narrative as a service to the other woman, and thus upholds the other's pain in their own account. Polynices' story, in Argia's words, becomes the story of Antigone's tears, desperate prayers, and futile connection with her doomed brother across the walls of the city (12.398–405). At this point, the master text, in the voice of old Menoetes, steps in to foreclose the dangerous witnessing-retelling of the plot, as the old guard stops Antigone from taking a turn and urges the two women to complete the burial before dawn (12.406).[31] But in this instance of radical formalism, the trace of this unruly idiom lingers in the narrative as a force that speaks for relationships and turns of events that challenge the dominant social imaginary keeping these becoming-women trapped and apart from each other. As Kelly Oliver puts it:

> Bearing witness, means not only listening to the other but also telling oneself to the other … My experience of myself comes through the narratives that I construct in order to tell myself and my life to another … I construct and reconstruct my experiences for another, even if I do not actually tell them the narrative that I have prepared for them. It is the bearing witness to the other itself, spoken or not, that gives birth to the I.[32]

A Poetics of Imperceptibility

Neither Hypsipyle nor Argia, and certainly nor Crotopus' unnamed daughter, with which this study opened, alter permanently the inexorable trajectory of the epic. And yet, their stories and actions, even when doubted or dismissed, target dominant regimes of perception and create stress points in the socio-symbolic order of the epic. They are brief but telling encounters in (and of) the text that shake the certainties of a bleak and pre-ordained narrative, as they preclude full comprehension and integration within what Elisabeth Grosz sees as a fundamentally deferential politics of identity:

> From the vantage point of (micro-) forces, wills to power, if politics constitutes itself as the struggle for recognition, the struggle for identity to be affirmed by the others who occupy socially dominant positions and among peers for mutual respect, it is a politics that is fundamentally servile; if identity is a "useful fiction," a subjectively apprehended cohesion which required personal and collective validation to take its place as a subject, then this identity is always governed, in advance, by the image and value of the other.[33]

Trying to enact love beyond recognition in the heart of an epic obsessed with domination, "unmarked" women such as Hypsipyle and Argia elude naming and thus point at plotlines and connections other than those allowed or expected by the powerful ones. They are tingly allusions to what kinds of other words exist that undermine the inevitability of the ones that seem to have prevailed. In their complexity and invisibility, they break free from the problematic binaries that keep toxic masculinity in power and all other values in the margins of the text. They are the traces of the narrative, authorial and political doubt and uncertainty that gnaws at this story of arrogance and what diffracts the predominantly male scopic gaze—of kings, soldiers, and the author alike— depriving it of its pleasure and conviction. They are the epic's *punctum,* to borrow from Roland Barthes's reflections in *Camera Lucida*: "The element that rises from the scene, shoots out of it like an arrow … sting, speck, cut, little hole … that pricks … but also bruises"[34] the sovereign assertion of the epic code and the epic frame from within which it spills over, "lightning like … [but] with the power of expansion … [as] a detail that fills the whole picture."[35]

Warning against the dull and dangerous reassurance of recognition, Deleuze seeks thought and experience in those dark moments when systems of meaning fail:

> Something in the world forces us to think. This something is an object not of recognition but of a fundamental encounter. What is encountered may be Socrates, a temple or a demon. It may be grasped in a range of affective tones: wonder, love, hatred, suffering. In which tone, its primary characteristic is that it can only be sensed.[36]

In this chapter, we traced Hypsipyle's and Argia's becoming-imperceptible. An incalculable force of formal resistance indifferent to recognition has left tears and traces all over the narrative before bowing to the epic's arresting wrath and authorial recognition. But the force of the random encounters remains, an assault on the pride and values of the epic text from the disruptive position of the imperceptible.

Notes

1. And especially in Book 2: see, e.g., Laius' ghost disguised as Teiresias (2.89–133); Harmonia's necklace (2.265–305); the Sphinx's ekphrasis (2.496–681).

2. For more on this domesticated Medusa, see Keith 2013.

3. For a reflection on the significance of this radical transition for Tydaeus and Polynices, see, e.g., Alston and Spentzou 2011, 176–92.

4. However, a trusted nurse is not always obsequious to authority. Consider, e.g., Myrrha's nurse and her enabling of incest at the expense of her master Cinyras in Ovid, *Metamorphoses* 10.298–502: on this see Spentzou 2019, 426–9.

5. I am inspired here by Quashie (2021), thinking of the aesthetics of Blackness as a "capacity of wondering and wandering" (82). As he puts it, "[w]e know subjunctivity as an expression of desired or conditional action. As such, subjunctive utterances, through their wishfulness, seem to create or manifest a scene for happening, as if the subjunctive is a spell that casts its subject into the suspension of an imaginary" (59).

6. Phelan 1993, 5.

7. For more discussions on the pitfalls of recognition see below, and Oliver 2001, esp. 23–49.

8. Phelan 1993, 27.

9. Phelan, 1993, 10.

10. Phelan, 1993, 10.

11. Phelan, 1993, 149.

12. Note here two other side-lined girls, Antigone and Ismene, plotting inaudible storylines in the privacy of their chamber, "in broken murmur" (*truncum murmur* 8. 618) beyond the access of the master narrative (Book 8.607–35, and esp. 618–19).

13. Thus reproducing an unsettling generic stereotype, that of the epic hero reluctant to drag his kingdom to war: see, e.g., Latinus in *Aeneid* 7 and 11.

14. On the Deleuzian stutter, see Wohl's chapter in this book.

15. Quashie 2021, 61.

16. For more on this "high-resolution" attention, see Alford 2020, esp. 36–41.

17. Deleuze 1989, 126.

18. Deleuze 1989, 125.

19. Horrifying views of which we are granted in 5.309–13. In a rare relaxation of the book's tight focalization through Hypsipyle, we watch the women being "allowed to see what they had dared do," the morning after the murders (*licuit sentire quid ausae* 5.303).

20. It is rather ironic then that in her lament for Opheltes, she likens the story she has offered to the Argives to a lullaby, when recalling the similar bedtime story she used to tell her baby to help him sleep. (5. 615–16)

21. See, e.g., Nugent 1996 on Hypsipyle's subordinate position to the Law of the Father; see Keith 2000, 57–64, on the absorption of Hypsipyle into the natural epic landscape and subsequent subordination of her into the Roman political order; see also Heslin 2016.

22. Augustakis 2010, 46. See also McAuley 2016, 301 and 387–8.

23. See, as an introduction, Olkowski 1999, esp. 32–58; Flieger 2000; Grosz 2002; Sharp 2009; and Dolphijn and van der Tuin 2012.

24. Deleuze and Guattari 1987, 276–7.

25. On which, see Pagan 2000.

26. For a sympathetic examination of the women's lament here, consider, e.g., Dietrich 1999.

27. Note also her dismissal of Theseus' authority and council, condemned as "slow" (*sententia lenti Theseos* 12.210–11) at the beginning of her flight away from the multiple and intersecting hierarchies of Argos, Thebes, and Athens.

28. And not only: "all she met pointed at her way, shuddering at her appearance, in awe of her miserable plight" (*demonstrat proxima quisque / obvius horrescitque habitus miseramque veretur* 12.220–21).

29. Olkowski 1999, 34.

30. A mighty impulse (*impetus ingens* 12.203) that has propelled and sustained Argia since the beginning of her nightly journey.

31. Note here the moment the guards reach the funeral pyre prepared by the women and the violent recalling of the women into modes of speaking compatible with the marginalized positions allowed to them by the master narrative: "gone was the respect that filled the words of each one until now. One would call it anger and hatred instead, so loud was the shrieking of discord" (*nusquam illa alternis modo quae reverentia verbis, / iram odiumque putes; tantus discordat utrimque / clamor* 12.461–3). See also Manioti 2016, who sees a sisterly-like bond developing between the two women through both likemindedness and competitive rivalry.

32. Oliver 2001, 206–7.

33. Grosz 2002, 471.

34. Barthes 1993, 26–7.

35. Barthes 1993, 45.

36. Deleuze 1994, 139.

CHAPTER 11
FORM AS PRECARIOUS SHELTER: GWENDOLYN BROOKS'S *IN THE MECCA*

Lucy M. Alford

With many others over the past two years, I have been thinking a lot about houses and housing, home, shelter, and enclosure. The Covid-19 pandemic intensified our awareness of inside and outside, proximity and distance to other people, chosen and unchosen relocations, chosen and unchosen confinements: shut-in, shelter-in-place, work-from-home, personal protective equipment. Those who had the luxury of working from home during lockdown confronted the collapse of inside and outside spaces, work and life boundaries, the crowding of family spaces, compounded caretaking responsibilities, the creation household pods, and the taking up of new home-based hobbies from living room workouts to breadmaking to birdwatching. Alongside the movement of all aspects of life into the enclosed home space, housing insecurity also increased. Evictions persisted despite temporary eviction moratoria; rents and housing prices increased despite the overwhelming number of furloughs and lay-offs, as did the vulnerability of homeless populations due to the shortage of social service resources. Crowding and the spread of Covid in prisons prompted an increase in house-arrest sentencings.

In the later stages of the pandemic and into the present, the movement "back to normal" has been accompanied by a steep rise in the number of those being evicted from their homes: according to the Eviction Lab at Princeton, in the last six months eviction rates have spiked to approach and even exceed pre-Covid levels due to housing shortage, inflation, and the lifting of national, state, and local anti-eviction measures and rent-assistance programs.[1] In short, the pandemic has intensified attention to housing and shelter as vital needs, sources of material security and physical safety, zones of contagion, confinement, and crowding, and sites of precarious community.[2]

Housing in and as Poetic Form

Housing structures are sites at which the material, the formal, and the structural come together, as well as the social, the political, and the physiological. The history of housing is a history of material forms by which people shelter their bodies from the elements, gather as families and communities, lay claim to property, and construct interiors that are separate, to greater and lesser extents, from their environments. To build an indoor dwelling is also to construct an outdoors.

Thinking about formed language and its relationship to material history, this construction of self-supporting structures that have standing as objects and spaces of inhabitation is deeply resonant with the construction of inhabitable structures using language as building material. Poems are both made objects and acts of making: formative of subjects, objects, arguments, addresses, cities, landscapes, worlds. Their structures of rhythm and rhyme create temporal patterns (what Husserl called "objects of time in the sense proper") through repetition, symmetries, and internal coherence: self-contained structural systems of formal necessity constructed out of nothing, out of absolute contingency.

Housing, shelter, and home have a long history of articulation in and as poetic form. As the subject of poems, certainly, but also in the lexicon of poetic form. There is a long and trans-traditional history linking poetic form to aspects of housing construction—so many metaphors for what formed language houses or shelters. These metapoetic figures of building, dwelling, and shelter can be found across diverse linguistic and aesthetic traditions. The Arabic line and the Hebrew stanza are both synonymous with "house" (*bait, bayit*), and the English stanza derives from room, or chamber—a stopping place for journeying "feet." Victoria Rimell has observed that "against and alongside competing metaphors of mobility," in imperial Roman literature and in Western culture more broadly "the literary imagination so often appears to live *inside,* in confined spaces."[3] Poetry's etymological origin in *poiesis*—the act of making or building—is a well-rehearsed standby and starting point in discussions of what poems are and what they do.

While the relationship between housing and poetic form has ancient roots, we find in the late nineteenth and through the twentieth centuries a proliferation of writings that tie the work of poetry to the work of building, and the structures of poetry to housing structures—from Emily Dickinson's 466 ("I dwell in Possibility / A fairer House than Prose") to the houses and home interiors that run through the work of Wallace Stevens and Elizabeth Bishop.[4] In modern philosophy, Walter Benjamin's unfinished *Passagenwerk,* or *Arcades Project,* traces the nineteenth-century obsession with interior dwelling-place (the house as a "shell") and the dispersal of this in the twentieth century's move toward porosity, migrancy, and transparency:

The difficulty in reflecting on dwelling: on the one hand, there is something age-old—perhaps eternal—to be recognized here, the image of that abode of the human being in the maternal womb; on the other hand, this motif of primal history notwithstanding, we must understand dwelling in its most extreme form as a condition of nineteenth-century existence. The original form of dwelling is existence not in the house but in the shell. The shell bears the impression of its occupant. In the most extreme instance, the dwelling becomes a shell. The nineteenth century, like no other century, was addicted to dwelling. It conceived the residence as a receptacle for the person, and it encased him with all his appurtenances so deeply in the dwelling's interior that one might be reminded of the inside of a compass case ... The twentieth century, with its porosity and transparency, its tendency toward the well-lit and airy, has put an end to dwelling in the old sense ... Today this world has disappeared entirely, and dwelling has diminished: for the living, through hotel rooms; for the dead, through crematoriums.[5]

Martin Heidegger's essays "Building Dwelling Thinking" and "... Poetically Man Dwells ..." likewise articulate an essential relationship between the acts of building and dwelling ("To build is already to dwell"), finding in both an essential poetic impulse of making and emplacing forgotten or unattended in the existential homelessness of the modern period.[6] Language becomes, for Heidegger, "the house of Being." More recently, Hebrew poetry scholar Vered Karti Shemtov has placed Heidegger's thinking on dwelling in vital tension with the Jewish understanding of "dwelling in text," reading how the latter plays out in twentieth- and early twenty-first-century poetry of Almog Behar, Dan Pagis, and the Israeli social movement protesting the housing shortage in Israel.[7] Reading these works in conversation, Shemtov illuminates an important tension in the relationship between politically and materially confined housing and the relatively unconfined (especially in Heidegger's usage of it) metaphor of "poetic dwelling," reflecting on what happens to the metapoetic figure of the poetic house when it is placed in dialogue with the political realities of housing limitation, exile, containment, and economic insecurity.

Thinking with the relationship between housing and poetic form requires a balancing act between the formal and materialist approaches. On the one hand, the transhistorical and trans-linguistic nature of this relationship indicates a through-running formal practice, and a parallel line of discourse, thought, and metaphorization about that formal practice. Thinking about the forms poems take allows us to consider their standing as objects and made spaces. Comparative formalism allows us to place poems in conversation with one another across times and contexts, across disparate conditions of creation, distribution, and reception. On the other hand, the historical specificity of any poem's moment of composition matters, bearing and reflecting the imprint of its material conditions: the social position of its author, the stability or precarity of their life and the surrounding lives. The poem—any poem—is both imprint and artefact of a physical life: its relation to others, its lifemeans, the available shelters and sustenances supporting or constraining the sheltering and sustaining of the poetic act of making.

An awareness of the ways in which the basic act of building and dwelling in sheltering structures has informed and inflected both poems and poetic theory cannot overshadow the difference between poetic and material shelters. It is easy, particularly when reading the work of poets writing in exile, for whom poetic language becomes a kind of portable homeland, to allow the metaphorical boundary to blur. A "home" in language is not the same as a real home, and a poetic house is not an adequate replacement for shelter, for safety, for housing security. At the same time, the relationship between shelter and poetic form sheds light not only on the ways in which poetic forms have been metaphorized in terms of this basic need, but also serve as articulations and embodiments of what house and home have meant for poets in particular historical moments—whether as an indication of abundance, as in the seventeenth-century Country House Poems convention, or as indications of precarity or displacement. Every dwelling place is a sign of labor (one's own or that of others) to make a certain kind of living possible; every dwelling place also therefore reflects the possibility of not-having. Every house is a structure built out of and against homelessness.

In the Mecca

It is difficult to think of a poetic work that engages more richly with both the formal and material histories of housing than Gwendolyn Brooks's 1968 volume, *In the Mecca*.[8] The volume brings together the longer history of poetry's formal relationship to housing with a semi-documentarian elegy to an actual building, to critique the material conditions of housing insecurity where it intersects with urban segregation and systemic racial inequality.

In the Mecca builds housing insecurity into its very form, while also leveraging that very formal precarity toward a new poetics that combines elegiac witness, social reflection, as well as a formal demolition. The volume as a whole offers a way of thinking about the poetic (or anti-poietic) work *not* of making and building but of unmaking, decreation, and destruction. In this chapter I first offer an overview of the building's history and significance, then a brief sketch of the volume as a whole before turning to focus on a single poem about a broken window.

The volume takes its name from the iconic Mecca building in Bronzeville on Chicago's Southside. Designed by Willoughby J. Edbrooke and Franklin Pierce Burnham, the building was constructed in 1892 as a lavish and expansive hotel for visitors to the World's Columbian Exposition. Its grand scale, encompassing an entire city block, and its distinctive design, three sides enclosing a large glassed-in atrium, were aimed (like the exposition itself) at putting Chicago on the map as an emerging American metropolis on par with New York. After the fair, it was converted to homes for Chicago's white elite. When the whites-only policy was reversed two decades later, Bronzeville became a majority-Black neighborhood, and the Mecca building likewise entered a new chapter of signification. It originally housed Black upper and middle class and was seen as an icon of the glamour and grandeur of the Black metropolis of Chicago's jazz era. As the district suffered and the building fell into disrepair after the First World War, it became a slum home to thousands of low-income Black families. During and after the Depression, there was no firm account of how many people lived in the Mecca's 176 units. In *Report from Part One*, Brooks refers to an estimated one or two thousand,[9] but higher estimates ranged from three to nine thousand individuals.[10] One journalist described people sleeping in closets, under stairs, under kitchen sinks, and likened the building to a massive, over-crowded prison composed of the wreckage of opulence.[11] Illinois Institute of Technology (IIT), which had purchased the Mecca in 1940, moved to tear it down and have the inhabitants removed from the premises. The inhabitants fought for a decade to prevent its demolition, but eventually lost the battle. In the winter of 1951–2, IIT razed the Mecca and replaced it with a building designed by Mies Van der Rohe called Crowne

Hall. Working as a secretary to one of the residents, a medical patent purveyor, in the forties, Brooks had a chance to survey the Mecca's interior.[12] A decade and a half after its demolition, she returned to the building in memory, with the aim "to touch every note in the life of this block-long block-wide building … to capsulize the gist of black humanity in general."[13]

In the Mecca was written in a period when Brooks's own sense of her work and her identity were being razed and rewritten from the foundations up. By the time it appeared, Brooks had already established herself as a major figure in American poetry. Her first volume, *A Street in Bronzeville* (1945), met with wide acclaim, and *Annie Allen* was awarded the Pulitzer Prize in 1950, making Brooks the first African American poet to receive the award. In the intervening years she had published a novel (*Maud Martha* 1953), a book of children's verse (*Bronzeville Boys and Girls* 1956), and her third volume of poetry (*The Bean Eaters* 1960). But her writing was to undergo a profound unmaking and redirection at end of the 1960s. She writes in *Report from Part One*: "Until 1967 my own blackness did not confront me with a shrill spelling of itself."[14] In 1967 she attended the Second Black Writers Conference at Fisk University, where she was for the first time confronted by and immersed in the energy, urgency, and intensity of New Black Arts Movement. Her description of the experience of the conference underscores the shock of the new, the dissolution of a prior selfhood, a rupture of political awakening. She writes,

> Suddenly there was New Black to meet. In the spring of 1967 I met some of it at the Fisk University Writer's conference in Nashville. Coming from white white white South Dakota State College I arrived in Nashville, Tennessee, to give one more "reading." But blood-boiling surprise was in store for me. First, I was aware of a general energy, an electricity, in look, walk, speech, *gesture* of the young blackness I saw all about me … I didn't know what to make of what surrounded me, of what with hot sureness began almost immediately to invade me. *I* had never been, before, in the general presence of such insouciance, such live firmness, such confident vigor, such determination to mold or carve something DEFINITE.[15]

The task, in her post-1967 writing, becomes channeling this new awareness (this "shrill spelling") of the world and her place in it through a radical overhauling of her approach to poetic form.[16] *In The Mecca* is the first volume in this overhauling.

Brooks described her plan for the volume, in this way:

> A book-length poem, two thousand lines or more, based on life in Chicago's old Mecca building.
>
> This poem will not be a statistical report. I'm interested in a certain detachment but only as a means of reaching substance with some incisiveness. I wish to present a large variety of personalities against a mosaic of daily affairs, recognizing that the *grimmest* of these is likely to have a streak or two streaks of sun.

> In the Mecca were murders, moves, lonelinesses, hates, jealousies. Hope occurred,
> and charity, sainthood, glory, shame, despair, fear, altruism. Theft, material and
> moral. "Mental cruelty."
>
> Mouse and moth.

The volume is divided into two parts. The first, entitled "In The Mecca" takes the form of a single long poem by the same name. The second part, "After Mecca," is much shorter, consisting of eleven poems. Critics reviewing the volume when it was published found fault with what they saw as a lopsided structure—decrying the way in which the fullness of the title poem "dominates" the "slight, mainly topical poems" that follow it.[17] But if we take Brooks's design of the volume as intentional—as we should, given the degree of highly crafted formal intricacy that defines her work across volumes—we find that the book's structure reflects and embodies the fullness and complexity of the Mecca building, the violence and void of its demolition, while also opening into a public space of Black life and Black arts.

In its break with received forms such as sonnet, ballad, and rhymed quatrains, the volume also formally manifests the poet's own intentional break with or demolition of the house of the poem—breaking down the very forms that had housed her language and thinking up to that point—structures that proved no longer adequate to reflect or respond to the new consciousness. As Stephanie Burt has written, Brooks's formal break both stemmed from and reflected a desire "to emulate, in the cadences of her own poems, the wildness of a rising generation."[18] Tyrone Williams has noted that, "in this respect Brooks' career differed from that of younger protégés like Carolyn Rodgers and Haki Madhubuhti, whose published works reveal few, if any, 'breaks' in form or content as radical as Brooks."[19]

But a break with intact verse forms is not a break with form itself. And, while *In the Mecca* does constitute a marked exit from formal enclosures such as sonnet, ballad, and sonnet-ballad, still ballad-fragments, sonnet-shards, and abundantly scattered rhyme and metricalities persist throughout the volume. Karen Jackson Ford has argued that Brooks's *desire* to break from these forms—most notably the ballad, the form most strongly associated with a Black American poetic tradition rooted in song and vernacularity—was not entirely realized; lingering traces of these "suspect" verse forms throughout the volume reveal a far more complex and ambivalent attachment to the traditions and communities to which they are tied: "*In the Mecca* intermittently relies on suspect conventional forms, then, even as it works to shape a revolutionary poetry, because these older forms, especially the ballad, still speak to and for the Meccans . . . Perhaps this is why *In the Mecca* is such a formally tortured poem."[20] For Ford, this suggests something resilient about the ballad form (particularly in the context of Black American poetics and social movements) and about the lyric impulse more broadly—its engrained (if ambivalent or "tortured") presence in Brooks's language, and its survival even amid willful suppression. Yet Brooks's "Work Proposed" note for the poem makes clear that the inclusion of these glinting fragments of lyric forms was quite intentional on the poet's part: "Writing tools are to include random rhyme, off-rhyme, a long-swinging free verse, blank verse, prose verse. The couplet, the sonnet, the ballad . . ."[21] "Music," too, is listed on Brooks's list of "high hopes" and "strict personal expectations" for the volume. Brooks's inclusion of the broken forms themselves (in fragmentary assemblage) suggests something vital about the role of deconstruction in the forging of a new poetics, and the possibility that disruptions of song might bend the lyre toward more revolutionary ends.

Fragmentary Chorus, or Choral Mosaic

Brooks's "sheaf of plans" for "In the Mecca" also makes clear her conscious intention to build the building into the poem's very form—its "uninterrupted flow of review" echoing the uninterrupted view across the block-length atrium from any floor; its "long sentences" hallway-like; its construction of "story on top of story": "It is to be Leisurely and massive . . . Mastery of 'style.' Subtle wit. Social width."[22] "In the Mecca," (the title poem and first section of the volume), extends for thirty pages. The entire poem takes place in the interior of the building, while the poems that comprise "After Mecca" take place, with one exception, outside on the street, on corners, at public monuments (the Chicago Picasso and the Wall of Respect), and, in two elegies for Medgar Evers and Malcolm X, in the public space of mourning.

"In The Mecca" opens with Mrs. Sallie ascending the long interior staircase after work, returning home to her children. This large single-parent family and a host of other characters form the cacophonous mosaic of very different lives playing out under one sprawling roof. The assemblage of these lives, pressed together in short fragmentary glimpses of different apartment interiors on different halls and floors, constitute the energy and density of the poem—in Brooks's words (as above), its "mosaic of daily affairs," its "murders, moves, lonelinesses, hates, jealousies," its "hope, … charity, sainthood, glory, shame, despair, fear, altruism. Theft, material and moral. 'Mental cruelty.' Mouse and moth."[23] Brooks's list begins with murders, and it is true that the fragmentary chorus of the poem's many inhabitants coalesces around a single missing child, Pepita. The search for the child takes us up and down hallways, inside apartments, and into repeated encounters with the indifferent intrusion of "The Law." As Jeni Rinner has observed, the structure holding one family from another, one character vignette from another, in the complex of the poem begins to fray and grow porous as the work progresses: "the stanzaic 'apartments' that enclose each character become increasingly porous; especially after Mrs. Sallie's revelation that Pepita is missing, stanzas contain more than one character's perspective."[24]

Pepita is (in name and form) the kernel, the seed at the heart of the poem. But the seed, the pepita, is both terminal (as illness, as wound) and germinal (as potential, as not-yet). Pepita's absence, and finally the discovery of her body, hidden under the cot of one of the Mecca's inhabitants, and tucked into an indent in the middle of a stanza, is the absence or abscess at the heart of a poem-building otherwise bursting with life and movement:

> Beneath his cot
> a little woman lies in dust with roaches.
> She never went to kindergarten.
> She never learned that black is not beloved.

Simultaneously postmortem and emerging at the moment of exodus (from the poem, from the first half of the volume), Pepita's absent voice inserts itself, rhymed and rhythmic like a shard of nursery song: "'I touch'—she once said—'petals of a rose. / A silky feeling through me goes!'"[25] In her notes on the project, Brooks wrote that she "wanted an end-stanza to end all end-stanzas! Directions to Myself—End-stanza like the self-pacification of the sea, after wild threshing." The end of the poem does not offer "closure" but an unsettling proliferation of movements and sounds. The dust and roaches that surrounded her corpse are replaced by the wrigglings of a baby bird, her chopped chirps rising:

> She whose little stomach fought the world had
> wriggled, like a robin!
> Odd were the little wrigglings
> and the chopped chirpings oddly rising.[26]

The violent tragedy that ruptures and rises from the closing of "In The Mecca" launches us, brokenly, into the second half. The childhood that began in the thronging interior of The Mecca is cut short, and we are cast into whatever comes after—after the poem, after lyric, after life, after the building itself.

Writing on this final quatrain, Charyl Clarke claimed that "In the Mecca" should be understood as a "post-modern elegy on the place of the lyric in African-American poetry" in the sense that the poem both "critiques and pays homage to the lyric, the ballad, the sermon, the slave narrative, the proverb, the psalm."[27] "The lyric cannot exist in the Mecca," writes Clarke, "neither can the reversal of class and race locations."[28] The line "[w]e part from all we thought we knew of love" (*In the Mecca* 28) signals "the painful parting with the lyric testament—at least in the Mecca. Lyric is sex, lyric is female, lyric is Western contamination—racial as well as artistic. Again the question of what is there to say, what is the language beyond the ending, beyond 'Farewell'? What can be reclaimed or recuperated? Certainly not Pepita—and perhaps not anyone else in the Mecca. There is damage here, irrevocable …"[29] Rejecting this reading of the "death" or "loss of the lyric"[30] in the poem, and the implied irrecuperability that lyric death implies, Ford argues that "the last quatrain of 'In the Mecca' surely cannot represent the death of lyric. Rising like Pepita's chirpings, expressing resistance and even, oddly, hope, lyric is what survives."[31] Clarke, too, suggests that the poem's final lines suggest the "possibility of renascence— outside the Mecca—the possibility of something 'black and electric' rising out of the rubble, perhaps even out of the dead Pepita's 'chopped chirpings oddly rising.'"[32]

And indeed, the words of one inhabitant, Alfred, resonate with this possibility, this wager—the sense of what life, sounds, movements might begin to rise out of the Mecca's wreckage, and what exits and unmakings that might entail:

. . . something in the Mecca
continues to call! Substanceless; yet like mountains,
like rivers and oceans too; and like trees
with wind whistling through them. And steadily
an essential sanity, black and electric,
builds to a reportage and redemption.
    A hot estrangement.
    A material collapse
that is Construction.[33]

"A material collapse / that is Construction." The poem offers us neither simple "death" (of lyric or futurity) nor any easy message about the survival of song as a metaphor for Black resilience or the human spirit. Song, too, is ensnared and enmired in the very systems it would exit or tear down. I see, in the last quatrain of "In the Mecca" and the ruptural hinge Brooks creates into the volume's second part, something closer to what Fred Moten spoke of, in a lecture at MIT Architecture on building, *Bildung*, and the projects, on the ways in which communities might learn from "our projects, our project" in cultivating an "architecture of movement," even of "radical displacement," rather than of occupying ground: activating displacement as a radical and insurgent sociality that does not replicate the brutality of subject-position-assertion, and the laying-claim to property.[34] In D.H. Melhem's words, "[i]n a destructive environment, she suggests, Black sanity will be curative, not by passive alienation but through a passionate 'estrangement' from prevailing values. 'Material collapse' will be the collapse of a materialistic society. Construction must involve essential change."[35]

The poem does not maintain its home in the Mecca but thrusts us into its after, into what Mai der Vang named displacement's "afterland," into the outdoors. To do this, the volume hinges at a window: first directing the gaze outside and glimpsing wild, creaturely movement there, then taking us *through* the window, in the very act of breaking it. In this way the window is the vantage through which the volume breaks in its passage from the interior of *In the Mecca* to the open and public spaces of *After Mecca*. What follows considers the window as a single built feature of housing construction: its long standing as metapoetic figure, and its formal shattering in the first two poems of *After Mecca*, with particular attention to the second poem, "Boy Breaking Glass."

Windows have been a central figure in the long history of interrelation between poetic form and housing structures: the window's constructed frame and fragile pane have served as compositional container, vantage point, lens, and light-source. This metapoetic figure has suggested not only poetry as framed composition but, more specifically, the site of lyric subjectivity—of I and eye, of self as perspectival position and perceptual lens. The eyes of the house are also windows to the soul and windows on the world. As a formal metaphor, the window has served its lifetime well—as opening frame for the invocational lark song reaching the ears of Bernart de Ventadorn's lovers; as optic frame for desire in Shakespeare's Sonnet 24. Poets from George Herbert to Charles Baudelaire, Emily Dickinson, Rainer Maria Rilke have used windows as figurations of the poetic act. If one goes looking for windows in modern and contemporary poetry, once finds them everywhere: looking in, looking out, keeping in and keeping out. Letting the light in, keeping the world (with its gusts, dust, and intruders—human and nonhuman) out.

Less has been said, though, of poetry's broken windows, despite the many ruptures of form, meaning, and subjectivity in the twentieth and twenty-first centuries. After the loaded interior of "In the Mecca," both of the first two poems in the second section, *After Mecca*, center on windows. The first poem, "To a Winter Squirrel" addresses a wild nonhuman creature, "unbaffleable; / with sentient twitch and scurry" from the vantage of an apartment window: "You out beyond the shellac of her look / and of her sill!" The gaze of the "she" moves "out beyond," and the wildness and free movement of the creature becomes equated with mountain and star. The second poem, "Boy Breaking Glass," breaks the window. Or rather, the poem hears in a boy's act of window-breaking a "cry of art"—a generative shattering of a confining formal frame.

"Boy Breaking Glass"[36]

> *To Marc Crawford*
> *from whom the commission*

Whose broken window is a cry of art
(success, that winks aware
as elegance, as a treasonable faith)
is raw: is sonic: is old-eyed première.
Our beautiful flaw and terrible ornament.
Our barbarous and metal little man.

"I shall create! If not a note, a hole.
If not an overture, a desecration."

Full of pepper and light
and Salt and night and cargoes.

"Don't go down the plank
if you see there's no extension.
Each to his grief, each to
his loneliness and fidgety revenge.
Nobody knew where I was and now I am no longer there."

The only sanity is a cup of tea.
The music is in minors.

Each one other
is having different weather.

"It was you, it was you who threw away my name!
And this is everything I have for me."

Who has not Congress, lobster, love, luau,
the Regency Room, the Statue of Liberty,
runs. A sloppy amalgamation.
A mistake.
A cliff.
A hymn, a snare, and an exceeding sun.[37]

Stephen Best has traced the shattered window (and the "cry of art, urging a rebuild[ing of] the human world") through the poem's fragmented syntax: "the shattering it precipitates moves *through* the poem like a stain or a metabolic enzyme, fracturing the chains in the poem's syntax along the way."[38] Observing sonic rather than syntactical shards, D. H. Melhem described the poem as a "shattered sonnet."[39] Indeed, remnants of the sonnet form can be found in iambic lines starting as early as the epigraph to Marc Crawford[40] (a near-perfect pentameter broken into four and six) and echoed in scattered rhymes (aware / premi*è*re, other / weather, runs / sun). While these formal patterns almost go unnoticed, they signal the formal frame that has been broken.

That Brooks chose the sonnet as the window broken by this poem is telling—both from the standpoint of lyric history and her own development as a poet. The sonnet's rectangular frame is, in the Anglophone tradition, a most iconic frame of lyric subjectivity—the stage of a composed gaze that fixes both lover and beloved in a structure of internal tensions and balances—a formal eye that "looks on tempests and is never shaken." Indeed, mastering, inhabiting, and subverting the sonnet has, since Brooks, become a vital line in Black American poetics, in the work of Rita Dove, Wanda Coleman, Terrance Hayes, Tyehimba Jess, and others. Brooks's own mastery of the sonnet form had helped to launch her career with *A Street in Bronzeville,* in which her neighborhood inhabited highly crafted portraits, most notably in sonnets and ballads, composed in her second-floor corner kitchenette window. Of this compositional vantage, she writes, "623 was right on the corner, the corner of 63rd and Champlain, above a real estate agency. If you wanted a poem, you had only to look out of a window. There was material always, walking or running, fighting or screaming or singing."[41]

The opening line of "Boy Breaking Glass" situates us in a state of syntactical ambiguity, with the word "whose" signaling a question, even as it links up to the title subject. In placing us between questioning and fragmentary continuation, the poem already foregrounds namelessness and breakage: "Whose broken window is a cry of art." Because of the lack of a question mark, the opening continues the sentence the title begins, sonically shadowed by the question, "whose?". The window broken by the boy was likely not his very *own* window, yet the "whose" places the window, broken, in the boy's possession: it becomes his in the act of breaking: *his* broken window. To break a thing thus becomes an act of claiming (or perhaps more rightly *creating*) through destruction or desecration.

This is the "cry of art." Or rather, "*a* cry of art." The indefinite article suggests plurality or non-designation. Moreover, it is not a cry *for* art, but a cry *of* art. Both the indefinite article "a" and the preposition "of" are fruitfully indistinct—a cry of art could be a cry of "art" or art's cry. Taking the latter reading (art's cry) as the more likely, the indefinitely pronoun intensifies: not *the* cry but *a* cry: a cry belonging to a "who" without name or place: "Nobody knew where I was and now I am no longer there." His possession is his act: a negative space that is both creation and cry—both of his own (un)making.

Yet if the boy has nothing "for him" except this "hole," this "desecration," if he has no belongings and belongs nowhere, he is nonetheless *ours*: "*Our* beautiful flaw." "*Our* terrible ornament." *Our* boy "is raw: is sonic: is old-eyed première." Out of the space of the broken window emerges a voice. The boy speaks now directly to us out of the poem: we who did not see him, who have helped create his reality and his namelessness. His voice confronts us with the force of art's cry: "I shall create! If not a note, a hole. If not an overture, a desecration." In the act of breaking, a parenthesis opens—a negative space: success "winks aware." Awareness winks in the broken window as "elegance," and as "a treasonable faith." In the boy's voice, lit with awareness, the reader is singled out in the discomfort of a collective responsibility (we) and in the exposure of singular address: "It was you, it was you who threw away my name! / And this is everything I have for me."

This is everything I have for me. "This" here refers not to the boy's name: that is gone. As he indicts, "we" have thrown it away. It belongs to the *this:* the broken window, the broken form that is the poem itself. His cry is the sound the poem makes, breaking into a different clearing in the final stanza. Shut out from spaces of privilege and comfort, his is an art of amalgamation, of cliffs, snares:

> Who has not Congress, lobster, love, luau,
> the Regency Room, the Statue of Liberty,
> runs. A sloppy amalgamation.
> A mistake.
> A cliff.
> A hymn, a snare, and an exceeding sun.

Brooks's poem of breakage and unmaking is a call to break silence, tear down walls, and exit the comfortable Regency Rooms of privilege, to stand outside with others in the hymn and snare of an exceeding sun. Both at its time of publication and re-reading today, Brooks's Mecca poems ask: What shape must the cry of art take now? What sheltering structures have we built or defended that we must tear down? What windows should be broken to let in air and street and sound? In place of a sealed glass pane, a jagged and glinting opening, an exceeding sun. In place of quiet composure, an audible cry, a shout, a holler, a hymn, a snare. As she writes in the final lines of the volume's final poem,

> It is lonesome, yes. For we are the last of the loud.
> Nevertheless, live.
> Conduct your blooming in the noise and whip of the whirlwind.

Notes

1. Estimations based on monitoring eviction filings in seven states and thirty-one cities. Details on the data sources and trends for individual cities can be found at Princeton Eviction Lab, "The Eviction Tracking System," Eviction Lab, https://evictionlab.org/eviction-tracking/ (accessed January 2, 2023). See also Covert 2022.

2. These are material conditions of our immediate contemporary moment and also part of a longer history of systemic precarity, of which housing is only one manifestation. It could go without saying that the events of the past few years have laid bare the material and physical precarity of human life, while also making starkly visible the unequal distribution of precarity across and within populations in our present historical moment. The pandemic has highlighted the ways in which even crises that render vulnerable all members of the population without exception nevertheless hit those already most vulnerable the hardest, accentuating and deepening longstanding disparities between race, class, gender, and disability groups. Environmental insecurity and climate change have long revealed similarly disparate impacts. On Greek tragedy and the pandemic, see Telò 2023a.

3. Rimell 2015, 1.

4. See Brogan 2005.

5. W. Benjamin 1999.

6. Heidegger 2001, 141–60 and 209–27.

7. Shemtov 2015.

8. Brooks 1968.

9. She writes in "Work Proposed for 'In the Mecca,'" "How many people lived there? Some say a thousand, some say two thousand" (Brooks 1972, 190).

10. Clarke 1995, 136–7.

11. J. B. Martin 1950, 91. Brooks includes the following excerpt from Martin's article on the Mecca (published in *Harper's Magazine* as part of a series on American architectural wonders) among the epigraphs to "In the Mecca": ". . . a great gray hulk of brick, four stories high, topped by an ungainly smokestack, ancient and enormous, filling half the block north of Thirty-fourth Street between State and Dearborn . . . The Mecca Building is U-shaped. The dirt courtyard is littered with newspapers and tin cans, milk cartons and broken glass . . . Iron fire escapes run up the building's face and ladders reach from them to the roof. There are four main entrances, two on Dearborn and two on State Street. At each is a gray stone threshold and over each is carved 'The Mecca'. . ." (Brooks 1968, 2).

12. Her employer, a resident in the Mecca, appears in the poem as the wonder-drug witch doctor, Reverend Williams. A section of the poem is also devoted to his mistreated wife Ida, who, in the poem, dies both starving and "in self defense," from abuse and/or neglect. Karen Jackson Ford (2010) has observed that this section comprises "a brief elegy in ballad form, one of the ways in which Brooks continues to ballad, or ballads continue to rise out of her poetry, even amid and despite her desire to break from her earlier forms after 1967."

13. Brooks 1972.

14. Brooks 1972, 84.

15. Brooks 1972, 85.

16. For a fuller account of Brooks's participations in the conference and her discussions with those present, see A. Jackson 2017, 94–102.

17. Rosenthal 1969.

18. Burt 2007, 84.

19. T. Williams 2022, 163.

20. Ford 2010, 385. For a resonant argument on Brooks's formal ambivalence toward the ballad form, see Goldsby 2006. On the vexed racialization of the ballad form, see V. Jackson 2016, 176–96, on "the spectral ideal of the ballad" in Paul Laurence Dunbar's "Haunted Oak" lynching ballad, and Glaser 2022, on the racialization of form in the lynching ballads of Sterling Brown, Gwendolyn Brooks, and others. Taking up Jacqueline Goldsby's critique of the "cultural logic" of lynching as it inhabits the ballad form as well as Brent Hayes Edwards's (2017) writing on the interplay of thought and music in jazz poetics, Glaser's examination of Black blues and ballad quatrains reads the form not only as a continuation of musical legacy but as "a form in which to test musicality as a raced concept," showing the ways in which "racialized form structures the precarity of black life" (Glaser 2022, 208).

21. Brooks, 1972. Ellipsis in original.

22. Brooks 1972.

23. Brooks 1968.

24. Rinner 2015.

25. Brooks 1968, 31.

26. Brooks 1968, 31.

27. Clarke 1995, 138–9.

28. Clarke 1995, 141.

29. Clarke 1995, 145.

30. Clarke 1995, 144.

31. Ford 2010, 386.

32. Clarke 1995, 145.

33. Brooks 1968, 30–1.

34. Moten 2022. For a rich analysis of *In the Mecca* in the context of the historic and present racialization of "urban renewal" and "urban decline," see Lowney 1998.

35. Melhem 1987, 166.

36. Reprinted by Consent of Brooks Permissions.

37. Brooks 1968.

38. Best 2018, 58.

39. Melhem 1987, 176.

40. Crawford, a Black writer and editor of *Time Capsule*, originally suggested that Brooks write a poem on Black ghetto youths. Of the "commission," Brooks writes, "Marc Crawford asked me to consider: How ghetto blacks, overwhelmed by inequity and white power, manage to live. Does a black boy, for example, turn his eyes away from the Statue of Liberty? How does he talk to himself, comfort himself? What beauties are at his disposal?" (Brooks 1972, 184–5). For a fuller discussion of the poem's origins and its place in the larger context of *In the Mecca*, see Melhem 1987, 153–89. See also Stephanie Burt's consideration of this poem in the context of a larger examination of youth and adolescence in *The Forms of Youth* (2007, 107–16).

41. Brooks 1972, 68–9.

PART IV
FORMS UNFURLING

CHAPTER 12
FORMALIZATIONS AT THE THRESHOLD: INTRODUCTIONS TO HORACE
Victoria Rimell

How to start reading classical texts? This is the root of the matter for me, the "radical" of the volume title.[1] The type and quality of attention to form in the act of classical philology is a *way of being*—characterized not just by an Aristotelian demand for "balance, closure, unity,"[2] but by objectification, disembodiment and the denial of relationality—that is inseparable from the corrupt history of "classics," in its co-formation with patriarchal white supremacy and imperialism.[3] Yet in my subfield of Latin literature, at least, this way of being (or its consequences for the modalities of our readings) still remains largely outside our awareness, even among those scholars who have long rejected what Gianni Vattimo's *Il pensiero debole* called *il pensiero forte*—the inherently violent or deadening exclusion of difference and precarity in the bid to excavate stable, singular meanings from inert texts.[4]

In this tentative chapter, I want to consider form, or taking form, in Latin poetry, at one of the sites at which it is most striking, intensive, and highly charged—the proem or opening poem of a book, where we encounter the shapes, framings, and orderings of a text for the first time. Horace *Odes* 1.1, in its manifest entanglement with *Satires* 1.1, is my starting/sticking point because these poems hold tandem paradigmatic status as programs for a classical Latin book, and for a particular way of reading or being in classical philology. I will stay—ineptly—with this opening, in part because the act of attending to or activating content-form,[5] within the fixed space of this chapter, is slow, undecided, requiring a change in pace and rhythm from faster generalizations, summary, or the fragmenting practice of excerption, but also because, through *SatOdes* 1.1, the challenge I hear in response to recent manifestos for an anti-racist classics is that of tolerating discomfort at the threshold, in the movement of formalization, before I am quite able to arrive.[6]

The Science of Programmatics

All first encounters are exposing, we might say, and they happen again and again. In the language of Gestalt therapy—in which "forms" are continually co-created as a journeying in relationship to moving environment—this is the start of a unit of experiential contact with the world, where the possibility of being changed by the other begins.[7] As Anne Dufourmantelle puts it in her duet with Derrida in *Of Hospitality*, a text which has been formative for me:

> When we enter an unknown place, the emotion experienced is almost always that of an indefinable anxiety. There begins the slow work of taming the unknown, and gradually the unease fades away. A new familiarity succeeds the fear provoked in us by the irruption of the "wholly other."

Thought, she reminds us, is

> a force of mastery. It is continually bringing the unknown back to the known, breaking up its mystery to possess it, shed light on it, name it.[8]

Dufourmantelle might be describing the operation of classical philology in response to the unruly otherness-in-relation of ancient poetry as it becomes a familiar and intelligible object to the trained classicist. Roman classicism, in particular, has come to be defined in scholarship by a canon of "programmatic" proems (Lucretius–Virgil–Horace–Ovid), and getting to know these interrelated "types" of openings has become emblematic of the conventions of reading and teaching classical Latin poetry since the 1980s. What I am calling the science of programmatics in the field of Latin literature responds to the processual experience of relating to a strange new text that is coming into being, by striving, pre-emptively, to obviate or transcend that process: the Latinist works to convert the act-event of inauguration, with its fresh, relational formalizations, into static topics, patterns, and declarations of authorial-generic identity that are dynamic only insofar as they are seen to activate paths within a plottable complex of tradition.[9] The "programmatic" curtails astonishment by harnessing a predictable future and projecting that closure onto the work's opening, so that meaning is not per-formed as (im)possibility but pre-formed as disciplinarily codified knowledge. The task for the Latinist, then as now, is to acquire the tools and skills required to overcome an uncanny or naive sense of being surprised and altered by a new, singular configuration of reality, within a live history of contestation, at the formally delineated threshold of a book: alterity quickly, or even in advance, becomes virtuosity; virtuality becomes actuality;[10] recognition takes the place of apprehension, insecurity, or hypervigilance; categorization overrides oddities or discontinuities; "polyphony" regulates excess; and form is a static functional device, an innovation dissected from affective vitality and from the overt movements of the proem's becoming, as we enter into it. That's what classical philology *is*.[11]

The exemplary status of Horace *SatOdes* 1.1 is multi-layered and inseparable from the notion that interpretation finds its ground in poetic and social form: *Sat.*1.1, published around 36/35 BCE, on the wrong side of the battle of Actium in 30, the year we think the *Epodes* were finished, is said to constitute "a story of Horace's formation" that offers a "blueprint for Horatian satire,"[12] while *Odes* 1.1, launched in the very different world of 23 BCE, displays, in the words of Roland Mayer's Green and Yellow, a "programmatic . . . engrafting of the Greek lyric tradition onto the stock of Roman poetry."[13] Horace is my threshold as he still stands as the cornerstone of Roman classicism and canonicity: in collected volumes, the earlier *Satires* are often printed after the *Odes*, as if to affirm the *Odes*' position at the apex of the canon, their embodiment of the classical body, and the extent to which they are *known*.[14] From the start, the barbed enmeshment of these works' two proemial poems, signaled bluntly in my *SatOdes* 1.1, is a relation kept at bay by programmatics: as Jonathan Culler writes, so soothingly, of Horace, "[s]atiric ventures he keeps for hexameter verse, while remaking the tradition of the lyric, with a wide range of discursive postures and topics of disquisition, from political issues to amorous entanglement."[15] Spiky iambics (and *Epode* 2's cynical fantasy of *beatus ille*) are another thorn in that "variety." Together with Virgil, his contemporary, and Ovid, a generation later, Horace has long come to represent the crafting of new poetic programs in Rome at the turn from Republic to Empire. As if to make room for their own elucidations, which will naturally enter the canon too, Robin Nisbet and Margaret Hubbard begin their Oxford commentary on *Odes* I with the words, "[t]he *Odes* of Horace are too familiar to be easily understood."[16] Michael Sullivan's 2021 article takes up the baton: "among the most familiar," he writes, "is surely *Carm.*1.1, which by virtue of its position might be designated 'exhibit A' of the phenomenon they [sc. Nisbet and Hubbard] describe." He adds: "As every student of Roman literature knows and every synoptic study of the *Odes* duly notes . . . Horace's dedicatory ode to Maecenas takes the form of a priamel, which, after elaborating a series of alternative vocations, culminates in a bold declaration of his ambition to be counted among the canonical nine Greek lyric poets."[17]

Horace's commentators do for Horace what Gian Biagio Conte does for Virgil in his influential article "Proems in the Middle."[18] After noting briefly the proem's liminal position between "speech outside of poetry" and "fully poetic speech," or "not yet song and song," Conte proceeds to master the Augustan proem by dividing content from poetics, and vaunting the "lucid desire for proportion—typical of the new Roman classicism—which attached an aesthetic value to [the] empirical and contingent opposition between two proemial functions," that is, the functions of announcing the work's content, and declaring its poetic program. These poetic inaugurations are mapped as a set of emergent, then solid conventions: they are not invitations to cross a threshold into the unknown, to re-experience what we know in relation to the new, but already-familiar "manifestos," pointing to a future already plotted. The programmatic has become a capacious device for the classical philologist, able to assimilate and correct all foreignness, non-humanness, stuttering or irritation, and to still all form as empirical structure, rather than, as Derrick Attridge puts it, "performed mobility," or in Lucy Alford's terms, an "attentional space."[19] It allows Mayer to acknowledge how "odd" the priamel of *Odes* 1.1. is, but then, leaving oddity aside, to make his case for its "neutrality" as "primarily a focusing device."[20] *Satires* 1.1, a poem that has been called puzzling, dislocated, experimental, a performance of loose connections, of formation and de-formation, can be at the same time summed up as paradigmatic, or as Gowers writes, a "blueprint for how to survive in uncertain times," a tirade of trite commonplaces that "bolster[s] a reassuring impression of familiarity," a "recipe for satire" and a "refresher course for first principles."[21] Within the regulating form of the programmatic, the remarkable, ungraspable singularity of the first satire is enfolded into "polyvocality," the "establishment of Horace's authorial voice"[22] in the "standard canon of program poems."[23] Whereas Horace, and even Maecenas, are vulnerable here, we might be momentarily perplexed (never left awkwardly in the hallway), but only until we get with the program. In the end—and we are always looking towards the end at the beginning[24]—the message is, as Sullivan writes on *Odes* 1.1: "[Horace's] programmatic priamel therefore harmonises archaic subject-matter and Hellenistic method in a manner which sets the tone for the entire poetic project to follow."[25] Or as William Fitzgerald puts it in his concluding comments on the poem, "[l]yric poetry itself is a varied spectacle, a potential anthology, and Horace *will be* included within this, while at the same time his own collection *will be* characterized by variety, hence his final boast [i.e. *Odes* 1.1.35–6]."[26]

I want to ask what might emerge when we consciously work against the instrumentalizing tendency to assimilate and define the other as same at the point where it is most acutely other—in its arrival, or in our initial focus on its contours or content-form. What is that encounter like—understood as a phenomenological process of getting to know (or attempting to relate to) this more or less familiar yet radically foreign other, as what Eugenie Brinkema calls the "energetic possibility of the detail and the particular"?[27] How might we process, or write down, the "affective dilemma" of what she terms "speculative thought derived from reading with form," whereby our faithfulness towards the text as other must always return it to death in the attempt to enliven it, or be alive with it?[28] In his electric and tender writing on El Anatsui's *Fading Cloth*, Stephen Best invites us to experience this aporia as a movement that is both a deferral of and an enactment of living with loss.[29] Yet is what Attridge names, in response to texts like *Of Hospitality*, a "fully responsive" or "hospitable" reading of monumentalized classical proems like Horace's even possible?[30] This question is especially pressured in our teaching, and in our field's outreach. The tendency is, as Dufourmantelle puts it, to "regally think the other (the guest)" before moving on to "examine another question," never, as Emmanuel Levinas explores, to "let [thought] lose its bearings."[31] Yet classicists have developed many other often ingenious ways of curtailing the oscillation Best sustains. We can call out more-or-less un-self-conscious formulations of irreducible alterity (thinking "we have reached out to the Other ... we in fact enclose ourselves in a narcissistic fantasy of self-reference"), while postponing the process of tracking how the "degree of alterity" that persists in the "political" encounter not just with "antiquity" but with particular texts impacts us as ungeneralizable individuals within a collective.[32] We can insist, as Don Fowler put it in his landmark *Classical Constructions: Readings in Postmodern Latin*,[33] that we are "making it up" all the way (within the confines of our interpretive communities), so that the truth that "meaning is constructed, not discovered" is made to constitute both an unconcealment of ethico-political responsibility and a re-concealment of the two-ness of relation—the capacity not just to meet but to *be met*, over and over, in a subject-subject rather than subject-object relation.[34] Or we can, like Eve Kosofsky Sedgwick, become "perverse readers" by enacting "a visceral near-identification with the writing ... at the level of sentence structure, metrical pattern, rhyme," a "kind of formalism" that for her was "one way of trying to *appropriate* what seemed the numinous and resistant power of the chosen objects" (1994, 3–4).[35] Alternatively, we can turn away from texts altogether, cramming all attempts to approach them "in the original" into the exclusionary history of ancient language "mastery," and stay instead with "telling and teaching the critical histories of the so-called discipline of Classics."[36] All these moves avoid the difficulty of acting on our responsibility to the other that is the ancient text, to accompany its stubborn resistance and singularity as it comes into being and impinges on us in our idiocultural reading of it.[37]

Priamel

If we don't deploy programmatics to turn form from a verb to a noun, what becomes of us when we cross the threshold(s) of *SatOdes* 1.1? Both poems involve, in different ways, a poetic form that we call the priamel, a term coined by German scholars from the medieval Latin *preambulum*, which was first used to describe a poem containing a series of seemingly disconnected paradoxical statements brought together wittily at the end. In modern scholarship, the priamel refers to a rhetorical form in which multiple examples, or others (depersonalized as "the foil"), lead up to or introduce a focal point, or "preferable" perspective ("the cap" or "climax") that marks an arrival in the here and now.[38] Long taken as emblematic of the lyric genre (famous examples include Sappho fragment 16, Pindar, *Olympians* 1.1–8, and fragment 221[39]), the priamel takes pride of place in classical philology's stock of programmatic forms, an exemplar of the "set piece" or "kind of generic composition"[40] that functions to re-enact on multiple levels the process of establishing what is "best," or first-class, *classicus*.[41] By the time we get to Horace, "the diversity of men's pleasures and pursuits was in fact an old literary topic. The prototype appears as early as Solon . . .": "not only the content but the form of our ode is traditional."[42] *Odes* 1.1, "probably the most famous priamel in Latin literature,"[43] is already poised to supplant its predecessor/counterpoint/ugly twin, *Sat*.1.1, in a kind of intertextual parallel process. The opening of *Sat*.1.1, also addressed to Maecenas, is described as an "inverted priamel,"[44] because instead of running through a series of others who are content with or resigned to their lot, before setting in relief the poet's preferences and ambitions, the poem catalogs people of different trades (many, like the soldier and farmer, reappear in *Odes* 1.1 as well as *Epodes* 2) who are always unhappy even if offered abundance or a different life, in uncertain and never explicit contrast with the evasive poetic persona. We never quite read here a 'but *I* on the other hand' (Sappho's ἔγω δὲ at fr. 16.4), which is available only fleetingly, implicitly, in the *raro* of lines 117–18 (*inde fit ut raro, qui se uixisse beatum / dicat* "And so it happens that rarely is there a man who can say he's lived a happy life"), an "indirect thank you to Maecenas for making him self-sufficient"[45] perhaps, unless this smug contented type is another foil to some putative (just as dodgy?) exterior position, after *beatus ille qui* (*Epode* 2.1). At the same time, as much as philology would want to isolate *Odes* 1.1 from satirical and iambic contagion, or to package its "retrospection" in the abstract as establishing "generic continuity,"[46] it is bound to admit that this is "an odd poem"[47] that stands "normal and expected proportions on their heads."[48] The "foil," in other words, takes up almost the entire ode, and as Kirk Freudenburg notes in his review of Michèle Lowrie's *Horace's Narrative Odes*, it seems to include or echo not little of what is distinctive about the "cap," or the poet's insistent "but me" (*me . . . me . . . me* 29–35):

The question I ask of the priamel is not "which one is Horace? The guy under the tree? Just the counterposed *me* of line 29?" but "which one isn't Horace?" Oddly, in the course of the poems that follow, we see that this poet will, in fact, raise a cloud of two of Olympic dust; he will launch ships of his own and contend for honor and immortality; and he will spend a good deal of time in subumbral sipping, unwary of falling limbs. The priamel runs us through options explored, even in promising not to explore them. And in the process, it reminds us of the multifarious nature of lyric itself.[49]

As Fitzgerald expands, again rooting us in the deradicalizing science of programmatics, "Horace *will not* so much stake his own place among the variety of lyric poetry, in which the priamel is the form which distinguishes a given poet's uniqueness, as embrace or *contain* it— all within his more various understanding of the lyric genre."[50] But what would it be to stay instead with (or *italicize*) the question of where we are in response to the shades of connection and contiguity in *SatOdes* 1.1? What does "variety" or the "multifarious" avoid, and what is made possible when we bring that avoidance into awareness?

No One and Me

What excites *me* in *SatOdes* 1.1 is the way in which the Priamel welcomes us into the dilemma of negotiating the relation between self and others, or self and not-self. On the edge of the book, it seems to animate, in a parallel process that invites inter-action, the attention to form that Alford describes as "itself an opening, a site of porosity between subject and object, or between subject and subject."[51]

And yet we—I—(false) start with no one, the "unpoetic"[52] *nemo*:

Qui fit, Maecenas, ut **nemo**, quam sibi sortem
seu ratio dederit seu fors obiecerit, illa
contentus uiuat, laudet diuersa sequentis?

How come, Maecenas, that no one alive is ever content
with the lot he chose, or the one fate has thrown in his way,
but praises those who follow other paths?

Even with the help of a rich classical commentary on "this first in a trio of diatribe satires," and despite, or because of all that I think I know about Latin literature, this is tough going, always a first encounter all over again. I'm stumbling in the dark through the reshaped hexameters, their conversational fragments hard to pattern. Because I don't know *who* this is I'm overhearing, although I'm almost sure he's taking the mickey as trite pub-philosopher character, and there's no way of knowing whether Maecenas, the addressee, is in on it or the butt of the jokes on conspicuous consumption, or both, I don't quite know who I am in relation, and how to respond.[53] Who are the anonymous interlocutors imagined to be? Do I laugh at, imagine laughing at them as one of the in-crowd? True to form, I am surging ahead. But actually, it's hard even to get beyond *nemo* in the first line—that could really include everyone, including the speaker, Maecenas, and me as audience, or I could neutralize it as "proverbial," or assert my power to differentiate (the philologist is nothing if not elite).[54] Horace's "Why are you laughing" (*quid rides?*) trips us/*me* up later in line 69, as *sermo* (conversation) dismantles the form of the hexameter: change the name, and the tale is told of you, he adds (*mutato nomine de te / fabula narratur* 69–70), a "programmatic warning"[55] that doesn't save me. Ditto the notion that such interjections are "typical of diatribe"—nobody, *nemo*, is immune from insatiability, or abuse. But there I go again, pushing on.

In my squirming response to the "inverted priamel" of lines 4–12 (every man is unhappy with their lot, and thinks he wants someone else's life), I too would rather be that other person who *isn't* already exhausted, "bowed by age, body shattered by service" (*grauis annis / . . . multo iam fractus membra labore* 4–5). Is it wise, or stupid, to sneer at what commentaries call this "human irrationality," not being happy with what you already have? It's a corny joke, remember: *mempsimoiria* is a typical diatribe theme.[56] On the other hand (*contra* 6), how could we possibly start reading any poem without imagining being in someone else's shoes, or imagining what it's like inside someone else's house just as we are invited in? The hackneyed is a false refuge, a flicker of something uncanny in the here and now.[57] Turn the tables and the envied trader's ship is tossed on high seas: further fantasies of security are required. Meanwhile *he* thinks being a soldier is better, as in battle you either win or the end is quick (*Sat.* 1.1.7–8):

> "militia est potior. quid enim? concurritur: horae
> momento cita mors venit aut uictoria laeta."

> "A soldier's life is better." Why? "You charge and then:
> It's a quick death in a moment, or a joyful victory."

The anxious merchant's "fickle" words here offer me an impossible choice, a moment of crisis. Gowers writes of *uictoria laeta* that this is a "a rare type in *Satires* I of hexameter ending . . . noun followed by adjective, both with short endings, by now old-fashioned and a nod to cumbersome martial epic. Triumphal cliché and plodding verse downplay the charms of the soldier's life."[58] As a ventriloquized relic of martial epic, the trader's words become satirizable, or perhaps self-satirizing—his grass-is-greener aspirations are not just poeticized fantasy, they collapse under the weight of their own pompous anachronism. This whole sketch is straight out of some dusty textbook, is it not? Yet the framing (*militia est potior. quid enim? concurritur*), like *qui fit?* (1), hones a dislocated, run-together hybrid that —like the rest of this "inverted priamel"—sits at that turning point of time (*horae / momento*) between clunky old hexameters and their clipped reshaping in the new now of Horace's "conversations." The question of how to respond to the ironic old schoolboy routine of unhappy men imagining stepping into someone else's life has now become the opening for me to desire to enter into this poem as someone else's—Horace's—process of (de)formation. This is the satiric event—if I do not on some level read *nemo . . . contentus uiuat* as including me, I cannot enter this restless world full of others I both know and do not know.

This moment is never over. Rather than setting up the program, the end of *Sat.*1.1 returns us to the beginning, and to no one (108–9):

> illuc unde abii redeo, qui **nemo**, ut auarus,
> se probet ac potius laudet diuersa sequentes

> I return to my starting point, that because of greed no one's
> content in himself, praising all others who follow different paths

Editors prefer *qui nemo ut auarus* (attested only in the lost Blandinius vetustissimus, V), over *nemon ut auarus*, on the grounds that, with *laudet diuersa sequentes*, it "recapitulates the start of the poem":[59] ring composition becomes an anchor for form, rather than an enactment of unfinished formalization/Gestalt that blurs the poet's "home stretch" into the pathetic circular strivings of the discontent—charioteers in the circus of life who always get outrun by someone richer (112–16). No one is naming any names here. Within the philological scaffold of form, Horace must always be the exception to *nemo*— the rare *beatus* ("the contented guest image . . . stands in for H."[60]); and the final lines of *Sat.*1.1 must, unsatirically, affirm the closural reshaping of "Lucilius's over-egged pudding into a form contained by proper limits,"[61] by way of already-classical Lucretius and Virgil (117–21):

> inde fit ut raro qui se uixisse beatum
> dicat et exacto contentus tempore uita
> cedat uti conuiua satur reperire queamus.
> iam satis est. ne me Crispini scrinia lippi
> compilasse putes, uerbum non amplius addam.

> Rarely can we find a man who says he's lived a happy life,
> who when his time is up is content to go,
> like a guest at a banquet who's had his fill.
> Well, enough of that. In case you think I've rifled the shelves
> of half-blind Crispinus, I'll not add a single word.

The dialogue with Virgil is "closest" in the "closural cluster of *satur* and *satis*"[62] (cf. *Ecl.* 10.70 *haec sat erit*; 10.77 *ite domum saturae, uenit Hesperus, ite capellae*), but the jolt of *iam satis est* seems both to affirm satisfaction and set a premature, violent limit on satiety. We are starting, not concluding; we can rarely find the man who (says he) is a contented guest, where *raro* is barely a softening of *nemo*, and beatitude is a well-soiled cliché, even before *Epode* 2. My introduction to Horace, overspilling with others' fullness, seems to re-enact the impossibility of hospitality as I approach its entry hall, a no man's land between outside and in.

One and the Other

Just as *nemo* returns on a loop in *Sat.*1.1, so the "foil" in *Odes* 1.1. takes up almost the entire poem. The signature *Maecenas* in the first line registers to me now as a satiric trace of inescapable vulnerability on the threshold of someone else's kingdom. But there is new security here, it seems, an enclosure/defense (*praesidium*), a sense of eavesdropping on something close to intimacy—*dulce decus meum*—that might spur me to begin *SatOdes* again (1–2):

> Maecenas atauis edite regibus,
> o et praesidium et dulce decus meum,
>
> Maecenas, birthed from royal stock,
> my protector and sweet glory,

But then we take a wide swerve towards those "others" (*sunt quos*), and visualize in lines 3–4 lurching in a chariot around the turning post, just avoided in the hanging *euitata*, with its long syllables, at the start of line 5 (3–8):

> sunt quos curriculo puluerem Olympicum
> collegisse <u>iuuat</u> metaque feruidis
> euitata rotis palmaque nobilis
> terrarum dominos euehit ad deos;
> <u>hunc,</u> si mobilium turba Quiritium
> certat tergeminis tollere honoribus;
>
> some with their chariot love to raise
> Olympic dust, and when their wheels skid hot
> around the turn, the noble palm exalts them
> to the gods—masters of the earth.
> This man when the mob of fickle Romans
> strives to lift him up to triple honors;

The first Asclepiad, a very different meter from the hacked-up hexameter of the *Satires*, but apparently just as experimental and avant-garde in Latin (as far as we know it makes its first appearance here[63]), lays out rhythm in a smoother form. But where am I in relation to this patron-poet duo, and to these "others"? Pushed away? Elevated from? Invited in? Made a witness? What kind of space for (disrupting) avoidance do I find in *euitata*? Am I doing it or watching it as I'm immersed in the dust, heat, and speed? Where in *Sat.*1.1 there was anxiety and restlessness in the strange-proverbial "others" striving in the circus of life, who might include the speaker, and *me*, here there is pleasure, *iuuat* (4); perhaps, in the ahistorical, asatirical "floating … present tense" of lyric, in which "not a crack remains to recall [the] shattering"[64] of civil war, it can be our pleasure too as we think ourselves into the thrill of those masters of the universe, rising to the gods—along with or like the poet, hoisted to a place Maecenas was born into effortlessly? That the "glory of an Olympic victory" has form (cf. Pindar and Libanius) takes the heat off; but in the cycle of *SatOdes* 1.1, the foil is always doubled, re-intensified, and I am reminded of all those bypassed losers at the back (*temnens extremos inter euntem*, *Sat.* 1.1.116).

Hunc (7) brings us down from many to one. This man is pleased if (big *if*) the crowd of mobile/unpredictable Romans strives to raise him up with triple honors: *honor* might be a synonym for *decus*—if so, how does poet relate to politician? How does fickle mob relate to Maecenas, and his power to elevate and promote? Nisbet and Hubbard note *ad loc.*, working backwards from the programmed end yet risking self-sabotage in touching the Gestalt of *SatOdes*, "the grandiloquence of the noun [*Quiritium*] is satiric; Horace is hinting at the drawbacks of other men's pursuits."

That man too, *illum*, is happy as he is—the pleasure of *iuuat* taken for granted now, although it feels diluted, almost erased (9–14):

> illum, si proprio condidit horreo
> quidquid de Libycis uerritur areis.
> gaudentem patrios findere sarculo
> agros Attalicis condicionibus
> numquam demoueas ut trabe Cypria
> Myrtoum pauidus nauta secet mare.

> That man, if he's stored in his own granary
> every speck swept up from Libyan floors.
> The man who adores splitting ancestral acres
> with a hoe, you'd never coax him—
> by the terms of Attalus—to swap lives with a sailor
> in his Cyprian hull, cleaving Myrtoan sea, terrified.

He's chuffed if he can sweep up the last bit of Libyan grain and store it all in his barn. The chaff has been blown away, rising into the air like dust, leaving the good stuff on the ground to be gathered up. A pleasure not in elevation, then, but in security, in putting away for the future in the owned barn, an enclosure embodied precarity can(not) enter (cf. *SatOdes* 1.1.44–8[65]). I seem to be moving into a different kind of pleasure now, earth-bound, not the impersonal *iuuat* but the long drawn-out present participle *gaudentem* (11), the farmer enjoying hoeing paternal fields: this "sympathetic sketch, drawn without satire"[66] [in the nick of time, but too late for *me*], leads up to "you'd never shift him from this" (*numquam demoueas*), not for all the wealth of Attalus, the second-century BCE king of Pergamon renowned for his love of luxury. Who's you? Maecenas? Us? A generalized, "you wouldn't," or "blurred you"?[67] Here at last we have a man content with his current status—although in the transference of *SatOdes*, not to mention *Epode* 2, the corny fantasy of being a farmer (*tu, consultus modo, rusticus*, *Sat.* 1.1.17) is someone else's embarrassment: the uncanny contradiction and joke of the proverbial cliché that is *actually so unrealistic now in practice* in *Sat*.1.1 seems to erupt here, in the spondaic reveling that is *gaudentem*. But still, now, the desire to change him, the intrusion of the desire to *mobilize—demoueas*—in this inaugural taking-form that we are making happen.

Then, in another swerve, an opaque subject: the farmer wouldn't be a sailor. But we do not know what the other, the sailor, wants, what he takes pleasure in, whether he ever imagines himself as another (as a soldier? *SatOdes* 1.1.6–8 and *Epod.* 2.5–6); whether *secet mare* ("splits the sea") sits in parallel with *findere agros* ("to split the fields"),[68] whether *pauidus nauta*, the scared sailor, is a devitalized, "proverbial" phrase,[69] and whether there is a pleasure in danger, if only for the fantasizing onlooker.

Luctantem at the start of line 15, still energized perhaps by *iactantibus Austris* (*SatOdes* 1.1.6), is another lurch. Or, if you like, "another gliding transition":[70] I might linger on the neat nestling of *Icariis fluctibus* within accusative object *luctantem Africum*, but at the same time the weird non-human agency of wrestling wind, and then the two-ness of wind-wrestling-waves, enlivens the storm and the merchant's affect (15–18):[71]

> luctantem Icariis fluctibus Africum
> mercator <u>metuens</u> otium et oppidi
> laudat rura sui; mox reficit rates
> quassas, indocilis pauperiem pati.

> The merchant fearing African winds as they
> wrestle Icarian waves praises the quiet
> of his home town and its fields; yet soon he mends
> his shattered boats, unused to the pain of poverty.

Icariis fluctibus seem to me as I per-form them to evoke the image of Icarus falling like a black dot from sky to sea, "a picturesque detail"[72] that cannot quite inhibit a rapid dive from (the hubris of?) *euehit ad deos* (6). As the alternative ways of living and being pile up, the fearing merchant (*mercator metuens*) enacts the unknown terror in *pauidus nauta* as a newly shaped affect, while the odd rub of *metuens otium ... / laudat*, in lyric's tight space, seems to ruffle the escapist (anxious) defense. In *SatOdes*, people again want to be someone else, not a sea trader at the mercy of the elements, but a simple type who sits at home and enjoys the countryside. The priamel is becoming a foil to itself as it expands and draws me in: the *mercator* dreams of stepping into another poem, but he is forced to suck it up and mend his boats, or face crippling poverty. We don't want to be him now, as fantasy yields to the constraint of form as a material happening.[73]

Then, a respite, perhaps, or a response to fear: *est qui*, making a pattern or contrast with *sunt quos* (19–25):

> est qui nec ueteris pocula Massici
> nec partem solido demere de die
> spernit, nunc uiridi membra sub arbuto
> stratus, nunc ad aquae lene caput sacrae.

multos castra iuuant et lituo tubae
permixtus sonitus bellaque matribus
detestata.

There's one who won't spurn cups of old Massic,
who wastes the best part of the day lying down,
now under the greenwood tree, now
softly close to sacred waters at their source.
Many men love camp, and the sound of trumpets
mixed with horns, and the wars that mothers
hate.

I catch a playfulness in *nec . . . spernit*, stretched out over lines 20–1 (well, he wouldn't say no), and in the Greekish repetition *nunc . . . nunc . . .* (21–2),[74] the sprightly pleasure of the now, and of a body—limbs stretched out under a tree, by a gently murmuring brook, with optional sound-effects from elsewhere (*Epod.* 2.23–8). The impersonal verb of line 4, *iuuat,* returns in line 23 as the plural *iuuant,* pleasure for the many (*multos,* cf. *sunt quos,* 3) in a different kind of sound, the cacophony of clarion and trumpet, announcing war. The noise carries far, high into the air, towards the frigid Jove or cold sky (25) that strikes me now, with *Epod.* 2.29–30, as a depersonalized counterpoint to hot-faced Jupiter, all epic-satiric puff, in *Sat.*1.1.20–2. But then again, as if staying with Icarus' fall, the loss of a son, and the terror of shattered ships, the hanging

bellaque matribus / detestata

Mothers, those disturbing others, subjects-always-in-relation, hate wars. Again, or increasingly, the priamel—a poetic form that cultivates a repeated movement to the limit and to the experience of the other before stopping me short—generates its own foils.[75] The enclave of personal lyric —emblematized after Sappho, it is said, by the priamel—is made unhomely by the madness and rage of the grieving mother. Compare and contrast the classic, violent form of the latest English commentary on this line:

"However hateful war is to mothers, H. was a realist and knew that there is no point in trying to argue men out of their pleasures."[76]

In the final foil to the foil, in lines 26–8, the hunter must forget his relationship to his "tender wife" as he focuses on his next prey, a deer about to be caught by his dogs, or—another foil—a boar who tears the finely spun enclosure and, perhaps, this time, escapes (25–8):

. . . manet sub Ioue frigido
uenator tenerae coniugis immemor,
seu uisa est catulis cerua fidelibus,
seu rupit teretis Marsus aper plagas.[77]

> ... The hunter stays out under a frozen sky,
> forgetting his gentle wife, whether the
> faithful hounds spy a deer, or a Marsian
> boar has ripped the fine-spun nets.

In a fleeting opening to curiosity and desire, I do not know what the hunter feels when separated from or "forgetting of" his wife, whom I meet coddled/trapped in his forgetting ...

> uenator *tenerae coniugis* immemor

... let alone what it is, for her, to be forgotten. Who does not forget? (*quis non* ... / *obliuiscitur? Epod.*2.37–8). Musurillo senses "after line 27 the structure seems to break down."[78] In this way, the poet arrives at himself, *me*.

If

> *me* doctarum hederae praemia frontium
> dis miscent superis, *me* gelidum nemus
> Nympharumque leues cum Satyris chori
> secernunt populo, si neque tibias
> Euterpe cohibet nec Polyhymnia
> Lesboum refugit tendere barbiton.
> quod si *me* lyricis uatibus inseres,
> sublimi feriam sidera uertice.
> (29–36)

> Me the ivy, prize of poets' brows, entwines
> with the gods above; me the cold grove and
> the gathering of light nymphs and satyrs
> draw out from the throng, if Euterpe the Muse
> won't deny me her flute, not Polyhymnia
> refuse to tune the Lesbian lyre.
> But if you include me among lyric poets
> I will hit the stars with my exalted head.

The poet's triumphant assertion, *dis miscent superis,* curiously close to or entwined with the apparent foil in line 6 (*euehit ad deos*), reforms the mixing of sounds in the inauguration of war, *permixtus sonitus.* There shall be a splitting off from the people (*secernunt populo*), from those others who have the power to elevate in 7, and before that, implicitly, from the crowds that cheer on the charioteer in lines 3–5. Secluded in his cool grove (*gelidum nemus* 30), "the poet is the very epitome of aesthetic detachment."[79] My response to the form of this epitome takes shape as a growing awareness that the triple condition (*si neque ... cohibet ... nec refugit tendere ... si inseres*) can fold back into the precarity of *si . . . turba . . .* and *si . . . condidit*, the aspirations of the politician and the grain farmer, in lines 7–9, and that, as Santirocco muses, and as Musirillo first noted, "it is tempting to identify the hedonist [of lines 19-22] with Horace himself."[80] The other is already here, in the comic gigantism of the poet knocking his head on the stars,[81] in the fickle *populus* that can elevate him or have him crash like Icarus, who got his comeuppance after getting too close to the sun, and in the dependency that haunts all those final "ifs." The problem, as ever, is not sameness/inclusion, but the quality of inter-relation.

Classical philology's long-running debate on whether Horace's preamble is argumentative or non-committal (that is, whether, as Kenney puts it, "the poet leads up to his theme by way of a series of rejections,"[82] or whether "the priamel here is largely neutral," giving "emphasis by means of contrast"[83]) is "complicated," as Fitzgerald captures recently, by the notion that Horace can appear "both in and out of the list," or foil.[84] In Santirocco's formative study, the entanglement of foil and climax, which would "violate the priamel structure," becomes the philologist's foil to a climactic conclusion of detachment ("*Set apart* from other men ... this picture of the poet *will recur* in many odes, but here, at the very outset of the collection, it functions as an *accurate gauge* of the *distance* Horace has travelled from satire to lyric"[85]). Similarly, although Fitzgerald tunes into the poem's movements between connection and separation, multiplication and deduction, the challenge of being with the other in *SatOdes* is again postponed. In this way of being, the pleasurable performance of variety—a nod, perhaps (how could it not be?) towards our politics of diversity—evades what Kevin Quashie describes as the "tussle of relation,"[86] and has us delight in a spectacle from afar. The priamel is, again, safely programmatic: "his own collection *will be* characterised by variety, hence his final boast."[87]

Still, I do not quite know where to begin.
How shall we start reading classical texts together?

Notes

1. Brinkema (2022, 20–1) parses this as a "return to the speculative *ground* or *roots* of what thinking can claim" which "involves reading without guarantee; its terms, affordances, and stakes cannot be declared and secured beforehand."

2. Freudenburg 2001, 6.

3. Freudenburg (2001, 6) writes in response to Henderson 1999, and alluding to Iser 1978: "That desire to authorize them [sc. Latin texts, esp. satire] in that way [i.e., as "singularly meaningful and trouble-free"] ... has to do with our being stubbornly human (not just stubbornly 'western'), and thus afraid of the chaotic and the unknown. We are, at some level, hardwired to make these misguided demands." While fear of the unknown is uncontroversially a feature of being human, such universalizing moves exemplify for me the concealment of the specificities of vulnerability and ethical responsibility in post-90s philology, which are often packaged (and again concealed) in the generalizable "ideology of the individual reader" (Fowler 2000, viii, *et passim*), a foundation to be confessed defensively, up front: or as Henderson puts it, albeit with gentle mockery of "the personal voice" (1999, x), "First, let's get *me* out of the way." See discussion to follow.

4. Vattimo 1983. It is worth noting that this is still the almost unchallenged status quo in the field of classical philology in mainland Europe and especially Italy, which produces a large portion of the world's professional Latinists in universities today.

5. On the interdependency of content and form as a spatio-temporal process, see Attridge 2017, 150–70; cf. Eyers 2017 (e.g., 9, 13), on troubling "the distinction between form and content," where form is often seen as an "immoveable and static encasement of a kinetic literary content, sluggish in its response to history"; Eyers's "theory of formalization" bears "synthetically within it the characteristics usually associated with form and content both."

6. E.g., Umachandran (2022) calls for "life transformation" in the relinquishing of "performances, self-conceptions, and repertoires of mastery." She adds, " 'I do not know where to begin even though I know we must' is a fine place to start." (27). Compare Derrida's elegiac oscillations in "Title to Be Specified" (2011, 194): "But your moment of discomfit, these doubts drifting about the waves or the semantic froth in the air, you don't dominate them. They leave you awash on the border of a shore where you want to arrive safe and sound or even, I would say, arrive *yourself*."

7. The particular experimental putting into practice of phenomenological method in Gestalt psychotherapy, as a theory of forms that offers immense stimulus for (theorizing) the practice of literary criticism, including what we are calling "radical formalism," is curiously nowhere in sight in recent works on the phenomenology of form: see, e.g., Brinkema 2014, 2018, Levine 2015, Eyers 2017, Best 2018, Moten 2003, 2018, Alford 2020, Quashie 2021 (who comes closest in referencing the form of this adjacent canon in his discussion of Buber 1970, at pp. 21–2). Key texts in the formulation of Gestalt therapy include Perls, Hefferline, Goodman 1951 and Perls 1969 and 1973.

8. Derrida and Dufourmantelle 2000, 26, 28.

9. This also summarizes, for me, the now long-standing status quo of Latinists' understanding of intertextuality, after Hinds 1998: for discussion, see Rimell 2019.

10. See Telò in this volume.

11. Contrast, for example, the politics of Padilla Peralta's enactment of "disorienting" immersion in the question of "Why Classics": https://classics.stanford.edu/dan-el-padilla-peralta-why-why-classics.

12. Gowers 2012, 58–60.

13. Gowers 2012, 58–60, and Mayer 2012, 63.

14. Cf. Farrell 2007, 175–6: "Horace himself is frequently regraded as one of the foundational theorists of 'the classical body.' "

15. Culler 2015, 58.

16. Nisbet and Hubbard 1970, xi.

17. Sullivan 2021, 49.

18. Conte 1992.

19. Attridge 2017; Alford 2020.

20. Mayer 2012, 63. "Focusing device" is Bundy's term (1986).

21. Gowers 2012, 58–61.

22. Gold 1992, 161–2.

23. Freudenburg 2001, 4.

24. "Radical formalism" might be said to stall or disable the telegraphic: see Telò in this volume on prolonging the intensity of moments.

25. Sullivan 2021, 70.

26. Fitzgerald 2016, 124 (my italics).

27. On the limits to this phenomenological process, which I keep in awareness here, see Moten 2018a.

28. Brinkema (2022, 29), alluding to Derrida's *Work of Mourning* (2001). Cf. Eyers 2017 and Quashie 2021. See also Phillips's and Purves's chapters.

29. Best 2018, 49: "This isn't merely clever. It isn't a move in the game of modernism. It's much more than that. It's a way of finding beauty, losing it, and, rather than getting attached to the loss, attaching instead to the movement from gold to trash."

30. Attridge 2017, 213–14 and 175–6.

31. Derrida and Dufourmantelle 2000, 30–2.

32. The Postclassicisms Collective (2020, 38), parsing Loraux's response to Vernant's powerful critique of the assimilation of antiquity (Vernant 1956 and Loraux 1993), before recasting our "responsibility to antiquity in political rather than ethical terms" (39), via Arendt and Foucault (39–44): no ancient texts are mentioned.

33. Fowler 2000.

34. See Quashie's formulation of "aliveness" as a term of relation (2021, 21–2).

35. Sedgwick 1994, 3–4.

36. Umachandran 2022, 27.

37. Cf. Henderson's efforts (1999, xii) to "make sure" the Latin texts he reads "still sing, transgressive, unpredictable," even as he "writes them down," or stoops to their level. Henderson's "mimetic response" (1999, x) flirts with the amoral and immoral in ways that perhaps now (from a position like Umachandran's) might look politically problematic, something like a perverse indulgence in complicity, or in what texts do to us/get us to do, that in the third decade of the twenty-first century seems to defang the very question of complicity. But if this is the critique, it is also worth remembering that Henderson's *modus scribendi*, self-consciously idiosyncratic and of its time, always disavowed a fantasy of purity that is inevitably re-enacted in the turn away from Latin and Greek texts in the name of ethics. As Alford puts it in her powerful coda (2021, 277), "the amorality of poetic attention is crucial to its aliveness."

38. For surveys and definition of the priamel in classical texts, see Krischer 1974, Race 1982, Kirby 1985, Faraone 2005.

39. Cf. Musurillo 1962; Fitzgerald 2016, 117; and Culler 2015, 58: "Horace re-creates many Greek lyric types— thus 1.1. is a priamel, listing his different choices of life (of soldier, farmer, sailors, etc.) while noting his preference for that of the poet."

40. Faraone 2005, 249, 264.

41. Philologists have their own foils for this, however: see, e.g., Gold (1992), who reads *Odes* 1.1. as a "classic priamel" and *Epode* 2 as "a parody of a priamel."

42. Nisbet and Hubbard 1970, 1–2.

43. Fitzgerald 2016, 119.

44. Gowers 2012, 59. Cf. Farrell 2007, 179.

45. Gowers 2012, 59.

46. Santirocco 1986, 17.

47. Mayer 2012, 61.

48. Kenney 1983, 16. Cf. Farrell 2007, 184: "Nevertheless, Horace's lyric body is not so sharply differentiated from his satiric body as some theorists might lead us to expect."

49. Freudenburg 1999, 236; see also Fitzgerald 2016, 124.

50. Fitzgerald 2016, 124–5 (my italics).

51. Alford 2020, 274.

52. Axelson 1945, 76–7.

53. For Freudenburg (2001, 15), this task "of determining who 'we' imagine ourselves to be in relation to the man who speaks from the page, and just how much we want to credit his sometimes trained and addled reasoning against us" is "narratological." Gold (1992) organizes responses to this dilemma by identifying four audiences for *Satires* 1.1, which allows her to manufacture a climactic philological disconnection: "the fourth audience, which is *farthest removed* from the text, is the actual audience" (166, my italics). Cf. The Postclassicisms Collective 2020, 37, on philology as a "solitary, isolationist" practice.

54. Gold (1992, 167) opens this up, then immediately closes it down and projects this philological closure onto the poet: "presumably *nemo* must also refer to Horace and Maecenas. But Horace carefully excludes himself and Maecenas from this group."

55. Freudenburg 2001, 8.

56. Cf. Gowers 2012, 64.

57. Cf. Gold 1992, 180 (with further bibliography), on the history of reading *Odes* 1.1 as a whole as hackneyed and unoriginal.

58. Gowes 2012, 65.

59. Gowers 2012, 82.

60. Gowers 2012, 84.

61. Gowers 2012, 84.

62. Gowers 2012, 84.

63. Although a relative, the greater or fifth Asclepiad, had been used by Catullus. The Asclepiad belonged to group of meters known as Aeolic, associated especially with Sappho and Alcaeus. In Horace's Latin lyric "it would seize the attention" (Kenney 1983, 15).

64. Oliensis 1998, 106.

65. Even if you have a thousand bushels of grain, "your stomach won't hold more than mine" (*non tuus hoc capiet uenter plus ac meus* 46).

66. Nisbet and Hubbard 1970, ad loc.

67. Culler 2015, 194, with further bibliography; cf. Gold 1992, 177, on *demoueas*, which she decides is only addressed to H.'s "internal audience."

68. Cf. D. West 1995, 4–6; cf. Santirocco 1986, 16–17 (arguing that H. "pointedly alludes" to his *Satires* in this "brief *mempsimoiria*").

69. Mayer 2012 ad loc.: "sailors are commonly called fearful."

70. Mayer 2012 ad loc.

71. Thanks to T. Phillips for chats on this.

72. Mayer 2012, ad loc.

73. Compare Eyers 2017, 32, on the "productivity of formal constraints."

74. Mayer (2012 ad loc.) notes that this correspondence of temporal adverbs is probably borrowed from Greek, νῦν μὲν νῦν δέ.

75. Santirocco 1986, 17: "Warfare and hunting are undercut by the perspectives from which they are viewed."

76. Mayer 2012, 62.

77. Compare *Epod.*2.31–2 (*aut trudit acris hinc et hinc multa cane / apros in obstantis plagas*).

78. Musurillo 1962, 230.

79. Oliensis 1998, 106.

80. Musurillo 1962, 238; Race 1982, 122 n13; Santirocco 1986, 18; Gold 1992, 182.

81. Cf. Farrell 2007, 189, with Nisbet and Hubbard 1970 ad loc.

82. Kenney 1983, 16. Cf. Musurillo 1962; Santirocco 1986, 15; Gold 1992, 181; D. West 1995, 6: "the expectation in the priamel is that the last item is preferred."

83. Mayer 2012, 62; cf. Race 1982, 122–4.

84. Fitzgerald 2016, 123.

85. Santirocco 1986, 18–19.

86. Quashie 2021, 131; cf. Brinkema 2014, xiv, on the "slow hard tussle of reading texts closely"; see also Cavarero 2016.

87. Fitzgerald 2016, 124 (my italics).

CHAPTER 13
QUITE A BIND: COUPLET, CONSTRAINT, CLAUSTROPHOBIA, I.E., OVID'S *IBIS*
Tom Geue

If we ask ourselves honestly what reading poetry does to us, and if we answer equally honestly, feeling pleasure is not the only answer we should admit. Sometimes, in fact, pleasure is barely in the mix at all. Poetry can mesmerize us, but not through any particular heart-stopping sublimity; it can fascinate us through boring us, can fix us to the spot via head-scratching, can make us groan in distaste through its difficulty, can send us to sleep with its sonic monotony, can make us zone or tune out by its repetitions. The arsenal of negative affect housed in poetry's potential is particularly relevant for the endless taxing procedures of reading classical verse, a stop-start affair of confusion, mix-ups, misunderstandings, laborious consultation of dictionaries and commentaries, mental translation, glitchy scansion.[1] In fact anyone who tells us that reading classical poetry is "pure pleasure" is lying through their teeth—for this is to downplay the much vaster geoformations of intellectual difficulty and struggle on which any pleasurable pay-off in this sphere is built. And sometimes, form is to blame.

Of course, pleasure and pain are bound experiences, and the voluntary seeking of the former can be a way of accessing the latter. Is reading Latin poetry a masochist's game then? Perhaps the question, at such a level of abstraction, isn't quite right. What I would like to argue in this chapter is that a *certain* feature of a *certain* poetic form—let us call it the repetitive nature of the Ovidian elegiac couplet—has a multivalent capacity built into it. The couplet's prescribed metrical pattern can be a source of mesmeric pleasure and captivation; but it can also be a way of trapping and suffocating us, creating something much more intense than the usual degree of boredom involved in reading classical verse.[2] At the risk of perpetrating a theoretical naivety that maintains a boundary between two inseparable phenomena (pain and pleasure), those of us dabbling in postcritical currents of literary criticism need to be careful, I think, not to reduce desperately the experience of literature to various subsets of an all-encompassing pleasure. Reading is not just about being "hooked" and coming back for more,[3] or "repairing" paranoia with pleasure;[4] in literature as in life, sometimes negative affects must be sat with and churned over rather than whisked too quickly away. So working with the sense of constraint is one of my key tasks. But what I would like this chapter to do, at the same time, is show how these possibilities of boredom and unpleasantness can inhere within form itself. There can be something deadening about a form's mercilessly repeated mantra—what Lucy Alford calls, apropos of Thom Gunn's early poetry, "the boredom of the perfect form."[5] Radical formalisms' capacious spirit may accommodate the depressing truth that form is not always a vehicle of liberation, but sometimes a machine of imprisonment.[6] An aesthetic encounter can be binding, a curse leaving us hard pressed to do much more than run with it.

Couplet and Constraint

This chapter is about a classical Latin poem penned by one of the smoothest ancient verse merchants of pleasure. We want to see what happens when he turns that verse to pain. Ovid's *Ibis* is a 650-odd-line curse poem wishing all bad things on his pseudonymized enemy Ibis from his agonized position in exile. The work starts as a long prayer for Ibis's misfortune in life and death, but duly disintegrates into an endless litany, couplet by couplet, of all the many ways and means Ovid would like to see Ibis suffer and die, with samples drawn from across the gamut of Greco-Roman mythology and history. The *Ibis* contains literally hundreds of utterances wishing myriad victimhood on its addressee, but the way it does so—in a mode of obscure, riddling speech largely deprived of simple names as intelligible pins of orientation[7]—means that the victim Ibis is not the only one cursed. The other target of the second-person address is you, me, us, the reader(s), who are forced to stop and puzzle over the exact stories contained in the couplets, and to whom and where they allude. Reading this poem in an edition with explanatory notes immediately deciphering these allusions actually cuts through a lot of the cognitive pain, and serves as a crutch of gloss that Ovid deliberately withheld from us. Few other poems from antiquity deploy and lay bare the endless excesses of intertextuality, of interpretation too, rooting us to the spot, making us scratch our heads, binding us into the search for parallel and meaning. In this poem, we too are transfixed, we too are stopped dead. Antonio La Penna was on to something when he called the poem, in his 1957 edition, "grigio e pesante."[8]

What I want to do in this chapter, however, does not have much to do with our intertextual fixation or compulsion, which has already been amply and beautifully analyzed by Alessandro Schiesaro.[9] My fixation, my compulsion will be rather different. I want to give a quick account of how Ovid uses a very simple formal technology—the elegiac couplet, now at a true high point of its historical evolution at Rome—to a very simple end: namely, producing a sadistic sense of bind or constraint. Such a will to bind is at the heart of the curse genre at large. Many have noticed the chilling overlap between the ethos of the *Ibis* and that of Greek or Latin curse tablets, or *defixiones*,[10] which seek to constrain the victim in their medium literally, metaphorically, however they can; these pieces, rolled or folded sheets of lead, with text in almost illegibly small letters, sometimes pierced with nails (hence *defixio*, from Latin *defigo*, fasten down), buried in the ground or nailed to a wall, try to crush the cursee into confinement with all the magic of their folding, fixing form.[11] There is something structural to this form of magic that foregrounds compression (rolled/folded), heaviness (lead), smallness (illegible letters), transfixing (nail-pierced), and oppression (burial underground). They try to squeeze the victim into a confined space—and this is the function partly played on by Ovid's naming of Callimachus' *Ibis* as an *exiguus libellus* (449). This kind of curse poem leverages the resources of Callimachean smallness to put pressure on its victim; they turn compression to claustrophobia.

But the *Ibis* of both Callimachus and Ovid have another very distinctive weapon of constraint at their disposal: the elegiac couplet, refined by Ovid over many years and thousands of polished verses of erotic, aetiological, and exilic discourse. My contention is that the *Ibis* is not just a specular inversion of Ovidian love elegy or its dark twin;[12] it is actually a fully fledged working out of an affordance always possessed by this repetitive meter, but never quite spun out to its logical conclusion. (By affordance I mean a kind of inherent capability of a particular form or medium, as popularized by Caroline Levine.)[13] The affordance of the elegiac couplet revealed in the *Ibis* is something we might call constraint or enclosure; and its affective travelling companion, we might call claustrophobia.[14]

First, a refresher on the basics. The form of the Ovidian couplet, illustrated through the critically burdened paradigm of the opening to *Amores* Book 1, looks like (1.1.1–2):

Arma graui numero | uiolentaque bella parabam
    edere, materia || conueniente modis.

I was getting ready to produce weapons and violent wars in heavy verse, with the content to match the meter.

- uu / - uu / - uu / - uu / - **uu** / - x
- uu / - uu / - || - **uu** / - **uu** / - (**fixed parts of the metrical pattern marked in bold**)

The distich stands as a display piece for Ovid's generic-metrical contrivances: hexameter for flirting with epic drive (*arma gravi numero uiolentaque bella*), pentameter for holding the action up. But there is also a strong sense here of the pentameter as vehicle for *sameness*. The idea of material rhyming with meter (*materia conueniente modis*) is patterned in the sonic duplication around both halves of the pentameter: -uu -uu - / -**uu** -**uu** -. As we will see, the relentlessly fixed point that is the second half of the pentameter serves as a way of condensing or compressing repetition; it is an echo that cannot be messed with. Just as Ovid starts his elegy with the best epic intentions of matching content to meter, so the end of his first couplet (as we will see, a charged spot in the scheme) is devoted, literally, to a kind of "metrical convenience"—an agreement, at all costs, with meter itself. In this chapter, we are concerned with the dark side of that conformity to form.

There has been some excellent scholarship of late on how we should understand the potentialities of the Ovidian elegiac couplet. In the older formalist tradition, Llewellyn Morgan's 2010 book *Musa Pedestris: Metre and Meaning in Roman Verse* was a crucial intervention. In Chapter 4 of this book, where Morgan deals with elegiac verse, he builds off Ted Kenney to show how the Ovidian couplet has particular limitations.[15] Not only does the final disyllable ending the distich become almost completely inflexible, but enjambment across couplets is almost eliminated entirely.[16] Contrary to the fluid and progress-driven hexameter then, there is a relentlessly stop-start quality to the Ovidian couplet; while every unit starts with the potential for freedom and movement felt in the initial hexameter, the pentameter promptly kills its buzz with a "certain breathlessness" identified by Heinze.[17] Onto the oscillation of freedom and constraint embodied by the couplet, we could superimpose a number of other oppositions spread across this unequal form that, in Morgan's scheme, lends itself especially to a constant antiphonal duet: continuity vs discontinuity, potency vs impotence, swell vs subsidence, energy vs running out of steam.[18] In Ellen Oliensis's recent scheme, we might add tumescence vs detumescence,[19] and finally, variation vs monotony,[20] as the hexameter starts strong with a string of open dactylic/spondaic options, only to be bound to certainty at its end, and for the pattern then to be repeated at micro-level within the pentameter, which moves from limited variation in its first two and a half feet, to the numbing inevitability of two and a half dactyls in its second half. Oliensis's new reading of the erotics of Ovidian elegy shows how on one hand the couplet lends itself to closure, but on the other, revels in the endlessness of eros by constantly resisting closure in the pentameter (indeed the two halves of this line are like two abortive hexameter openings), and by constantly repeating the experience with a new couplet.[21] This is true, but I'm not sure the story of the *Ibis*'s (as opposed to the love elegy's) metrical spirit can be spun so pleasurably. Rather, building on Georg Luck's observation about the pentameter "becoming its own echo," stopping and reversing, and "closing in on itself,"[22] I would read the rhythmic messaging of the Ovidian couplet as a compulsive reinscription of the same old story: opening with a series of metrical *possibilities* at the beginning of the hexameter, which inevitably end in constraint; and making that story even more severe in the pentameter, where the more flexible first half of the verse terminates in the iron-clad rhythm fixed in the second half, -uu -uu -. This is a meter, I would say, that teases us with freedom only to stage the ultimate sealing victory of constraint.

This mechanical and brutally efficient technology of the couplet works in tandem with several of the punitive themes of the *Ibis*, all falling under this rubric of constraint: among them, imprisonment, impediment, burial, burdening, strangulation, choking, piercing, transfixing, crushing, confining, and entrapment. Below, I give a few selected examples of how perfectly metrical form accomplishes these violent procedures. But for now, a general example to make concrete some of the patterning I am pushing for. Near the beginning of the poem, Ovid directly co-ordinates this new *Ibis* of his with the lost Callimachus poem of the same name and same target. As we read, slowly, lingeringly, pay attention to the distribution of the words across the parts of each verse, and the sonic repetition baked in:

Nunc quo Battiades inimicum devovet Ibin,
Hoc ego devoveo teque tuosque modo.

- - / - uu / - uu / - - / - **uu** / - **x**
- uu / - uu /- // - **uu** / - **uu** / -

Now in the same way Battiades curses his enemy Ibis, so I curse you and yours.

Each line contains its own face-off of aggressor vs victim, Battiades, i.e., Callimachus vs Ibis in the hexameter, Ovid vs *his* Ibis in the pentameter. But if we associate respectively the first parts of each line with freedom, the second with constraint, a spellbinding arrangement emerges. First, the victors, Battiades and ego, are given the freer initial parts of their verses, and the victims *Ibin* and *teque tuos* are assigned the more constrained final parts. Second, rhythmic mirroring works in both effectively to drill that inexorable last part of the verse even more: *-des inimicum devovet ibin* marshals the full power of the hexameter ending -uu -x to make the curse rain down *twice* on Callimachus' Ibis head; *hoc ego devoveo* -uu -uu proleptically weights its two and a half dactyls behind the object of Ovid's curse, droned in the same predictable terminal cadence, as inevitable as death and taxes. While internal mirroring does a job of "nailing" the curse here, the main thing I want to point out is the way the victims are constrained within the inflexibly fixed containers of their line ends. To the victor belongs the range of metrical possibility reserved for the beginning; to the victim, the claustrophonic/-phobic certainty of the end.

Nailing It

As I said above, this "nailing," binding, whatever you want to call it, takes place via many means and metaphors in the *Ibis*. Let us start with the constellation around piercing, impaling, transfixing—and I mean transfixing in its double sense of both penetrating with a sharp implement and rooting us to the spot through some kind of incantatory aesthetic encounter, a form of death in life.[23] As a verse version of a *defixio*, the *Ibis* is dead set fixated on hammering its enemy, and us, with pointy projectile after pointy projectile. And again, the elegiac couplet delivers the blow. Check out the following examples (327–8, 531–2, 541–2, 567–8):

> quaeque in Adimantum Phyllesia regna tenentem
> a Iove venerunt, te quoque tela petant.

> - uu / - - / - - / - uu / -uu / - x
> - uu / -- / - // - **uu** / - **uu** / -

May the spears directed from Jupiter against Adimantus, ruling the Phyllesian kingdom, strike you too.

> utque coturnatum periisse Lycophrona narrant,
> haereat in fibris fixa sagitta tuis.

> - uu / - - /- uu / - uu / - uu/ - x
> - uu / - - / - // - **uu** / - **uu** / -

As they say fell the buskin-donning Lycophron, let the arrow stick fast in your flesh.

inque tuis opifex, vati quod fecit Achaeo,
noxia luminibus spicula condat apis.

\- uu / - uu / - - / - - / - uu / - x
\- uu / - uu / - // - **uu** / - **uu** / -

May the maker bee do what he did to the Achaean seer: sink in your eyes a vicious sting.

ossibus inque tuis teli genus haereat illud,
traditur Icarii quo cecidisse gener.

\- uu / - uu /- - / - uu / - uu /- x
\- uu / - uu /- // - **uu** / - **uu** / -

May that brand of weapon stick fast in your bones—it's said Icarius' son-in-law fell by the same.

All of these mini-curses pertain to missiles thrown, death by dart, barb, javelin. But feel for a second how the final, fixed part of the verse is marshalled to drive the weapon right in—in a sense, the invariability of the rhythm makes the missile stick fast. In the first example, the victim Ibis and the mode of attack are crammed into the second half of the pentameter; this closure of victim within the closed half of the pentameter was something we saw above, in *teque tuosque modo* (56). We see similar strategies in examples two and three—in both cases reserving the jab for the final thrust of the pentameter, *fixa sagitta tuis* (532) / *spicula condat apis* (542). In the last example, the metrical slot picked to stick in the weapon is the last part of the hexameter, *haereat illud* (567), with its equally non-negotiable rhythm. Metrical fixity, in other words, is called up for the task of transfixing.

The *Ibis*'s need to nail and transfix is perhaps partly also a compensatory reflex of its risky poetics of the scattergun: constant skipping from one mythological paradigm to another means a potential loss of focus. Indeed, the apparent formlessness of the poem at the macro-level—its floating across loosely associated clusters of couplet with little apparent rhyme or reason[24]—perhaps makes it necessary to overstress a compulsive orientation at the micro-level, a constant coming back to the same sonic place. The poem's saturation with endless comparisons creates the ever-present threat of distraction from the main game; but Ovid also has a way of rhythmically casting our attention back from vehicle to ultimate tenor, Ibis, and once again the last part of the pentameter is a critical tool for shunting us back on track. We have seen how this segment of the verse's familiar rhythm can recall the focus on "you" in *teque tuosque modo* (56) and *te quoque tela petant* (328). This structure is leveraged at several other moments of the poem (503–4, 595–6, 606–7):

quique Lycurgiden letavit, et arbore natum,
    Idmonaque audacem, **te quoque rumpat aper**.

The boar who killed the son of Lycurgus, and the man born from a tree, and bold Idmon— may he burst you as well.

> utque coturnatum vatem tutela Dianae,
>   dilaniet vigilum **te quoque turba canum**.

As the guardians of Diana did to the buskin-donning bard, may a crowd of watchful dogs tear you up.

> qua sua Penteliden proles est ulta Lycurgum,
>   haec maneat teli **te quoque plaga novi**.

As his own offspring took revenge on Lycurgus the Pentelid, so may this blow of a new weapon be in store for you too.

Where the first part of the couplet flies off into different mythical territory every couple of lines, the last part is often tasked with reminding us precisely who, in the final analysis, the object of all this death and destruction is. Drumroll: you, Ibis. The predictable and monotonous closure puts a stop on the poem's proliferating variation. There are so many ways to die, but death in the end is always the same; the full weight of the second half of the pentameter helps puncture and punctuate, preventing us from wandering, bringing us back to the same place, stopping *Ibis* in his tracks. The end of the couplet is a particularly hospitable place for the sameness of death (637–8):

> denique Sarmaticas inter Geticasque
> his precor ut vivas **et moriare locis**.

Ultimately, I pray that you live in these regions among Sarmatian and Getic arrows—and die among them.

Even within the *Ibis*'s constrained terms of reference, life (*vivas*) belongs in the first part of the line; after the caesura, there is always only one thing for it.

Crushing It

If you were to describe the strict scheme of the Ovidian elegiac couplet as a kind of crushing inevitability, nowhere is that metaphor better literalized than in the *Ibis*. This roll-call of curses is full of moments of bodily confinement, closure and crush—and Victoria Rimell has written wonderfully on the affective significance of these images of space constricting around bodies in the *Ibis*, squeezing out our panicked gasps of last-ditch anxiety.[25] Two of Rimell's postcard images of claustrophobia in this poem also happen to be very interesting test cases for our theory about the metrics of constraint.[26] Take the example of the bronze bull invented by Perillus for the tyrant Phalaris—an archetypal torture device involving the imprisonment of a human within a bronze bull, and a flame applied underneath to slowly roast the occupant to death. Ovid devotes a couple couplets to this nightmare, and they are both testament to form deployed as horrific constraint (437–8, 439–40):

> aere Perilleo veros imitere iuvencos,
> ad formam tauri conveniente sono.

> - uu / - - / - - / - uu /- uu / - x
> - - / - - / - // - **uu** / - **uu** / -

May you ape real bulls with Perillus' bronze, with the sound fitting the shape of the bull.

> utque ferox Phalaris, lingua prius ense resecta
> more bovis Paphio clausus in aere gemas.

> - uu / - uu / - - / - uu / - uu / - x
> - uu / - uu / - // - **uu** / - **uu** / -

Like wild Phalaris, tongue first pruned with the sword, may you growl like an ox trapped in the Paphian style.

In the first couplet, note how the idea of sameness, imitation, repetition is squashed into the end of both hexameter (*imitere iuvencos*) and pentameter (*conveniente sono*; the darker version of the *conveniente modis* seal on the first couplet of the *Amores*, above). The pentameter is in fact a haunting synesthetic experience, whose avowed statement of a "matching sound"—a sound matching a visual form of the bull, that is—is almost undermined by the distinct rhythms in both halves of pentameter: *ad formam tauri / conveniente sono*. Ovid shows the dissonance involved in crushing a human into a bull, the *inconvenience* of making it perforce sound like one. In the second couplet, again, a classic curse-use of the second half of the pentameter to double down on enclosure, as the word *clausus* lands precisely on the most constrained part of the couplet: again, metrical inflexibility tightens the screw, subjects the victim, both Ibis and us readers trapped at the end of that second person, to suffer the horrible shutdown at the rhythmic level. We might note the same pattern in another lynchpin of bodily confinement, the couplet on Thyestes (545–6):

> ut puer Harpagides referas exempla Thyestae,
> inque tui caesus **viscera patris eas**.

Like the son of Harpagus, may you repeat the example of Thyestes: chopped up, may you enter your father's bowels.

The son, chopped up for ease of consumption, enters the bowels of his father precisely at the most gut-punching part of the verse; trapped in his dad's digestive tract like Perillus and Phalaris inside the bull, the meter helps us feel, at gut level, what it is to be stuck inside.

Rimell's second totem example works just as well, in a slightly different circle of hell:[27]

> aut ut Anaxarchus pila minuaris in alta,
> ictaque pro solitis frugibus ossa sonent.

> - uu /- - / - - /- uu / - uu / - x
> - uu / - uu / - // - **uu** / - **uu** / -

Or like Anaxarchus, may you be reduced in a deep mortar, your crushed bones to sound instead of the usual grain

As Rimell points out, Anaxarchus is the degree zero of the *Ibis*'s poetics of claustrophobia and bodily dissolution:[28] he is literally ground up into a million little pieces. But note again what the pentameter does with sound to accomplish such obliteration. Anaxarchus' remains undergo a grim metamorphosis whereby they sound like pounded grain—*ictaque*, inevitably pointing us to ictus, the Latin word for metrical beat, advertising the sound of the pounding within this terrifying mortar they call the pentameter. The entire line is mirrored—two and a half dactyls a piece, capturing the morphing of bones into grain, *ossa* into *frugibus*; but it is also maximally dissolved, i.e., has the greatest number of short syllables that the pentameter can possibly bear, as if the grinding took place in our ears via a merciless metrical granulation. Here the pentameter acts as a vehicle of the most destructive pressure conceivable, squeezing a body into infinitesimally small fragments.

In fact images of crush and weight drag everywhere in the *Ibis*—and everywhere the unrelenting metrical constraints pile on the pressure. In the following run of examples, look how the pressure Ibis exerts on the earth at birth comes back in the various permutations of burden and burial (221–2, 313–14, 355–6, 461–2):

> qui simul impura matris prolapsus ab alvo
> Cinyphiam foedo corpore pressit humum,

> - uu / - - / - - / - - / - uu / - x
> - uu / - - / - // - **uu** / - **uu** / -

As soon as he fell from his mother's dirty womb, and pressed the Cinyphian earth with his disgusting body.

> utque Iovis Libyci templum violare parantes,

acta noto vultus condat harena tuos.

- uu / - uu / - - / - uu / - uu / - x
- uu / - - / - // - **uu** / - **uu** / -

Like those ready to violate the temple of Libyan Jupiter, may the sand, driven by the south wind, bury your face.

> quaeque parare suis letum patruelibus ausae
> Belides assidua colla premuntur aqua.

- uu / - uu / - - / - uu / - uu / - x
- uu / - uu /- // - **uu** / - **uu** / -

Or in such a wife as were the daughters of Belus, who dared to plot death for their cousins, their necks bent by carrying water upon water.

> aut, ut Cassandreus domino non mitior illo,
> saucius ingesta contumuleris humo.

- - / - - / - uu / - - / - uu /- x
- uu / - - / - // - **uu** / - **uu** / -

Or like the man of Cassandrea, no gentler than that master, may you be buried, wounded, under piles of earth.

In each case, Ovid throws the full overwhelming weight of the pentameter's end upon the oppression and pressure contained, or should I say constrained, within: of earth in *corpore pressit humum, condat harena tuos, contumuleris humo*, and of water in *colla premuntur aqua*.

Choking It

Such crushing has its violent companion in the concatenation of couplet fates set up around asphyxiation or choking—and again, the pentameter end does a lot of heavy lifting (550–1, 555–6, 570–1, 591–2):

> utve Syracosio praestricta fauce poetae,
> sic animae laqueo sit via clausa tua.

- uu / - uu / - - / - - / - uu / - x
- uu / - uu /- // - **uu** / - **uu** / -

Or as happened to the Syracusan poet whose throat got strangled, so may your breath's passage be shut by a noose.

utque duobus idem dictis modo nomen habenti,
praefocent animae Cnosia mella viam.

- uu / - uu / - - / - uu / - uu / - x
- - / - uu / - // - **uu** / - **uu** / -

And like the man who bears the same name as the two already mentioned, may Cretan honey choke your breath's passage.

utque loquax in equo est elisum guttur acerno,
sic tibi claudatur pollice vocis iter.

- uu / - uu / - - / - - / - uu / - x
- uu / - - / - // - **uu** / - **uu** / -

And as the chatty throat was smashed in the maple horse, so may the way of your voice be stopped with a thumb.

comicus ut liquidis periit, dum nabat, in undis,
et tua sic Stygius strangulet ora liquor.

- uu / - uu / - uu / - - / - uu / - x
- uu / - uu /- // - **uu** / - **uu** / -

As the comic poet drowned as he swam in the clear water, so may the Styx's waves throttle your mouth.

The first three examples visualize choking as a process of "stopping the way" of breath or speech—and no coincidence that the word for way, *via* or *iter*, is stopped in its tracks by the circuit breaker of the second half of the pentameter. In the last example, the same part of the line is used to "stifle" the mouth, starting with *strangulet*. It is almost as if the endless end-stopping of the pentameter, its constant capping with an identical rhythm, dramatizes the breakdown in speech of which the verses struggle to talk. Where language fails under a thumb closing in on the throat, the metronomic predictability of -**uu** -**uu** - still gasps out its sound, a mechanical paralysis perhaps best taken as death throes in verse.

This process of strangling speech is part of the *Ibis*'s fundamental function: as a long monologue of an unhinged Ovid, it is designed to drown out other speech. In fact, unlike other Ovidian elegy, which is littered with internal speakers,[29] the *Ibis* only makes space for about three lines of quotation, all in the voice of those most iron-clad utterers of performative speech, the Fates. This short clip, capping the prayer prelude of the poem before we enter the litany zone, also uses the end of the pentameter as a means of adding wait to the grim certainty of fate's prophecy (245–6):

et, ne longa suo praesagia diceret ore,
"fata canet vates **qui tua**," dixit, "**erit.**"

And to avoid articulating the long prophecy with her own mouth, she said "a bard to sing your fates there will be."

In fact in this poem, not even the Fates really want to speak (*ne longa suo praesagia diceret ore*)—they hand over all binding verbal tasks to Ovid himself. But what they do say is massaged into immovable futurity with the full power of the pentameter's familiar pattern. **Qui tua dixit erit**, as if to draw out, with the juxtaposition of past verb of saying and future verb of being, that there is barely a difference between them; as Ovid and the Fates say, so it will be. We know by then, by now, there is only one way this can go.

No Way Out

In this poem about just how many ways we might will death on an enemy and a reader, it perhaps makes a perverse form of sense that the most determined part of the couplet, we might even say the couplet's death, carries and *imposes* so much weight. Over and over again the end of the pentameter functions with brutal efficiency to imprison, shut up, enclose, transfix, crush, oppress, bury, choke. All the good stuff. This technology of constraint is a negative capability, an evil affordance of form.

We might note in closing that these sorts of metaphors of restriction, enclosure, imprisonment, etc., are precisely the accusations that formalists and historicists throw at each other, to make the other not just an impoverished reader of literature, but almost a threat to the very freedom of the human subject.

> Hatreds of formalism are all alike. Accused of abandoning the world, its misfortunes, its tumults and things, one is asked to accede to Fredric Jameson's call for a "literary or cultural criticism which seeks to avoid imprisonment in the windless closure of the formalisms."[30]

> With this development being so marked at so many important levels, it was only to be expected that many would feel it as an ever-narrowing straightjacket, and therefore long to break free.[31]

Needless to say I find these accusations a little over the top, and I would say the polemic waged by both sides of the formalist-historicist divide sometimes itself strays into the realm of the suffocating. When Eugenie Brinkema starts her *Life-Destroying Diagrams*, a new cutting edge work of radical formalism, with a famous Fredric Jameson passage about the primacy of historical-political interpretation of literature, but with all the occurrences of the word "political" crossed out and overwritten with "formal,"[32] I cannot help feeling some blood boil at this gimmick—but then gimmicky is precisely the kind of dismissal that Brinkema would expect from a (part)historicist critic, part critic of historicism, such as myself, whose critiques of formalism, in her eyes, are all the same. Are we stuck in a cell of our own dialectical oscillation between formalism and historicism? And as a group of primarily white, middle-class critics who tend not to see the insides of any prison except those conjured up in metaphor, should we really keep exaggerating like this?

Or: where would I position myself in this debate, a key feature of which seems to be the mutual fatigue, not to say boredom, of its contenders? Ultimately, I am probably neither so radical as a formalist or a historicist as to think that one or the other mode is an intolerable straitjacket limiting us. Indeed, outside the world of a *Radical Formalisms* volume, I would gravitate much more naturally to the question of the historicity of forms, and why forms phase in and out over time, and what affective possibilities particular forms enable or foreclose at any particular moment. In terms of the chapter I have written here, I am also not convinced that I have been able to transcend the old formalism, which seeks to show form as a *supplement* to meaning. In some ways, this chapter has been a conventional analysis of how Ovid "uses" the couplet to "convey" or "express" something—a project to which radical formalism might have some objections. The only way I can have hoped to have approached that radical formalism is by insisting that the thing conveyed is not necessarily meaning, but feeling. The poem's metrical constraint subjects us to the horror of claustrophobia.

While the mutual resentment between formalists and historicists can get a little overbaked, the accusations above also show us, I think, that criticism itself is propelled by a congealing sense of boredom and claustrophobia—boredom, that is, with and towards forms of criticism that are perceived to have ossified into unproductive and mechanical habits. The moment we feel criticism has become predictable or routine, calcified in its own forms—whether those be concerned with form or history—we lose patience. We try to mix it up. It is this resistance to sclerotization—to borrow a term Terry Renaud uses of the periodic emergence of various new lefts in the surges of twentieth-century revolutionary politics[33]—that puts the radical in radical formalisms. The sense is that we can and should bust out of the critical prisons of our own making; that we can aim at a way of stretching or snapping the ties that bind us to particular critical forms, whether to old formalism or to the dominant contextualist paradigm; that we can even break free of the discursive prison-houses locking us into a constant oscillation between form and history, to get out there, to breathe in the fresh air, to enjoy something *else*.

Yet these critical and discursive constraints are not something we *can* fully escape. We are bound to them. That is partly because constraint is structural to form, and form is structural to life. Indeed I have tried to show in this chapter that the constraint we often feel in reading can be a property of form itself. In my chosen case study, Ovid's *Ibis*, the unvarying nature of metrical form is a crucial vehicle of fascination and spellbinding. It makes us feel the fixity and inevitability of death in an OTT, highly repetitive mode; and perhaps it binds us through its constrained rhythms just as much as its inaccessible "meaning." Indeed the poem's notorious obscurity helps to tune us out of meaning and into the binding nature of rhythm. One of the *Ibis'* pin-up monsters, with whom I would like to shut myself up, is the Sphinx, from Greek σφίγγειν "bind, squeeze, strangle," a terrifying creature who literally kills by its unintelligible phraseology (377–8):

ut quos, obscuri victos ambagibus oris,
legimus infandae Sphinga dedisse neci

\- - / - - / - - / - - / - u u / - x
\- uu / - - / - // - **uu** / - **uu** / -

As those, defeated by the riddles of her opaque mouth, whom we read that the Sphinx gave over to ineffable death

Where death is inexpressible, *infandae*, we "read" beyond the words to the same old rhythm beating out our familiar impossible bind, that monotonous cadence killing us as we puzzle: *Sphinga dedisse neci, Sphinga dedisse neci.* A radical formalism might not just try to break the monotony, but revel in it; listen to that binding rhythm, get lost in its tiring traps, rather than try to work out what the hell the Sphinx means. And again: *Sphinga dedisse neci, Sphinga dedisse neci.* And . . .

Notes

1. On glitchy formalism, see Telò's chapter.

2. For similar aesthetic dynamics in Greek tragedy, see Telò 2020b.

3. Felski 2020.

4. On paranoid and reparative reading, see Sedgwick 2003 (ch. 4). See also Introduction.

5. Alford 2020, 246.

6. See Telò 2020b (esp. ch. 2 and Epilogue), on the complex interplay of liberation and imprisonment in the pleasure of death-driven aesthetics.

7. On name suppression in the *Ibis*, see Krasne 2012, 44–83, and Geue 2019 (ch. 2).

8. La Penna 1957, x.

9. Schiesaro 2011.

10. For the shared space between *Ibis* and *defixio*, see Zipfel 1910 and Watson 1991.

11. For an introduction to the nature of ancient curse tablets, see Gager 1992, 3–41; for more recent work on the social function and history of the technology, see McKie 2022 and Woolf 2022.

12. On the continuity between *Ibis* and other Ovidian elegy through the genesis of woundedness, see Krasne 2012, 39–40.

13. Levine 2015 (ch. 1). For a critique of Levine, see the Introduction.

14. The generic quality of *Ibis* is complex, as elegy converges or is mixed in with iambus: on the pleasure-in-pain of iambic form, see Telò 2019.

15. See Morgan 2010, 348, and Kenney 1982 (cf. Kenney 2002).

16. Morgan 2010, 348.

17. See Morgan 2010, 351, and Heinze 1919, 76.

18. Morgan 2010, 352.

19. Oliensis 2019, 154.

20. Oliensis 2019, 155–6.

21. Oliensis 2019, 156–8.

22. Luck 1969, 28, quoted in Morgan 2010, 354–5.

23. For similar imagery in the iambic pleasure-in-pain, see Telò 2019.

24. For an attempt to restore some method to the madness and to shed light on the organization of said associative clusters, see Krasne 2012.

25. See Rimell 2015, 308–11.

26. Rimell 2015, 309.

27. Rimell 2015, 308–9.

28. "It is curious that, as Ovid puts it, Anaxarchus' pulverized bones 'sound out' (*sonent* 572): this is, we might say, the song of *Ibis*, the 'fruit' of its curse. *Ibis* becomes a poem about what drives Ovidian poetics, about whether poetry can live on in a world governed by the specular inversion of absolute, tyrannical security—pure, boundless terror, the safe room turned torture chamber, the poison without the cure. There is, we suspect, no way back from this" (Rimell 2015, 309).

29. E.g., the *Fasti*; or the *Heroides*, maximally written in other people's voices. The *Ibis*'s experiment with the endless utterances of the Ovidian first-person speaker is perhaps counterevidence to Natoli (2017)'s claims about Ovidian loss of speech in exile.

30. Brinkema 2022, 251.

31. North 2017, 182, on increasing specialization, and the tightening of the "historicist-contextualist" paradigm in literary studies.

32. Brinkema 2022, xvi.

33. Renaud 2021.

CHAPTER 14
OPEN FORM IN NATHANIEL MACKEY
Sean Alexander Gurd

In addition to his work as a radio broadcaster, as the editor of *Hambone*, and as a cultural and literary critic, Nathaniel Mackey has become known for two ongoing creative projects. The first is a serial epistolary novel, *From a Broken Bottle Traces of Perfume Still Emanate*, in which a certain N. writes to his friend the Angel of Dust about the adventures of his musical improvisation ensemble. The second is a single long poem comprised of two intertwined series entitled *Song of the Andouboulou* and *Mu* respectively.[1] The writing in these works hovers uncannily on the threshold of what some might lazily call "making sense"—there is always a setting, a sense of narrative, a relatively stable set of characters, but it is often hard to tell exactly what is being described, as though the goal were to produce an aura or a feeling rather than an unequivocal narrative. Indeed, Mackey has espoused the Zukofskian formula that poetry is a function operating in the space between language and music;[2] he reaches often to musical models—African American jazz in the avant-garde tradition, as well as Andalusian deep song, are particularly important; and in a significant essay called "Sound and Sentiment, Sound and Symbol," he invokes both Victor Zukerkandl's philosophy of music and Steven Feld's ecomusicology as analogues and provocations to his poetics. Such emphases seem to call up, even to demand, a formalistic enquiry, and so he seems like an ideal authority to consult in the interests of a renewed formalism such as we are contemplating in these pages.

But Mackey drops hints that he is nervous about formalism. In a letter in the first volume of *From a Broken Bottle Traces of Perfume Still Emanate,* Mackey's narrator N. writes:

> I'm troubled by the apparent fatalism intrinsic to form, the threat of conservatism the centralness of "form" to "conformity" seems to imply.[3]

N. expresses his concerns about the fatalism and conformism of form in the middle of a train of thought about what he calls "phantom objectivity,"[4] which, he says, refers "to a situation … where we find ourselves haunted by what we ourselves initiate."[5] Now "Phantom objectivity" is likely a reference to the Marxist notion that commodities reify social relations, particularly as this is discussed in the opening pages of Georg Lukács's "Reification and the Consciousness of the Proletariat."[6] In N.'s interpretation, commodity fetishism is also commodity *fatalism*: what we initiate becomes a form to which we must conform, from which we can never escape. As Lukács put it, when the commodity became "the universal category of society as a whole," the result was that it "became crucial for the subjugation of men's consciousness to the forms in which this reification finds expression and for their attempts to comprehend the process or to rebel against its disastrous effects and liberate themselves from servitude to the 'second nature' so created."[7] "Phantom objectivity," in other words, may be said to name a situation in which we are forced to adhere to forms of our own making—even when we resist.

The hypothesis that, as "phantom objectivity," forms create spaces we compulsively return to—they don't haunt us; we haunt them—offers one way to understand some crucial details in Mackey's poetics. Themes developed early recur throughout the work, sometimes over a span of decades, and they are less motifs than platforms or frames within which he can develop new performances again and again. In what has become a basic architectural feature of his poetry, a longer poem will be followed by some number of briefer poems, each presented beneath a horizontal line (As though they were footnotes, commentary, or scholia); these shorter poems respond to, comment on, or elaborate the longer first poem in an open-ended number of ways.[8] Similarly, in *Blue Fasa* Mackey uses the image of the resonating strings on a sitar: his later work resounds with themes and images in his early work as those strings resonate with the melodic line played on the sitar's primary strings. Linking form with "phantom objectivity" may also help us look beyond Mackey to more general problems of art and aesthetics. It recognizes, for instance, that art's modern mode of being is grounded in a capitalist logic: divorced from the messy business of production, enjoying a kind of simple purity from which have been purged all questions about the circumstances of the author or the social system which supported the work, an aesthetic form *is* a commodity in the Marxist sense. In what is arguably one of the most important works on art of the twentieth century, Theodor Adorno's *Aesthetic Theory* argued that the independence of the work of art is itself an artifact of modern capitalist commodification and, in a contradiction of the kind that Adorno was unusually brilliant at detecting, was itself an expression of capitalist logic, even as it seemed to create a space separate from it. But the perspective of thinkers like Marx, Lukács, and Adorno has a weakness; it depends entirely on an assessment of the industrialist-capitalist predicament of modernity, and fails to recognize that non-modern cultures can develop similar cultural logics, similar object-fetishisms or formalisms. For example, the Greco-Roman system of culture promoted standardizations in architecture, poetry, and music, which allowed a finite set of forms to appear at geographically disparate locations and over a great span of time. There were ancient "systems of objects" (the phrase is Baudrillard's)[9] comparable to modern commodification. In consequence, classicism must contend with a crushing double logic: on the one hand, its objects of study have a "phantom objectivity" arising from the specific historical relations governing their ancient production; on the other hand, the discourse of classicism itself has been reabsorbed into a modernity that uses it as a leading facilitator of the mystification of commodities.[10] Hence classicism risks an unusually high level of conformism, since it must adhere to both an ancient and a modern commodity logic.

The problems inherent in "classicism" are my concern, not Mackey's. But I find his approach to the challenge of form provocative and useful for thinking through my own preoccupations. And in fact Mackey does engage some ancient Greek material. Thus, for example, in *Bedouin Hornbook* N. continues his thoughts on the "conformism" surrounding form by turning to Greek Pythagorean notions of the harmony of the spheres:

> Music got pulled in not only because I'm a musician but because of the longstanding tradition that uses musical form as the symbol par excellence of a cosmic status quo, the so-called "harmony of the spheres." Any such harmony, if it exists, does so at our expense I'm convinced.[11]

Ancient fantasies about heavenly music were associated with musical reformists who sought to promulgate and enforce precise musical intonations, usually grounding their efforts in mathematical measurements.[12] Thus while empirical observers like the fourth-century philosopher Aristoxenus acknowledged that there was an infinity of possible fine-tunings,[13] theorists like Archytas, Plato, and even Ptolemy sought instead to specify a finite group of tuning standards in relation to which practical musics could either adhere or fall away. This normative musicology sought to support its project of disciplining music by associating the tunings it endorsed with celestial objects and movements. That tradition has continued into the modern world: indeed one way to characterize modern European music is to say that it is the story of constant attempts to assure a fixed standard of definite intonations, rigorously enforced in practice and continuously justified with reference to a normative concept of nature. This is at once a formalism and a classicism, evincing just the top-down tendencies towards cultural domination N. worries about in *Bedouin Hornbook*. He reacts by pointing to the violent social forces that unmask such musics as authoritarian: "you don't have to listen long," he writes, "to realize that the music coming down from on high can't be heard from the noise the police helicopters make."[14]

In Lukács's diagnosis of commodity fetishism, there is no possibility of stepping outside the system: only the commodity can be used to resist commodification. This leads to a tactical aporia: how, given the inescapability of the commodified world, can one work towards a different, more liberated state of being? How does one change one's fate, conform a little less? N.'s answer is distinct from that of Marx or Lukács; he looks not to political action but to a transformed artistic practice. It's not enough, writes N., for musical composers to simply cover their own tracks, producing music that seems direct and spontaneous. They need to go further, to undo composition, to de-compose (to invest, he says, in the aroma of "compost" that still rises from the verb "compose").[15] As a model, he offers Pharoah Sanders' solo on John Coltrane's "My Favorite Things," on *Live at the Village Vanguard Again!* Pharoah's tone on this solo, he says, has a "hovering, hivelike quality;" it "troubles every claim to a 'composed' approach."

N. identifies the poetics underlying these tonal qualities as improvisatory and "imprecise." The latter word worries him, and he returns to it in the next letter, where he adds that "imprecision" only ever emerges "in relation to an alien frame of reference." Referring to the griots of Mauritania, whose musical modes are hard to identify by western standards but are easy to identify by Mauritian audiences, N. argues that the alternative to "conformist form" is a music that emphasizes the "notional" rather than the "notational": Pharoah Sanders's sound "refuse[s] to be contained by any locatable, unequivocal point on the notational grid."[16] (Again I am reminded of schisms in Greek musicology, where Neoplatonic approaches tended to associate the *ethos* or feeling of a piece of music with the pitch set it used, while those working in the more empirical Aristoxenian tradition attributed *ethos* to the much more intangible quality of appropriateness in a performance's combination of elements.[17])

Improvised, intonationally free, noisy and uncomposed, Sanders's tone is an emblem of what Mackey elsewhere calls "open form":

> Noise is whatever the system, in a particular situation, is not intended to transmit, be the system a poem, a piece of music, a novel, or an entire society. Open form (itself a discrepant, oxymoronic formulation, not unlike Williams' "variable foot") is a gesture in the direction of noise.[18]

"Whatever the system is not intended to transmit" in the context of mainstream European music theory is timbre and "expressive variation" in both rhythm and tuning.[19] Theory describes precise, as-it-were Archimedean pitch points, while individual players may stray from these. Sanders's tone gestures—more than gestures—in this direction, and so it stands for "open form" not only because it is improvised within an expansive modal framework, but because its modality of expression gestures away from the closed system defined by the musical discourse that defines "harmony." He does not play "notes:" he buzzes, hisses, rasps, his tonality an "asthmatic ambush" of the notion of tone. It is the sound of the commodity object—the "note"—coming nearly undone.

The title of half of Mackey's long poem, "Song of the Andoumboulou," draws its inspiration from mythological figures among the Dogon of West Africa, about which Mackey learned from ethnographic studies.[20] The Andoumboulou feature in a relatively minor way in this body of material; they are an intermediary generation in the early history of the world, in this one respect rather like the ancient Greek Titans. Mackey describes them as follows:

> I couldn't help thinking of the Andoumboulou as not simply a failed, or flawed, or earlier form of human being but a rough draft of human being we continue to be. The commonplace expression "man's inhumanity to man" has long acknowledged our Andoumboulousness. The song of the Andoumboulou is one of striving, strain, abrasion, an all but asthmatic song of aspiration. Lost ground, lost twinness, lost union and other losses variably inflict that aspiration, a wish, among others, to be we, that of the recurring two, the archetypal lovers who visit and revisit the poems, that of some larger collectivity an anthem would celebrate.[21]

The two halves of this extended gloss describe conflicting but complementary temporalities: on the one hand, the Andoumboulou are a first, rough draft of humanity, and as such figures for a humanity that is also in an ongoing condition of inchoition. Thus, in a sense, the Andoumboulou have an orientation to the future, a futural charge. But in the second half of the paragraph we learn that this aspiration is inflected by "lost ground, lost twinness, lost unity." The sense of loss seems to me to have a praeteritive charge; what is lost is something we *had*, or something we might have had, back then. The Andoumboulou thus operate in a moment that is both straining towards the future and longing for the past.

Taken together, the conditions of (futural) incompletion and (praeteritive) lostness describe a present of insecurity, of almostness that Mackey designates here with the pneumatic figures of asthma and aspiration. Such a condition is evoked elsewhere in other terms. In a 2014 interview with Andrew R. Mossin, Mackey compared his writing to prayer:

> Prayer is an act of union or seeking union that has to guard against presuming to have attained it. I've been influenced by listening to devotional music from Asia—the Bauls of Bengal, dervish music, Indian bhajans, Pakistani qawwali, and so on—and by reading devotional literature such as that by Ibn Arabi, Rumi, Mina Bai, and Kabir. One finds, in both the music and the literature, an always unsettled relationship between union and separation. I've recently been reading *Divine Flashes* by Fakhr-al-Din Iraqi, a thirteenth-century Persian poet. It's filled with passages like this One:

> I want union with him
> He wants separation from me
> So I abandon my desire
> to His

> Perhaps, as in the relationship between John Donne the cleric and John Donne the poet, poetry as a practice of displacement is prayer's way of standing guard or prayer's hedge against presumption, a way of remaining true to estrangement, keeping watch.[22]

Mackey illustrates his point with a few lines from an early poem, "John Coltrane arrived with an Egyptian lady," which has the subtitle "belated prayer:"

> no sheet of sound enshroud
> the Fount of this fevered
> Brook becoming one
> with God's eye, not
> a one of these notes

> come near to the brunt
> of the inaudible
> note I've been reach-
> ing towards[23]

This poem is, presumably, a response to and an invocation of Coltrane's sound, and perhaps also of the increasingly urgent spirituality of his recordings from *A Love Supreme* onward. Mackey describes it as a *via negativa* which "acknowledges limit and separation" (177). Thus the "sheets of sound" (a cliché for describing Coltrane's approach to improvisation) veil no hidden or mystic unity with "God's eye;" the "I" of the poem strives after an "inaudible note," which is never even approximated by the sound of the player's horn. Striving for transcendence is combined with an articulation of the impossibility of achieving it, perhaps resonating with Rumi's famous image of the Nay or reed flute, which sings of its longing for the bush from which it was cut. Mackey writes: "the very sound calls to mend the cutting which brought it into being and which it laments. The sound subsists as that cutting. The *nay* not only mourns but embodies separation."[24]

Often this perspective is played out in the poetry itself, which presents itself mid-step, as it were, in the process of taking flight:

> a drum's head it was we walked on,
> beats parsed out by ghost feet,
> protoghost feet our feet had
> become. It was a dream of beaten
> > earth,
> beaten air, beaked extravagance,
> birds we'd eventually be.[25]

The title of this poem, "Sound and Sentience," evokes Steven Feld's *Sound and Sentiment,* a study of myth and music among the Kaluli that has been very influential for ecomusicology and sound studies. Mackey worked with it extensively in the important essay "Sound and Sentiment, Sound and Symbol."[26] There he cites Feld's claim that among the Kaluli "poetic language is bird language";[27] here, it is as though "we" are almost birds, the sound of the drum almost become bird language. That "almost" is a recurrent motif; thus "we", here, are not even ghosts, but only protoghosts, ghosts in the process of becoming. This passage articulates, we might say, a state of being mid-transformation, almost spiritualized, almost poetry.

In an essay called "Cante Moro," which addresses and extrapolates from Lorca's interpretation of Andalusian deep song and the aesthetic phenomenon of *duende,* Mackey draws attention to the fact that *duende* "often has to do with a kind of longing that has no remedy, not simply loss, unrequited love and so forth, but what Lorca calls 'a longing without object.'"[28] This unmitigated longing, Mackey says, has a *sound.*

…the voice becomes troubled. Its eloquence becomes eloquence of another order, a broken, problematic, self-problematizing eloquence. Lorca also quotes [Manuel] Torre as having told a singer, "you have a voice, you know the styles, but you will never triumph, because you have no *duende*." So you see that *duende* is something beyond technical competence or even technical virtuosity. […] Lorca tells a story of the Andalusian singer Pastora Pavón, also known as La Niña de los Peines. He tells of her singing in a little tavern in Cádiz one night before a group of flamenco aficionados. He says that when she finished singing she was met with silence. Her voice, though technically perfect, and her virtuosity, though impressive, didn't move anyone. "When Pastora Pavón finished singing," Lorca writes, "there was total silence, until a tiny man, one of those dancing manikins that rise suddenly out of brandy bottles, sarcastically murmured 'Viva Paris!' as if to say: 'Here we care nothing about ability, technique, skill. Here we are after something else.'" Which is not to say that you get there by not having skill. You get there by not being satisfied with skill. It's the other side, the far side of skill, not the near side. Then Lorca goes on to say:

> As though crazy, torn like a medieval weeper, La Niña de los Peines got to her feet, tossed off a big glass of firewater and began to sing with a scorched throat, without voice, without breath or color, but with duende. She was able to kill all the scaffolding of the song and leave way for a furious, enslaving duende.[29]

We find a similar sound-beyond-technique in Mackey's reflections on the Andoumboulou. The "Song of the Andoumboulou" on the record *Les Dogon* is a funeral song, but what Mackey responded to was a kind of tone, which he associated directly with duende,

> [The Song of the Andoumboulou] is related in my mind to *duende* and to flamenco by that raspy tonality that is resorted to in the voice of the singer of the "Song of the Andoumboulou," which is the thing that really struck me. I seem to be very susceptible to these raspy vocal qualities.[30]

The singers on this record do indeed sing with a roughness of voice that bears comparison with deep song, at the very least in its avoidance of the kind of glossy pure tone favored in European art music and American musical theater.

The notion of "discrepant engagement" (also the title of his first book of criticism) is one of Mackey's more well-known ways of imagining this raspiness.

> [Discrepant Engagement] is an expression coined in reference to practices that, in the interest of opening presumably closed orders of identity and signification, accent fissures, fracture, incongruity, the rickety, imperfect fit between word and world. Such practices highlight—indeed inhabit—discrepancy, engage rather than seek to ignore it. Recalling the derivation of the word *discrepant* from a root meaning "to rattle, crack," I relate discrepant engagement to the name the Dogon of west Africa give their weaving block, the base on which the loom they weave upon sits. They call it "the creaking of the word." It is the noise upon which the

word is based, the discrepant foundation of all coherence and articulation, of the purchase upon the world fabrication affords.[31]

The idea of the "creaking of the word" comes from the 1948 *Dieu d'eau: entretiens avec Ogotemmêli* (translated as *Conversations with Ogotemmêli* in 1965), in which Marcel Griaule reports, in the edited words of the Dogon philosopher Ogotemmêli, in the moment when the Dogon learned to weave from an ancestor spirit whose mouth was the stage upon which the first act of weaving was performed:

> At sunrise on the appointed day the seventh ancestor Spirit spat out eighty threads of cotton; these he distributed between his upper teeth which acted as the teeth of a weaver's reed. In this way he made the uneven threads of a warp. He did the same with the lower teeth to make the even threads. By opening and shutting his jaws the Spirit caused the threads of the warp to make the movements required in weaving. His whole face took part in the work, his nose studs serving as the block, while the stud in his lower lip was the shuttle.
>
> As the threads crossed and uncrossed, the two tips of the Spirit's forked tongue pushed the thread of the weft to and fro, and the web took shape from his mouth in the breath of the second revealed Word.
>
> For the Spirit was speaking while the work proceeded. As did the Nummo in the first revelation, he imparted his word by means of a technical process, so that all men could understand. By doing so he showed the identity of material actions and spiritual forces, or rather the need for their cooperation.
>
> The words that the Spirit uttered filled all the interstices of the stuff: they were woven in the threads, and formed part and parcel of the cloth. They were the cloth. And the cloth was the word.[32]

This tale equates weaving with speaking: it is an alternative genealogy, you might say, for the notion of *text*. The first act of weaving is literally a kind of utterance, with the loom represented by the movement of the mouth: "the interlacing of warp and weft endured the same words, the new instruction which became the heritage of mankind and was handed on from generation to generation of weavers to the accompaniment of the clapping of the shuttle and the creaking of the block, which they call 'the creaking of the word.'"[33] Mackey turns the block into a bass (it "sings base," he says)[34] and reads its sound as "noise," that is as a sonic element that is meant to be excluded from the textile word: at once fundamental (bass/base) and extraneous (noise).

But Mackey makes no effort to creak when he reads, or to score poems that would or should be uttered with a raspy tone of voice. Instead, it is the collocation of different images, not of word-sounds, that produces the discrepancy he says is central to his poetics. As he put it in that 1997 interview, "the process of bringing things together that are, in the most widely accepted senses of the term, 'disparate' and 'disengaged,' bringing them into contiguity with one another, is analogous to the roughness you get and the rub you get when you bring things that are not homogeneous together."[35] Developing Lorca's proposition that *duende* "draws near places where forms fuse together into a yearning superior to their visible expression,"[36] Mackey characterized it as the occupation of the voice by "another voice;"[37] but I don't think these propositions can be assimilated to a purely sonic poetics. This notion of discrepancy is located in the world of signified things, rather than the "music" of the spoken word, and is even used to explain sonic concepts. Whatever sounds inspired them, his poetics of juxtaposition seem to be grounded in reference.

Indeed, there are times when even music seems to acquire a kind of propositional meaning. A case in point is an episode in *Bedouin Hornbook*, in which Lambert, a member of the band whose adventures in musical improvisation are the substance of the novel's narrative, proposes to the rest of the group that they should engage a drummer. He does so by performing a piece of music on saxophone and harmonica. The piece, Lambert says, is called "Prometheus" (117). What is remarkable, for our purposes at least, is the fact that it is described *as though it were speech*:

> The piece began in a rather straight-ahead vein, its opening phrases built around an arpeggiated B-flat triad by way of which the most commonly accepted particulars regarding Prometheus were once again served up. Lambert was careful to begin with Prometheus' birth to the Titan Iapetus and the Oceanid Clymene, going on to make a point of the clever way in which Prometheus remained neutral during the revolt of the Titans, thereby ingratiating himself with Zeus. Falling back on a riff or two reminiscent of "Confirmation," he told of the grudge Prometheus nursed against the Olympians for destroying the Titans and of how he revenged himself by favoring humans at the gods' expense. (In a parenthetical aside that displayed a boplike reverence for the opening phrase's chord configuration, Lambert made reference to a rather late tradition which maintained that it was Prometheus who with earth and water—his own tears according to some, Lambert pointed out—had fashioned the body of the first mortal.) He took his time going into the well-known and oft-repeated details of the meeting at Sicyon. Zeus's anger at having chosen a pile of bones as his portion of the sacrifice, his decision to withhold fire from humans and then the trip Prometheus made to Hephaestus's forges on the island of Lemnos all came vividly to life with Lambert's more pronounced, more prominent use of Trane-inspired 16ths.[38]

At a crucial moment, the performance modulates. Thus far he has been playing "tonally:" he builds his opening phrases "around an arpeggiated B-flat triad;" quotes Charlie Parker's "Confirmation," displays "boplike reverence for the opening phrase's chord configuration" and plays "Trane-inspired 16ths." But then he moves into a style drawn more from Pharoah Sanders or Albert Ayler. Now he "growled, spat, split notes, railed, bellowed, and shrieked." And in this extra-tonal playing, this display of "technique beyond technique," as Mackey put it in explaining *duende*, N. hears a critique of the myth: he tells us that Lambert's new sonic palette comes "by way of maintaining that the

Prometheus myth in the form in which we know it represents a classic case of 'blaming the victim.'"[39] In this sense the music seems to mirror or contain an internal emblem of Mackey's poetics, in which the rasp signals discrepancy, "noise," and in doing so provides a space or voice for the excluded.

But my argument seems to have gone off the rails. Far from the "uneasy fit between word and world" that Mackey associates with discrepant engagement, here we have a musical form of expression that can, it would seem, be clearly and accurately translated into recognizable meanings. Did I get it wrong? Is Mackey perhaps not a formalist at all, even in the name of open form, because he so strongly emphasizes ideas, images, and myth? Does the translatability of Lambert's saxophone solo into a critical discourse on the meaning of Prometheus not bespeak a radical commitment to reference?

Maybe I've made an assumption we need to question. Who says that forms only happen in the ear, that sound is the privileged point of access for formal investigations? Maybe we should adopt this refinement: sound, sheer sound, has no form until someone starts to recognize patterns in it: whether these patterns are words or rhythm, sound or image, matters less than that they impose a perceivable periodicity on what we hear. And it is only then, only at the point when we can discern elements and appreciate how they are combined, that we can begin to assess a thing's form. "Formal analysis" depends on our impression of the syntax and rhythm of elements, *whatever* these elements are.

That observation cuts both ways: it not only allows for forms to occur within the realm of reference, but it also implies that reference may itself be mostly or entirely formal. Here let me ask a question that is perhaps so obvious we might have forgotten about it: what sense or meaning does the *Prometheus* myth actually have? Does *it* tell a story that maps on to prosaic, regular experience? The answer is surely that it does not: from antiquity onward this myth has required high levels of exegetical energy in order to transform it into usable meaning. On its own, it says about as much as a piece of music does (at least under normal conditions). Recognitions of this fact are not hard to find. One might think of Lévi-Strauss's extended argument, in *Mythologiques*, that myth and music are symmetrical images of each other. Indeed, Myth's reluctance to disclose anything like simple meaning has been a well-known part of modern attempts to handle it, beginning at least with Vico. Samuel Taylor Coleridge proposed that myths were, as he put it, *tautegorical*: in opposition to allegories, which said something other than what they seemed to say, a myth only said what it said. It said *this* (*tauton*), not something else or other (*allon*).[40]

Let us return to Lambert's *Prometheus*. It seems, at first, as though the musical performance was readily translated into a myth, which we could therefore take as its meaning, its widely understood reference. But a reconsideration suggests that there are two formal systems at play in this scene: a piece of music and a myth. They are brought together when Lambert declares that his piece will be called "Prometheus." What follows, I would suggest, is in fact not a translation from the one into the other, but rather N.'s narrative of the results of *his* juxtaposing these disparate materials in an act of listening. What we read, in other words, comes from an act of discrepant engagement, myth rubbing up against music to produce an energetic response. One sign that this is a better way to understand the scene is that the piece does not produce an univocal response: some in the audience take umbrage at it, and a vigorous debate ensues. Multiple acts of discrepant engagement lead to a scene characterized by even further dissonance as reactions start to occur.

The epigraph to Mackey's *Whatsaid Serif* draws from Ellen Basso's study of Kalapalo storytelling, *A Musical View of the Universe*. According to Basso, the Kalapalo require a

> whatsayer, who is a crucial actor in the situation. The whatsayer may be someone who asked to begin the narrative or the recipient of a story that exemplifies explanatory principles needing clarification during the course of some other situation.[41]

As the book's title implies, the sequence of songs in *Whatsaid Serif* is concerned with exegetical dialogues. But the "whatsayer" in Mackey's work, who seems to alternate between demands for explanation and unhelpful interpolations, seems more like an oppressive presence, someone who would eliminate the rough voice, the immanent rasp, of the poetry.

<pre>
                        Thus it
        was these words broke my sleep,
                                woke
        me: *Heard it who seldom spoke,*
          "No remedy," flamenco's gnostic
        moan . . . Standing, I sank, felt
             nothing, though the spun words
          rocked my waking, shook me,
            spun from when body caught soul,
                                    soul
        body,
            "Tongue too familiar with
          tooth," I complained, blue
                            Davidic
        harp, Ethiopian moan. Monophysite
            lament, one we, Ouadada, that
        we would include, not reduce to us . . .
        He to him, she to her, they to them,
                                opaque
          pronouns, "persons" whether or not we
        knew who they were . . .

                            Whoosh, what we
        needed, movement,   except the what-sayer,
</pre>

> obsessed, asking what. "Was it a woman
> he once was in love with?" "Was it a lie
> he'd long since put it all behind?"[42]

I admit to feeling some discomfort at these lines. For the first half of the passage, Mackey's lyric "I" articulates a series of phrases with clear points of reference in his critical writings: "no remedy" a reference to the *sin remedio* of deep song, affect of *Duende*;[43] "spun words" the weaving that engenders the notion of the "creaking of the word." In some ways, the passage reads like a catalogue of interpretive keywords, an expansive gloss on each of which would amount to a full articulation of Mackey's poetics as it has been expressed in his criticism.

But whatever the exegetical value or valence these phrases might have, the catalogue here is capped by the intrusion of a "whatsayer," whose obsessive questions block the movement "we needed." The whatsayer's questions seem exegetical: they assume that the poetry is about something, that there is a biographical meaning somewhere ("a woman he once was in love with"). I have started to worry that no matter how carefully I stay in the margins, as it were, with observations about Mackey's metapoetic thought, I am going to end up being another whatsayer blocking the longed-for flight of this poem's "I." What's the difference, in the end, between biography, history, and poetics? All are, in their way, orders of stabilization, methods of capture. The nervousness expressed in these lines about the whatsayer could well bespeak a resistance to interpretation on all such planes. Why, after all, should I assume that this work wants anything like a "reading" from me anyway? Such a line of thought heads towards the unsettling conclusion that Mackey is indeed interested in a kind of formal closure. There *is* a line drawn around the work, insofar as it repels such exegetical whatsayers. "Open form" would amount to another modality of closure.

But this isn't quite right, for just a few poems later, the "I" of *Whatsaid Serif* itself proves a whatsayer:

> I was the whatsayer.
> Whatever he said he said I would
> say so what.[44]

A great deal depends on who "he" is—and even speculating about that makes me into the whatsayer we've been angsting about. But let's just say for the sake of the argument that "he" is indeed the exegetical whatsayer of the earlier poems, whose questions seemed to block needed movement. Here, "I" would be unasking the exegetical questions of before, unveiling them as insignificant or meaningless ("so what?"). The consequence, in the immediately subsequent lines, is movement—though it is a very ambiguous kind of movement, which invokes the forced migration of African slaves towards Porto Novo. An act of unterpretation—saying "so what" to the exegetical whatsayer—seems both to liberate and destroy liberty, as though "free," like "we," must remain asymptotic. Whatsaying is less an act of blockage *imposed* on the poetry's will-to-fly than a process of confrontation which guarantees the condition of being *almost* which is so consistent throughout the poetry. Whatsaying is dialogue, a *pas-de-deux* of asking and unasking, an unending process of suspension.

The band whose adventures *From a Broken Bottle Traces of Perfume Still Emanate* narrates is in the grip of an unusual phenomenon. At certain moments, not predictable to the musicians themselves, cartoon speech-bubbles or "balloons" emerge out of the player's instruments: these balloons contain texts that are like oracles, revelatory of the music or of the state of mind of the musicians or, not uncommonly, entirely enigmatic and the subject of much discussion and controversy. But as the band's reputation grows, the possibility that balloons might emerge during a performance becomes, as it were, part of the performance, so that audiences hope for this event and comment on it afterward. In *Late Arcade*, N. refers to these balloons as "captions," a moment within the music when a kind of meaning becomes available to the audience.[45] The band becomes uneasy with this: they prefer a music that eschews such lazy self-interpretation. In an attempt to reset the balance between music and meaning, they distribute real (i.e., rubber) balloons to the audience in advance, with the instruction that they may do what they like with them.[46] Possible prophylaxis (as one character punningly puts it) against the musical captions, the gesture of distributing balloons makes of musical meaning an active, collaborative action.

N. and his bandmates imagine these rubber balloons as "captured breath":

> We agree that a balloon is nothing if not captured breath. That it contains or seeks to contain something too inchoate to be contained we also agree. That the comic-strip balloon and the literal balloon, the rubber balloon, have that much in common we see as well. We agree that using containment (would-be containment) to open things up is a kind of coup. That putting the audience's will or wish to containment literally in their hands carries an element of poetic justice has also occurred to us. That it carries an element of poetic license as well has occurred to us too. That tradition of balloons as a sign of ceremony does recruit color, as you say, to the binding of breath, much as music does. We couldn't have said it better, except we'd maybe keep going and say balloons are in a sense already music, a ritual disbursement of caught or constricted breath meant to consecrate, even where it borders on asthma (if not especially where it borders on asthma), the blessing breath is. If asthma can be thought of as a wildfire, we'd say, balloons are a controlled burn. They marshal caught or constricted breath intimating breath's possible extinction, festive recruit's cautionary aspect or address. Balloons are also, we'd go on to say, chromatic festivity's dark tone, dark temper, so much depending on sacks of air. We'd want festive lightness given a gravity of sorts, each audience member holding a balloon as though it were his or her own lung.[47]

"Using containment (would-be containment) to open things up:" the band's strategy, in effect, is to take literally an audience's desire to caption their music, and in doing so, to create a new space of energized openness. Open form as the result of conflictual proximity, less coordination than layering. Whereas the musical balloons had emerged from the *players*, and thus risked seeming like an exegetical cut-off, these balloons are given to the audience and become symbols of their ability to talk back. The performance becomes inclusive through a series of acts of partial closure. N.'s description of this process represents it as a rediscovery of color: the balloons "recruit color" to the binding of breath and are "chromatic festivity's dark tone"—language that blends musical chromaticism with the discordant rasp of *duende*, which Lorca had called "the Pharoah's black torso" and Mackey had evoked as *cante moro*, "black song."

As musical captions or inflatable rubber toys, the balloons embody a recognition that "breath" signifies liability to capture, frailty, and exposure; as "chromatic festivity's dark tone" they remind us that breath has implications in the politics and aesthetics of tone, whether this is musical tone or skin tone. In 2017 Mackey published an essay entitled *Breath and Precarity* in which he linked a poetics of the breath with a commitment to life as fragile and precarious, and a tradition of what he calls "radical pneumatism." *Breath and Precarity* begins as a meditation on the aesthetics of breath in the "New American Poetry," particularly as these were articulated by Charles Olson in his influential 1950 essay "Projective Verse." Olson proposed that the poetic line "comes (as I see it) from the breath, from the breathing of the man who writes, at the moment that he writes;" Mackey emphasizes in particular Olson's assertion that "a projective poet will go down through the workings of his own throat to the place where breath comes from"—this place being the heart. (Olson's formulation, "the HEAD, by way of the EAR, to the SYLLABLE/the HEART, by way of BREATH, to the LINE" is in its way a renovation of Aristotelian ideas: for Aristotle there were two distinct communicative systems, the one leading from *nous* to *logos* via the mouth, the other from the heart to the voice via the breath.[48]) He finds this poetics of breath paralleled in the musical phraseology of saxophonists like John Tchicai, Sonny Rollins, and Ben Webster. On the sax as in poetry, he finds an emphasis on pneumatism which reveals that without breath we cannot live and that, for many on the planet, the ability to breathe is constantly threatened. Commenting on Ben Webster's performance of "Tenderly" on *King of the Tenors*, Mackey writes:

> it advances an essay on fragility and frailty with a certain lightness of touch, a fleetingness of nuance and lightness according with the diagnostic finesse I've long wondered about and that I still wonder about. Leakage, air's propensity to escape or be taken away, seems to both halo and haunt the piece, giving it a ghost escort or the intimation of ghostliness, making it also, whatever else it is, the tenderness of address it obviously is, a meditation on transience, mentality, expiration. On the other hand, such radical pneumatic practice parallels Olson's assertion that "breath allows *all* the speech-force of language back in (speech is the 'solid' of verse, is the secret of a poem's energy) . . . a poem has, by speech, solidity." In Webster's *Tenderly* and other such work, breath is rendered solid, bodied forth as texture, tactility, palpability, an abrading aurality one feels one could reach out and touch. Is its implied purchase, the solidity it bestows on breath, a resilient measure making

breath all the better to be held on to? Granted solidity, audiotactility, does breath become less airy and thus less fleeting, less ephemeral? Is radical pneumatism as much a holding action as an elegiac lament?[49]

The solidity that we encounter here, this "audio-tactility," is a kind of insistence; it "wields a lever against present conditions" (15), aims to "transmute or alchemize anti-black violence, harassment, and predation" (17). The pneumatism of poetry and jazz is a way of resounding with Eric Garner's "I can't breathe," which itself rhymes brutally with Franz Fanon's observation that "we revolt simply because, for many reasons, we can no longer breathe" (17). Pneuma solidifies *not* into speech, but into "the line," another term we find at work in both poetry and jazz, designating the concrete presence of what is constitutionally at risk.

So let us listen to Mackey's line, which he described in an interview as seeking to achieve a certain level of jaggedness and which (as we saw above) he affiliates with William Carlos Williams's notion of the "variable foot." Mackey takes it to be of vital importance that Williams heard in "black rhythm" the sound of a limp, what we might call a swung gait.[50] In *Patterson,* as Mackey points out, Williams linked the "limp" of swing with the subjugation of those who made the music, further connecting this with the choliambic or "limping iambic" associated first with Hipponax.[51] Mackey glosses: "this would be a way of talking about the 'variable foot,' less an aid to scansion than a trope—the travestied, fractured foot."[52] He then links this with "the Fon-Yoruba orisha of the crossroads, the lame dancer Legba." Legba becomes a figure for the rub or rasp of discrepant engagement. He is a "master of polyrhythmicity and heterogeneity;" his "impairment taken to higher ground, remediated, translates damage and disarray into dance."[53] It is, to put this otherwise, a condition of loss, absence, or precarity, sublated.

And it is in this limping polyrhythmicity that I suspect a place to have been cleared—maybe we should call it an orchestra or a dancing floor—for an unknown arrivant, something like an audience, but different from the exegetical whatsayer. In the first volume of *From a Broken Bottle,* N. offers a brief meditation on John Chernoff's pioneering work of ethnomusicology, *African Rhythm and African Sensibility,* drawing particular attention to Chernoff's interpretation of Ghanaian drumming as intensely polyrhythmic, "best considered as an arrangement of gaps where one may add a rhythm, rather than as a dense pattern of sound."[54] N. concludes that "polyrhythmic drumming implies an absent, additional rhythm, a furtive beat one's own listening supplies or one's dancing echoes."[55] An easy enough hypothesis to test: what makes you tap your foot or dance would less be some precise, thumping pulse, but the presence of two or more rhythmic patterns rubbing together. The idea has been called "participatory discrepancy."[56] Applied to Mackey's poetry, we might observe that rhythmic raggedness and the use of heterogeneous materials are both constructed so as to imply an absence, to create that sense of present precarity suspended between (futural) incompleteness and (praeterite) loss; into this precarious present we may add our own elements by singing or dancing along.[57]

Such rhythm has a swinging gait that makes us dance, as it were. But dancing is not marching: we do not dance in lockstep, but each with a slightly different lilt, our reactions adding to and extending the rhythm as it was stated to us. Here if I could add a scholion I would say that this is not just a poetics: it is the articulation of the kind of criticism such writing might expect. A critic would not merely explain or judge, but would join in, writing beside the work, their own paragraphs articulating an idiomatic version of textual rhythm. I don't want to underestimate how radical such a proposal is: open form would demand a criticism that is as far from authority as one can imagine. One would become another voice, one would add a layer. One would be with the text, beside the text, not above or apart from it. Between music and myth, as between text and paracrit, then, an act of engaged difference. Mackey emblematizes this with the word "ythm," which he explains as "clipped rhythm, anagrammatic myth."[58] We might think of the two defining operations of his poetics: the gap that opens to others, recalled in the "clipping" of rhythm; and the juxtaposition of disparate materials in the "anagrammatization" of myth.

As a kind of epigraph to the half of his long poem called *Mu*, Mackey cites Jane Harrison's speculation in *Themis* that "the first *mythos* was simply the interjectional utterance *mu*."[59] What Harrison meant by this is difficult to discern. She could have been proposing little more than an etymology of the word *mythos*, via a reminiscence of the role of the tragic chorus in punctuating narrative action with mythical narratives.[60] But a later passage suggests a different, more remarkable interpretation. Interjections are not just punctuation marks in ritual action: they are an early phase in the emergence of language.

> Language, after the purely emotional interjection, began with whole sentences, *holophrases*, utterances of a relation in which subject and object have not yet got their heads above water but are submerged in a situation. [...] The holophrase shows us man entangled as it were in his own activities, he and his environment utterly involved. He has as yet no "soul," but he has life, and he has it abundantly.[61]

Mu might therefore designate the earliest phase in this model of linguistic progress, the "entwined interjection" that occurs even before the emergence of holophrases, something like a primary vocal materialization on which language as we know it was gradually elaborated. If so, it would occupy a linguistic temporality akin to the anthropological temporality of the Andoumboulou, the first draft of humanity which humanity itself is. Harrison might be implying that narrative itself is merely a habit of crafting meaning around the weave of an interjectional music, as though the sequences of vowels and consonants were there first, the meanings found later; and Mackey would seem to agree, since he remarks that *Mu* is a song of "momentary utterance extended into ongoing myth, an impulse towards signature, self-elaboration, finding and losing itself."[62]

I, of course, hear other resonances in *mu*. Not just the zen negation *mu* that opens the way to further meditative practice. Not just the hominin utterance *hmmm* that David Mithen theorized was the vocal practice from which language and music later evolved,[63] or the 'pataphilological *ha* that, for Alfred Jarry, symbolized the primate origins of language.[64] Not just the originary utterance *Om*, containing all sound, on which a lifetime of contemplation can be spent and which traditionally begins the recitation of Sanskrit verse.[65] For me, *Mu* is above all the sound of the aulos—*mumu mumu mumu*, in Aristophanes' unforgettable transcition.[66] The roaring or booming aulos, instrumental interjection in tragedy, the voice of ritual continuity and sacrifice, instrument of transport and transformation, mistrusted by Plato for its polyvocality, by Aristotle for its irrationality: one way to read this instrument is to say that it provides the burr or rasp to Greek musical performance. And of course one might think of the aulete in dithyramb and tragedy as at once a leader and an answerer, a whatsayer who propels through sound and gesture the narrative told by the chorus.

The aulos was famous for its sonic polyformity, its ability to be bent beyond its own sound. In the technique called the *syrigmos*, auletes made noises described as "serpentine" or "bestial;" such sounds were used in musical narratives to represent the death sounds of monsters who existed before the Olympian order. The instrument could also be played broken or "clipped:" in one story, the aulete Midas' mouthpiece broke and he completed his performance playing "in the manner of a syrinx"—which seems to mean not that he hissed and buzzed but that he converted the aulos into a pan-pipe, blowing over the top of the bore. Similarly, in a section of Mackey's reading of *Song of the Andoumboulou* 16, Hafez Modirzadeh played the saxophone without its mouthpiece, a sometime syrinx or broken aulos (though he called it "conch sax").[67] The saxophone sounds almost like a human voice, talking along or under Mackey's poetry, articulating myths one can perhaps only hear if one speaks at the same time.

Notes

1. The five novels of *From a Broken Bottle Traces of Perfume Still Emanate* are Mackey 2010 (Comprising *Bedouin Hornbook, Djbot Baghostus' Run*, and *Atet A.D.*, all published earlier), Mackey 2008 and 2017. The long poem, in book form, appears in Mackey 1985, 1993b, 1998, 2006, 2011, 2015, and 2021b. Writing on Mackey is widespread: I have learned particularly from Mallot 2004, Zamsky 2006, Simpson 2003, O'Leary 2000, Nielsen 2000, Mossin 2014, Lavery 2004, Jenkins 2016, Finkelstein 2008, Edwards 2000, Burge 2013, and Reed 2014, 171–206.

2. "Poetry may be defined as an order of words that as movement and tones (rhythm and pitch) approaches in varying degrees the wordless art of music as a kind of mathematical limit" (Zukofsky 1967, 19), cited by Mackey in Mackey 2005, 180, and 1987, 30.

3. Mackey 2010, 72.

4. Mackey 2010, 72.

5. Mackey 2010, 72.

6. I think Mackey's main point of reference here is "Reification and the Consciousness of the Proletariat" in Lukács 1971.

7. Mackey 2010, 86.

8. "They have an unsettled relation to the poem that precedes them and the poem that follows them" (Mackey 2005, 296); "They revisit in many instances, but they revisit in a way that's differentially marked. There's a great deal of revisitation in my writing anyway; these do it in a way that's marked visually and underscored visually in the way that they are put on the page, where they're placed at the bottom of the page, beneath a line" (Mackey 2005, 297).

9. Baudrillard 1996.

10. Walter Benjamin's ruminations on classicism and neoclassisism throughout the *Arcades Project* thematize the heavy ideological labor classicism has always been required to do in the capitalist era. See especially the "exposés" of 1935 and 1939 (W. Benjamin 1999, 4 and 15), but also throughout his notes (W. Benjamin 1999, 107, 157, 217, 405 and especially 694). I am less convinced by his association of the citation of classical models with *all* revolutionary moments: his own documentation suggests only that classicism is the language of choice for bourgeois revolutions.

11. Mackey 2010, 72.

12. Barker 2007 and Creese 2010.

13. I outline this argument in more detail in Gurd 2019.

14. Mackey 2010, 73.

15. Mackey 2010, 74.

16. Mackey 2010, 78.

17. See Gurd 2019, 139–41.

18. Mackey 1993a, 20.

19. See, for example, Iyer 2002.

20. Griaule 1965.

21. Mackey 2006, xi.

22. Mossin 2014, 176–7.

23. Mossin 2014, 177; the poem is in Mackey 1985, 66–7.

24. Mackey 2005, 196. On Mackey and Sufism, see Burge 2013.

25. Mackey 2006, 86.

26. Mackey 1987.

27. Mackey 1987, 31, citing from Feld 1990, 34.

28. Mackey 2005, 185.

29. Mackey 2005, 182. Citing from García Lorca 1980, 40.

30. Mackey 2005, 294.

31. Mackey 1993a, 19.

32. Griaule 1965, 27–8.

33. Griaule 1965, 29.

34. Mackey 1993a, 19.

35. Mackey 2005, 294.

36. Mackey 2005, 184.

37. Mackey 2005, 186.

38. Mackey 2010, 117.

39. Mackey 2010, 118.

40. His coinage was taken up by Schelling. See "Coleridge on Allegory and Symbol," https://www.oxfordhandbooks.com/view/10.1093/oxfordhb/9780199644179.001.0001/oxfordhb-9780199644179-e-19#oxfordhb-9780199644179-div1-83

41. Mackey 1998, unnumbered page. See Basso 1985, 15.

42. Mackey 1998, 14–15.

43. "One of the phrases which recur a great deal in canto jondo is the phrase *sin remedio*, 'without remedy.' You'll also hear the assertion *no hay remedio,* 'there is no remedy.' Pepe de la Matrona, who has one of the darkest, gruffest voices you'll ever hear (more an extended, variegated growl than a voice), sings a song called 'Remedio no Tengas,' which means 'you would have no remedy.'" (Mackey 2005, 185).

44. Mackey 1998, 22.

45. Mackey 2010, 531.

46. Mackey 2010, 76–7.

47. Mackey 2010, 78.

48. Olson, "Projective Verse," cited in Mackey 2021a, 4.

49. Mackey 2021a, 12–13.

50. Mackey 1993a, 242–3.

51. Mackey (1993a, 243), citing W. C. Williams 1995, 53.

52. Mackey 1993a, 243.

53. Mackey 1993a, 244.

54. Mackey 2010, 134.

55. Mackey 2010, 134–5.

56. See Keil 1987, endorsed by Mackey (2005, 207).

57. Mackey 2010, 135. See Chernoff 1979.

58. Mackey 2006, xiii.

59. Harrison 1912, 330.

60. "Each step in the ritual action is shadowed as it were by a fresh interjection, till the whole combines into a consecutive tale" (Harrison 1912, 330).

61. Harrison 1912, 474.

62. Mackey 1993b, xiii.

63. Mithen 2006.

64. See Gurd 2018a.

65. See Katz 2018.

66. Aristophanes, *Knights* 10.

67. Mackey 2005, 234.

CHAPTER 15
CHAL CHAL CHAL: APOLLONIUS' TALOS TALES (AND MEDEA'S)
Mario Telò

What does it mean to think of politics not just as form but, more specifically, an intensive formalistic force expressed as a depersonalized, insurrectionary surge? Speaking of the surge of demonstrations provoked by the murder of George Floyd, Angela Davis has voiced the need for thinking about how we respond to what she calls "the lost intensity of the moment"[1]—that is, how we prolong the intensity of the moment of protest into its aftermath. We might then consider the relation, etymological and conceptual, between intensity and insistence. As a spatial stretching, *in-tensity* (from *in* + *tendere*, "to stretch") is part of the conceptual field covered by *in-sistence* (from *in* + *sistere*, "to remain"), which connotes a temporal expansion, a prolonged remaining in place that stretches the body but also the structural, formal contours of the social.[2] In this chapter, I explore the possibilities of this political stretching by focusing on a specific formal intensity in Apollonius' *Argonautica*: the metallic sound of a brazen disability or hyperability, an insurrectionary insistence, clanging forth from the exertions of the giant Talos. In this exploration, I will embark on an exercise of radical formalism, which, as I will expound at the end, I intend as both a practice of hyper-formalistic reading and as an instrument of radical, that is, emancipatory metapolitics.

Non-ableist embodiment can be enacted in poetic deformation, in the very making of form, what Mallarmé calls "the crisis of verse."[3] Considering the work of poet Amber DiPietra, Petra Kuppers observes that in her poems "the pain of scratched eyes emerges as a site of phoneme production, as productive typos, as a production machine that creates and sounds itself into the world even in the presence of pain."[4] Elsewhere, Kuppers describes her experience in reading a poem by Philip Dowd as an encounter of three disabilities—her own, Dowd's, and that of Hephaestus, featured in these lines:

Cerebral palsy moves as in tides
Sometimes high, sometimes low,
And I must follow.

Tidally something cosmic
Moves through me
The comic
The forge
Hephaestus . . .

In Kuppers's experience:[5]

> To read this poem, I gasp, quickly, as the lines chop across my breath, making me weigh the length of each syllable, the cost of the word. The intake and outflow of breath are audible to me as I read, again and again, following the punctuations into pauses … [Hephaestus] doesn't just hasten away, unthinking … His foot is an undefined mass, yet-to-be-shapen … I can hear that hammer coming down, hammering matter into fiery shape … The weight of the hammer, "a muscular contraction": words are heavy, and create a new beginning.

In my analysis of Apollonius' Talos—who joins the dis- and hyper-ability of the Olympian god and the metallic ontology of his female assistants in the *Iliad*[6]—I wish to heed the mimetic synergy of muscular contraction, chopped (or "cripped") breath, and hammering metallic cadence that shake the Cretan giant's daily encumbered movements and release an impersonal, recalcitrant force against ableist subjectivity and subjectivity as such.

To bring out the aesthetico-political overlap of intensity, form, and disability discernible in the intimate encounter between Talos and his enemy Medea, I will read the scene in light of Jacques Derrida's *Glas*, originally published in 1974 and recently reissued as *Clang*, which shows us a posthumanist Derrida,[7] a Derrida interested in the "logic of sensation," or in the biopolitics of sound.[8] Organized around two columns or towers—Hegel's and Genet's—*Glas* presents itself as the graphic juxtaposition of two (conceptual) constructions, two "erections" (in both the architectural and sexual sense), as Derrida explicitly characterizes them. Yet, as Catherine Malabou has observed, for Derrida "erection is maintained"—graphically—"through infinite spacing, punctuating holes made by cuts, amputations, missing limbs, stumps, decapitations."[9] This breaking of integrity, verticality (or rectitude), and straightness[10]—a non-ableist corporeality—is encapsulated in the minoritarian force of a phonestheme, *glas*, the din caused by letting "wordstones from the gantries of high towers … fall into scattered rubble, or pile into a cairn marking a tomb."[11] The evocative force of *glas* can also be conceptualized in these terms: "One gags or chokes somewhat as one pronounces *gl/cl*, as though one's speech were *impaired* by a clot of saliva, mucus, milk."[12] This impairment is a surplus beyond the opposition of life and death—what Naomi Waltham-Smith calls a "shatter," which "harks back to the shards, splinters, explosions, splatter, peals of bells, and eruptions of uproarious laughter in *Glas* where Hegelian metaphysics is *volé en éclats*."[13] In the course of my analysis, I will connect the impairing and impaired intensity of *glas* with *chal* in *chal-keios* ("made of bronze"), the adjective that diffuses impressions of the giant's metallic substance into the textual atmosphere.[14]

Before turning to Apollonius' Crete—which is under the protection of Talos when the Argonauts approach it—I wish to dwell briefly on the hyper-present of American politics, as reflected in a short satiric video by queer comedian Randy Rainbow, a parody of "The Trolley Song," from the 1944 Judy Garland film *Meet Me in St. Louis*. Here, Missouri Republican senator Josh Hawley, confronted by Rainbow, in the guise of a cable news anchor, about his role in the January 6 Capitol attack, declares, in a gesture of blatant projection, "I'm not going to back down before a liberal mob"—a statement that seamlessly segues into Randy's queer reperformance of the queer refrain *clang, clang, clang*, an iconic metallic sound, both of the trolley and the bell.[15] Fragmenting and expanding into an onomatopoetic overload, *clang clang clang* issues an alternative language:[16] *yap, yap, yap*; *crap, crap, crap*; *bitch, bitch, bitch*; *mitch, mitch, mitch*; *push, push, push*; *yuk, yuk, yuk*; *bang, bang, bang*; *creep, creep, creep*; and, inevitably, *trump, trump, trump*[17]—which replace, among others, *ding, ding, ding*; *zing, zing, zing*; *thump, thump, thump*; and *bump, bump, bump* in the Garland song. Just as *yu(c)k* is caught between a laughter and an interjection of disgust, between sense and nonsense, verbs like *push* but also proper nouns (*Trump* and *Mitch*) are turned into quasi-profanity, automated tics, the rhythmic clamor of engines or quasi-automated somatic routines (laughing, defecating, intercourse). Language does not simply disintegrate into sound; it becomes noise, what David Theo Goldberg has called, in reference to rowdy protests, "the punctuation in the political conversation," or "a perturbing intrusion … into structure and form,"[18] we might say of a dissensual Real. In our daily lives, we are constantly exposed, as Waltham-Smith notes, to the sound of biopolitics:

> the cries of suffering, the screams of torture, the shouts of protest, the shattering of explosions, or the dog whistles of the far right, or … the sound of the tube gates opening to let precarious workers take the first train home in the morning or … the pulses by which ocean tomographers "auscultate" the planet to reveal the negative impact of neoliberal capitalism on ocean temperatures and global climate change.[19]

In this landscape, as she observes, we witness "the proximity between the weaponization of the sound and its use as a tool of resistance … between violence and counterforce … between the sound of a tear-gas grenade and a Molotov cocktail, between governmentality and *la génération ingouvernable*."[20] In Rainbow's lyrics, a mischievous lingering on the phonography of onomatopoeia; the queer transformation of ordinary political noise into the *jouissant* formalism, hypermimetic and nonsensical, of a twitch; and a subversively impish attachment to letterality generate a counter-insurrectionary intensity.[21]

This intensity encompasses yet exceeds laughter, marking an interobjective fusion of human and non-human, or a minoritarian intrusion of the mechanical, or the robotic, into the human. There is also a marked political force of genderqueer disidentification in the insurrectionary noise *clang clang clang*, not just because of Rainbow's own flamboyant gay persona, his becoming Judy Garland and splintering into all the people on the trolley (male and female), but also because the verbal repetition converges with the immobile motion of the trolley's looping engine—and of the trolley itself, fixed against the rear-projected scenery—conveying an intense sense of time out-of-joint, to use a phrase favored in various theorizations of queer temporality.[22]

Even before Rainbow's parodic homage, Garland, with her *clang clang clang-ing*—"too much intensity, too much physicality, too little glamour, too little heterosexual rapport with the dancing boys"[23]—performs and models for the gay male viewer a kind of "sissy insurgency."[24] The word *siss-y* itself, an adjective resulting from the amputation and phonetic expansion of *sis-ter*, releases a lisping sigmatism.[25] A metallic intensity can be found in Garland's "kinesics of suffering," in the cyborgic metamorphosis foisted upon her by the cruel aesthetic conventions of the movie industry, which starkly limited her performative mobility, imposing rigid protocols of posture and deportment, stiffening her legs and arms, constraining her torso and head, that is, subjecting her body to a torturous makeover, to the same necropolitical orthopedics that, as we will see, wear down Talos' own corporeality through quotidian labor.[26] In the performance of "The Trolley Song," she is squeezed in a rigid corset that makes her movements machinic, like those of the wheels of the contraption used on set to simulate movement.[27] There is a sense in which Judy Garland, while acting in *The Wizard of Oz*, is not just Dorothy but also the Tin Woodman, a successor of Talos.[28]

A creaking sigmatism is among the formal intensities emitted by Talos himself in the half-line—*surinx haimatoessa kata sphuron* ("blood-bearing vein by the ankle" 1647)— that introduces his vulnerable anatomical locus, part of the cumbersome metallic ensemble of his body. Installed by Zeus as the guardian of Europa on Crete, mighty yet precarious, Talos is forced to monitor the island with a serial clanging,[29] in spite of his physical disability or because of his hyperability, as we read in Apollonius' account of the Argonauts' first encounter with him (1638–47):

τοὺς δὲ Τάλως χάλκειος, ἀπὸ στιβαροῦ σκοπέλοιο
ῥηγνύμενος πέτρας, εἶργε χθονὶ πείσματ' ἀνάψαι
Δικταίην ὅρμοιο κατερχομένους ἐπιωγήν.   (1640)
τὸν μέν, χαλκείης μελιηγενέων ἀνθρώπων
ῥίζης λοιπὸν ἐόντα μετ' ἀνδράσιν ἡμιθέοισιν,
Εὐρώπῃ Κρονίδης νήσου πόρεν ἔμμεναι οὖρον,
τρὶς περὶ χαλκείοις Κρήτην ποσὶ δινεύοντα·
ἀλλ' ἤτοι τὸ μὲν ἄλλο δέμας καὶ γυῖα τέτυκτο   (1645)
χάλκεος ἠδ' ἄρρηκτος, ὑπαὶ δέ οἱ ἔσκε τένοντος
σύριγξ αἱματόεσσα κατὰ σφυρόν ...

Breaking (*rhêgnumenos*) rocks from the sturdy cliff, *Talos, made of bronze* (*Talôs chalkeios*), prevented them from attaching ropes to the land, while they were coming down to the Dictaean harbor of anchorage. For Europa's sake, Cronus' son had established him as the island's guardian, who would *circle around* (*dineuonta*) Crete *three times* (*tris*) [a day] with his feet *made of bronze* (*chalkeiois*), he who, at the time of the demigods, was the only one left of *the bronze root* (*chalkeiês ... rhizes*) of men born from ash trees. All his body and limbs were made of bronze and were unbreakable (*ar-rêktos*), but under the tendon he had a blood-bearing vein (*surinx*) by the ankle.

While the overlap of phonemic intensities between *Tal* and *chal* is striking in itself, in the narrative report that every day Talos goes around the island three times, the adjective *chalkeios* appears three times:[30] it is as though the textual microcosm from line 1638 to

1644 were the island itself, and in stumbling three times on the same adjective, the reader's eyes were engaged in a repetitious, circular journey equivalent to Talos' daily rounds—and thus were immersed in the giant's own temporal out-of-jointness. A relic of another time, stationed on the island at Zeus' behest, Talos appears unwilling to accede to the law of epochal transition, of temporal movement. The tight sequence *tal- chal-* created by the juxtaposition *Talôs chalkeios* invites us to linger on the initial syllable of *chalkeios* and imagine it as an alternative name, with the result that the metallic ontology of the giant becomes at once his identifying marker and a source of disidentificatory intensity through the mutilation of the full word and the replacement of *tau* with *chi*. Even though he is depicted as breaking rocks, instrumentalizing them as weapons—a position as a subject, underscored by *ar-rêktos* ("unbreakable" 1646)—Talos is, like a fossil, the mobile trace of a deracinated ancestrality breaking the rhythm of an apparently homogeneous present. The broken materiality of the rocks replicates Talos' own separation from the mass of bronze, through which his epoch persists as metallic flesh.

Mimicking the plodding movement of enfleshed metallic joints stripped out of their congenial materiality, the refrain that emerges from the triple repetition—*chal chal chal* (1638, 1641, 1644)—is not unlike *clang clang clang* in "The Trolley Song," just as Talos resembles a fragile, ungrounded tower, always on the verge of collapse.[31] *Chal* in fact, with its initial *chi*, an aspirated voiced velar, is nearly equivalent to *glas*, which, as Bennington and Wills say in their introduction to Derrida's book, indicates "the fact, event and performance of a bell ringing." When it is pronounced, the word, they say, paraphrasing Derrida, "begins as a guttural, quasi-metallic, perhaps even industrial clamor or pure noise."[32] *Chal chal chal* resonates with Talos' robotic exertions, with what we might call the crip or queer creaking in his gait, as he lumbers around the island, translating his metallic disability or hyperability into a triple intensity. The resonant power of *Tal-* in *Talos* breaks off *chal* from *chalcheios*, giving it an autonomous existence that matches Talos' hyperability as one who is at once broken and unbroken (*a-rrhêktos*). The word break generated by the autonomous force of the phonestheme *tal-* in relation to *chal-* reproduces Talos' defensive (and anti-social?) impetus, breaking rocks along the shore, preventing invaders from mooring, from attaching their bodies (and their boats) to the support of the land. Talos' rock-breaking could be seen not just as a function of his guard duty but also as a protest against the labor that has been imposed on him, an insurrection against the idea of bodily wholeness that his disability contests. The refrain *chal chal chal*, the broken-rock form of *chalkeios* emerging hauntologically from the power of *Tal-* in the process of close reading, invites a mimetic quasi-performance of disability, a ghostly inhabitation of crip embodiment. Derrida connects *glas* with *gala*, *galaxy*, and *galactic*, a term that, in his essay—a confrontation of Hegel and Genet graphically produced through juxtaposed columns—indicates a Genetian, queer alternative to Hegelian dialectic.[33] *Galactic* expresses, in fact, an unruly network of connections woven by the juxtaposition itself. As Derrida puts it, "[t]he colossi" (that is, Hegel and Genet) "exchange an infinite number of overlaps, of winks, double each other up at every opportunity, interpenetrate each other, stick and unstick, passing the one into the other."[34]

When the narrative focus switches from Talos to Medea, his adversary, we can see a similar exchange of intensities—"vibratory motion[s]" and "resonation[s]," in Brian Massumi's definition, flows of becoming; such intensities recall Eve Sedgwick's description of the queer as a "continuing moment [and] movement" across that is "recurrent, eddying."[35] I suggest that we read the intervention of Medea in the episode as galactic or, we might say, *chal-actic*, and in the rest of the chapter I will explain what this characterization implies interpretively. Thinking of non-ableist corporeality through the phrase "Talos made of bronze" and the contagious *chal-actic* he disseminates makes us conceive "of vibration as a mode of being, a way of inhabiting the flesh ... that speaks to the possibility fundamental to indeterminacy," that is to say, to "that state of being in-between," as Dionte Harris puts it, which "breathes new ... life into what we mean when we say *Blackness, gender, sexuality*."[36] Re-reading Medea—Apollonius' as well as Euripides'—in light of Talos' disability opens up the possibility of theorizing radical formalism as vibrational feminism.

When Medea prepares her magical arts to defeat Talos, we stumble upon the hyper-vibratory formalism of what Richard Hunter calls "the most striking alliteration in the *Argonautica*": *ptucha porphureoio proschomenê peploio pareiaôn* ("She drew a fold of her purple robe over both cheeks" 1661–2).[37] This alliteration—an agglutination of labial intensities—is usually taken as the mimetic rendition of a spell.[38] At the same time, this phonetic persistence merges bodily parts and prosthetic supplements, rendering Medea's *peplos* ("robe") as a constitutive part of her body, like her cheeks. The brazenness of Talos conveyed by *chal chal chal* is matched by the textile materiality of Medea expressed by *ptucha porphureoio peploio*, whose repetitive *p* sounds also connect with the *surinx*, the single vein that nourishes Talos' body—human and non-human, disabled and hyper-abled—while evoking a wind instrument that operates through repetitive puffing.

If we focus on Medea's prayer and perform what D. A. Miller would call a "too close reading,"[39] we notice a disassembling and dissemination of elements from the narrative of Talos. The phrase *chalkeioio Talô* ("brazen/bronze Talos") is twice preceded by *tris* ("three times"), connected by commentators with the protocols of ritual magic, and by *peri ... dineousai*, a circling around in the air of the "Fates of Death", the spirits of the night invoked by Medea (1665–88):

ἔνθα δ' ἀοιδῇσιν μειλίσσετο, μέλπε δὲ Κῆρας (1665)
θυμοβόρους, Ἀίδαο θοὰς κύνας, αἳ περὶ πᾶσαν
ἠέρα δινεύουσαι ἐπὶ ζωοῖσιν ἄγονται.
τὰς γουναζομένη τρὶς μὲν παρακέκλετ' ἀοιδαῖς,
τρὶς δὲ λιταῖς· θεμένη δὲ κακὸν νόον, ἐχθοδοποῖσιν
ὄμμασι χαλκείοιο Τάλω ἐμέγηρεν ὀπωπάς· (1670)
λευγαλέον δ' ἐπὶ οἷ πρῖεν χόλον, ἐκ δ' ἀίδηλα
δείκηλα προΐαλλεν, ἐπιζάφελον κοτέουσα.
Ζεῦ πάτερ, ἦ μέγα δή μοι ἐνὶ φρεσὶ θάμβος ἄηται,
εἰ δὴ μὴ νούσοισι τυπῇσί τε μοῦνον ὄλεθρος
ἀντιάει, καὶ δή τις ἀπόπροθεν ἄμμε χαλέπτει, (1675)

ὡς ὅ γε, χάλκειός περ ἐών, ὑπόειξε δαμῆναι
Μηδείης βρίμῃ πολυφαρμάκου· ἂν δὲ βαρείας
ὀχλίζων λάιγγας ἐρυκέμεν ὅρμον ἱκέσθαι,
πετραίῳ στόνυχι χρίμψε σφυρόν· ἐκ δέ οἱ ἰχώρ
τηκομένῳ ἴκελος μολίβῳ ῥέεν. οὐδ᾽ ἔτι δηρόν   (1680)
εἱστήκει προβλῆτος ἐπεμβεβαὼς σκοπέλοιο·
ἀλλ᾽ ὥς τίς τ᾽ ἐν ὄρεσσι πελωρίη ὑψόθι πεύκη,
τήν τε θοοῖς πελέκεσσιν ἔθ᾽ ἡμιπλῆγα λιπόντες
ὑλοτόμοι δρυμοῖο κατήλυθον, ἡ δ᾽ ὑπὸ νυκτί
ῥιπῆσιν μὲν πρῶτα τινάσσεται, ὕστερον αὖτε   (1685)
πρυμνόθεν ἐξεαγεῖσα κατήριπεν· ὥς ὅ γε ποσσίν
ἀκαμάτοις τείως μὲν ἐπισταδὸν ἠωρεῖτο,
ὕστερον αὖτ᾽ ἀμενηνὸς ἀπείρονι κάππεσε δούπῳ.

There she sang soothing songs, and she celebrated the soul-devouring Fates, the swift she-dogs of Hades, who, *circling around* (*peri . . . dineuousai*) the entire sky, are set upon mortals. Supplicating them, she summoned them *three times* (*tris*) with songs, *three times* (*tris*) with prayers; with bad intentions, she cast a spell on the *eyes* (*ommasi*) of Talos *made of bronze* (*chalkeioio*) with her *gaze* (*opôpas*) full of hatred; she gnashed baneful anger against him, and, vehemently enraged, she *sent* (*proiallen*) *destructive phantasms* (*aidêla deikêla*) against him. Father Zeus, great astonishment is rising in my mind, if death does not come upon us only with diseases and blows, and someone *hurts* (*chaleptei*) us from afar, just as he, even though *made of bronze* (*chalkeios*), gave in to the strength of Medea *of many drugs* (*polu-pharmakou*), subdued. While *lifting* (*ochlizôn*) heavy rocks to prevent them from arriving at the anchorage, he knocked his ankle against the edge of the rock; from him *serum* (*ichôr*) similar to melted lead poured forth. And standing upon a jutting *cliff* (*sko-**peloio***), he did not stay for long; but as an *enormous* (***pelô**riê*) *pine tree* (***peuk**ê*) on the top of the mountains, which lumberjacks with their swift *axes* (***pele**kessi*) left still *half-chopped* (*hêmi-**plêga***) when they descended out of the forest, is first shaken by breezes at night and then falls down, cut off from the base, thus he, with his indefatigable feet, swayed while standing and then, in turn, collapsed, powerless, with boundless noise.

One has the impression that the repetitive energy of Talos' daily triple circuit around Crete (*peri . . . dineuonta*) has seeped into textual form, as though the motion of the giant persists even as Medea tries to stop it through a diffusion of metallic intensities. In the line that follows the phrase *chalkeoio Talô* (1670), the adjective *leugaleon* ("baneful") modifies *cholon* ("bile, anger"), the anger that Medea directs against Talos: together, *leu**gal**eon* and ***chol**on* contain *chal*, the noisy intensity of Talos' bronze dis- or hyper-ability, while the assonant phrase *aidêla / deikêla proiallen*, with its triple sequence of *êla, êla, alle(n)*, seems to further prolong it.

The viscous materiality that is attached to *cholos* ("bile, anger") seems also to carry forward traces of Talos' ostensible metallic solidity, his disabled solidity, while the circulation of bronze intensities continues in the transition between lines 1675 and 1676, where the verb **chal**-*eptei* ("he hurts") is followed by **chal**keios ("made of bronze"), producing another impression of a *chal-axy*. When, just before her spell, Medea says that Talos may be mortal, even if his body is "wholly of bronze" (*pan-chalkeon*), we can take this adjective as an announcement of this *chal-axy*, this pervasive metallic atmosphere. Medea, who is described as *polu-pharmakos*, seems to enact the deconstructive ambiguity of the *pharmakon*—healing and hurting, antidote and poison, making Talos persist in the very language meant to destroy him.[40] Formal intensity is a *pharmakon* because it is a force for appearance in disappearance; it carries hauntological insistence. Defeated by Medea's incantation, Talos falls and dies when his ankle strikes a sharp rock while once again futilely "lifting" (*ochlizôn*) boulders against his enemies—an action in which the verbal rendition of "lifting" contains the intensity of his impending collision. When Derrida discusses the intensive power of *glas/clang*, he envisions the articulation of the phonestheme *gl/cl* as a vocal contortion, something similar to gagging or choking. Even though he moves, bringing forth his apparent kinetic agency, Talos is immobilized by his master, by Zeus' Law, or the Law that Zeus is, that is, by the task, ordered by Zeus, of lifting rocks, designated by a word whose intensive substance impedes the giant, as intimated by *chl* in the phonetic constitution of *ochlizô*. This relation between Talos and Zeus, which establishes yet unsettles the borders of ability, disability, and hyper-ability, also reflects back on the poetic voice's own subjection to *Zeu pater* (1673). The invocation facilitates the narrative ego's insinuation into the textual space as the indirect pronoun *moi*, rendered motionless by stupor (*thambos*),[41] becoming Talos, emotionally partaking of his metallic *zôê* while speaking of, that is, objectifying Talos.

Something similar to saliva or mucus, the blood serum, expressed by the enigmatic word *ichôr*, that is concentrated in Talos' only vein, is at once Talos' vital fluid and the marker of his disabled embodiment, of the ontological impairment aggravated by his death-driven labor. The moment of Talos' fatal fall coincides with the outpouring, the liberation of this vital fluid, all compressed in the narrow space of a single blood vessel. It is not just that death is a liberation for the oppressed giant; there is also the sense of an impersonal, depersonalized energy freed, brought into the open, as indicated by the syntactical isolation—a sign of resistance—in which the sudden outflow, a literal ex-cess, of *ichôr* is placed. The etymology of *ichôr* is contested, but a compelling connection has been made between it and *ichar* (ἴχαρ), a term, translated by the scholiast and in modern dictionaries as "burning desire" (*epithumia*), which occurs in Aeschylus' *Suppliant Women* (850), where it expresses the persistence of rage and grief of the female refugees, who are commanded by their Egyptian cousins (or the Egyptian herald) to abandon the altars they are clinging to, to interrupt their protest, to stop shouting (*keleuô boas methesthai* 849), to bring their cacophonic resistance—their "madness" (*phreni g'asan*) —to an end.[42] The *ichôr* spurting at the moment of Talos' death is, thus, a biological force of interruption, an unbound impersonal volition, the dissensual conation of disability, and a materialized intensity dispersed like the Danaids' desperate shouting or the phonestheme *chal*-, which turns poetic texture into an insurrectionary *chal*-axy.[43]

The volitional intensity that links Talos to Medea, while maintaining its impersonal force, also manifests itself at the moment that the giant falls, a collapse whose radically formalistic potential has consequences for the reading not only of Apollonius, but also of the prologue of Euripides' *Medea*. When Talos dies, an epic simile assimilates him to a tree half cut with axes by lumberjacks, shaken by the winds at night, and crashing to the ground. As Hunter observes, "[t]he passage evokes Homeric similes comparing the fall of warriors to the collapse of trees ... thus continuing the presentation of Medea's triumph as a single-combat."[44] But if we apply, once again, a too-close reading, one that, as Miller puts it, heeds "fracture points in [an] image's presumed obviousness," we can arrive at a different reading, an experiment in overanalysis that illustrates the ethical and political stakes of radical formalism. The feminine vehicle of Talos in the simile, the "gigantic, monstrous pine tree," accompanied by the feminine pronoun *tên*, creates an effect of excess, of spilling out, emphasized by the alliterative persistence (triple once again) of ***pelôriê*** ... ***peukê*** ... ***pelekessi*** ("monstrous ... pine tree ... with axes"), which brings Medea herself into the picture. In the prologue of Euripides' *Medea*, the pine tree cut off by axes to build the Argo (*peukê*) is a patent figuration of Medea herself, cut off from her family, and about to cut herself off from her children, whom she will kill, in a re-enactment of her cutting her brother to pieces (1–6):[45]

Εἴ θ' ὤφελ' Ἀργοῦς μὴ διαπτάσθαι σκάφος
Κόλχων ἐς αἶαν κυανέας Συμπληγάδας,
μηδ' ἐν νάπαισι Πηλίου πεσεῖν ποτε
τμηθεῖσα πεύκη μηδ' ἐρετμῶσαι χέρας
ἀνδρῶν ἀρίστων οἳ τὸ πάγχρυσον δέρος
Πελίαι μετῆλθον ...

If only the hull of the Argo had not flown through the dark blue *Clashing Rocks* (*Sum-**plê**gadas*) to the land of the Colchians and *the pine tree* (***peukê***), cut off in *the glades of mount Pelion* (*na**paisi Pêl**iou*) *had never fallen down* (***pesein pote***) and those among the best heroes who were after the Golden Fleece *for the benefit of Pelias* (***Peliai***) had not equipped their hands with oars.

Pelôriê ... ***peukê*** ... ***pelekessi*** ("monstrous ... pine tree ... with axes") in Apollonius—a striking echo of ***Pêliou** pesein ...* ***peukê***—urges us to reconsider the Euripidean prologue from a radically formalistic perspective. Although commentators are silent on the matter, the confusing quasi-homonymy between mount Pelion (*Peliou*) in Thessaly—the site of the environmental mutilation supplying wood for the first ship—and king Pelias (*Peliai*), the Argonauts' master, generates an alliterative labial contagion, which exceeds the triangularity ***peukê Pêliou pesein*** and encompasses *Sum-**plê**gades* and *na**paisi***.

What is the significance of the refrain *plê-, pêl-, pel-*? The proximity with *peukê* cryptically conjures—through the effect of a spectral conflation and anagrammatic recombination—the word *peleku(s)* ("ax"), the weapon that lethally strikes the Thessalian wood. In Ennius' rendition of the Euripidean prologue, axes appear as the instruments that fell the wood of Mount Pelion with the cutting edge of an enjambment (*securibus /*

caesa).[46] Furthermore, reading for labials, as the refrain invites us to do, leads us to analyze *napaisi* as *na-paisi*, to see, that is, Medea's children hidden or contained in the forest—as though the prologue subliminally overlaid the children's onto the trees. This is an exercise of "over-reading" or radical "overanalysis," which one may be reluctant to perform out of fear of falling into the "fanciful," of being accused of self-indulgent hermeneutic excess.[47] Yet the alternative is to constrain interpretation within the bounds of the normative by noticing the alliteration as simply a striking expressive emphasis, presenting it as a decorative actuality more than a formal virtuality, an ornamental, self-evident, insignificant fact rather than an affective, not immediately signifying relation generative of an effect of reading experienced as a productive position of hermeneutic passivity, as it were, at once critical and post-critical.[48]

Uttered by the tragic Nurse, the refrain *plê-, pêl-* , *pel-* emanates the labiality of maternal care perverted into the too-intimate attachment of a lethal penetration. The traumatic tic of *plê-, pêl-, pel-* litters the synchronic or synoptic space of the prologue with the deforested debris of Mount Pelion as well as the sensory-expressive remainders of the infanticidal blows to come. The nomadic force of the Euripidean Nurse's labial intensities—a formal care or motherly form against *secur*-itarian violence, the Argonauts' *ax*-ology—looks forward to Ennius' rendition of the prologue in his own *Medea*:[49]

> *utinam ne in nemore **Pelio securibus***
> ***caesa** accidisset abiegna ad terram trabes,*
> *neve inde navis inchoandi exordium*
> *coepisset, quae nunc nominatur nomine*
> *Argo, quia Argivi in ea delecti viri*
> *vecti **pe**tebant **pel**lem inauratam arietis*
> *Colchis imperio regis **Pel**ia **per** dolum:*
> *nam numquam era errans mea domo efferret **ped**em*
> *Medea, animo aegro, amore saevo saucia.*

If only the firwood timber had not fallen to the ground in the Pelian grove, hewn by axes, and if only the ship had not taken from there the first steps to a beginning—the ship that is now known by the name of Argo, since selected Argive men traveling in her sought the Golden Fleece of the ram from the Colchians, at the behest of king Pelias, by trickery. For never would my mistress, Medea, going astray, have set her foot outside the house, sick in her mind, wounded by savage love.[50]

Here the return of the refrain *pe- pe- pe- pe-* underscores the de-subjectivization of the Argonauts, whose colonial quest for the Golden Fleece (*petebant pellem*) seems to be haunted or even taken over by *Pel*ion itself, by the first target of their extractivist violence, a mountain made mobile, capable of circulating, by its traumatic wounding, an inanimate agent that assimilates the aggressor (*petebant*) to the victim (*pellem*), the subject to the object.[51] This agent, "cut by axes," conflates the children with Medea herself, the mutilated subject or object (as indicated by the punning resonance of her name with *tmêtheisa*),[52] rejecting and separating herself from Jason's protective pretense, his *securitarian* excuses, his thinly disguised neglect.[53] *Pe-, pe-, pe-, pe-* is thus the eerie cadence of Medea's foot (*pedem*), a "Lesbian phallus," preemptively driving (and treading upon) the Argonauts' action even before they have met her.[54]

There is an ethical and political dimension to this practice of overanalysis, which "pushes to the extreme the always potentially interminable impulse toward disintegration, dissolution, deconstruction, and decomposition characteristic of any form of analysis":[55] an approximation to *lysis*, an aesthetic practice of deindividuation (or disabling of individuation), to use Fred Moten's terminology.[56] In a reading of Plato, Derrida, and Fanon, Moten sees *lysis*—the deeply antinormative component of *analysis* that *overanalysis* valorizes—as "separation and the breaking down of walls, refutation as well as redemption," an "inhabitable possibility."[57] We can say that *chal chal chal* in Apollonius and *plê pêl pel* and *pel pe pel* in Euripides and Apollonius are examples of the intensive power of language, or the transformation of language into what Deleuze calls style, a minoritarian force that emerges when, in his words, a "spark flash[es] and break[s] out of language itself," when "words produce sparks leaping between them, even over great distance."[58] These sparks seem to circulate, proliferating, if, in the passage of Apollonius, we read *skopeloio*—Talos' cliff, formally located, in the midst of ***pelôriê peukê pel**ekessin*— as *sko-**pel**oio* and see the "cut" in *hêmi-**plê**ga*, modifying the tree struck down by the woodcutters in the simile, as not merely a cut, but as the traumatic resonance of the Argonauts' environmental violence against Mount ***Pê**lion*. The resonance even extends to the Sym***plê**gades*—one of the fatal encounters of the Argonauts in the previous part of the poem, which the synergy or the non-ableist assemblage of Medea and Talos revives.[59] Medea's tragic story, with its distinctive symbols, is transformed into a nomadic energy, both bound by a particular configuration of sound and unbound in its insurrectionary power of circulation and transformation. The *lysis* of overanalysis—an aesthetic, hermeneutic analog of the abolition that Medea symbolizes[60]—radically deindividuates the signifiers into unbound sounds and resonances, dissolving them into a formal virtuality, an "animated *clameur*,"[61] into the "inhabitable possibility" by which the pine tree shades into the ax; Talos into Medea; the victim into the aggressor; the object into a subject.[62]

The discovery of the affinity (or lytic interchangeability) between Medea and Talos, a mutual deterritorialization, brings us back to *chalkeios*, the word with which we began. *Chalkeios*, in fact, vibrates with the same sounds as *Kolchêis*, a woman from Colchis, i.e., Medea. In the resistant *chalaxy* that I have explored, little more than an exchange of aspirated intensities separates Talos and Medea, the bronze giant and the woman from Colchis. In line 1670, the word order that describes Medea's spell-casting gaze against Talos—with *ommasi* and *opôpas* at the edges of the line—figures a reciprocal mirroring, an optic interchange. Beyond their connective capacity, the verbal intensities making up this *chalaxy* seem to be endowed with an autonomous force, a kind of insistent, bronze resilience, which is, in a sense, the very stubbornness of poetic form.[63]

The insistent metallic intensities of Talos, and therefore of Medea, can also be read as feminist intensities through the mediation of Jack Halberstam's *Gaga Feminism*.[64] In this book, ringing is a prominent motif, and so is one of its source objects, the iconic telephone in Lady Gaga's eponymous song and video with Beyoncé from 2010, which, in Halberstam's words, "burbles and beeps, hiccups and repeats, insistently, calling and ringing, ringing and calling and chaining us all to the charisma of the pop beat even as heterosexuality itself seems like an event in a distant past."[65] Ringing here is the intense murmur of a queer and trans, anarchic feminism, which seeps into the musical cadence of Halberstam's language. The fact that, as Halberstam explains, the name Lady Gaga itself arose through a digital glitch, an auto-correction of the phrase "Radio Ga Ga," adds a further metallic ring to the "gaga" through a chain of associations:[66] first, the 1984 song by Queen, with its metallic sound, and then the accompanying video, a pastiche of the Fritz Lang silent film *Metropolis*, in which humans become prostheses of machinery and a robot is transformed into a female cyborg. In *Metropolis*, the futuristic-fascist fantasy— where "modernization ... appears as a process ... where the body's natural rhythms are subordinated to the rhythms and the tempo of the industrial clock"[67]—is haunted by the colonizer's fear that technology is affected and infected by the latent dissensual agency of the "spirits of colonized labor that produced it."[68] Through this chain of associations, the name Lady Gaga becomes a marker both of Halberstam's anarchic feminism and of a metallic formalism. This metallic formalism comes through in Halberstam's declaration of gaga feminism as distinct from Lady Gaga herself: "from the get-go—religion is a no-no and *God* has *got* to *go-go*."[69]

In this percussive insistence and guttural intensity, the insurrectionary formalism of metallic mimeticism, we can locate an emancipatory politics (feminist, queer/trans, cyborgic), as we can in Talos' *chal(k), chal(k), chal(k)* and Medea's *col(kh), col(kh), col(kh),* which also bring to mind what Legacy Russell has called "glitch feminism." Russell's feminist manifesto celebrates the glitch—the digital failure, another metallic intensity —"as a vehicle of refusal." This "glitch," like the metallic *chal-axy* in Apollonius' poetic form, "creates a fissure within which new possibilities of being and becoming manifest" themselves.[70] It is a phonetic excess conjuring a surplus intensity that resists and transcends the pre-packaged boundedness of the status quo.

We can regard the *chal-axy* in Apollonius as an example of what Eugenie Brinkema calls "speculative form," which she presents as an effect of close reading arising from an attempt, as she puts it, "not to describe something that is already in the text—received as a commodity by the audience—but rather to talk about how the form itself is surprising and speculative."[71] This *chal-axy* is a mode of insurrectional poetry, of what Moten calls "socio-poetic insurgency," an "improvisational, anarchically principled (dis)organization" or "a poetics of recombination marked precisely by an ongoing anarchic seizure, excess and intensification."[72] It feeds on the radicality of the useless, on what becomes illegible by being of no use. As a hermeneutic judgment, "uselessness" establishes hierarchies of what counts and what does not for the interpretive exercise, but it may conversely be reclaimed as the resistance of form, a locus of radical anti-normativity, of a quasi-depersonalized force irrupting into, stalling (or disabling), and shaping the hermeneutic encounter.[73] The *chal-axy* I have posited models radical formalism as an aestheticized expression of radical impossibility, which I take to be the affirmative negativity necessary for emancipatory change—a subjunctive negativity underscored, in the last line of Apollonius' episode, by the juxtaposition of the "no-strength" of *a-menênos* and the "no-demarcation" of *a-peironi*, of disabled embodiment and deindividuation (1687).[74] I am not afraid of advocating radical formalism as an *engagé* impressionism, or a counter-hermeneutics of impressionism, an experience of radical closeness that lets form exert a pressure on us. Through this impressionism, we can locate the noise of the (im)possible, unruly configurations of utopia with its inbuilt negative force. The insistence of Argonautic poetic texture, Medea's gaga (or *chal chal*) feminism, Talos' crip motions, the repeated exertions of his bronze body, partake of a utopia that lets go of inevitably normativizing futural thinking, finding an ungrounded ground in the perpetual present of a minoritarian political insistence, of glitchy, insurrectionary intensities beyond and against the subject.

Notes

1. Davis 2020.

2. Massumi (2002, 26) observes that "intensity would seem to be associated with nonlinear processes: resonance and feedback that momentarily suspend the linear progress of the narrative present from past to future." Edelman (2004, 3) conceives of queerness "as resistance to the viability of the social while insisting on the inextricability of such resistance from every social structure."

3. Mallarmé 2001. I discuss the relation between form and de-formation in Telò 2023b (Introduction). In reference to the work of Laura Moriarty, Durgin (2009, 169) underscores the convergence between post-language poetry and disability studies, observing how "certain poets," while not identifying as disabled, "make *poesis* itself the site of forging post-ableist subjectivity."

4. Kuppers 2011, 79. For Kuppers, disability poetics, which she calls "poetry-ing," entails "a widening of the poem"—"blowing up the page, not in an explosion, but in a material density, a cloud pillow, a texturing of languages, densely entwined with our bodies, our geopolitical locations, our temporalities."

5. Kuppers 2006.

6. On the disability and hyperability of Hephaestus and his cyborgic assistants, see Dolmage 2006, Raphael 2015, Brockliss 2019, and Silverblank and Ward 2020, 511–14.

7. Derrida 2021.

8. "Logic of sensation" has a Deleuzian coloration: see Deleuze 2003. On the phrase "biopolitics of sound," see esp. Waltham-Smith 2021.

9. Malabou 2016, 242.

10. Bringing out the queerness in Adriana Cavarero's feminist valorization of "inclination" (2016), J. Butler (2021, 50–1) connects "rectitude" with "rectum": "If the upright posture requires or implies the rectum, then a certain form of inclination is presupposed by a form of rectitude built upon its denial."

11. O'Keeffe 2021, 19 (in a review of the new edition of *Glas*).

12. Thus, Bennington and Wills (2021, xvii [my emphasis]), paraphrasing (Derrida 2021, 158) in their introduction to the new edition of *Glas (Clang)*. They add that "*Gl* or *Cl* is a vocal

contortion, requiring the rapid articulation of two very different phonemes . . . to activate the back of the throat and the tongue as it were on the edge of physiological capacity." The phonesthetic disability of *gl* is exemplified by *aveugle* ("blind").

13. Waltham-Smith 2021, 22. On the protesting intensity of the sound of laughter, see Neyra 2020, 14–16.

14. The link between *glas* and *chal* is suggested by Derrida himself when he says that "the clang is first of all (**clas**, *chiasso, classum, classicum*) the blast from a trumpet used to call (**calare**), convoke, gather together as such a *class* of Roman people" (2021, 100; my bold). On the sound of the trumpet in Greek literature, see Nooter 2019a and 2019b, 284–8.

15. https://www.youtube.com/watch?v=07II_EJlcYg

16. On onomatopoeia, the device that reveals the non-referentiality of language in spite (or because) of mimeticism, see Attridge 1984 and, for a new conceptualization, Nooter in this volume.

17. "Yap, Yap, Yap, Went Ted Cruz / Crap, Crap, Crap Went McCarthy / Bitch, Bitch, Bitch Went the Base / Mitch, Mitch, Mitch Went McConnell As His Neck Tried to Swallow his Face /. . . Push, Push, Push Go Their Puppets / Yuk-Yuk-Yuk Go the Dems / "Fuck, Fuck, Fuck" Goes Liz Cheney /. . . / Creep, Creep, Creep Went the Creeper / Grump, Grump, Grump Went Rand Paul / Trump, Trump, Trump Went Jim Jordan / . . . /Duh, Duh, Duh Went De Santis / Bang, Bang, Bang Went the Feds / . . . as their Party Implodes, Gerrymanders, Corrodes, and Colludes . . .?" The attention to these phenomena may be the domain of what Gurd (2018a, 55) has called '*pataphilogy*, which is focused on "the audible glyph of language" and on "forms of time that . . . seem . . . to tie the line of history into a knot or a Möbius strip."

18. Goldberg 2021, 203.

19. Waltham-Smith 2021, 15.

20. Waltham-Smith 2021, 15–16.

21. On letterality, see Kornbluh 2019.

22. On queerness as out-of-joint temporality, see, e.g., Edelman 2004, Freeman et al. 2007, and Telò and Olsen 2022, 2–3.

23. Thus Cohan (2005, 133), who speaks of Esther Smith, the character played by Garland in *Meet Me in St. Louis*, as "the excess radiating from her girlish 'in-between' persona."

24. Ross 2022. On Garland's androgyny and "boyishness," see Dyer 2004.

25. On *surigmos* as "sigmatic whistling," see Porter 2007, 8. On "sissiphobia," see Ross (2022, 14), referring to Margaret Walker. On sigmatism in Euripides' *Medea*, see Telò 2020b, 98–100.

26. On Garland's "kinesics of suffering," see McLean (2002, 8), who observes that Garland's "arms, perhaps as a result of how much mental effort she was exerting to coax her body into the required gesture-posture parameters, usually seem to move stiffly in and out of positions rather than flowing smoothly from one to the other."

27. Dyer (2004, 159) suggests that "*Meet Me in St. Louis* is a celebration of Garland's peppiness; yet this film also shows the awkwardness of this pep, the need to contain it."

28. On the queerness of the Tin Woodman, see Pugh 2008.

29. Raphael (2015, 183) notes that "Talos is a hybrid entity"; "he is . . . metallic, like Hephaestus' Maidens; he combines exceptional ability (size, strength) with an unusual and fatal weakness; and defeating him requires unusual means." Cassidy (2018, 445) observes that Talos "is a symbol of isolation, vulnerability and innocence, a creature whose demise, although appropriate for the heroic post-mythic world, is treated with a sympathetic undertone."

30. See Hunter 2015, 300: "In the most common version attested after Apollonius, Talos runs three times *per day* around Crete." See also Livrea 1973 ad loc.

31. See O' Keeffe 2021, 19, on the image of the tower in *Glas*: "*Glas* detours around *tours*—erect structures figuring philosophy's proud edifices, phallic emblems of right and privilege, cocksure intimations of Absolute Knowledge, no less." Lovatt (2013, 335) suggests that Talos' height is "a position of power" that is also "a position of vulnerability."

32. Bennington and Wills in Derrida 2021, xvi–xvii.

33. See esp. Hayes 2017 and O'Keeffe 2021.

34. Derrida 2021, vii.

35. Massumi 2002, 26, and Sedgwick 1993, xii.

36. D. Harris 2022, 12–13. See also Goodman 2009, 79: "[The] differential ecology of vibrational effects directs us toward a nonanthropocentric ontology of ubiquitous media, a topology in which every resonant surface is potentially a host for contagious concepts, percepts, and affects."

37. On the subliminal wedding symbolism of this gesture, see Cassidy (2018), who discusses its inevitably ominous allusion to the tragic ending of Medea and Jason's marriage.

38. For readings of the magic language and imagery of the passage, see, e.g., Paduano 1971, N. Powers 2002, and Cassidy 2018.

39. Miller 2021, 15.

40. On the Derridean *pharmakon* in Homeric epic, see esp. Bergren 1981.

41. Hopkinson (1988, 199) notes that "the narrator makes a rare personal appearance." On the etymology of *thambos* and its relation to "immobility," see Vanicek 1877, 1130.

42. On the connection between ἰχώρ and ἴχαρ, see Bolling 1945.

43. Tom Phillips draws my attention to the similarity between the phrase *têkomenôi ikelos molibôi* ("similar to melted lead") and the description of Medea in 3.1018–21 ("inside her mind she was warming up, melted [*têkomenê*], just like dew around the roses melts [*têketai*] warmed by the rays of dawn"), which, as he observes, "puts Talos' and Medea's bodyliness into unsettling adjacency, another reminder of the disturbingly unregulated material intensities that bubble just under the apparent strictures of conation and self-awareness."

44. Hunter 2015, 305. On these lines' epic allusivity or anti-epic polemic—the only interpretive angles in the existing scholarship—see also Lovatt 2013, 336.

45. On Medea's self-cutting, see Telò 2020b, 90–113. S. Butler (2015) suggests a model of intertextuality predicated on sound, not conditioned by semantics.

46. On this detail in Ennius' rendition, see Fantuzzi 1989, 126.

47. On the neoliberal valorization of the "the simple, the obvious, and the commonsensical" against overanalysis as the domain of negativity and paralysis, see McEleney 2021.

48. On this theoretical point, see Telò 2020b, 279–82, and 2023b (Introduction).

49. Lines 208–16 Jocelyn.

50. Goldberg and Manuwald 2018 (Loeb translation).

51. Boyle (2006, 72) says that, compared to Euripides, Ennius "has adopted a . . . more alliterative, heavy, periphrastic style." But perhaps the Greek/Latin binarism commonly used to analyze Ennius' rendition should be reconsidered. A *pe- pi- pe-* refrain also occurs in Phaedrus, *Fables* 4.7.6–7, where the fable writer ventures into a deliberate remake of Ennius: *utinam nec umquam **Pelii** in nemoris iugo / **pinus bipenni** concidisset Thessala* ("If only the Thessalian pine tree on the forest's height had collapsed because of the double-edged ax"). The assimilation between subject and object, victim and target is underscored by the alliterative juxtaposition *pinus bipenni*.

52. On Medea's name and the participle *tmêtheisa* in the Euripidean prologue, see Konstan 2007.

53. I am here playing on the etymology of *securitas* (presupposing *sine cura*, that is, "neglect") and its paretymological resonances with *secus, securis* ("ax"). See Sanyal 2021.

54. On the lesbian phallus, see J. Butler 1993, 55–6; see also Musser 2018 (ch. 3). On the phallic foot in Euripides' *Medea*, see Buchan 2008.

55. McEleney (2021, 20), referring to the discussion of *ana-lysis* and *lysis* in Derrida 1998, 27. See also Telò 2023b (ch. 5).

56. See Moten 2013, 766, and 2018a, 140–246.

57. Moten (2018a, 224) considers the accusation of self-indulgent nihilism that *lysis* may raise; this accusation is that the idea that "lysis morphs into autopsy so that nonbeing's generativity—as it is manifest in noise, chatter, gobbledygook, pidgin's social refusal of imposed and impossible intersubjectivity—is taken for sterility, its flow taken for aridity." Moten responds by citing what he calls Fanon's "animating claim, his animated *clameur*," as exemplified in this passage from *Black Skin, White Masks* (1967, xii): "there is a zone of nonbeing, an extraordinarily sterile and arid region, an incline stripped bare of every essential from which a genuine new departure can emerge."

58. Deleuze 1995, 141.

59. See 2.411–25 and 611–18. See Fantuzzi 1989, 122–3.

60. A symbol of the abolition of family, reproduction, and even, to an extent, gender, Medea is a figure of feminist abolitionism, on which see Davis, Dent, Meiners, and Richie 2022. Staging Euripides' play in prison, Rhodessa Jones views Medea as the quintessential imprisoned woman, the icon of women in jail: see Fraden 2001, 47–53.

61. For this phrase of Moten, see above.

62. Suggesting a connection with [Plato], *Minos* 320c4–8—where Talos is said to have been made by Minos into a political guardian who defended the laws of Crete inscribed on brazen tablets—Tom Phillips observes in correspondence: "*Lysis*/desubjectivization as material dissolution is, in this intertextual coupling, projected into literary history as the dissolution of fixed, signifying, crafted 'chalcheic' materiality by the bronze body of the fully (again) metallic Talos . . . and, more pressingly, by the transubstantiation of that body into glitch-ridden sound, purveying force unpredictably. Bronze tablets have been liquefied and dissipated on the textual surface. This operation reads easily as a counterweight to a hermeneutics of closure that would seal the Talos episode off in a superseded, primordial history, securely displaced by narrative's onward (impersonal) trajectory, namely by ostentatiously reversing/refusing [Plato]'s explanatory maneuver, and presenting us with a different kind of history: Talos not a lawgiver to be learned from, but an affective forcefield to which we (re)awaken."

63. On the stubbornness of form, see esp. Eyers 2017.

64. Halberstam 2012.

65. Halberstam 2012, 64.

66. As the producer Rob Fusari explains, "I typed 'Radio Ga Ga' in a text and it did an autocorrect so somehow 'Radio' got changed to 'Lady.' . . . It was actually a glitch." See Peters 2012, 25.

67. Golding 2019, 317.

68. Golding 2019, 319. See also Cowan 2007, 237 and 241.

69. Halberstam 2012, 64.

70. Russell 2020, 11. See Telò 2023b (ch. 5). Erik Gunderson suggests to me that the *Argonautica* could be characterized as a "glitchy epic." On the glitch as a mechanism of aesthetic transformation, see also Brinkema 2022, 167–70.

71. Brinkema 2019, 69.

72. Moten 2018b, 36 and 51.

73. For a critique of the utilitarian rhetoric of the "useful" and a re-evaluation of the "useless," see Ahmed 2019; for Ahmed, "to queer use can be to linger on the material qualities of that which you are supposed to pass over." See also Harney and Moten 2021 for a critique of what they call "the usufruct of man." See Telò 2023b (Introduction).

74. On poetic subjunctivity as a space of possibility, see Quashie 2021 (ch.3).

CONTRIBUTORS

Lucy M. Alford is Assistant Professor of Literature at Wake Forest University, specializing in modern and contemporary American and comparative poetics. As both a practicing poet and teacher of poetry, Alford is particularly interested in sensory life, experimentation, and the roles of habit, constraint, and play in poetic processes. She is the author of *Forms of Poetic Attention* (2020), which examines the forms of attention both required and produced in poetic language, bringing both philosophical and cognitive inquiry into conversation with the inner workings of specific poems. Alford's poems have appeared in *Harpur Palate, Literary Matters, The Warwick Review, Streetlight, Atelier,* and *FENCE.*

Shane Butler is the Hall Professor in the Humanities at Johns Hopkins University. With primary interests in aesthetics and queer theory, he has published widely on classical literature and its reception, Renaissance humanism, the history of sensation, the phenomenology of reading, and the history of sexuality. His most recent monographs are *The Ancient Phonograph* (2015) and *The Passions of John Addington Symonds* (2022). Recent edited volumes include *Deep Classics: Rethinking Classical Reception* (2016) and, with Sarah Nooter, *Sound and the Ancient Senses* (2018).

Ren Ellis Neyra is Associate Professor of English at Wesleyan University, an affiliated faculty member with African American Studies, and, currently, the Coordinator of the Social, Cultural, and Critical Theory Certificate hosted by Wesleyan's Center for the Humanities. Ellis Neyra writes and teaches in the fields of Caribbean and Latinx studies of aesthetics (focusing especially on poetry, music, and cinema), as well as literary and critical theory. Ellis Neyra is the author of *The Cry of the Senses: Listening to Latinx and Caribbean Poetics* (2020) and is currently writing two book manuscripts: "Re-reading: the Violence of Relation" and "Caribbean Non-sovereignty." Articles related to these manuscripts have recently appeared or are forthcoming in *Small Axe Journal, sx salon, Modern Philology,* and *differences.*

Tom Geue teaches Latin at the Australian National University. He has written about Roman satire, anonymous Roman literature, and the repressions of slavery in Virgil's *Georgics.* His 2019 book, *Author Unknown,* proposed some new ways of working with anonymous authorship; the next instalment will hopefully treat the ultimate anonymous author, the enslaved amanuensis co-authoring alongside Virgils and Horaces. In the meantime, he is writing something between intellectual history and classical scholarship, called *Major Corrections: the Materialist Philology of Sebastiano Timpanaro* (forthcoming). It seeks to show technical philology and militant Marxism working together towards a future of full human flourishing.

Sean Alexander Gurd is Professor of Classics at the University of Texas at Austin. He has active research interests primarily in the areas of ancient theater (especially tragedy), ancient music, and any part of intellectual culture that interfaced with the concept of art (or technē). He has a secondary but related interest in twentieth-century avant-gardes, particularly in the Americas. He is the director of the *Ancient Music and Performance Lab,* which is dedicated to exploring innovative ways of integrating arts practice with humanities scholarship. He has written four monographs: *Iphigenias at Aulis: Textual Multiplicity, Radical Philology* (2006), *Work in Progress: Literary Revision as Social Performance in Ancient Rome* (2012), *Dissonance: Auditory Aesthetics in Ancient Greece* (2016), and *The Origins of Music Theory in the Age of Plato* (2019). He has edited *Philology and Its Histories* (2010), and co-edited *'Pataphilology: An Irreader* (2018). With Pauline LeVen he edited the Bloomsbury *Cultural History of Western Music in Antiquity* (forthcoming). He is an editor of <u>Tangent</u>, an imprint of punctum books dedicated to publishing innovative books and projects that touch on classical antiquity.

Allannah Karas is Assistant Professor of Classics at the University of Miami. She has published on classical reception in the work of Black visual artist Bob Thompson and on the dynamics of *peithô* ("agreeable compulsion") and rhetoric in Aeschylus' *Oresteia.* Her first book project examines the latent violence of *peithô* as presented and problematized by ancient Greek poets, dramatists, and orators.

Sarah Nooter is Professor of Classics and Theater and Performance Studies at the University of Chicago. She is the author of *When Heroes Sing: Sophocles and the Shifting Soundscape of Tragedy* (2012), *The Mortal Voice in the Tragedies of Aeschylus* (2017), and *Greek Poetry in the Age of Ephemerality* (2023). She is co-editor with Shane Butler of *Sound and the Ancient Senses* (2018) and editor of the journal *Classical Philology.* She also has a volume of translation coming out called *How to Be Queer: An Ancient Guide to Sexuality.*

Sarah Olsen is Associate Professor of Classics at Williams College. She is the author of *Solo Dance in Archaic and Classical Greek Literature: Representing the Unruly Body* (2021). She is also the co-editor, with Mario Telò, of *Queer Euripides* (2022) and co-editor, with Zoa Alonso Fernández, of *Imprints of Dance in Ancient Greece and Rome* (forthcoming). Her current research focuses on female intimacy in Euripidean tragedy.

Tom Phillips is Senior Lecturer in Classical Literature at the University of Manchester. His publications include *Pindar's Library: Performance Poetry and Material Texts* (2016), *Untimely Epic: Apollonius Rhodius'* Argonautica (2020), and articles on Greek and Latin lyric poetry.

Alex Purves is Professor of Classics at University of California, Los Angeles. She is the author of *Space and Time in Ancient Greek Narrative* (2010) and *Homer and the Poetics of Gesture* (2019), as well as editor of *Synaesthesia and the Ancient Senses,* with Shane Butler (2013), and *Touch and the Ancient Senses* (2018).

Patrice Rankine is Professor of Classics at the University of Chicago. He is author of *Ulysses in Black: Ralph Ellison, Classicism, and African American Literature* (2006), *Aristotle and Black Drama: A Theater of Civil Disobedience* (2013), and a coeditor of *The Oxford Handbook of Greek Drama in the Americas* (2015). He has also written a post-pandemic reflection on Black life, literature, and drama in relation to classical themes, titled *Theater and Crisis: Myth, Memory, and Racial Reckoning in America, 1964–2020* (forthcoming). His works in progress include a book-length study of the Icarus myth across Black American art, literature, and drama.

Victoria Rimell is Professor of Latin at the University of Warwick. Her research, which spans many different authors and genres, engages critically with major themes in Roman literature and culture and aims to promote dialogue between classical philology and modern philosophical and political thought. Her latest books are *The Closure of Space in Roman Poetics* (2015), *Ovidio,* Remedia Amoris: *Introduzione, Testo, Commento* (2022) and (ed. with Elena Giusti) *Virgil and the Feminine* (*Vergilius* special issue, 2022).

Efrossini Spentzou is Reader in Latin Literature and Classical Reception at Royal Holloway University of London. She is the author of *Readers and Writers in Ovid's Heroides: Transgressions of Gender and Genre* (2003), *The Roman Poetry of Love: Elegy and Politics in a Time of Revolution* (2013), and (with Richard Alston) *Reflections of Romanity: Discourses of Subjectivity in Imperial Rome* (2011). She has co-edited (with Don Fowler) *Cultivating the Muse: Struggles for Power and Inspiration in Classical Literature* (2002) and (with William Fitzgerald) *The Production of Space in Latin Literature* (2018). She is the lead of Myth and Voice Initiative, a storytelling community and citizenship project.

Mario Telò is Professor of Rhetoric, Comparative Literature, and Ancient Greek and Roman Studies at the University of California, Berkeley. He is the author of *Aristophanes and the Cloak of Comedy* (2016), *Archive Feelings: A Theory of Greek Tragedy* (2020), *Greek Tragedy in a Global Crisis: Reading through Pandemic Times* (2023), *Resistant Form: Aristophanes and the Comedy of Crisis* (2023), and *Reading Greek Tragedy with Judith Butler* (forthcoming) as well as co-editor of *Greek Comedy and the Discourse of Genres* (2013), *The Materialities of Greek Tragedy* (2018), *Queer Euripides* (2022), *Niobes: Antiquity Modernity Critical Theory* (2024), and *The Before and the After: Critical Asynchrony Now* (2024).

Victoria Wohl is Professor of Classics at the University of Toronto. She studies the literature and culture of classical Greece. Her publications include *Intimate Commerce* (1998), *Love Among the Ruins: The Erotics of Democracy in Classical Athens* (2002), *Law's Cosmos: Juridical Discourse in Athenian Forensic Oratory* (2010), *Euripides and the Politics of Form* (2015), and (as editor) *Probabilities, Hypotheticals, and Counterfactuals in Ancient Greek Thought* (2014). She is currently working on the poetics of the Presocratic philosophers.

BIBLIOGRAPHY

Adorno, T. W. 1991. "Punctuation Marks." In *Notes to Literature*, Volume 1, 91–7. New York.

Ahmed, S. 2019. *What's the Use? On the Uses of Use*. Durham, NC.

Albrecht-Crane, C. 2011. "Style, Stutter." In *Gilles Deleuze: Key Concepts*, edited by C. J. Stivale, 142–52. New York.

Alexander, M. 2020. *The New Jim Crow: Mass Incarceration in the Age of Colorblindness*. New York.

Alexiou, M. 2002. *The Ritual Lament in Greek Tradition*. Lanham, MD.

Alford, L. 2020. *Forms of Poetic Attention*. New York.

Alston, R., and E. Spentzou. 2011. *Reflections of Romanity: Discourses of Subjectivity in Imperial Rome*. Columbus, OH.

Amos, E. 1995. *Interview of Emma Amos by bell hooks, November 13, 1994*. New York.

Amos, E. 1999. "Measuring Content." In *Looking Forward, Looking Black*, edited by J. Isaak, 38–9. Geneva, NY.

Andrews, B. 1996. *Paradise and Method: Poetry and Praxis*. Evanston, IL.

Andújar, R. 2015. "Revolutionizing Greek Tragedy in Cuba: Virgilio Piñera's *Electra Garrigó*." In *The Oxford Handbook of Greek Drama in the Americas*, edited by K. Bosher, F. Macintosh, J. McConnell, and P. Rankine, 361–79. Oxford.

Anker, E., and R. Felski. 2017. "Introduction." In *Critique and Postcritique*, edited by E. Anker and R. Felski, 1–28. Durham, NC

Appiah, K. A. 2018. *The Lies That Bind: Rethinking Identity*. New York.

Attridge, D. 1984. "Language as Imitation: Jakobson, Joyce, and the Art of Onomatopoeia." *MLN* 99.5: 1116–40.

Attridge, D. 2017. *The Singularity of Literature*. London.

Auerbach, E. 1984. "Figura." In *Scenes from the Drama of European Literature*, 11–76. Minneapolis.

Augoustakis, A. 2010. *Motherhood and the Other: Fashioning Female Power in Flavian Epic*. Oxford.

Axelson, B. 1945. *Unpoetische Wörter: Ein Beitrag zur Kenntnis der lateinischen Dichtersprache*. Lund.

Badiou, A. 2013. *Philosophy and the Event*. Cambridge.

Barker, A. 2007. *The Science of Harmonics in Classical Greece*. Cambridge.

Barnard, J. L. 2021. *Empire of Ruin: Black Classicism and American Imperial Culture*. Oxford.

Barone, J. 2016. "Revisiting Michael Richards' Art in the Age of Black Lives Matter." *The New York Times*, August 11, 2016. https://www.nytimes.com/2016/08/12/arts/design/revisiting-michael-richards-art-in-the-age-of-black-live-matters-lower-manhattan-cultural-council-governors-island.html

Barthes, R. 1978. *A Lover's Discourse: Fragments*. New York.

Barthes, R. 1993. *Camera Lucida: Reflections on Photography*. London.

Barthes, R. 2005. *The Neutral*. New York.

Barzilai, S., and M. W. Bloomfield. 1986. "New Criticism and Deconstructive Criticism, Or What's New?" *NLH* 18.1: 151–69.

Bassi, K., and J. P. Euben. 2010. "Introduction." In *When Worlds Elide: Classics, Politics, Culture*, edited by K. Bassi and J. P. Euben, ix-xxi. Lanham, MD.

Basso, E. B. 1985. *A Musical View of the Universe: Kalapalo Myth and Ritual Performances*. Philadelphia.

Baudrillard, J. 1996. *The System of Objects*. New York.

Beasley, J. D. 1927. "Icarus." *JHS* 47.2: 222–33.

Beck, D., ed. 2021. *Repetition, Communication, and Meaning in the Ancient World*. Leiden.

Benjamin, A. 2021. "The Politics of Informed Form: Plato and Walter Benjamin." In *The Politics of Form in Greek Literature*, edited by P. Vasunia, 103–24. London.

Benjamin, W. 1999. *The Arcades Project*. Cambridge, MA.

Bennett, C.-L. 2021. *Checkout 19*. London.

Bergren, A. 1981. "Helen's Good Drug: *Odyssey* 4.1–305." In *Contemporary Literary Hermeneutics and Interpretation of Classical Texts*, edited by S. Kresic, 201–14. Ottawa.

Berlant, L., and L. Edelman. 2019. "What Survives." In *Reading Sedgwick*, edited by L. Berlant, 37–62. Durham, NC.

Berman, A. 1988. *From the New Criticism to Deconstruction: The Reception of Structuralism and Post-Structuralism*. Urbana, IL.

Best, S. 2018. *None Like Us: Blackness, Belonging, Aesthetic Life*. Durham, NC.

Best, S., and S. Marcus. 2009. "Surface Reading: An Introduction." *Representations* 108.1: 1–21.

Betegh, G. 2013. "On the Physical Aspect of Heraclitus' Psychology." In *Doctrine and Doxography: Studies on Heraclitus and Pythagoras*, edited by D. Sider, and D. Obbink, 225–61. Berlin.

Biles, Z. P. 2011. *Aristophanes and the Poetics of Competition*. Cambridge.

Blanchot, M. 1982. *The Space of Literature*. Lincoln, NE.

Blanchot, M. 1997. *Friendship*. Stanford, CA.

Blier, S. P. 2017. *Art and Risk in Ancient Yoruba: Ife History, Power, and Identity, c. 1300*. Cambridge.

Blumenberg, H. 1988. *Work on Myth*. Boston.

Bollack, J., and H. Wismann. 1972. *Héraclite ou la séparation*. Paris.

Bolling, G. M. 1945. "The Etymology of ΙΧΩΡ." *Language* 21.2: 49–54.

Bottici, C. 2007. *A Political Philosophy of Myth*. Cambridge.

Bottici, C. 2014. *Imaginal Politics: Images Beyond Imagination and the Imaginary*. New York.

Bowie, A. M. 1993. *Aristophanes: Myth, Ritual and Comedy*. Cambridge.

Boyle, A. J. 2006. *Roman Tragedy*. New York.

Brinkema, E. 2014. *The Forms of the Affects*. Durham, NC.

Brinkema, E. 2016. "Violence and the Diagram: Or, *The Human Centipede*." *Qui Parle* 24.2: 75–108.

Brinkema, E. 2019. "We Never Took Deconstruction Seriously Enough (On Affects, Formalism, and Film Theory)." (An Interview with E. Brinkema by J. Anger and T. Jirsa) *Iluminace* 31.1: 65–85.

Brinkema, E. 2022. *Life-Destroying Diagrams*. Durham, NC.

Brockliss, W. 2019. "Out of the Mix: (Dis)ability, Intimacy, and the Homeric Poems." *CW* 113.1: 1–27.

Brogan, J. V. 2005. "'Inessential Houses' in Stevens and Bishop." *The Wallace Stevens Journal* 29.1: 25–33.

Brooks, C. 1947. *The Well Wrought Urn: Studies in the Structure of Poetry*. Orlando, FL.

Brooks, G. 1968. *In the Mecca*. New York.

Brooks, G. 1972. *Report from Part One*. Detroit, MI.

Buber, M. 1970. *I and Thou*. Edinburgh.

Buchan, M. 2008. "'Too Difficult for a Single Man to Understand': Medea's Out-Jutting Foot." *Helios* 35.1: 3–28.

Budelmann, F. 2013. "Alcman's Nightscapes (Frs. 89 and 90 *PMGF*)." *HSCP* 107: 35–53.

Budelmann, F., and T. Phillips, eds. 2018a. *Textual Events: Performance and the Lyric in Early Greece*. Oxford.

Bibliography

Budelmann, F., and T. Phillips. 2018b. "Introduction." In *Textual Events: Performance and the Lyric in Early Greece*, edited by F. Budelmann and T. Phillips, 1–28. Oxford.

Bullitt, J., and W. Jackson Bate. 1945. "Distinctions between Fancy and Imagination in Eighteenth-Century English Criticism." *Modern Language Notes* 60.1: 8–15.

Bundy, E. L. 1986. *Studia Pindarica I-II*. Berkeley, CA.

Burge, S. R. 2013. "Music, Mysticism, and Experience: Sufism and Spiritual Journeys in Nathaniel Mackey's Bedouin Hornbook." *Contemporary Literature* 54: 271–302.

Burnett, A. 2005. *Pindar's Songs for Young Athletes of Aegina*. Oxford.

Burt, S. 2007. *The Forms of Youth: Twentieth-Century Poetry and Adolescence*. New York.

Burt, S. 2016. "What is this Thing Called Lyric?" *Modern Philology* 113.3: 422–40.

Bury, J. B. 1898. *The* Nemean *Odes of Pindar*. London.

Butler, J. 1993. *Bodies That Matter: On the Discursive Limits of Sex*. New York.

Butler, J. 2021. "Leaning Out, Caught in the Fall: Interdependency and Ethics in Cavarero." In *Toward a Feminist Ethics of Nonviolence: Adriana Cavarero with Judith Butler, Bonnie Honig, and Other Voices*, edited by T. J. Huzar and C. Woodford, 46–62. New York.

Butler, S. 2015. *The Ancient Phonograph*. New York.

Butler, S. 2018. "Principles of Sound Reading." In *Sound and the Ancient Senses*, edited by S. Butler and S. Nooter, 233–55. London.

Butler, S. 2022. *The Passions of John Addington Symonds*. Oxford.

Campbell, D. A. 1982. *Greek Lyric*, Volume 1. Cambridge, MA.

Cassidy, S. 2018. "Wedding Imagery in the Talos Episode: Apollonius Rhodius, *Argonautica* 4. 1653–88." *CQ* 68.2: 442–57.

Cavarero, A. 2016. *Inclinations: A Critique of Rectitude*. Stanford, CA.

Chantraine, P. 1968. *Dictionnaire étymologique de la langue grecque: histoire des mots*. Paris.

Chase, C. 1986. *Decomposing Figures: Rhetorical Readings in the Romantic Tradition*. Baltimore, MD.

Chernaik, J. 1972. *The Lyrics of Shelley*. Cleveland.

Chernoff, J. M. 1979. *African Rhythm and African Sensibility: Aesthetics and Social Action in African Musical Idioms*. Chicago.

Childs, A. 2021. "Variations and Old Master Narratives: Bob Thompson in the Wake of Art History." In *Bob Thompson: This House Is Mine*, edited by D. Tuite, 58–68. New Haven.

Clarke, C. 1995. "The Loss of Lyric Space and the Critique of Traditions in Gwendolyn Brooks's 'In the Mecca.'" *The Kenyon Review* 17: 136–47.

Clay, D. 1970. "Fragmentum Adespotum 976." *TAPA* 101: 119–29.

Cohan, S. 2005. *Incongruous Entertainment: Camp, Cultural Value, and the MGM Musical*. Durham, NC.

Coker, G. 1978. *The World of Bob Thompson*. New York.

Comay, R. 2021. "Lumpendialectic—or, Tragedy and Revolution (Again)." Unpublished keynote lecture delivered at the "Tragedy and Philosophy" conference, University of London, Goldsmiths, June 10.

Comay, R., and F. Ruda. 2018. *The Dash—the Other Side of Absolute Knowing*. Cambridge, MA.

Conte, G. B. 1992. "Proems in the Middle." In *Beginnings in Classical Literature*, edited by F. M. Dunn and T. Cole, 147–59. Cambridge.

Cook, W. W., and J. Tatum. 2012. *African American Writers and Classical Tradition*. Chicago.

Cooper, C. 2022. "Fallen: Generation, Postlapsarian Verticality + the Black Chthonic." *Rhizomes: Cultural Studies in Emerging Knowledge* 38. http://rhizomes.net/issue38/pdf/cooper.pdf.

Couloubaritsis, L. 1989. "La notion d'*aion* chez Héraclite." In *Ionian Philosophy*, edited by K. J. Boudouris, 104–13. Athens.

Covert, B. 2022. "After the Eviction Moratorium," *The New Republic*, July 5. https://newrepublic. com/article/166774/eviction-moratorium-new-york-housing-court

Cowan, M. 2007. "The Heart Machine: 'Rhythm' and Body in Weimar Film and Fritz Lang's *Metropolis*." *Modernism/modernity* 14.2: 225–48.

Creese, D. E. 2010. *The Monochord in Ancient Greek Harmonic Science*. Cambridge.

Culler, J. 2015. *Theory of the Lyric*. Cambridge, MA.

Dale, A. M. 1969. "The Hoopoe's Song." In *Collected Papers*, edited by E. G. Turner and T. B. L. Webster, 135–6. Cambridge.

Davis, A. Y. 2020. "Race at a Boiling Time: The Fire This Time." https://www.youtube.com/watch?v=3I22E2Sezi8.

Davis, A. Y., G. Dent, E. R. Meiners, and B. E. Richie. 2022. *Abolition. Feminism. Now.* Chicago.

Deichgräber, K. 1963. *Rhythmische Elemente im Logos des Heraklit*. Mainz.

Deleuze, G. 1989. *Cinema 2: Time Image*. Minneapolis.

Deleuze, G. 1990. *The Logic of Sense*. New York.

Deleuze, G. 1994. *Difference and Repetition*. New York.

Deleuze, G. 1995. *Negotiations (1972–1990)*. New York.

Deleuze, G. 1997. "He Stuttered." In *Essays Critical and Clinical*, 107–14. London.

Deleuze, G. 2003. *Francis Bacon: The Logic of Sensation*. Minneapolis.

Deleuze, G. 2006. *Nietzsche and Philosophy*. New York.

Deleuze, G., and F. Guattari. 1987. *A Thousand Plateaus: Capitalism and Schizophrenia*. Minneapolis.

De Man, P. 1978. "The Epistemology of Metaphor." *Critical Inquiry* 5.1: 13–30.

De Man, P. 1979. *Allegories of Reading: Figural Language in Rousseau, Nietzsche, Rilke, and Proust*. New Haven, CT.

De Man, P. 1983. "Hegel on the Sublime." The Messenger Lectures. https://archive.org/details/bb-paul-de-man-the-messenger-lectures-1983/Paul+de+Man_Hegel_on_the_Sublime.mp3

De Man, P. 1986. *The Resistance to Theory*. Minneapolis.

De Man, P. 1996. *Aesthetic Ideology*. Minneapolis.

Derbew, S. 2019. "(Re)membering Sara Baartman, Venus, and Aphrodite." *Classical Receptions Journal* 11: 336–54.

Derrida, J. 1976. *Of Grammatology*. Baltimore.

Derrida, J. 1978. *Writing and Difference*. Chicago.

Derrida, J. 1996. *Archive Fever: A Freudian Impression*. Chicago.

Derrida, J. 1998. *Resistances of Psychoanalysis*. Stanford, CA.

Derrida, J. 2001. *The Work of Mourning*. Chicago.

Derrida, J. 2005. *Rogues: Two Essays on Reason*. Stanford, CA.

Derrida, J. 2011. *Parages*. Stanford, CA.

Derrida, J. 2020. *Geschlecht III: Sex, Race, Nation, Humanity*. Chicago.

Derrida, J. 2021. *Clang*. Minneapolis.

Derrida, J., and A. Dufourmantelle. 2000. *Of Hospitality: Anne Dufourmantelle Invites Jacques Derrida to Respond*. Stanford, CA.

Dickie, M. 1990. "Talos Bewitched: Magic, Atomic Theory, and Paradoxography in Apollonius *Argonautica* 4.1638–88." *Papers of the Leeds Latin Seminar* 6: 267–96.

Diels, H., and W. Kranz, eds. 1951. *Die Fragmente der Vorsokratiker*, Volume 1. Zurich.

Dietrich, J. 1999. "*Thebaid*'s Feminine Ending." *Ramus* 28.1: 40–53.

Dilcher, R. 1995. *Studies in Heraclitus*. New York.

Dolmage, J. 2006. "'Breathe upon Us an Even Flame': Hephaestus, History, and the Body Rhetoric." *Rhetoric Review* 25.2: 119–40.

Dolphijn, R., and I. van der Tuin. 2012. "A Thousand Tiny Intersections: Linguisticism, Feminism, Racism, and Deleuzian Becomings." In *Deleuze and Race*, edited by A. Saldanha and J. M. Adams, 129–43. Edinburgh.

Doniger, W. 2010. "Claude Lévi-Strauss's Theoretical and Actual Approaches to Myth." In *The Cambridge Companion to Lévi-Strauss*, edited by B. Wiseman, 196–215. Cambridge.

Douglass, F. 1994. *Autobiographies*. New York.

Dover, K. J. 1972. *Aristophanic Comedy*. Berkeley.

Bibliography

Du Bois, W. E. B. 2018. *The Souls of Black Folk*. Gorham, ME.

Dunbar, N., ed. 1998. *Aristophanes: Birds*. Oxford.

Duncan, A. 2005. "Gendered Interpretations: Two Fourth-Century b.c.e. Performances of Sophocles' *Electra*." *Helios* 32: 55–79.

Dunn, F., ed. 1996. *Sophocles'* Electra *in Performance*. Berlin.

Durgin, P. F. 2009. "Post-Language Poetries and Post-Ableist Poetics." *Journal of Modern Literature* 32.2: 159–84.

Dworkin, C. 2003. *Reading the Illegible*. Evanston, IL.

Dyer, R. 2004. "Judy Garland and Gay Men." In *Heavenly Bodies: Film Stars and Society*, 137–200. New York.

Easterling, P. E. 1973. "Repetition in Sophocles." *Hermes* 101: 14–34.

Eccleston, S.-M., and D. Padilla Peralta. 2022. "Racing the Classics: Ethos and Praxis." *AJP* 143.2: 199–218.

Edalatpour, J. 2019. "Michael Richards Retrospective at Stanford Art Gallery." *MetroActive*, February 27. http://www.metroactive.com/arts/Michael-Richards-A-Loss-of-Faith-Brings-Vertigo-Stanford-Art-Gallery-Exhibit.html.

Edelman, L. 2004. *No Future: Queer Theory and the Death Drive*. Durham, NC.

Edelman, L. 2022. "On Solidarity." In *Proximities: Reading with Judith Butler*, edited by D. Sanyal, M. Telò, and D. R. Young. *Representations* 158.1: 93–105.

Edmunds, L., ed. 1990. *Approaches to Greek Myth*. Baltimore.

Edwards, B. H. 2000. "Notes on Poetics Regarding Mackey's 'Song.'" *Callaloo* 23: 572–91.

Edwards, B. H. 2017. *Epistrophies: Jazz and the Literary Imagination*. Cambridge, MA.

Ellis, R. 2021. "Beyond the Human Condition: Duration and Virtuality in Heraclitus." *Ramus* 49: 41–69.

Ellis Neyra, R. 2020. *The Cry of the Senses: Listening to Latinx and Caribbean Poetics*. Durham, NC.

Epstein, D., and D. L. Steinberg. 2003. "Inventing Id-TV on the Jerry Springer Show." *Discourse* 25.3: 90–114.

Eyers, T. 2017. *Speculative Formalism: Literature, Theory, and the Critical Present*. Evanston, IL.

Fanon, F. 1952. *Peau noire, masques blancs*. Paris.

Fanon, F. 1967. *Black Skin, White Masks*. New York.

Fantuzzi, M. 1989. "La censura delle Simplegadi: Ennio, *Media*, fr. 1 Jocelyn." *QUCC* 31.1: 119–29.

Fantuzzi, M., and R. L. Hunter. 2004. *Tradition and Innovation in Hellenistic Poetry*. Cambridge.

Faraone, C. A. 2005. "Catalogues, Priamels, and Stanzaic Structure in Early Greek Elegy." *TAPA* 135.2: 249–65.

Farnell, L., ed. 1930–2. *The Works of Pindar I-III*. London.

Farrell, J. 2007. "Horace's Body, Horace's Books." In *Classical Constructions*, edited by S. J. Heyworth, P. G. Fowler, and S. J. Harrison, 174–93. Oxford.

Farrington, L. E. 2005. *Creating Their Own Image: The History of African-American Women Artists*. Oxford.

Fearn, D. 2017. *Pindar's Eyes: Visual and Material Culture in Epinician Poetry*. Oxford.

Feld, S. 1990. *Sound and Sentiment: Birds, Weeping, Poetics, and Song in Kaluli Expression*. Philadelphia.

Felski, R. 2020. *Hooked: Art and Attachment*. Chicago.

Ferrari, F. 2010. *Sappho's Gift: The Poet and her Community*. Ann Arbor.

Ferreira da Silva, D. 2014. "Toward a Black Feminist Poethics: The Quest(ion) of Blackness Toward the End of the World." *The Black Scholar* 44.2: 81–97.

Finglass, P., ed. 2007. *Sophocles:* Electra. Cambridge.

Finkelstein, N. 2008. "Nathaniel Mackey and the Unity of All Rites." *Contemporary Literature* 49: 24–55.

Fisher, T. 2013. "Making Sense: Jacques Rancière and the Language Poets." *Journal of Modern Literature* 36.2: 156–74.

Fitzgerald, W. 2016. *Variety: The Life of a Roman Concept*. Chicago.

Flieger, J. A. 2000. "Becoming-Woman: Deleuze, Schreber, and Molecular Identification." In *Deleuze and Feminist Theory*, edited by I. Buchanan and C. Colebrook, 38–63. Edinburgh.

Foley, H. P. 2014. *Reimagining Greek Tragedy on the American Stage*. Berkeley.

Ford, K. J. 2010. "The Last Quatrain: Gwendolyn Brooks and the Ends of Ballads." *Twentieth Century Literature* 56.3: 371–95.

Foster, S. L. 2019. *Valuing Dance: Commodities and Gifts in Motion*. Oxford.

Fowler, D. 2000. *Classical Constructions: Readings in Postmodern Latin*. Oxford.

Fraden, R. 2001. *Imagining Medea: Rhodessa Jones and Theater for Incarcerated Women*. Chapel Hill, NC.

Freeman, E. et al., 2007. "Theorizing Queer Temporalities." *GLQ* 13: 177–95.

Freud, S. 1920. *Beyond the Pleasure Principle. SE* 18: 1–64

Freudenburg, K. 1999. Review of M. Lowrie, *Horace's Narrative Odes* (Oxford, 1997). *CP* 94.2: 234–38.

Freudenburg, K. 2001. *Satires of Rome: Threatening Poses from Lucilius to Juvenal*. Cambridge.

Gager, J. G., ed. 1992. *Curse Tablets and Binding Spells from the Ancient World*. Oxford.

Gantz, T. 1993. *Early Greek Myth*. Baltimore.

García Lorca, F. 1980. *Deep Song and Other Prose*. New York.

Gaudlitz, E. 2010. "Stuttering in Beckett as Liminal Expression Within the Deleuzian Critical-Clinical Hypothesis." *Deleuze Studies* 4: 183–205.

Gelzer, T. 1996. "Some Aspects of Aristophanes' Dramatic Art in the *Birds*." In *Oxford Readings in Aristophanes*, edited by E. Segal, 194–215. Oxford.

Geue, T. 2019. *Author Unknown: The Power of Anonymity in Ancient Rome*. Cambridge, MA.

Gilroy, P. 1993. *The Black Atlantic: Modernity and Double-Consciousness*. Cambridge.

Glaser, B. 2022. "The Black Quatrain and America's Racialized Poetics." In *A Companion to American Poetry*, edited by M. M. Balkun, J. Gray, and P. Jaussen, 201–15. Hoboken, NJ.

Glissant, É. 1989. *Caribbean Discourse: Selected Essays*. Charlottesville, VA.

Glissant, É. 1997. *Poetics of Relation*. Ann Arbor, MI.

Goff, B., and M. Simpson. 2008. *Crossroads in the Black Aegean: Oedipus, Antigone, and Dramas of the African Diaspora*. Oxford.

Gold, B. K. 1992. "Openings in Horace's *Satires* and *Odes*." In *Beginnings in Classical Literature*, edited by F. M. Dunn and T. Cole, 161–85. Cambridge.

Goldberg, D. T. 2021. *Dread: Facing Futureless Futures*. Cambridge.

Goldberg, S., and G. Manuwald, eds. 2018. *Fragmentary Republican Latin: Ennius*, Volume 2. Cambridge, MA.

Goldhill, S. 2020. *Preposterous Poetics: The Politics and Aesthetics of Form in Late Antiquity*. Cambridge.

Golding, D. 2019. "The Darker Side of Fritz Lang's *Metropolis*: Coloniality in Modernist Cinema." *Postcolonial Studies* 22.3: 303–24.

Goldsby, J. 2006. *A Spectacular Secret: Lynching in American Life and Literature*. Chicago.

Goodman, S. 2009. *Sonic Warfare: Sound, Affect, and the Ecology of Fear*. Cambridge, MA.

Gowers, E., ed. 2012. *Horace: Satires Book I*. Cambridge.

Grabe, M. E. 2002. "Maintaining the Moral Order: A Functional Analysis of 'The Jerry Springer Show.'" *Critical Studies in Media Communication* 19: 311–28.

Greenwood, E. 2010. *Afro-Greeks: Dialogues between Anglophone Caribbean Literature and Classics in the Twentieth Century*. Oxford.

Griaule, M. 1965. *Conversations with Ogotemmeli: An Introduction to Dogon Religious Ideas*. London.

Griffiths, E. 2018. *The Printed Voice of Victorian Poetry*. Oxford.

Gross, D. M. 2006. *The Secret History of Emotion: From Aristotle's Rhetoric to Modern Brain*. Chicago.

Grosz, E. 2002. "A Politics of Imperceptibility: A Response to 'Anti-racism, Multiculturalism, and the Ethics of Identification.'" *Philosophy and Social Criticism* 28.4: 463–72.

Bibliography

Gunderson, E. 2021. "Theology's Shadow." In *Classical Philology and Theology: Entanglement, Disavowal, and the Godlike Scholar*, edited by C. Conybeare and S. Goldhill, 199–224. Cambridge.

Gurd, S. A. 2016. *Dissonance: Auditory Aesthetics in Ancient Greece*. New York.

Gurd, S. A. 2018a. "Introduction: Elements of 'Pataphilology." In *'Pataphilology: An Irreader*, edited by S. A. Gurd and V. W. J. van Gerven Oei, 21–60. Goleta, CA.

Gurd, S. A. 2018b. "Auditory Philology." In *Sound and the Ancient Senses*, edited by S. Butler and S. Nooter, 184–97. London.

Gurd, S. A. 2019. *The Origins of Music Theory in the Age of Plato*. London.

Gurd, S. A. 2022. "Listening to the 'Egg.'" In *Hearing, Sound, and the Auditory in Ancient Greece*, edited by J. Gordon, 111–42. Bloomington, IN.

Gurd, S. A., and V. W. J. van Gerven Oei, eds. 2018. *'Pataphilology: an Irreader*. Goleta, CA.

Hack, D. 2016. *Reaping Something New: African American Transformations of Victorian Literature*. Princeton, NJ.

Hairston, E. A. 2016. *The Ebony Column: Classics, Civilization, and the African American Reclamation of the West*. Knoxville, TN.

Halberstam, J. 2012. *Gaga Feminism*. Boston.

Hall, S. 2021. *The Fateful Triangle: Race, Ethnicity, Nation*. Cambridge.

Hamilton, J. 2003. *Soliciting Darkness: Pindar, Obscurity, and the Classical Tradition*. Cambridge, MA.

Harris, D. 2022. "The Smear: Vibrational Flesh and the Calculus of Black Queer Becoming in Barry Jenkins's *Moonlight*." *differences* 33.1: 1–27.

Harris, S. L. 2021. "Emma Amos: Color Odyssey." In *Emma Amos: Color Odyssey*, edited by S. L. Harris, 18–41. Athens, GA.

Harrison, J. E. 1912. *Themis*. Cambridge.

Hayes, J. 2017. "Derrida's Queer Root(s)." In *Derrida and Queer Theory*, edited by C. Hite, 164–83. Goleta, CA.

Hegel, G. W. F. 1975. *Hegel's Aesthetics: Lectures on Fine Art*, Volume 2. Oxford.

Heidegger, M. 2001. *Poetry, Language, Thought*. New York.

Heinze, R. 1919. *Ovids Elegische Erzählung*. Leipzig.

Henderson, J. 1999. *Writing Down Rome: Satire, Comedy and other Offences in Latin Poetry*, Oxford.

Hershbell, J. P., and S. A. Nimis. 1979. "Nietzsche and Heraclitus." *Nietzsche-Studien* 8: 17–38.

Heslin, P. 2016. "The Perfect Murder: the Hypsipyle Epyllion." In *Family in Flavian Epic*, edited by N. Manioti, 89–121. Leiden.

Heuman, G. 1994. *"The Killing Time": The Morant Bay Rebellion in Jamaica*. Knoxville, TN.

Hinds, S. 1998. *Allusion and Intertext: Dynamics of Appropriation in Latin Poetry*. Cambridge.

Hoefmans, M. 1994. "Myth into Reality: The Metamorphosis of Daedalus and Icarus (Ovid, *Metamorphoses*, VIII, 183–235)." *L'Antiquité Classique* 63: 137–60.

Holman-Hunt, D. 1969. *My Grandfather: His Wives and Loves*. London.

Holmes, D. 2019. *Philosophy, Poetry, and Power in Aristophanes's* Birds. Lanham, MD.

hooks, bell 1993. "Straighten Up and Fly Right: Making History Visible." In *Emma Amos: Paintings and Prints 1982–92*, edited by The College of Wooster Art Museum, 15–28. Wooster, OH.

Hopkinson, N., ed. 1988. *A Hellenistic Anthology*. Cambridge.

Horky, P. S., ed. 2019. *Cosmos in the Ancient World*. New York.

Hume, C. 2006. "Improvisational Insurrection: The Sound Poetry of Tracie Morris." *Contemporary Literature* 47.3: 415–39.

Hunter, R., ed. 2015. *Apollonius of Rhodes: Argonautica Book IV*. Cambridge.

Iser, W. 1978. *The Act of Reading: A Theory of Aesthetic Response*. Baltimore.

Iyer, V. 2002. "Embodied Mind, Situated Cognition, and Expressive Microtiming in African-American Music." *Music Perception* 19: 387–414.

Jackson, A. 2017. *A Surprised Queenhood in the New Black Sun: The Life & Legacy of Gwendolyn Brooks*. Boston.

Jackson, V. 2016. "Specters of the Ballad." *Nineteenth-Century Literature* 71.2: 176–96.

Jackson, Z. 2020. *Becoming Human*. New York.

Jakobson, R. 1960. "Linguistics and Poetics." In *Style in Language*, edited by T. Sebeok, 350–77. Cambridge, MA.

Jakobson, R. 1962. "Why 'Mama' and 'Papa'?" In *Selected Writings*, Volume 1, 538–45. The Hague.

Jakobson, R. 1981. "What is Poetry?" In *Selected Writings*, Volume 3, 740–50. The Hague.

Jebb, R., ed. 1924. *Sophocles: The Plays and Fragments. Part VI: The* Electra. Cambridge.

Jenkins, G. M. 2016. "'Re: Source:' African Contexts of Nathaniel Mackey's Ethics." *African American Review* 49.1: 35–52.

Jenkyns, R. 1982. *Three Classical Poets*. Cambridge, MA.

Kahn, C. H. 1960. *Anaximander and the Origins of Greek Cosmology*. New York.

Kahn, C. H. 1979. *The Art and Thought of Heraclitus*. Cambridge.

Kahn, C. H. 1983. "Philosophy and the Written Word: Some Thoughts on Heraclitus and the Early Greek Use of Prose." In *Language and Thought in Early Greek Philosophy*, edited by K. Robb, 110–24. La Salle, IL.

Katz, J. T. 2018. "Gods and Vowels." In *Sound and the Ancient Senses*, edited by S. Butler and S. Nooter, 153–70. Routledge.

Keil, C. 1987. "Participatory Discrepancies and the Power of Music." *Cultural Anthropology* 2: 275–83.

Keith, A. 2000. *Engendering Rome: Women in Latin Epic*. Cambridge.

Keith, A. 2013. "Medusa, Python, Poine and the Argive Ritual." In *Ritual and Religion in Flavian Epic*, edited by A. Augoustakis, 303–18. Oxford.

Keizer, H. 2000. "Eternity Revisited: A Study of the Greek Word *Aion*." *Philosophia Reformata* 51: 53–71.

Kenney, E. J. 1982. "Ovid." In *The Cambridge History of Classical Literature*, Volume 2: *Latin Literature*, edited by E. J. Kenney and W. V. Clausen, 420–57. Cambridge.

Kenney, E. J. 1983. "The Key and the Cabinet: Ends and Means in Classical Studies." *PCA* 80: 7–18.

Kenney, E. J. 2002. "Ovid's Language and Style." In *Brill's Companion to Ovid*, edited by B. W. Boyd, 27–89. Leiden.

Kincaid, J. 1990. *Lucy*. New York.

Kincaid, J. 2022. "The Art of Fiction No. 252." Interview by Darryl Pinckney. *The Paris Review*. (Spring): 160–92.

Kirby, J. T. 1985. "Toward a General Theory of the Priamel." *CJ* 80.2: 142–4.

Kitzinger, R. 1991. "Why Mourning Becomes Elektra." *CA* 10: 298–327.

Konstan, D. 1990. "A City in the Air: Aristophanes' *Birds*." *Arethusa* 23.2: 183–207.

Konstan, D. 1997. "The Greek Polis and its Negations: Versions of Utopia in Aristophanes' *Birds*." In *The City as Comedy: Society and Representation in Athenian Drama*, edited by G. W. Dobrov, 3–22. Chapel Hill, NC.

Konstan, D. 2007. "Medea: A Hint of Divinity?" *CW* 101: 93–4.

Konstantinou, A. 2015. "Tradition and Innovation in Greek Tragedy's Mythological 'Exempla.'" *CQ* 65: 476–88.

Kornbluh, A. 2019. *The Order of Forms: Realism, Formalism, and Social Space*. Chicago.

Kostelanetz, R. 2018. *Radical Formalism: Yet More Fulcra Poems*. Ridgewood, NY.

Krasne, D. 2012. "The Pedant's Curse: Obscurity and Identity in Ovid's *Ibis*." *Dictynna* 9. https://journals.openedition.org/dictynna/912.

Krischer, T. 1974. "Die logischen Formen der Priamel." *Grazer Beiträge* 2: 79–91.

Kuppers, P. 2006. "Disability Culture Poetry: The Sound of the Bones. A Literary Essay." *Disability Studies Quarterly* 26.4. https://dsq-sds.org/article/view/809/984.

Kuppers, P. 2011. "Poetry-ing: Feminist Disability Aesthetics and Poetry Community." *ELN* 49.2: 73–82.

Kurke, L. 1991. *The Traffic in Praise: Pindar and the Poetics of Social Economy*. Ithaca, NY.

Kurke, L. 1999. *Coins, Bodies, Games, and Gold: The Politics of Meaning in Archaic Greece*. Princeton, NJ.

Kurnick, D. 2020. "A Few Lies: Queer Theory and Our Method Melodramas." *ELH* 87.2: 349–74.

LAEP = Everest, K., et al., eds. (1989–). *The Poems of Shelley I–V*. Harlow.

Laks, A. 2015. "Sommeils présocratiques." In *Le sommeil: approches philosophiques et médicales de l'Antiquité à la Renaissance*, edited by V. Leroux, N. Palmieri, and C. Pigné, 29–50. Paris.

Laks, A., and G. W. Most, eds. 2016. *Early Greek Philosophy*. Cambridge, MA.

Lambert, S. 2020. "'The Real Dark Side, Baby': New Sincerity and Neoliberal Aesthetics in David Foster Wallace and Jennifer Egan." *Critique* 61: 394–411.

La Penna, A., ed. 1957. *Ibis*. Florence.

Lavery, M. A. 2004. "The Ontogeny and Phylogeny of Mackey's 'Song of the Andoumboulou.'" *African American Review* 38.4: 683–94.

León, C. 2021. "Risking Catachresis: Reading Race, Reference, and Grammar in 'Women.'" *Diacritics* 49.2: 61–71.

Lesjak, C. 2019. "A Democracy of Forms: Levine, Latour, and New Formalism." *Historical Materialism*. https://www.historicalmaterialism.org/book-review/democracy-forms-levine-latour-and-new-formalism

LeVen, P. 2018. "The Erogenous Ear." In *Sound and the Ancient Senses*, edited by S. Butler and S. Nooter, 212–32. London.

Levinas, E. 1969. *Totality and Infinity: An Essay on Exteriority*. Pittsburgh.

Levinas, E. 1985. *Ethics and Infinity: Conversations with Philippe Nemo*. Pittsburgh.

Levinas, E. 2000. *God, Death, and Time*. Stanford, CA.

Levine, C. 2015. *Forms: Whole, Rhythm, Hierarchy, Network*. Princeton, NJ.

Levitan, W. 1985. "Dancing at the End of the Rope: Optatian Porfyry and the Field of Roman Verse." *TAPA* 115: 245–69.

Lilja, S. 1968. *On the Style of the Earliest Greek Prose*. Helsinki.

Lippard, L. 1991. "Floating Falling Landing: An Interview with Emma Amos." *Art Papers* 15.6: 13–16.

Livrea, E., ed. 1973. *Apollonii Rhodii Liber Quartus*. Florence.

Lloyd-Jones, H., and N. Wilson, eds. 1990. *Sophoclis Fabulae*. Oxford.

Lobato, J. H. 2017. "Conceptual Poetry: Rethinking Optatian from Contemporary Art." In *Morphogrammata: The Lettered Art of Optatian*, edited by M. Squire and J. Wienand, 461–93. Stuttgart.

Loraux, N. 1993. "Éloge de l'anachronisme en histoire." *Le Genre Humain* 27: 23–40.

Loraux, N. 1998. *Mothers in Mourning*. Ithaca, NY.

Lovatt, H. 2013. *The Epic Gaze: Vision, Gender and Narrative in Ancient Epic*. Cambridge.

Love, H. 2010. "Truth and Consequences: On Paranoid Reading and Reparative Reading." *Criticism* 52.2: 235–41.

Lowney, J. 1998. "'A Material Collapse That Is Construction': History and Counter-Memory in Gwendolyn Brooks's *In the Mecca*." *MELUS* 23.3: 3–20.

Lowrie, M. 1997. *Horace's Narrative Odes*. Oxford.

Luck, G. 1969. *The Latin Love Elegy*. London.

Lukács, G. 1971. *History and Class Consciousness: Studies in Marxist Dialectics*. Cambridge, MA.

Lunt, P., and P. Stenner. 2005. "*The Jerry Springer Show* as Emotional Public Sphere." *Media, Culture, & Society* 27: 59–81.

Mackey, N. 1985. *Eroding Witness*. Urbana, IL.

Mackey, N. 1987. "Sound and Sentiment, Sound and Symbol." *Callaloo* 30: 29–54.

Mackey, N. 1993a. *Discrepant Engagement: Dissonance, Cross-Culturality, and Experimental Writing*. Cambridge.

Mackey, N. 1993b. *School of Udhra*. San Francisco.

Mackey, N. 1998. *Whatsaid Serif*. San Francisco.

Mackey, N. 2005. *Paracritical Hinge: Essays, Talks, Notes, Interviews*. Madison, WI.

Mackey, N. 2006. *Splay Anthem*. New York.

Mackey, N. 2008. *Bass Cathedral*. New York.

Mackey, N. 2010. *From a Broken Bottle Traces of Perfume Still Emanate: Bedouin Hornbook, Djbot Baghostus's Run, Atet a.d.* New York.

Mackey, N. 2011. *Nod House*. New York.

Mackey, N. 2015. *Blue Fasa*. New York.

Mackey, N. 2017. *Late Arcade*. New York.

Mackey, N. 2021a. *Breath and Precarity*. Berkeley.

Mackey, N. 2021b. *Double Trio*. New York.

MacPherson, S. 2017. "The Political Fallacy." *PMLA* 132: 1214–19.

Mahoney, A. 2007. "Key Terms in *The Birds*." *CW* 100.3: 267–78.

Malabou, C. 2016. "Philosophy in Erection." *Paragraph* 39.2: 238–48.

Malamud, M. 2019. *African Americans and the Classics: Antiquity, Abolition and Activism*. London.

Mallarmé, S. 2001. "Crisis of Verse." In *Norton Anthology of Theory and Criticism*, edited by V. Leitch, 841–51. New York.

Mallot, J. E. 2004. "Sacrificial Limbs, Lambs, Iambs, and I Ams: Nathaniel Mackey's Mythology of Loss." *Contemporary Literature* 45.1: 135–64.

Manioti, N. 2016. "Becoming Sisters: Antigone and Argia in Statius' *Thebaid*." In *Family in Flavian Epic,* edited by N. Manioti, 122–42. Leiden.

Marcus, L. S. 1996. *Unediting the Renaissance: Shakespeare, Marlowe, Milton*. London.

Martin, C. J. 2012. "Emma Amos in Conversation with Courtney J. Martin." *Nka: Journal of Contemporary African Art* 30.1: 104–13.

Martin, J. B. 1950. "The Strangest Place in Chicago." *Harper's Magazine* (December 1). https://harpers.org/archive/1950/12/the-strangest-place-in-chicago/.

Martínez, M. E. 2004. "The Black Blood of New Spain: Limpieza de Sangre, Racial Violence, and Gendered Power in Early Colonial Mexico" *The William and Mary Quarterly* 61.3: 479–520.

Martínez, M. E. 2008. *Genealogical Fictions: Limpieza de Sangre, Religion, and Gender in Colonial Mexico*. Stanford, CA.

Massumi, B. 2002. *Parables for the Virtual: Movement, Affect, Sensation*. Durham, NC.

Matuszewski, R. 2022. "When a Man Is an Island: Introductory Remarks on Being Alone in Antiquity." In *Being Alone in Antiquity*, edited by R. Matuszewski, 1–22. Berlin.

Maxwell, B. 1980. "The Steytler Recordings of Alfred Lord Tennyson: A History." *Tennyson Research Bulletin* 3.4: 150–57.

Mayer, R., ed. 2012. *Horace: Odes Book 1*. Cambridge.

McAuley, M. 2016. *Reproducing Rome: Motherhood in Virgil, Ovid, Seneca and Statius*. Oxford.

McEleney, C. 2021. "The Resistance to Overanalysis." *differences* 32.2: 1–38.

Mckie, S. 2022. *Living and Cursing in the Roman West: Curse Tablets and Society*. London.

McLean, A. L. 2002. "Feeling and the Filmed Body: Judy Garland and the Kinesics of Suffering." *Film Quarterly* 55.3: 2–15.

Melhem, D. H. 1987. *Gwendolyn Brooks: Poetry & the Heroic Voice*. Lexington, KY.

Meyer, M. 2014. *Reading Nietzsche through the Ancients: An Analysis of Becoming, Perspectivism, and the Principle of Non-Contradiction*. Berlin.

Mihaylova, S. 2015. "The Radical Formalism of Suzan-Lori Parks and Sarah Kane." *Theatre Survey* 56.2: 213–31.

Miller, D. A. 2021. *Second Time Around: From Art House to DVD*. New York.

Minchin, E. 2021. "The Creation of a Storyrealm: The Role of Repetition in Homeric Epic and Alice Oswald's *Memorial*." In *Repetition, Communication, and Meaning in the Ancient World*, edited by D. Beck, 373–92. Leiden.

Mithen, S. J. 2006. *The Singing Neanderthals: the Origins of Music, Language, Mind, and Body.* Cambridge, MA.

Morgan, L. 2010. *"Musa Pedestris": Metre and Meaning in Roman Verse.* Oxford.

Mossin, A. R. 2014. "'The Song Sung in a Strange Land:' an Interview with Nathaniel Mackey." *The Iowa Review* 44.3: 172–92.

Most, G. W. 1995. "Reflecting Sappho." *BICS* 41.1: 15–38.

Moten, F. 2003. *In the Break: The Aesthetics of the Black Radical Tradition.* Minneapolis.

Moten, F. 2013. "Blackness and Nothingness (Mysticism in the Flesh)." *SAQ* 112.4: 737–80.

Moten, F. 2017. *Black and Blur: Consent Not to Be a Single Being.* Durham, NC.

Moten, F. 2018a. *The Universal Machine.* Durham, NC.

Moten, F. 2018b. *Stolen Life.* Durham, NC.

Moten, F. 2022. "Building and Bildung Und Blackness: Some Architectural Questions for Fela." MIT Architecture: NOMAS Lecture (April 6). https://www.youtube.com/watch?app=desktop &v=EW1aR3rHeZE.

Moten, F., and S. Harney. 2004. "The University and the Undercommons: Seven Theses." *Social Text* 22.2: 101–15.

Moten, F., and S. Harney. 2013. *The Undercommons: Fugitive Planning and Black Study.* New York.

Moten, F., and S. Harney. 2021. *All Incomplete.* Oakland.

Moyer, I., A. Lecznar, and H. Morse, eds. 2020. *Classicisms in the Black Atlantic.* Oxford.

Mueller, M. forthcoming. *Sappho and Homer: A Reparative Reading.* Cambridge.

Musser, A. J. 2018. *Sensual Excess: Queer Femininity and Brown Jouissance.* New York.

Musurillo, H. 1962. "The Poet's Apotheosis: Horace *Odes* 1.1." *TAPA* 93: 230–9.

Mylonas, G. 1940. "Athens and Minoan Crete." *HSCP* 51: 11–36.

Nancy, J.-L. 2009. *The Fall of Sleep.* New York.

Natoli, B. 2017. *Silenced Voices: The Poetics of Speech in Ovid.* Madison, WI.

Nersessian, A. 2020. *The Calamity Form: On Poetry and Social Life.* Chicago.

Netz, R. 2020. *Scale, Space, and Canon in Ancient Literary Culture.* Cambridge.

Nielsen, A. L. 2000. "N + 1: Before-the-fact Reading in Nathaniel Mackey's Postcontemporary Music." *Callaloo* 23.2: 796–806.

Nietzsche, F. 1962. *Philosophy in the Tragic Age of the Greeks.* New York.

Nisbet, R. G. M., and M. Hubbard, eds. 1970. *A Commentary on Horace Odes Book I.* Oxford.

Nonnenberg, S. 2019. "Stanford Presents 'Michael Richards: Winged.'" *Palo Alto Weekly* (February 14). https://www.almanacnews.com/news/2019/02/14/stanford-presents-michael-richards-winged

Nooter, S. 2012. *When Heroes Sing: Sophocles and the Shifting Soundscape of Tragedy.* Cambridge.

Nooter, S. 2017. *The Mortal Voices in the Tragedies of Aeschylus.* Cambridge.

Nooter, S. 2018. "Sounds of the Stage." In *Sound and the Ancient Senses,* edited by S. Butler and S. Nooter, 198–211. London.

Nooter, S. 2019a. "The War-Trumpet and the Sound of Domination in Ancient Greek Thought." *Greek and Roman Musical Studies* 7.2: 235–49.

Nooter, S. 2019b. "The Prosthetic Voice in Ancient Greece." In *The Voice as Something More,* edited by M. Feldman and J. Zeitlin, 277–94. Chicago.

Nooter, S. 2020. "The Fourth Level of Life: White Noise in the *Homeric Hymn to Aphrodite* and Plato's *Phaedrus.*" *Parallax,* 26.2: 133–50.

Nooter, S. 2022. "Tragedy: Reconstruction and Repair." *CP* 117.2: 229–33.

North, J. 2017. *Literary Criticism: A Concise Political History.* Cambridge, MA.

Nott, J. C., and G. R. Gliddon. 1854. *Types of Mankind: Or, Ethnological Researches, Based upon the Ancient Monuments, Paintings, Sculptures, and Crania of Races, and upon Their Natural, Geographical, Philological and Biblical History.* Philadelphia.

Nugent, G. 1996. "Statius' Hypsipyle: Following in the Footsteps of the *Aeneid*." *Scholia* 5.1: 46–71.

O'Keeffe, B. 2021. "Transing Derrida." *American Book Review* 42.5: 19–31.

O'Leary, P. 2000. "Deep Trouble/Deep Treble: Nathaniel Mackey's Gnostic Rasp." *Callaloo* 23.2: 516–37.

Oliensis, E. 1998. *Horace and the Rhetoric of Authority*. Cambridge.

Oliensis, E. 2019. *Loving Writing/ Ovid's* Amores. Cambridge.

Oliver, K. 2001. *Witnessing: Beyond Recognition*. Minneapolis.

Olkowski, D. 1999. *Gilles Deleuze and the Ruin of Representation*. Berkeley.

O' Meally, R. G. 2007. *Romare Bearden: A Black Odyssey*. New York.

O'Neill, M. 1989. *The Human Mind's Imaginings: Conflict and Achievement in Shelley's Poetry*. Oxford.

Oyeyemi, H. 2005. *The Icarus Girl: A Novel*. New York.

Paduano, G. 1970–1. "L'episodio di Talos: osservazioni sull'esperienza magica nelle *Argonautiche* di Apollonio Rodio." *SCO* 19: 46–67.

Pagan, V. 2000. "The Mourning After: Statius *Thebaid* 12." *AJP* 121: 423–52.

Page, D. L. 1955. *Sappho and Alcaeus: An Introduction to the Study of Ancient Lesbian Poetry*. Oxford.

Page, D. L. 1962. *Poetae Melici Graeci*. Oxford.

Page, D. L. 1968. *Lyrica Graeca Selecta*. Oxford.

Parker, L. P. E. 1997. *The Songs of Aristophanes*. Oxford.

Parks, S.-L. 2006. *365 Days, 365 Plays*. New York.

Paschen, E., and R. P. Mosby, eds. 2001. *Poetry Speaks: Hear Great Poets Read Their Work from Tennyson to Plath*. Naperville, IL.

Patton, S. 2002. "Emma Amos: Art Matters." *Nka: Journal of Contemporary African Art* 16.1: 40–7.

Payne, M. 2006. "On Being Vatic: Pindar, Pragmatism, and Historicism." *AJP* 127.2: 159–84.

Payne, M. 2010. *The Animal Part: Human and Other Animals in the Poetic Imagination*. Chicago.

Payne, M. 2013. "The Understanding Ear: Synaesthesia, Paraesthesia and Talking Animals." In *Synaesthesia and the Ancient Senses*, edited by S. Butler and A. Purves, 43–52. Durham, NC.

Payne, M. 2018. "Fidelity and Farewell: Pindar's Ethics as Textual Events." In *Textual Events: Performance and the Lyric in Early Greece*, edited by F. Budelmann and T. Phillips, 257–74. Oxford.

Pedley, J. G. 2012. *Greek Art and Archaeology*. Upper Saddle River, NJ.

Perloff, M. 2021. *Infrathin: An Experiment in Micropoetics*. Chicago.

Perls, F. 1969. *Gestalt Therapy Verbatim*. Moab, UT.

Perls, F. 1973. *The Gestalt Approach and Eye Witness to Therapy*. Mountain View, CA.

Perls, F., Hefferline, R. E. and R. Goodman. 1951. *Gestalt Therapy: Excitement and Growth in the Human Personality*. London.

Peters, M. A. 2012. "On the Edge of Theory: Lady Gaga, Performance, and Cultural Theory." *Contemporary Readings in Law and Social Justice* 4.1: 25–37.

Pfeiffer, R. 1968. *History of Classical Scholarship From the Beginning to the End of the Hellenistic Age*. Oxford.

Pfeijffer, I. 1999. *Three Aeginetan Odes of Pindar*. Leiden.

Phelan, P. 1993. *Unmarked: The Politics of Performance*. London.

Philen, R. C. 2005. "Reflecting on Meaning and Myth: Claude Lévi-Strauss Revisited." *Anthropos* 100: 221–8.

Phillips, T. 2015. "Echo in Euripides' *Andromeda*." *Greek and Roman Musical Studies* 3: 53–66.

Phillips, T. 2018. "Words and the Musician: Pindar's Dactylo-Epitrites." In *Music, Text, and Culture in Ancient Greece*, edited by T. Phillips and A. D'Angour, 73–98. Oxford.

Pickering, P. E. 2000. "Verbal Repetition in 'Prometheus' and Greek Tragedy Generally." *BICS* 44: 81–101.

Bibliography

Porter, J. I. 2000. *Nietzsche and the Philology of the Future*. Stanford, CA.

Porter, J. I. 2005. "What Is 'Classical' about Classical Antiquity? Eight Propositions." *Arion* 13.1: 27–61.

Porter, J. I. 2007. "Lasus of Hermione, Pindar and the Riddle of S." *CQ* 57.1: 1–21.

Porter, J. I. 2010. *The Origins of Aesthetic Thought in Ancient Greece: Matter, Sensation, Experience*. Cambridge.

Porter, J. I. 2016. *The Sublime in Antiquity*. Cambridge.

Postclassicisms Collective. 2019. *Postclassicisms*. Chicago.

Powers, M. 2018. *Diversifying Greek Tragedy on the Contemporary US Stage*. Oxford.

Powers, N. 2002. "Magic, Wonder, and Scientific Explanation in Apollonius, *Argonautica* 4.1638–93." *PCPhS* 48: 87–101.

Pozzi, D. C. 1985–6. "The Pastoral Ideal in *The Birds*." *CJ* 81.2: 119–29.

Przybyslawski, A. 2002. "Nietzsche Contra Heraclitus." *The Journal of Nietzsche Studies* 23: 88–95.

Pugh, T. 2008. "'There Lived in the Land of Oz Two Queerly Made Men': Queer Utopianism and Antisocial Eroticism in L. Frank Baum's Oz Series." *Marvels & Tales* 22.2: 217–39.

Purves, A. 2015. "Ajax and Other Objects: Homer's Vibrant Materialism." *Ramus* 44: 75–94.

Purves, A. C. 2016. "Feeling on the Surface: Touch and Emotion in Fuseli and Homer." In *Deep Classics: Rethinking Classical Reception*, edited by S. Butler, 67–85. London.

Purves, A. 2019. *Homer and the Poetics of Gesture*. Oxford.

Purves, A. Forthcoming. "Alcman, Sappho and the 'Lyric Present.'" In *Time, Tense and Genre in Ancient Greek Literature*, edited by C. Bloomfield and E. Hall. Oxford.

Purves, A., and V. Wohl. Forthcoming. "Now, Sleep." In *Making Time for Greek and Roman Culture*, edited by K. Gilhuly and J. Ulrich. New York.

Pyle, F. 2014. "Skylark-Image: Or, the Vitality of Disappearance." *European Romantic Review* 25.3: 319–25.

Quashie, K. 2021. *Black Aliveness, or a Poetics of Being*. Durham, NC.

Race, W. H. 1982. *The Classical Priamel from Homer to Boethius*. Leiden.

Rancière, J. 2004. *The Flesh of Words: The Politics of Writing*. Stanford, CA.

Rancière, J. 2011. *Mute Speech: Literature, Critical Theory, and Politics*. New York.

Rankine, P. 2006. *Ulysses in Black: Ralph Ellison, Classicism, and African American Literature*. Madison, WI.

Rankine, P. 2013. *Aristotle and Black Drama: A Theater of Civil Disobedience*. Waco, TX.

Rankine, P. 2019. "The Classics, Race, and Community-Engaged or Public Scholarship." *AJP* 140.2: 345–59.

Raphael, R. 2015. "Disability as Rhetorical Trope in Classical Myth and *Blade Runner*." In *Classical Traditions in Science Fiction*, edited by B. M. Rogers and B. E. Stevens, 176–96. Oxford.

Reed, A. 2014. *Freedom Time: The Poetics and Politics of Black Experimental Writing*. Baltimore.

Reiner, P., and D. Kovacs. 1993. "ΔΕΔΥΚΕ ΜΕΝ Α ΣΕΛΑΝΝΑ: The Pleiades in Mid-Heaven (*PMG* Frag. Adesp. 976 = Sappho, Fr. 168b Voigt)." *Mnemosyne* 46.2: 145–59.

Renaud, T. 2021. *New Lefts: The Making of a Radical Tradition*. Princeton, NJ.

Renehan, R. 1969. *Greek Textual Criticism: A Reader*. Cambridge, MA.

Retamar, R. F. 1974. "Caliban: Notes towards a Discussion of Culture in Our America." *The Massachusetts Review* 15.1–2: 7–72.

Ribeyrol, C. 2013. *"Étrangeté, Passion, Couleur": L'hellénisme de Swinburne, Pater et Symonds (1865–1880)*. Grenoble.

Rich, A. 2012. *Tonight No Poetry Will Serve: Poems 2007–2010*. New York.

Rimell, V. 2015. *The Closure of Space in Roman Poetics: Empire's Inward Turn*. Cambridge.

Rimell, V. 2019. "After Ovid, after Theory." *IJCT* 26: 446–69.

Rimmon-Kenan, S. 1980. "The Paradoxical Status of Repetition." *Poetics Today* 1: 151–9.

Rinner, J. 2015. "From Bronzeville to the Mecca and After: Gwendolyn Brooks and the Location of Black Identity." *MELUS* 40.4: 150–72.

Roelofs, M. 2005. "Racialization as an Aesthetic Production: What Does the Aesthetic Do for Whiteness and Blackness and Vice Versa." In *White on White/ Black on Black*, edited by G. Yancy, 83–124. Landham, MD.

Rohde, E. 1925. *Psyche: The Cult of Souls and the Belief in Immortality Among the Greeks*. New York.

Rosenmeyer, P. A. 1991. "Simonides' Danae Fragment Reconsidered." *Arethusa* 24.1: 5–29.

Rosenthal, M. L. 1969. "'In the Mecca' (Review)." *The New York Times Book Review*, March 2.

Ross, M. B. 2022. *Sissy Insurgencies: A Racial Anatomy of Unfit Manliness*. Durham, NC.

Rossetti, W. M., and A. C. Swinburne. 1868. *Notes on the Royal Academy Exhibition, 1868*. London.

Roynon, T. 2013. *Toni Morrison and the Classical Tradition: Transforming American Culture*. Oxford.

Roynon, T. 2021. *The Classical Tradition in Modern American Fiction*. Edinburgh.

Rubery, M. 2014. "Thomas Edison's Poetry Machine." *19: Interdisciplinary Studies in the Long Nineteenth Century* 18. https://19.bbk.ac.uk/article/id/1447/

Rugg, R. 2008. "Radical Inclusion 'Til It Hurts: Suzan-Lori Parks's *365 Days/365 Plays*." *Theater* 38: 53–75.

Rugg, R. 2009. "Dramaturgy as Devotion: 365 Days/365 Plays of Suzan-Lori Parks." *PAJ* 31.1: 68–79.

Ruiz, A. 2016. "Radical Formalism." *Women & Performance: a journal of feminist theory* 26.2–3: 233–40.

Russell, L. 2020. *Glitch Manifesto: A Manifesto*. London.

Saint-Amour, P. 2020. Review of C. Levine, *Forms: Whole, Rhythm, Hierarchy, Network* (Princeton, 2015). http://mtwebsit.blogspot.com/2020/06/paul-saint-amour-reviews-forms-whole.html

Santirocco, M. S. 1986. *Unity and Design in Horace's Odes*. Chapel Hill, NC.

Sanyal, D. 2021. "Race, Migration, and Security at the Euro-African Border." *Theory & Event* 24.1: 324–55.

Sasamoto, R. 2019. *Onomatopoeia and Relevance: Communication of Impressions via Sound*. London.

Sassi, M. M. 2018. *The Beginnings of Philosophy in Greece*. Princeton, NJ.

Saul, S. 2003. *Freedom Is, Freedom Ain't: Jazz and the Making of the Sixties*. Cambridge, MA.

Schaeffer, P. 1966. *Traité des objets musicaux: Essai interdisciplines*. Paris.

Schechner, R. 1981. "Restoration of Behavior." *Studies in Visual Communication* 7: 2–45.

Schofield, M. 2019. "*Diakosmêsis*." In *Cosmos in the Ancient World*, edited by P. S. Horky, 62–73. Cambridge.

Schiesaro, A. 2011. "'Ibis Redibis.'" *MD* 67: 79–150.

Scott, D. 2010. *Extravagant Abjection: Blackness, Power, and Sexuality in the African American Literary Imagination*. New York.

Scott, P. G. 1972. "The Proof of Tennyson's Achilles Over the Trench." *Tennyson Research Bulletin* 2.1: 38–9.

Sedgwick, E. K. 1993. *Tendencies*. Durham, NC

Sedgwick, E. K. 2003. *Touching Feeling: Affect, Pedagogy, Performativity*. Durham, NC.

Segal, C. 1974. "Arrest and Movement: Pindar's Fifth Nemean." *Hermes* 102: 397–411.

Serpell, C. N. 2014. *Seven Modes of Uncertainty*. Cambridge, MA.

Sethi, A. 2005. "'I Didn't Know I Was Writing a Novel.'" *The Guardian*, January 10. https://www.theguardian.com/books/2005/jan/10/fiction.features11.

Sexton, J. 2016. "Afro-Pessimism: The Unclear Word." *Rhizomes: Cultural Studies in Emerging Knowledge* 29. http://www.rhizomes.net/issue29/sexton.html.

Sharp, H. 2009. "The Impersonal is Political: Spinoza and a Feminist Politics of Imperceptibility." *Hypatia* 24.4: 84–103.

Shemtov, V. K. 2015. "Poetry and Dwelling: From Martin Heidegger to the Songbook of the Tent Revolution in Israel." *Prooftexts* 35.2–3: 271–90.

Siegel, J. 1967. "Robert Thompson and the Old Masters." *Harvard Art Review* 2.1: 10–14.

Silverblank, H., and M. Ward. 2020. "Why Does Classical Reception Need Disability Studies?" *Classical Receptions Journal* 12.4: 502–30.

Simpson, M. 2003. "Trickster Poetics: Multiculturalism and Collectivity in Nathaniel Mackey's 'Song of the Andoumboulou.'" *MELUS* 28: 35–54.

Sims, L. S. 2021. "A Tale of Two Bobs." In *Bob Thompson: This House Is Mine*, edited by D. Tuite, 136–42. New Haven, CT.

Slater, N. W. 1997. "Performing the City in *Birds*." In *The City as Comedy: Society and Representation in Athenian Drama*, edited by G. W. Dobrov, 75–94. Chapel Hill, NC.

Smalls, J. 2018. "'Expressive Camouflage': Classicism, Race, and Homoerotic Desire in the Male Nudes of Richmond Barthé." *Panorama* 4.1: 1–12.

Smith, A. 2014. *How to Be Both*. London.

Smith, I. 2002. "Misusing Canonical Intertexts: Jamaica Kincaid, Wordsworth and Colonialism's 'Absent Things.'" *Callaloo* 25.3: 801–20.

Smith, J. M. 1855. "From Our New York Correspondent." *Frederick Douglass's Paper*, January 12.

Snell, B. 1953. *The Discovery of the Mind: The Greek Origins of European Thought*. Oxford.

Speliotis, E. 2018. "Singing a New Song." *Claremont Review of Books* 18.3. https:// claremontreviewofbooks.com/singing-a-new-song/

Spentzou, E. 2019. "Orpheus, Byblis, Myrrha: Towards a Matrixial Ethics of Encounter in Ovid's *Metamorphoses*." *International Journal of the Classical Tradition* 26.4: 417–32.

Spillers, H. 2003. *Black, White, and in Color: Essays on American Literature and Culture*. Chicago.

Spivak, G. 1999. *A Critique of Postcolonial Reason: Toward a History of the Vanishing Present*. Cambridge, MA.

Squire, M. 2017. "POP ART: The Optical Poetics of Publilius Optatianus Porphyrius." In *The Poetics of Late Latin Literature*, edited by J. Elsner and J. Hernández Lobato, 25–99. Cambridge.

Steintrager, J. A., and Chow, R. 2019. "Sound Objects: An Introduction." In *Sound Objects*, edited by J. A. Steintrager and R. Chow, 1–19. Durham, NC.

Stouck, J. 2011. "Abject Hybridity in Helen Oyeyemi's *The Icarus Girl*." *Ariel: A Review of International English Literature* 41: 89–112.

Sullivan, M. B. 2021. "Horace's Programmatic Priamel." *JRS* 111: 49–73.

Suter, A. 2003. "Lament in Euripides' *Trojan Women*." *Mnemosyne* 56.1: 1–28.

Svenbro, J. 1993. *Phrasikleia: An Anthropology of Reading in Ancient Greece*. Ithaca, NY.

Symonds, J. A. 1880. *New and Old: A Volume of Verse*. London.

Symonds, J. A. 1890. *Essays Speculative and Suggestive*. 2 Volumes. London.

Symonds, J. A. 1893a. "Recollections of Lord Tennyson: An Evening at Thomas Woolner's." *Century Magazine* 46.1: 32–7.

Symonds, J. A. 1893b. *In the Key of Blue and Other Prose Essays*. London.

Symonds, J. A. 1967. *The Letters of John Addington Symonds*. 3 Volumes. Detroit, MI.

Symonds, J. A. 2016. *The Memoirs of John Addington Symonds: A Critical Edition*. London.

Sze, G. 2019. "The Consolatory Fold: Anne Carson's *Nox* and the Melancholic Archive." *Studies in Canadian Literature* 44: 66–80.

Tamás, A. 2021. "Catullus' Sapphic *Lacuna*: A Palimpsest of Absences and Presences." In *Unspoken Rome: Absence in Latin Literature and its Reception*, edited by T. Geue and E. Giusti, 19–34. Cambridge.

Telò, M. 2019. "Iambic Horror: Shivers and Brokenness in Archilochus and Hipponax." In *The Genres of Archaic and Classical Greek Poetry: Theories and Models*, edited by M. Forster, L. Kurke, and N. Weiss, 271–97. Leiden.

Telò, M. 2020a. "The Politics of *Dissensus* in Aristophanes' *Birds*." In *Aristophanes and Politics: New Studies*, edited by R. M. Rosen and H. P. Foley, 214–47. Leiden.

Telò, M. 2020b. *Archive Feelings: A Theory of Greek Tragedy*. Columbus, OH.

Telò, M. 2023a. *Greek Tragedy in a Global Crisis: Reading through Pandemic Times*. London.

Telò, M. 2023b. *Resistant Form: Aristophanes and the Comedy of Crisis*. Goleta, CA.

Telò, M. 2025. "Multidisciplinary Theory in Ancient Greek and Roman Studies." In *Multidisciplinary Theory*, edited by J. Di Leo. London.

Telò, M., and S. Olsen. 2022. "Queer Euripides: An Introduction." In *Queer Euripides: Re-Readings in Greek Tragedy*, edited by S. Olsen and M. Telò, 1–20. London.

Tennyson, A. 1851. "Ring Out, Wild Bells." *Frederick Douglass's Paper* (August 21).

Tennyson, A. 1855. "The Charge of the Light Brigade at Balaklava." *Frederick Douglass's Paper* (January 12).

Tennyson, A. 1877. "Achilles Over the Trench." *The Nineteenth Century* 2.6: 1–2.

Tennyson, A. *c.* 1884. "Manuscript Notebook of Poem Drafts, Including 'Achilles Over the Trench' and Other Verses." Morgan Library, New York, MA 464.

Tennyson, A. 1907. *Poems*. 2 Volumes. London.

Tennyson, C. 1956. "The Tennyson Phonograph Records." *British Institute of Recorded Sound Bulletin* 3: 2–8.

Tennyson, H. 1897. *Alfred Lord Tennyson: A Memoir by His Son*. 2 Volumes. London.

Tennyson, L. 1933. *From Verse To Worse*. London.

Terada, R. 2001. *Feeling in Theory: Emotion After the "Death of the Subject."* Cambridge, MA.

Terada, R. 2008. "After the Critique of Lyric." *PMLA* 123.1: 195–200.

Terada, R. 2009. *Looking Away: Phenomenality and Dissatisfaction, Kant to Adorno*. Cambridge, MA.

Thompson, C. 1999. "Remembering Bob." In *Bob Thompson: Fantastic Visions, Paintings & Drawings*, edited by Michael R. Gallery, 3. New York.

Tinsley, O. N. 2008. "Black Atlantic, Queer Atlantic: Queer Imaginings of the Middle Passage." *GLQ* 14.2–3: 191–215.

Trubetzkoy, N. S. 1969. *Principles of Phonology*. Berkeley.

Tuite, D. 2021. "This House Is Mine: Bob Thompson's Private Allegories." In *Bob Thompson: This House Is Mine*, edited by D. Tuite, 30–50. New Haven, CT.

Umachandran, M. 2022. "Disciplinecraft: Towards an Anti-racist Classics." *TAPA* 152.1: 25–32.

Valéry, P. 1957. *Oeuvres*. Paris.

Vanicek, A. 1877. *Griechisch–Lateinisch Etymologisches Wörterbuch*. Leipzig.

Vasunia, P., ed. 2022a. *The Politics of Form in Greek Literature*. London.

Vasunia, P. 2022b. "Introduction." In *The Politics of Form in Greek Literature*, edited by P. Vasunia, 1–19. London.

Vattimo, G. 1983. *Il pensiero debole*. Milan.

Vernant, J.-P. 1965. *Mythe et pensée chez les Grecs: Études de psychologies*. Paris.

Vieira, C. 2013. "Heraclitus' Bow Composition." *CQ* 63: 473–90.

Voigt, E.-M. 1971. *Sappho et Alcaeus: Fragmenta*. Amsterdam.

Vries, L. de. 2003. "Bruegel's 'Fall of Icarus': Ovid or Solomon?" *Simiolus* 30: 4–18.

Walters, T. L. 2007. *African American Literature and the Classical Tradition: Black Women Writers from Wheatley to Morrison*. New York.

Waltham-Smith, N. 2021. *Shattering Biopolitics*. New York.

Warren, C. 2018. *Ontological Terror: Blackness, Nihilism, and Emancipation*. Durham, NC.

Watson, L. C. 1991. *Arae: The Curse Poetry of Antiquity*. Leeds.

Weiss, N. 2017. "Noise, Music, Speech: The Representation of Lament in Greek Tragedy." *AJP* 138: 243–66.

Werner, A. 1962. "The Vatican." *Horizon: A Magazine of the Arts* 4.3: 22–49.

West, C. 1982. *Prophesy Deliverance! An Afro-American Revolutionary Christianity*. Philadelphia.

West, D., ed. 1995. *Horace Odes I: carpe diem*. Oxford.

Whitman, C. H. 1964. *Aristophanes and the Comic Hero*. Cambridge, MA.

Wilamowitz-Möllendorf, U. von. 1886. *Isyllos von Epidaurus*. Leipzig.

Wilderson, F. B. III. 2010. *Red, White, and Black: Cinema and the Structures of U.S. Antagonisms.* Durham, NC.

Wilderson, F. B. III. 2020. *Afropessimism.* New York.

Williams, T. 2022. "Radical Mimesis: Conceptual Dialectics and the African Diaspora." In *A Companion to American Poetry*, edited by M. M. Balkun, J. Gray, and P. Jaussen, 158–66. Hoboken, NJ.

Williams, W. C. 1995. *Patterson.* New York.

Wilson, D. 1873. *Caliban: The Missing Link.* London.

Wilson, E. 2018. *Homer Odyssey.* New York.

Wilson, J., and L. Hamalian, eds. 1985. "Bob Thompson: His Life and Friendships." *Artist and Influence* 3: 107–42.

Wilson, R. 2013. *Shelley and the Apprehension of Life.* Cambridge.

Winckelman, J. J. 1972. *Writings on Art.* New York.

Wohl, V. 2015. *Euripides and the Politics of Form.* Princeton.

Wohl, V. 2020. "The Sleep of Reason: Sleep and the Philosophical Soul in Ancient Greece." *CA* 39: 126–51.

Wohlfart, G. 1991. *Also sprach Herakleitos: Heraklits Fragment B 52 und Nietzsches Heraklit-Rezeption.* Freiburg.

Wolfskill, P. 2017. "Love and Theft in the Art of Emma Amos." *Archives of American Art Journal* 55.2: 46–65.

Wolfskill, P. 2022. "Making Art about Art: Emma Amos's Foundations in London." *Nka: Journal of Contemporary African Art* 50.1: 116–30.

Wolfson, S. J. 2006. "Introduction: Reading for Form." In *Reading for Form*, edited by S. J. Wolfson and M. Brown, 3–24. Seattle.

Woolf, G. 2022. "Curse Tablets: The History of a Technology." *Greece and Rome* 69.1: 120–34.

Woolner, A. 1917. *Thomas Woolner, R.A., Sculptor and Poet: His Life in Letters.* New York.

Wordsworth, W. 1807. "I Wandered Lonely as a Cloud." https://www.poetryfoundation.org/poems/45521/i-wandered-lonely-as-a-cloud

Worman, N. 2021. *Tragic Bodies: The Edges of the Human in Greek Drama.* London.

Zamsky, R. L. 2006. "A Poetics of Radical Musicality: Nathaniel Mackey's Mu." *Arizona Quarterly* 62: 113–40.

Zimmerman, B. 1983. "Utopisches und Utopie in den Komödien des Aristophanes." *WJA* 9: 57–77.

Zimmerman, M. 2006. "Heidegger, Buddhism, and Deep Ecology." In *The Cambridge Companion to Heidegger*, edited by C. Guignon, 293–325. Cambridge.

Zipfel, K. 1910. "Quatenus Ovidius in Ibide Callimachum Aliosque Fontes Inprimis Defixiones Secutus Sit." Leipzig.

Zukofsky, L. 1967. *Prepositions: the Collected Critical Essays of Louis Zukofsky.* London.

Index

fugitivity, 20, 22
Fyfe, James, 38

Garland, Judy, 250–1, 261n26
Garner, Eric, 242–3
gaze, 166–7, 171–4, 189, 191
Gestalt therapy, 196, 210n7
Gilroy, Paul, 14
Gladstone, William, 32, 33, 35–7, 39–40, 47
Glissant, Édouard, 8, 40–1
Goldberg, Theo, 250
Goldhill, Simon, 2
Gordon, George William, 38–9
Gowers, Emily, 202
grammar, viii
Greek Tragedy & Jerry Springer (Parks), 161–2
Griaule, Marcel, 236
Gross, Daniel M., 29
Grosz, Elisabeth, 178
Guattari, Felix, 143, 175
Guerilla Girls collective, 55
Gunn, Thom, 214

Hack, Daniel, 41, 44
Haden, Charlie, 55
Haitian Revolution, 44, 44–5
Halberstam, Jack, 258–9
Harris, Dionte, 253
Harrison, Jane, 244
Hartman, Geoffrey, 113
Hartman, Saidiya, 41
Hawley, Josh, 249–51
Hegel, G. W. F., 107–8, 109, 118, 119
Heidegger, Martin, 183
Hephaestion, 70, 77, 81, 82n4
Hephaestus, 20, 22, 23, 248–9
Heraclitus, x, 8
    aphorisms, 140, 147, 150n20
    B50 fragment, 147–8
    B62 fragment, 145
    B88 fragment, 145
    cosmic transformation, 140
    formal symmetry, 139–41
    kosmos, 138–48
    pedagogical fantasy, 147
    Peri Physeôs, 138–41, 149n7
Heraclitus, B52 fragment
    asyndeton, 142, 150n19
    cosmic cycle, 143–5, 146
    cosmic organization, 143–4
    first lines, 140–1
    Kahn's reading, 141, 143, 147
    language, 139
    logos, 141, 142, 144, 147
    narrative of rectification, maturation, and
        mastery, 141–2

Nietzsche's reading, 138–9, 149n6,
    149n11
paizôn, 138–9, 141, 142, 146–8
pesseuôn, 138, 141, 142, 146–8
playing child figure, 138
punctuation, 142–3, 149–50n16, 150n18,
    152n42
and reproduction, 146, 151n34
sovereignty, 143–4
structure, 143, 148, 150n24
stutter, 143–8, 149n8, 151–2n39, 151n37,
    151n38, 152n42
syntax, 139
hermeneutic practice, 3
Hipponax, 243
historicism, 2
    critiques of formalism, 225–6
historicist hermeneutics, 5–6
history, 124
Homer
    eagles, 116–17
    Iliad, 20, 23, 28–9, 32–8, 144, 249
    Odyssey, 82n6, 121n36
Homeric Hymn to Apollo, 93
Horace, x, 196–209
    commentators, 198
    Odes 1.1, 196, 197–9, 200–9
    preamble, 209
    programmatics, 196–200, 201
    Satires 1.1, 196, 197–8, 200–9
Horizon: A Magazine of the Arts, 60, 61
hospitality, 123
houses, housing and home, 181, 181–4
    broken windows, 189–92
    evictions, 181, 193n1
    "In The Mecca" (poem Brooks), 187–9
    In the Mecca (volume Brooks), 184–7
    inequality, 193n2
    insecurity, 184
    as poetic form, 181–4
    poetry's relationship to, 181–92
    shortages, 183
Hubbard, Margaret, 198
Hume, Christine, 100, 104n44
Hunt, Holman, 33
Hunter, Richard, 253, 256
hybridity, 26, 27
hylomorphism, 50

Ibis (Ovid), x, 214–27, 228n28
    apparent formlessness, 219
    bodily dissolution, 221–2
    choking, 223–5
    claustrophobia, 216, 220–3
    constraint, 221
    couplets, 214, 215–17

Index

Index

Index